CHILD POVERTY: AFRICAN AND

CHILD POVERTY: AFRICAN AND INTERNATIONAL PERSPECTIVES

Jaap E. Doek
A.K. Shiva Kumar
David Mugawe
Shimelis Tsegaye
(eds.)

Antwerp – Oxford – Portland

Distribution for the UK:
Hart Publishing Ltd.
16C Worcester Place
Oxford OX1 2JW
UK
Tel.: +44 1865 51 75 30
Fax: +44 1865 51 07 10

Distribution for Switzerland and Germany:
Schulthess Verlag
Zwingliplatz 2
CH-8022 Zürich
Switzerland
Tel.: +41 1 251 93 36
Fax: +41 1 261 63 94

Distribution for the USA and Canada:
International Specialized Book Services
920 NE 58th Ave Suite 300
Portland, OR 97213
USA
Tel.: +1 800 944 6190 (toll free)
Tel.: +1 503 287 3093
Fax: +1 503 280 8832
Email: info@isbs.com

Distribution for other countries:
Intersentia Publishers
Groenstraat 31
BE-2640 Mortsel
Belgium
Tel.: +32 3 680 15 50
Fax: +32 3 658 71 21

Child Poverty: African and International Perspectives
Jaap E. Doek, A.K. Shiva Kumar, David Mugawe and Shimelis Tsegaye (eds.)

© 2009 The African Child Policy Forum

Cover photographs: © iStockphoto.com/Peeter Viisimaa – 'Big smile' and © iStockphoto.com/Lucian – 'African family'

ISBN 978-90-5095-929-2
D/2009/7849/38
NUR 828

No part of this book may be reproduced in any form, by print, photoprint, microfilm or any other means, without written permission from the publisher.

PREFACE

Africa is in the midst of unprecedented socioeconomic transformation. The pace of economic progress is encouraging, as is the democratisation process now underway in a number of African countries. Armed conflicts in Africa have declined considerably.

Despite this, the continent is still ridden with scathing inequality and raging poverty. Children are the first in line to be disproportionately affected by inequality and poverty. It is obvious that, while poverty hurts every human being, it is most threatening and harmful to children, leaving them unable to enjoy their rights, reach their full potential, or participate in society as full members. In the worst of cases, poverty leaves children vulnerable to premature death.

The catalogue of current facts and statistics on child poverty and child wellbeing portray a deplorable situation, which has to be reversed if millions and millions of children are not to continue dying or suffering various forms of deprivation.

African governments have the primary political and moral responsibility for this. Lack of resources should not be an excuse for inaction. The non-fulfilment or violation of rights is not always related to economics – more importantly it is due to the lack of political commitment. For instance, five African countries (Democratic Republic of Congo (DRC), Ethiopia, Nigeria, Tanzania and Uganda) account for over half of all newborn deaths in Africa, with a total between them of almost 600,000 in 2004; yet three of these countries had military expenditures per GDP among the highest in Africa. Ethiopia's military expenditure was 3.7 per cent of GDP, while DRC's was 3.0 per cent, and Uganda's 2.5 per cent.

Significantly also, a recent report by The African Child Policy Forum (ACPF) on child wellbeing found that there was no intrinsic relationship between a country's level of economic development and the extent to which a government is committed to child wellbeing and action against child poverty. Using a simple and powerful advocacy and analytical tool, the Child-Friendliness Index (CFI), the report compared the CFI ranking of governments with their ranking for economic status as measured by GDP per capita. The analysis revealed that a number of governments (for example, Malawi, Burundi, Madagascar, Rwanda, Burkina Faso, Mali, Kenya and Uganda) were able to score high in "child-friendliness" despite relatively low levels of per capita national income. Thus, the child-friendliness rankings of

Malawi and Burundi, for example, were found to be 38 and 30 places higher respectively than those countries' GDP per capita rankings. In contrast, some governments with relatively high scores for GDP per capita were found to be in the least child-friendly category: for example, Equatorial Guinea ranked first of the countries in the study in terms of GDP per capita, but its CFI ranking was 37 places lower, indicating both a lack of political will and the fact the country's high economic performance is not benefiting children. The same was found to be true for the governments of Swaziland, Gambia and Angola, all of which scored low on the CFI despite relatively high per capita incomes.

Thus enhanced political commitment can be seen to be the single most important precondition for success in the fight against child poverty. That commitment, if passionate, genuine and unequivocal, translates into policies backed by sufficient budgets to ensure fair distribution of national resources, free universal access to basic primary health care, and basic education services. Examples of important instruments for tackling child poverty abound: the experiences of South Africa, Kenya and other countries have shown that cash transfer schemes, school feeding programmes and the abolition of user fees for health and school services have proved successful.

There is, however, one central predicament that well-intentioned governments face in any attempt to tackle child poverty: there is no well-researched factual information available on child poverty and/or the array of possible related policy options with which they might inform their decisions and actions.

This book is a first step towards understanding the problem of child poverty. It presents new papers alongside revised and updated versions of others presented at the International Policy Conference on the African Child, organised by The African Child Policy Forum in Addis Ababa in 2008.

The authors of the papers in this book are world-renowned scholars and experts on poverty, and their contributions are extremely valuable in addressing child poverty. It is our great hope that the observations and conclusions in this book will be of use to policy makers, child rights advocates, and academics worldwide.

Assefa Bequele, PhD
Executive Director
The African Child Policy Forum

TABLE OF CONTENTS

PREFACE v

ACKNOWLEDGMENTS xv

ABOUT THE AFRICAN CHILD POLICY FORUM xvii

LIST OF CONTRIBUTORS xix

PART I
CHILD POVERTY: A RIGHTS PERSPECTIVE

CHILD POVERTY: AN OVERVIEW
   Jaap E. Doek 3

1. Eradication at Last? 3
   1.1. Children in Poverty and Their Human Rights 5
   1.2. Eradication of Child Poverty: How? 7
2. Actions at the National Level 8
3. Actions at the International Level 10
4. Final Observations and Conclusions 13
5. References 14

CHILD RIGHTS, CHILD WELLBEING AND CHILD POVERTY
   Yanghee Lee 17

1. Human Rights Commitments and Pledges: An Overview 17
2. Convention on the Rights of the Child 20
3. Key Features of the Convention 21
4. Concluding Observations 24

THE HUMAN RIGHTS APPROACH TO PUBLIC POLICY IN ADDRESSING CHILD POVERTY
Magdalena Sepúlveda Carmona 27

1. Introduction 27
2. Human Rights Approach to Public Policy Regarding Children Living in Poverty 28
3. Universality and Indivisibility 30
4. Equality and Non-Discrimination 31
5. Transparency 32
6. Participation and Inclusion 32
7. Final Observations 33
8. References 34

CHILD RIGHTS AND ECONOMIC POLICY
Richard Jolly 35

1. Introduction 35
2. Rights, Goals, Policy and Partnerships 36
3. Needs, Country by Country 36
4. Mobilisation for Action 40

CHILD POVERTY: THE GENDER DIMENSION
Meredeth Turshen 43

1. Opening Observations 43
2. Social Transfers to Reduce Child Poverty 48
3. Health Programmes for Children and Youth 49
   3.1. Programmes for Reproductive Health 49
      A. Pharmacies as a Source for Youth-Friendly Care 49
      B. Games for Reproductive Health 50
      C. Facing the Challenges of New Reproductive Technologies ... 50
      D. Programmes to Combat AIDS 52
      E. Using Games to Reach Children and Youth 52
      F. Peer Education: Not a Cheap Fix 53
      G. Men as Partners Programme 54
      H. Exploring the Intersections Between Youth, Gender and AIDS 55
      I. Newspaper for Young People 55
         a. *Straight Talk*, Uganda 55

	J. Multimedia Soap Opera	55
	a. *Soul City*, South Africa	55
	K. Creating Participatory Radio with Children	56
4.	Concluding Comments	56
5.	References	57

CHILD MALNUTRITION: CHANGING PERCEPTIONS AND POLICY IMPLICATIONS
Urban JONSSON 59

1.	Introduction	59
2.	Science and Ethics – Theory and Practice	60
3.	Early Paradigms	62
	3.1 The Period Before 1950	62
	3.2 The Era of the Protein Deficiency Paradigm (1950–1973)	63
4.	From Mono-Causality to Multi-Causality (1973–1980)	64
5.	A Focus on the Community (1978–1990)	66
6.	Towards a Consensus (1990–1995)	67
7.	Back to Mono-Causality – A Period of Micronutrient Malnutrition Programmes (1995–2005)	69
8.	Renewed Interest in PEM and Multi-Causality (2005 – present)	70
9.	Development as Outcome and Process	71
10.	The Investment in Nutrition Approach	72
11.	The Human Rights-Based Approach to Nutrition Paradigm	74
12.	Different Policy Implications	76
13.	Conclusion	77
14.	References	78

PART II
CHILD POVERTY IN AFRICA

CHILD POVERTY AND DEPRIVATION IN AFRICA
Shimelis TSEGAYE 83

1.	Background and Purpose	83
2.	What We Mean by Child Poverty	84
3.	What We Know About Child Poverty in Africa	85
	3.1. Household Poverty and Deprivation	87
	3.2. The Extent of Child Deprivation	92

		A.	Health and Nutrition Deprivation 92

        A. Health and Nutrition Deprivation 92
        B. Deprivation in Water and Sanitation 101
        C. Deprivation in Shelter and Clean Living Environment 104
        D. Education Deprivation 105
  3.3. Deprivation Among Vulnerable Groups of Children 109
        A. Child Labourers and Child Slaves 109
        B. Orphans and Street Children 112
        C. Child-Headed Households 117
        D. Conclusion 119
4. The Way Forward 120
5. References 122

WHICH AFRICAN GOVERNMENTS ARE CHILD-FRIENDLY? WHICH ONES ARE NOT AND WHY?
    Assefa BEQUELE 131

1. Introduction 131
2. The Child-Friendliness of African Governments 132
3. How Protective Are African Governments of Their Children? 132
4. Ranking of Governments for Child Provision 134
5. How Do Rich and Poor African Countries Score in Budgetary Commitment? 137
6. Most and Least Child-Friendly Governments 138
7. Economic Status and Child-Friendliness 141
8. Conclusion 144

CLAIMING THE FUTURE: AN INTERNATIONALIST PERSPECTIVE
    Stephen LEWIS 145

PART III
TACKLING CHILD POVERTY: POLICY EXPERIENCES IN INDUSTRIALISED AND DEVELOPING COUNTRIES

CHILD POVERTY: AN INTEGRATED APPROACH
    Dharam GHAI 157

1. Introduction 157
2. Different Ways of Measuring Poverty 157

	2.1.	Incomes, Basic Needs and Human Rights 157
3.		Differences and Commonalities 159
4.		Adult Versus Child Poverty 161
5.		Strategies for Poverty Elimination 163
6.		Implementation Problems 165
7.		Conclusion.. 167

THE ABOLITION OF CHILD POVERTY AND THE RIGHT TO SOCIAL SECURITY: A POSSIBLE UN MODEL FOR CHILD BENEFIT?
Peter TOWNSEND 169

1. Acknowledgements by the Author 169
2. Introduction 170
3. Consequences of Child Poverty and Multiple Deprivation............ 171
4. Using Child Rights to Defeat Child Poverty 174
5. International Responsibility for Funding: 1) Transnational
   Corporations (TNCs) 177
6. International Responsibility for Funding: 2a) International Agencies:
   Safety Nets.. 181
7. International Responsibility for Funding: 2b) International Agencies:
   General Aid... 183
8. A Currency Transfer Tax: New Resources for Child Benefit and
   Social Security 186
9. Social Security and Child Benefit in Developing Countries........... 189
10. The Child Support Grant in South Africa 191
11. Child Benefit in the UK.. 194
12. Conditional and Unconditional Child Benefit 197
13. Summary and Conclusion: A Universal Child Benefit 197
14. References 200
Appendix I: The Millennium Development Goals 205
Appendix II: Child Mortality and Poor Conditions of Health 206

CHILD POVERTY AND SOCIAL INCLUSION IN COUNTRIES IN TRANSITION AND IN OECD COUNTRIES
Marta SANTOS PAIS 209

1. Introduction 209
2. A Region in Transition 210
3. Child Poverty in OECD Countries 213
4. Looking Ahead 217

COMBATING CHILD POVERTY AND SOCIAL EXCLUSION IN EUROPEAN UNION COUNTRIES: LESSONS FOR POLICY AND PRACTICE
Hugh FRAZER 219

1. Introduction 219
2. Extent and Nature of Child Poverty 221
3. Six Preconditions for Effective Action 223
   3.1. Political Priority and Public Support 223
   3.2. Mobilisation of All Actors. 223
   3.3. Commitment to Children's Rights. 224
   3.4. Effective Mainstreaming and Coordination 224
   3.5. Strategic Approach Based on Clear Objectives 225
   3.6. Good Data and Analysis 226
4. A Comprehensive Policy Framework 226
   4.1. Adequate Income 227
   4.2. Access to Services 228
   4.3. Ensuring Care and Protection 229
   4.4. Promoting Participation 230
   4.5. Three Cross-Cutting Themes 231
5. Effective Delivery 231
   5.1. Partnership, Networking and Participation. 232
   5.2. The Local Dimension 232
   5.3. Continuity 233
   5.4. Flexible and Tailored Responses 233
   5.5. A Community Development Approach 233
   5.6. Regular Monitoring and Evaluation 234
6. Conclusion. 234
7. References 235

TACKLING CHILD POVERTY: LESSONS FROM INDIA
A.K. SHIVA KUMAR 237

1. Introduction 237
2. India and Sub-Saharan Africa 238
3. The Indian Experience 240
4. Identifying the Linkages 243
   4.1. Public Investments 243
   4.2. Public Management 244
   4.3. Public Participation 244

	4.4.	Public Vigilance	245
	4.5.	Public Values	246
5.	Establishing the Connections		247
6.	Conclusion.		249
7.	References		250

CASH TRANSFER PROGRAMME FOR VULNERABLE CHILDREN: A POLITICAL AND POLICY CHOICE FOR THE GOVERNMENT OF KENYA – 2002–2008
Roger PEARSON and Carlos ALVIAR 251

1. Introduction 251
2. Cash Transfer Programmes in Africa Compared to the Rest of the World, and the Role of International Development Partners in Helping to Build Such Programmes 253
3. Poverty and Wealth in Kenya 256
4. The Core Poverty Programmes in Kenya in 2004 259
5. Policy Discussions Leading to the Genesis of the Kenya Programme ... 260
6. Policy Discussion, Capacity Building and Targeting in Phase Two 263
7. Conclusion 271
8. Acknowledgements 272
9. References 273

PART IV
THE IMPACT ON CHILDREN OF THE GLOBAL FOOD, FINANCIAL AND ECONOMIC CRISES

THE GLOBAL FOOD CRISIS: OBSERVATIONS
Jeffrey D. SACHS 277

WHAT WILL BE THE IMPACT OF THE GLOBAL ECONOMIC CRISIS ON CHILD POVERTY IN SUB-SAHARAN AFRICA?
Andy SUMNER and Sara WOLCOTT 283

1. Introduction 283
2. Impact of Economic Crises on Child Poverty 284
3. Tracking Transmission of Financial Crises to Child Poverty 285
   3.1. Methodological Issues 285

		3.2.	Conceptual Linkages 287

- 3.2. Conceptual Linkages 287
- 4. Child Poverty Impacts: Evidence 289
  - 4.1. Children and Household Income Poverty Impacts 289
  - 4.2. Children, Inequality and Distribution of Impacts 291
  - 4.3. Child-Specific Indicators and Non-Income Poverty Impacts 294
- 5. Sub-Saharan Africa, Children and the Current Crisis 297
  - 5.1. Pre-Crisis Macro-Economic Vulnerabilities and Impacts so Far 297
  - 5.2. Poverty and Child Vulnerabilities 299
    - A. Invest in Better Child Poverty and Vulnerability Early Warning Tracking Systems 301
    - B. Explicitly Link These New Tracking Systems to the Following 301
- 6. Conclusions 302
- 7. References 303

THE IMPACT OF THE WORLD FOOD CRISIS ON CHILDREN REQUIRING FOOD ASSISTANCE IN ETHIOPIA: A NOTE
Jakob Mikkelsen 307

- 1. Background 307
- 2. Ethiopia's Malnourished Children 308

ACKNOWLEDGMENTS

The African Child Policy Forum (ACPF) expresses its appreciation to International Child Support (ICS) and Plan International for their financial and technical support.

A special word of thanks also goes to Mark Nunn for copy-editing this book.

ABOUT THE AFRICAN CHILD POLICY FORUM

The African Child Policy Forum (ACPF) is a pan-African policy and advocacy centre on child rights. ACPF was established with the conviction that putting children first on the public and political agenda and investing in their wellbeing are fundamental for bringing about lasting social and economic progress in Africa and its integration into the world economy.

The work of ACPF is rights-based, inspired by universal values and informed by global experiences and knowledge. The Forum aims to provide a platform for dialogue; contribute to improved knowledge about the problems facing children in Africa; identify policy options; and strengthen the capacity of NGOs and governments to develop and implement effective pro child-policies and programmes.

P.O. Box 1179, Addis Ababa, Ethiopia
Telephone: +251 116 62 81 92/96
Fax: +251 116 62 82 00
E-mail: info@africanchildforum.org
Website: www.africanchildforum.org
              www.africanchild.info

LIST OF CONTRIBUTORS

Mr. Carlos Alviar
  Cash Transfer Specialist, UNICEF Kenya

Assefa Bequele, PhD
  Executive Director, The African Child Policy Forum (ACPF)

Magdalena Sepúlveda Carmona, PhD
  UN Independent Expert on Human Rights and Extreme Poverty

Prof. Jaap E. Doek
  Chair, UN Committee on the Rights of the Child (UNCRC), 2001–2007

Prof. Hugh Frazer
  Director of the Combat Poverty Agency of the Irish Government, 1987–2001

Prof. Dharam Ghai
  Senior Advisor to the Director-General, International Labour Organization (ILO), Geneva
  Executive Director, UN Research Institute for Social Development (UNRISD), 1987–1997

Prof. Sir Richard Jolly
  Deputy Executive Director, United Nations Children's Fund (UNICEF), 1982–96
  Architect, *Human Development Report*, 1996–2000

Urban Jonsson, PhD
  Regional Director for UNICEF, Eastern and Southern Africa (ESARO), 1998–2003
  International consultant on Human Rights and Development

Prof. A.K. Shiva Kumar
  Development economist and adviser to UNICEF India

Prof. Yanghee Lee
  Chair, UN Committee on the Rights of the Child

List of Contributors

Mr. Stephen Lewis
   Co-Director of AIDS-Free World

Mr. Jakob Mikkelsen
   Head of Nutrition and Education, World Food Programme (WFP) Ethiopia

Mr. David Mugawe
   Deputy Executive Director, ACPF

Prof. Marta Santos Pais
   Director, UNICEF Innocenti Research Centre

Mr. Roger Pearson
   Senior Social Policy Specialist, UNICEF Ethiopia

Prof. Jeffrey D. Sachs
   Director, The Earth Institute, Columbia University

Prof. Andy Sumner
   Head of Graduate Programmes and Research Fellow, Vulnerability and Poverty Reduction Team Institute of Development Studies, University of Sussex, UK

Prof. Peter Townsend
   Professor of International Social Policy, LSE, and Emeritus Professor of Social Policy, Bristol University

Mr. Shimelis Tsegaye
   Programme Coordinator, ACPF

Prof. Meredeth Turshen
   Edward J. Bloustein School of Planning and Public Policy, Rutgers University

Ms. Sara Wolcott
   MA Student at the Institute of Development Studies, Sussex, UK

PART I
CHILD POVERTY:
A RIGHTS PERSPECTIVE

CHILD POVERTY: AN OVERVIEW

Professor Jaap E. DOEK
Chair, UN Committee on the Rights of the Child (2001–2007)

1. ERADICATION AT LAST?

There are no poor children, but a lot of poor people. And therefore there are many poor parents, and families, and the children of those families live in poverty. Poverty is usually presented and discussed as a problem of income. This is confirmed, for example, by the Millennium Development Goal to eradicate extreme poverty by reducing by half the proportion of people living on less than a dollar a day. In 2000 the United Nations solemnly pledged to achieve this goal by 2015.

Children are not poor in this traditional sense of the word, but around 1 billion children live in poverty. This fact should trigger a massive investment of financial and human resources equal to global actions to address the current economic and financial crisis.

Because, as stated in *A World Fit for Children*:

> "Chronic poverty remains the single biggest obstacle to meeting the needs, protecting and promoting the rights of children...
>
> ...[Children] are hardest hit by poverty because it strikes at the very roots of their development, their growing bodies and minds. Eradication of poverty and reduction of disparities must therefore be a key objective of development efforts."

The same emphasis is made in the words of the United Nations Member States in 2002:

> "We reaffirm our vow to break the cycle of poverty within one single generation, united in the conviction that investment in children and the realization of their rights are among the most effective ways to eradicate child poverty." (WFFC par. 7(2))

With all these beautiful words of commitment and determination, the burning question is: do we know how to reduce the number of children living in poverty? And, if so, what kind of progress, if any, are we making?

For a starter: the first part of this question assumes that we know what we mean by "children living in poverty". But who are these children, and how do they figure in existing poverty reduction policies? Studies have found that information about the specific needs and problems of children is often lacking in debates on poverty.

There are also apparently different concepts of child poverty, resulting in different measurements and approaches to the issue (Minujin et al., 2006; Roelen & Gassman, 2008); this notwithstanding, we should emphasise that child poverty is more than income poverty. With this in mind, the working definition that UNICEF proposes in its 2005 *Report on The State of the World's Children* (p. 18) is a very useful one:

> "Children living in poverty experience deprivation of the material, spiritual and emotional resources needed to survive, develop end thrive, leaving them unable to enjoy their rights, achieve their full potential or participate as full and equal members of society."

One would expect, in light of all the commitments mentioned above, that the recent development and implementation of Poverty Reduction Strategy Papers (PRSPs) in many developing countries would come with a lot of attention paid in said PRSPs to children living in poverty. Unfortunately that is hardly the case.

This does not mean that in developing countries no actions are taken to address the needs of children living in poverty; but there seems to be more analytical description of the various factors that cause children to live in poverty, and of the devastating impact this has on the child's full and harmonious development, than there is information on large-scale targeted and successful programmes to reduce or end child poverty.

This is apparently a complex problem that cannot be solved by single or simple measures – for example, by providing poor families with children with state-subsidised incomes. It is also clear from various studies that children live in poverty not only in developing countries, but also in countries in transition and in rich countries (UNICEF, 2006).

Despite the overt international commitment to break the cycle of poverty within a generation, and a number of actions taken at national level in both the developing and the developed parts of the world, very many children still live in poverty. In the following paragraphs I will discuss some aspects of this problem and their responses.

1.1. CHILDREN IN POVERTY AND THEIR HUMAN RIGHTS

For many years, children living in poverty were not given much specific attention. From a global perspective, that changed significantly over the course of the 1990s.

The driving force behind increased attention to child poverty was and is in my opinion the ratification and implementation of the UN Convention on the Rights of the Child (CRC) in (at time of writing) 193 countries.

Firstly: The efforts made to implement the CRC made policy makers, NGOs, UN agencies (UNICEF, 2005) and other relevant stakeholders increasingly aware of the fact that poverty deprives children of almost all their human rights and undermines the child's rights to survival and development (Article 6); to the highest attainable standard of health (Article 24); to education (Article 28); to engagement in play, recreational and cultural activities (Article 31); to participation in society (Article 12); and to protection (Articles 19, 32, etc.).

In 2005, approximately 316,000 children died in sub-Saharan Africa because of a lack of immunisation; in this region in 2004, a baby's chance of dying from diarrhoea was 520 times that of a baby born in Europe or the United States. In countries such as Ethiopia, Rwanda and Uganda, four out of five children use surface water, or have to walk more than 15 minutes to find a protected water source. 38 million children were out of school in sub-Saharan Africa in 2004 (Mugawe, 2008). These are just some of many available examples of the serious and chronic violations of the human rights of children caused by the fact that they have to live in poverty.

Secondly: Through the lens of the human rights of children, we can see how multifaceted and complex child poverty is. It causes many problems in the lives of children; but the violations of children's rights are also important factors in maintaining the chronic nature of poverty in general, and in contributing to the intergenerational cycle of poverty. As underscored by Lee (2008), the human rights of children as enshrined in the CRC must be the framework of our actions to reduce and eradicate child poverty. Such actions are also by implication the best possible contributions to the eradication of poverty in general, because children live in poverty due to the fact that their parents and families are poor.

The CRC also reminds us of the plight of the individual child.[1] We do have macro figures (more estimates) available concerning the consequences of poverty for children (and many more than presented on the African children), but we know very little that is supported by evidence of the impact of poverty on the individual child.

Turshen (2008) observes that national bureaus of statistics do not publish data on child poverty disaggregated by sex since child poverty is a reflection of family circumstances; but in the light of the right to non-discrimination (Article 2 CRC), it is important to collect more information on possible differences in impact of poverty on the lives of boys and girls. Similar observations can be made regarding the other rights that are qualified by the CRC Committee as General Principles (Doek, 2007): the right of the child to have their best interests applied as a primary consideration in all actions affecting them (Article 3 CRC), and the right of the child to express her/his views and to participate in society (Article 12).

In short: it is crucial and imperative to promote a child rights-based programming of our efforts to eradicate child poverty. In this field, a considerable body of experiences and ideas already exists, with a strong emphasis on active and meaningful child participation (Theis, 2004; Hart, 2004); we must build on this basis in developing and implementing our actions to eradicate child poverty.

Finally: The CRC provides an excellent framework for these actions: it is an important tool in reminding the governments of the 193 States that have ratified it of their obligations to take the necessary measures for the progressive realisation of the economic, social and cultural rights of children.

Carmona (2008) argues that the traditional distinction between civil and political rights on the one hand, and economic, social and cultural rights on the other, is artificial:

> "All human rights impose a plurality of duties, and each of those duties potentially requires different degrees of State involvement as well as different levels of resources. There is no water tight division between the obligations by the two categories of rights."

The commitment of states parties to the CRC entails both entitlements of children and obligations of states. For instance: states parties to the CRC recognise the right of the child to a standard of living adequate for the child's physical, mental, spiritual, moral and social development (Article 27(1)) – in short, for the full and

---

[1] The CRC is the UN Convention on the Rights of the Child (single, not plural: children).

harmonious development of her or his personality (Preamble to CRC). While acknowledging the primary responsibility of parents in this regard, the states took upon themselves the obligation to take appropriate measures to assist parents and others responsible for the child in implementing this right, and to provide, in cases of need, material assistance and support programmes, particularly with regard to *nutrition, clothing* and *housing*.

With reference to Article 27 of the CRC, it can indeed be said that children are recognised as subjects of the right to adequate nutrition. This right can also be found in Article 24, which provides among other things that states parties shall pursue the full implementation of the child's right to the highest attainable standard of health, and shall take, in particular, appropriate measures:

> "... to combat disease and malnutrition, including within the framework of primary health care, through, inter alia, the application of readily available technology and through the provision of nutritious food and clean drinking water..." (Par. 2 under c)

The prevention of malnutrition is no longer a voluntary act of charity or benevolence, but an obligation. In the child rights-based approach, an "acceptable" level of malnutrition cannot exist. All children have the right to be equally well nourished.

The CRC-based approach also requires states parties to address in their policies, programmes and laws exclusions, discrimination and disparities, including via special protective measures and affirmative action to ensure that all children, including the most disadvantaged and excluded, enjoy their rights.

1.2. ERADICATION OF CHILD POVERTY: HOW?

Given the available information, we have quite a complete picture of the various factors, circumstances and conditions that force people to live in poverty. We also know how poverty affects the life of children, and how it becomes a chronic problem transferred from generation to generation.

Healthy economic growth is undoubtedly one of the factors that may contribute to a reduction of poverty. But the common belief that people living in poverty will benefit from this growth via a "natural" process of trickling down is hardly supported by empirical evidence.

The "laissez-faire" policy of the national and international free-trade market is not by itself reducing poverty: on the contrary, as is shown by the current financial and economic crisis.

There is a large degree of consensus that the multifaceted and complex nature of poverty is best, most comprehensively and most effectively addressed via a human rights-based approach. For children living in poverty the CRC is their most important tool for breaking the cycle of poverty. True as all this may be, it still leaves us with the question "How?".

Let me try to summarise the answers based on experiences in different parts of the world.

In the first place, the "how?" question requires answers and actions at the national level.

2. ACTIONS AT THE NATIONAL LEVEL

1. Develop and implement comprehensive national plans of action for the full implementation and realisation of the rights of children as enshrined in the CRC. Make these a matter of high priority. As Lee (2008) rightly put it, we need to sprint to action. The development of such plans should not be used as an excuse for not taking immediate actions when and where needed; but for the mid and long term, comprehensive action plans are necessary.

2. These plan should be developed and implemented with the integrated and well-coordinated involvement of key ministries (such as – for example – those of social and family affairs, health, education, labour and justice), all relevant NGOs, and other elements of civil society, such as associations of professionals working with and for children, private corporations, UN agencies operating in-country, and – last but not least – children and parents.

   This may look like a complicated process but it is necessary to muster broad societal support and involvement in efforts to reduce child poverty. This public participation is also important because available information shows that the sustainability of programmes is significantly higher when local communities are encouraged to have a clear ownership role (Kumar, 2008).

3. Ensure that monitoring, reporting and evaluation of the results of various programmes is an integral part of these plans, with assignment of these activities to independent inspectorates, research institutes and independent human rights institutions, in this case by children's rights ombudsperson or commissioner.[2]

---

[2] See for more information in this regard General Comment No 2 of the CRC Committee on the Rights of the Child.

4. The specific content of the plan, in terms of concrete social and other programmes and legislation, will differ from country to country. But it is possible to identify certain key elements of an effective national action plan to eradicate poverty. These are as follows:

   a. Public awareness-raising and educational campaigns to establish an understanding of the impact of poverty on the development of children, not only by explaining the negative consequences of poverty for children, but also by presenting the positive results of investing in children. One dollar spent on providing children with a healthy start in life may save seven dollars in costs spent on health and other problems. Studies show that one dollar invested in the elimination of (the worst forms of) child labour and making education available for all children will produce a return of USD 6.7 (IPEC/ILO, 2003).
   Arguments based on calculations/estimates of benefits versus invested money (costs) can be a powerful tool in the national political arena.
   In doing this we should not lose sight of the many immaterial benefits for children freed from the cycle of poverty; but in our efforts to promote the implementation of children's rights, we should collect and use more "hard" data on the benefits of this implementation. For instance, considerable attention is paid to financing and costing early childhood education, but relatively few studies have been done on cost-benefit ratios.[3]

   b. Measures to promote employment with a focus on underemployed or non-employed poor families – in particular single parent families (most of the time single women), in order to ensure adequate income.

   c. Inclusion in Poverty Reduction Strategy Papers (PRSPs), where applicable, of prioritised actions and services that will benefit children, such as immunisation and other primary health care services, free education, social benefits, and legislative measures to protect the rights of all children without any discrimination (O'Malley, 2004).

   d. Development and implementation of social transfer programmes, in cash and/or in kind, using them to support child involvement in education, to improve nutrition, and to protect children from child labour. The positive impact of cash transfer programmes for vulnerable children has been well documented (Pearson, 2008), and there are more examples of successful cash transfer programmes – such as the Oportunidades

---

[3] See *Funding the Future: Strategies for Early Childhood Investment, Costing and Financing*, Coordinators' Notebook, No 30, 2008 (an international resource for early childhood). For some information on economic losses due to failure to provide for early childhood, particularly in the areas of malnutrition and education, see Notebook No 30 p. 24-26 on empirical evidence from Eastern and Southern Africa.

programme in Mexico, which resulted in a 57 per cent rise in visits to health clinics in rural areas, a significant reduction in under-five mortality, and improved school attendance and completion (UNICEF, 2005).[4] In Brazil, the Bolsa Escola initiative resulted (for example) in 90 per cent school attendance (Townsend, 2008).

e. Measures related to investment, legislative and organisational actions to improve provision of and access to basic services such as housing, health care services, education and affordable transportation (Frazer, 2008).
    Studies of the Organisation for Economic Co-operation and Development (OECD) countries show a strong correlation between levels of social expenditure and child poverty. The higher the level of social expenditure (countries with a high level include, for example, Belgium, Sweden, Norway and Finland), the lower the child poverty rate.[5] A recent study by the ACPF showed that Africa's 12 most "child-friendly" governments followed a two-pronged approach to success: instituting appropriate laws to protect children, and ensuring adequate budgetary commitments to child-related services (African Child Policy Forum, 2008).

f. Measures to reverse and halt the spread of HIV/AIDS (cf. the Millennium Development Goals), because HIV contributes to the poverty of children and undermines the quality of their childhood (Lewis, 2008). These measures should be given very high priority. They require strong national and international actions, and we know that they are necessary. We cannot waste time and we are in fact running out of it (Lewis, 2006).

3. ACTIONS AT THE INTERNATIONAL LEVEL

One of the important, and often not fully recognised, features of the CRC is its call for international solidarity and cooperation, with particular attention to the needs of developing countries. For instance:

> "States Parties undertake to promote and encourage international cooperation with a view to achieving progressively the full realization of the right recognised in the present article (that is: the right to highest attainable stand of health). In this regard, particular account shall be taken of the needs of developing countries." (Article 24, par. 4 CRC)

---

[4] See (for example) a reduction of dropout rates in the third year of primary school of 14.8% for girls and 22.4% for boys, and a 25% increase in secondary school attendance in rural areas.

[5] Poverty rate from Luxembourg Income Study 2000, and social expenditure as a percentage of GDP from OECD social expenditure database 2004.

Similar provisions can be found in Article 28 (the right to education) and article 23 (the rights of children with disabilities), while in other articles explicit reference is made to international cooperation (Article 4 and 17) or to the need for multi-lateral measures (Articles 34 and 35).

International cooperation can take different forms, but currently the most important tool is Official Overseas Development Assistance (ODA). The rich countries (OECD) committed themselves some decades ago to contributing 0.7 per cent of their GDP to such international assistance. So far, most of these rich countries have failed miserably in meeting this commitment, despite a lot of repeated promises to the contrary.

It is necessary to increase our efforts to ensure that the rich countries live up to their promises. ODA can play an important role in supporting targeted national measures (e.g. national action plans as described above) to reduce and eradicate child poverty.

In its Concluding Observations, the CRC Committee should systematically remind states of their ODA promises, strongly recommending that they meet the internationally agreed standard commitment of 0.7 per cent of their GDP, and that they use it also for promoting and supporting the realisation of the rights of children.

International Institutions like the World Bank and UNDP should give the eradication of child poverty a much more prominent place on their agendas.

The World Bank does undertake efforts to reduce poverty, but only 10 per cent of its loans are allocated for social protection (i.e. USD 2.4 billion – in contrast, the UK, for example, spent USD 210 billion on social protection in 2005 alone). Much more is needed to eradicate poverty and enhance the full development of children living in it.

Townsend (2008) draws attention to the role of trans-national corporations, but his most challenging proposal is to introduce a Currency Transfer Tax, an idea already presented by Tobin in 1972. This would be a tax of 0.1 per cent on all currency transactions in the world, which would create a fund of USD 400 billion per year. If that is too far-reaching, an extra tax of 0.2 per cent on all currency transactions at airports would generate an annual fund of USD 280 billion.

This percentage is "peanuts" in light of the fact that the current standard tax for such transactions is already 2 to 3 per cent. Such a transfer tax, if allocated to universal child benefit, would immediately improve the life chances of hundreds of millions of children and pave the way for the emergence of social security systems in low-income countries, therefore radically reducing mass poverty; yet Townsend (2008) reports that the UN High-level Panel on Financing for Development (the Zedillo Panel) established in 2001 described the merits of this tax as "highly controversial", stating that "further rigorous study would be needed to resolve the doubts about the feasibility of such tax". There is no information indicating that that the necessary rigorous study has been conducted. It is therefore urgent to conduct this research immediately, to find out what the real difficulties are with implementing this tax, and to consider – if, as Townsend suggests, it is necessary – practicable alternative models of Transfer Tax.

There is a clear need to pursue this idea, with the maximum involvement of the NGO world, governments of low-income countries, trans-national corporations and UN agencies, with a view to establishing an international child benefit fund.

Many more and other international actions to eradicate child poverty should be taken by bodies such as – for example – the EU. But the recent food and financial and economic crises pose new and serious challenges for international solidarity and actions to reduce poverty.

To deliver a supplementary food ration to a malnourished child or to a pregnant or breastfeeding woman is at time of writing 50 per cent more expensive than it was a year ago. This means that organisations like the World Food Programme need to raise an additional 50 per cent of resources (Mikkelsen, 2008). Rich countries should provide the needed additional resources; but the likelihood that this will happen is very slim. Wouldn't it be great if we had that universal child benefit fund?

It is not possible yet to give a specific picture of the impact of the current financial and economic crises on child poverty, but there are enough indicators to assume that it will be severe (Sumner and Wolcott, 2008).

The World Bank estimates that due to these crises, newly poor people in 2009 will number 65 million more than the 130–155 million newly poor people in 2008 as a result of the food and oil crises. For sub-Saharan Africa it is estimated that the GDP will be down 3.5 per cent, resulting in an increase of poverty of 7 per cent. Millions more children will therefore live in poverty, and the non-income dimensions of this poverty in the areas of health, nutrition and education will be significant.

Sumner and Wolcott (2008) propose two things:

- Invest in better early warning tracking systems for child poverty and vulnerability, including *inter alia* a rapid qualitative appraisal of poverty impacts
- Link these tracking systems to planning of child-specific responses and social protection and pro-child public expenditures, to indicators of the underlying causes of child vulnerability, and to the Millennium Development Goals framework.

This tracking and evaluation is particularly important because of the global nature of the affecting crises and the threat they pose to aid and public expenditures.

4. FINAL OBSERVATIONS AND CONCLUSIONS

What emerges from the above discussion and other observations is the following:

1. Our efforts to eradicate child poverty have to be based on the systematic, comprehensive and well-coordinated implementation of the Convention on the Rights of the Child. This approach is important because it acknowledges the fact that child poverty is more than income poverty. We have to address the many non-income dimensions and impacts of this poverty, in particular with regard to the right to an adequate standard of living including housing, nutrition and clothing, the right to health care in all its dimensions, the right to education, the right to be protected from all forms of violence and exploitation, the right to participate, the right to a family life, the right to engage in play and recreational and cultural activities, and so on.
   This is also important because of the fact that 193 states in the world have committed themselves to implementing the rights of the child, and in doing so took upon themselves the obligation to take all necessary measures (see Article 4 of the CRC) for the progressive and full realisation of these rights.
   This approach should not prevent us from taking immediate and short term actions when necessary in situations of (armed) conflict, natural disasters or food, oil or financial crises.
2. This child rights-based approach at national level should be accompanied by a strong international solidarity (as expected under the CRC) and effective international cooperation. It remains crucial that the OECD countries meet their repeated commitments to spent 0.7 per cent of their GDP on Official

Development Assistance. At the 2009 G20 meeting the rich countries (again) promised to provide extra money for developing countries to address the negative impact of the financial and economic crisis.
3. In this regard, an active and persistent advocacy role must be played by the CRC Committee, the NGO community and UNICEF and other UN agencies, with the full involvement of children, their parents, and as far as possible the corporate world, in particular the trans-national corporations. This advocacy should be framed not only by the CRC and the *World Fit For Children* action plan, but also by the Millennium Development Goals.

Finally, and to set specific goals for all this:

1. Let us as a matter of priority develop the tracking system and linkages proposed by Sumner and Wolcott (2008).
2. Let us as a further matter of priority plan and undertake all necessary actions to establish the International Fund for the Rights and Welfare of Children as proposed by Pearson (2008).

5. REFERENCES

African Child Policy Forum (2008). *The African Report on Child Wellbeing. How child friendly are African governments?* Addis Ababa: The African Child Policy Forum.
Carmona, M.S. (2008). *The Human Rights Approach to Public Policy in Addressing Child Poverty*. Paper presented at the Third International Policy Conference on the African Child. 12–13 May 2008. Addis Ababa: The African Child Policy Forum.
Doek, J.E. (2007). "The CRC General Principles", in: *18 Candles. The Convention on the Rights of the Child Reaches Majority*, p. 31–42 (2007, Institut International des droits de l'enfant/IDE).
Frazer, H. (2008). *Combating Child Poverty and Social Exclusion in European Union Countries: Lessons for Policy and Practice*. Paper presented at the Third International Policy Conference on the African Child. 12–13 May 2008. Addis Ababa: The African Child Policy Forum.
Hart, J. et al. (2004). *Children Changing their World. Understanding and Evaluating Children's Participation in Development* (Plan International UK 2004).
IPEC/ILO (2003). *Investing in Every Child. An Economic Study of the Costs and Benefits of Eliminating Child Labour* (IPEC/ILO Geneva December 2003).
Kumar, A. K. S. (2008). *Tackling Child Poverty: Lessons from India*. Paper presented at the Third International Policy Conference on the African Child. 12–13 May 2008. Addis Ababa: The African Child Policy Forum.
Lee, Y. (2008). *Child Rights, Child Wellbeing and Child Poverty*. Paper presented at the Third International Policy Conference on the African Child. 12–13 May 2008. Addis Ababa: The African Child Policy Forum.

Lewis, L. (2008). *Claiming the Future: An Internationalist's Perspective*. Speech delivered at the Third International Policy Conference on the African Child. 12–13 May 2008. Addis Ababa: The African Child Policy Forum.

Lewis, L. (2006). *Race against time. Searching for Hope in Aids-Ravaged Africa* (CBS Massey Lectures, second edition 2006, House of Anansi Press Inc.).

Mikkelsen, J. (2008). *The Impact of the World Food Crisis on Food Assistance: A Case from Ethiopia*. Paper presented at the Third International Policy Conference on the African Child. 12–13 May 2008. Addis Ababa: The African Child Policy Forum.

Minujin, A. et al. (2006). "The definition of child poverty: a discussion of concepts and measurements". *Environment and Urbanization*, Vol. 18, No 2, 481–500 (2006).

Mugawe, D. (2008). *Child Poverty in Africa*. Paper presented at the Third International Policy Conference on the African Child. 12–13 May 2008. Addis Ababa: The African Child Policy Forum.

O'Malley, M.K. (2004). *Children and Young People Participatory in PRSP Processes: lessons from Save the Children's Experience* (Save the Children Fund, London 2004).

Pearson, R. (2008). *Kenya's Cash Transfer programme: from Inception to Adolescence 2002-2008*. Paper presented at the Third International Policy Conference on the African Child. 12–13 May 2008. Addis Ababa: The African Child Policy Forum.

Roelen, K. and Gassman, F. (2008). *Measuring Child Poverty and wellbeing. A literature Review*. Maastricht Graduate School of Governance Working Paper Series No 2008/WP001 (March 2008).

Sachs, J. D. (2008). *The impact of the global food crisis: Observations*. Speech delivered via videoconferencing at the Third International Policy Conference on the African Child. 12–13 May 2008. Addis Ababa: The African Child Policy Forum.

Sumner, A. & Wolcott, S. (2008). *What will be the Impact of the Global Economic Crisis on Child Poverty in sub-Saharan Africa?* Addis Ababa: The African Child Policy Forum.

Theis, J. (2004). *Promoting Rights-Based Approaches. Experiences and Ideas from Asia and the Pacific* (Save the Children, Sweden 2004).

Townsend, P. (2008). *The Abolition of Child Poverty and the Right to Social Security: A Possible UN Model for Child Benefit?* Paper presented at the Third International Policy Conference on the African Child. 12–13 May 2008. Addis Ababa: The African Child Policy Forum.

Turshen, M. (2008). *Child Poverty: The Gender Dimension*. Paper presented at the Third International Policy Conference on the African Child. 12–13 May 2008. Addis Ababa: The African Child Policy Forum.

UNICEF (2007). *Innocenti Social Monitor 2006. Understanding child poverty in South-Eastern Europe and the Commonwealth of independent States* (UNICEF Florence 2006) and Report Card No 6 on The Wellbeing of Children in the Rich Countries (Innocenti Research Centre UNICEF Florence 2007).

UNICEF (2005). *The State of the World's Children 2005: Childhood under Threat*

CHILD RIGHTS, CHILD WELLBEING AND CHILD POVERTY

Professor Yanghee LEE
Professor, Sungkyunkwan University
Chairperson, UN Committee on the Rights of the Child

1. HUMAN RIGHTS COMMITMENTS AND PLEDGES: AN OVERVIEW

The year 2008 marked the 60th anniversary of the UN Declaration of Human Rights (UDHR). The Declaration laid the foundation for the rights of every human being, covering economic, social, cultural, political, and civil rights. Two decades after the Declaration, two legally binding landmark human rights treaties were adopted: the International Covenant on Civil and Political Rights and the International Covenant on Economic, Social and Cultural Rights. Since then, treaties that address the rights of specific groups of people, including children, women, migrant workers, racial minorities, and people facing torture, have also been adopted. As of May 3, 2008, the newest Convention, the Convention on the Rights of Persons with Disabilities, and its Optional Protocol, have entered into force. Central to these human rights treaties are the following concepts:

- universality and inalienability: everyone in the world possesses these rights, which cannot be taken away;
- indivisibility: all rights have equal status and cannot be ranked;
- inter-dependence and inter-relatedness: realisation of a right may depend, wholly or in part, upon the realisation of other rights;
- equality and non-discrimination: every human being is equal and is entitled to his/her rights without any discrimination.

Let me briefly outline the various commitments and pledges made by the international community up to now in relation to the rights of the child and the issue of poverty. I do this with a purpose. The purpose is to emphasise that we have spent many years on making promises and setting the standards. I cannot argue that improvements have not been made, because they have indeed. However, in order for the promises not to be left as rhetoric, we need constantly to remind ourselves of the various promises we have made. We need critically to assess different endeavours, make necessary changes, and continue to strive to keep our promises.

At the World Summit for Children in 1990, the world pledged universal access to primary education by 2000, yet 130 million or more primary school-aged children were not in school by then. On September 8, 2000, the General Assembly adopted the United Nations Millennium Declaration, and the Millennium Development Goals (MDGs) within the Declaration. One hundred and eighty nine (189) nations committed themselves to achieve these Development Goals by 2015, which can be summarised as follows:

1. reduce by half the proportion of people living in extreme poverty (that is: on less than a dollar a day) and also the proportion of people that suffer from hunger;
2. ensure that all boys and girls complete a full course of primary education;
3. eliminate gender disparity in primary and secondary education, preferably by 2005 and at all levels by 2015;
4. reduce by two thirds the mortality rate among children under five;
5. reduce by three quarters the maternal mortality ratio;
6. halt and begin to reverse the spread of HIV/AIDS and the incidence of malaria and other major diseases;
7. integrate the principles of sustainable development into country policies; reverse loss of environmental resources. Reduce by half the proportion of people without sustainable access to safe drinking water. Achieve significant improvement of at least 100 million slum dwellers by 2020;
8. develop a global partnership for development, which includes the commitments (among others) to develop further an open trading and financial system, to address the least developed countries' special needs, to deal comprehensively with developing countries' debt problems, to develop decent and productive work for youth, and to provide access to affordable essential drugs in developing countries.

These MDGs recognise that extreme poverty has many dimensions – not only low income, but also vulnerability to disease, exclusion from education, chronic hunger and under-nutrition, lack of access to basic amenities such as clean water and sanitation, and environmental degradation such as deforestation and land erosion – that threaten lives and livelihoods.

On May 2002, the UN General Assembly held a Special Session on Children. It was attended by 69 Summit-level participants and 190 high-level national delegations. Attendees committed their governments to a time-bound set of specific goals for children and young people, and also agreed on a basic framework for achieving these goals. A Plan of Action for "Creating a World Fit for Children" was adopted, promising the following:

- promoting healthy lives;
- providing quality education;
- protecting against abuse, exploitation and violence;
- combating HIV/AIDS;
- mobilising resources;
- follow-up actions and assessment – including regular monitoring of progress at the national and international levels in the achievement of these goals.

The Plan of Action for the realisation of these promises is based on the commitment of the member States of the UN to, among others, the following principles and objectives:

1. put children first. In all actions related to children the best interests of the child shall be a primary consideration;
2. eradicate poverty: invest in children. We reaffirm our vow to break the cycle of poverty within a single generation, united in the conviction that investments in children and the realisation of their rights are among the most effective ways to eradicate poverty. Immediate action must be taken to eliminate the worst forms of child labour;
3. leave no child behind. Each girl and boy is born free and equal in dignity and rights; therefore, all forms of discrimination affecting children must end;
4. care for every child. Children must get the best possible start in life. Their survival, protection, growth and development, in good health and with proper nutrition, is the essential foundation of human development. We will make concerted efforts to fight infectious diseases, tackle the major causes of malnutrition[1], and nurture children in a safe environment that enables them to be physically healthy, mentally alert, emotionally secure, socially competent and able to learn;
5. listen to children and ensure their participation. Children and adolescents are resourceful citizens capable of helping to build a better future for all. We must respect their right to express themselves and to participate in all matters affecting them, in accordance with their age and maturity.

These and the other six principles and objectives are clearly a reflection of, and based in, the Convention on the Rights of the Child, and are also in part a confirmation of

---

[1] Re developments regarding efforts to address malnutrition, see the chapter contributed by Urban Jonsson to this book, *Child Malnutrition: Changing Perceptions and Policy Implications.*

the MDGs. They also make it very clear that the Member States of the UN consider the eradication of poverty by a strong call for investment in children a top priority, together with their commitment to make the best interests of the child a primary consideration in these and all other actions affecting children.[2]

More recently, on December 11 2007, the *World Fit for Children + 5* Special Session was held, and the pledges of the Heads of States at the 2002 Special Session were reaffirmed.

2. CONVENTION ON THE RIGHTS OF THE CHILD

The Convention on the Rights of the Child (CRC) just celebrated its nineteenth birthday last year. Many would say that the Convention has now 'come of age'. The Convention on the Rights of the Child was adopted and ratified by the UN General Assembly on November 20, 1989 and entered into force on September 2, 1990. The CRC was the first binding instrument in international law to deal with the rights of children, and it provides the highest level of international standards and guidelines for regional and national implementation.

The major accomplishment of the first 19 years of the CRC is that children have become more visible. Now there seems to be a certain degree of consensus that children are indeed bearers of rights. Unfortunately, there still exist many children who suffer from major violations of their rights, living in very harsh conditions, systematically discriminated against, abused, and denied participation in decision making processes. The CRC is the most comprehensive treaty affecting them, and contains 42 detailed provisions enshrining the rights of children in all areas of their lives. It is the first international instrument that covers the economic, social, cultural, civil and political rights, including special protection measures, of all persons under 18 years of age. The CRC is the only international human rights treaty that has almost universal ratification. To date, still with the exception of the United States of America and Somalia, there are 193 ratifications.

The Convention has been supplemented with two Optional Protocols. The Optional Protocol on the involvement of children in armed conflict, raising the minimum age for involvement in armed conflict to 18, entered into force on 12 February 2002. The Optional Protocol on the sale of children, child prostitution and child pornography strengthens the Convention's protection in these areas, and entered into force on 18 January 2002. Today, 118 States are party to the

---

[2] For more specific information on actions to eradicate poverty, See also the Plan of Action in the document *A World Fit For Children*, para. 18 and 19.

Optional Protocol on the involvement of children in armed conflict, and 124 States are party to the Optional Protocol on the sale of children, child prostitution and child pornography. Although the United States of America has not ratified the CRC, it ratified the two Optional Protocols. The initial reports submitted by the US government on the implementation of these Optional Protocols were considered during the Committee's session in May 2008. The Committee on the Rights of the Child, with its 18 very dedicated members, is effectively therefore monitoring implementation of three human rights treaties, with more than 400 total ratifications.

3. KEY FEATURES OF THE CONVENTION

- Definition of the child: everyone below the age of 18 years, unless, under the law applicable to the child, majority is attained earlier
- Non-discrimination
- Best interest of the child
- Right to life: appropriate health care, access to health care, hygiene, nutrition, environmental sanitation, prevention of accidents
- Right to development: appropriate child care, education, play, cultural activities
- Right to protection from all forms of physical or mental violence, economic, sexual and all other forms of exploitation, torture and other cruel, inhuman or degrading treatment or punishment.
- Right to participation, including the right to express views, to access information, and to freedom of association and freedom of peaceful assembly
- Training and dissemination of CRC.

The four General Principles identified by the CRC as fundamental for the realisation of all the other rights are as follows:

- Non-discrimination
- The best interests of the child
- Survival and development
- Respect for the views of the child.

Almost all of the articles in the CRC, either directly or indirectly, address the issue of poverty. This applies obviously, for example, to the right to benefit from social security (Article 26) and the right to an adequate standard of living (Article 27), and to the obligations of states parties to support and assist parents and other caretakers in the performance of their child rearing responsibilities (Article 18(2) and (3) and Article 27(3) and (4)); but it also applies to the rights to protection – in particular for children with disabilities (Article 23) – and to the rights to highest attainable standard of health (Article 24), education (in particular to free primary education (Article 28)), engagement in play and recreational activities, participation in cultural activities (Article 31), and the right to be registered immediately after birth (Article 7). Many other articles can be mentioned, but it is already very clear that states parties, in order to implement the Convention fully, must tackle the issues of poverty and social exclusion head-on.

Now, let us focus on the broader concept of poverty: definition, measurement, scope and nature.

It has been said repeatedly that poverty has many dimensions, and that it threatens all aspects of childhood. Furthermore, we are all too aware that poverty in childhood is the root cause of poverty in adulthood. There is a trans-generational aspect to poverty, and it contributes to many different negative consequences, including violence, discrimination, exploitation, disability, and delinquent behaviour: consequences that are addressed in many provisions in the CRC.

More importantly, there is a strong gender implication to poverty. The girl child is faced with the multiple effects of poverty. At the same time, research indicates that educating girls and empowering them is the key to the reduction of poverty.

The United Nations views poverty to be more than material deprivation – rather, it includes:

> "…deprivation of resources, capabilities, choices, security and power necessary for the enjoyment of an adequate standard of living and other civil, cultural, economic, political and social rights."

What, then, is adequate standard of living? How can we define and measure poverty? Does it mean the same for all societies?

The UN declaration from the World Summit on Social Development, which took place in Copenhagen in 1995, defines absolute poverty as follows:

> "a condition characterised by severe deprivation of basic human needs, including food, safe drinking water, sanitation facilities, health shelter, education and information. It depends not only on income but also on access to services."

The World Bank, on the other hand, defines poverty in absolute terms: extreme poverty means living on less than USD 1 per day; moderate poverty means living on less than USD 2 a day. Additionally, of course, there is the concept of poverty in terms of relative deprivation, 50 or 60 per cent below the median national income.[3] Regardless of how one defines poverty, the effects of poverty on children are characteristically the same: very serious and lifelong.

Let us now focus on how to measure poverty. Poverty must be measured not only in terms of income poverty or material deprivation. It must go beyond monetary terms, to include non-monetary indicators of income poverty, such as outcomes for children living in overcrowded housing, ability to establish and maintain social relationships, ability to feel good about oneself, and the ability to cope and adapt to external influences as well as internal/psychological influences.

Poverty experienced in childhood is different from poverty experienced as an adult. It threatens and undermines all aspects of childhood, and physical, intellectual, and socio-emotional development. In addition, it prevents children from enjoying equal opportunities, and creates social, economic, and gender disparities that ultimately contribute to the vicious cycle of poverty. Therefore, poverty must be measured differently for children.

According to UNICEF's Report Card No. 6, *Child Poverty in Rich Countries 2005*, higher government spending on family and social benefits is associated with lower child poverty rates. Moreover, poverty rates depend not only on the level of government support, but on the manner of its dispensation. Relationship between social expenditures and child poverty rates depends not only on the level of government support, but on the manner of its dispensation and on the priorities governing its allocation.

I would like to go back to the fact that the CRC has an almost universal ratification record, and to the fact that almost all articles of the CRC are related to the issue of poverty and its effects on children. When a government ratifies a Convention, it makes a promise, not only to the international community, but to its children, to fulfil its obligations. In other words, the will of a government dictates implementation.

---

[3] A study of the UNICEF's Innocenti Research Centre Report Card 6 on Child Poverty in Rich Countries 2005 (UNICEF, Florence 2005) draws the child poverty line at 50% of a country's current median income. Results show that in the rich countries, the proportion of children living in families with an income below 50% of the median income ranges from less than 5% (in, for example, Finland, Norway and Sweden) to more than 15% (e.g. the UK, Portugal, Italy and the USA – the latter with a figure of more than 20%). In other words, child poverty is not only a problem in developing countries.

When it comes to the issue of child poverty, this is when governments must demonstrate that they have lived up to their promises. We have enough evidence that increases in government spending for social benefits and education have a direct bearing on reductions in child poverty and on the improvement of the wellbeing of children.

4. CONCLUDING OBSERVATIONS

Many would agree that the twentieth century was the century of the child. In my view, nineteen years into the existence of the Convention on the Rights of the Child, the twenty-first century should be the century of accountability for all actors involved in the lives of all children. We – and I mean the collective "we" – have made a lot of promises. In fact, too many promises have gone unfulfilled. I will not repeat what many of us have said so many times: no more talk, but action. I would rather make the following observations and humbly offer some suggestions.

There is a consensus that poverty has many facets, and that it must be addressed in a multi-faceted manner. Promotion of the wellbeing of the child cannot be done in isolation. We have to address the issue of the rights of the child in a holistic and multi-sectoral fashion. The rights of the child cannot be considered without considering the economic, social, political, and attitudinal situation of a particular country. As I mentioned earlier, the inter-relatedness and inter-dependence of human rights cannot be stressed more.

On the one hand, we have not completely addressed the multiple dimensions of child poverty, nor have we addressed it in relation to other issues such as globalisation, decentralisation, privatisation, climate change, soaring prices of crude oil, and availability and access to basic needs, such as food, water, etc. It is known at time of writing that 33 countries could be subject – immediately – to civil unrest as a result of the current food crisis.

On the other hand, I am afraid that perhaps we have emphasised too much the "multi" nature of the problem. We have not tried to look at the big picture.

Everyone has created and worked in "silos", believing that if each did her or his job well, then somehow all the pieces would eventually fit together well. The problem is that the pieces do not and will not fit together without deliberate, focused effort to *make* them fit together, and fit together well.

I would like to make the analogy of the similarities and differences between a mosaic and a simple patchwork. Both contain many different pieces. A producer of a mosaic would have an image of their completed product. He, she, or they would use different pieces to complete a "plan". On the other hand, a simple patchworker would use their different pieces haphazardly.

The producer signifies political will, social will, and all the stakeholders at the national, regional, and international levels, including children. The pieces symbolise different programmes, policies, professionals, organisations, both human and financial resources, etc.: an image that is "multi" in every sense of the word. The end products of the two production processes look quite different: a mosaic has all the pieces fitting beautifully, creating a beautiful picture; whereas a simple patchwork simply looks as if different pieces have just been put together. What then, is our desired end product, the big picture? A "World Fit for Children." A world where every child will be able to realise her or his rights.

I am confident that we can assist in developing a blueprint for a beautiful mosaic: a blueprint whereby political, religious, and social differences can be put aside. Hopefully, we will leap one giant step forward into making Africa Fit For Children.

I grew up with the knowledge of a famous Ethiopian marathon runner, Abebe Biquila. Being a marathon runner myself, I know that pacing oneself to the end is very important. However, when it comes to children and child poverty, we cannot pace any longer. There are no pace-makers – nor should there be pace-makers, in this race to reducing child poverty.

Now is the time to sprint.

THE HUMAN RIGHTS APPROACH TO PUBLIC POLICY IN ADDRESSING CHILD POVERTY

Magdalena Sepúlveda Carmona
United Nations Independent Expert on the Question of Human Rights and Extreme Poverty

1. INTRODUCTION

It is quite significant for me that my first activity after being appointed as United Nations Independent Expert on the question of human rights and extreme poverty is to contribute an article on child poverty. It is my intention to make children's concerns one of the main priorities of my mandate as UN Independent Expert.

I have been asked to write on the human rights approach to public policies addressing poverty. It is a considerable challenge to approach such a vast topic in this rather brief contribution. Therefore, I will not attempt to cover the topic in detail, but rather will underline some aspects relevant to our discussion.

I am going to address the topic from a specific outlook, which, in this case, is a legal framework. By adopting such an approach, I do not intend to suggest that a human rights approach alone is sufficient to address child poverty. Economic growth, adequate levels of public expenditure, international assistance and cooperation, rules of international trade, the fight against corruption, among several other factors, are all crucial for poverty reduction. As has been stressed on numerous occasions, a multidimensional approach is required.

Nonetheless, I stress the point that for an effective public strategy that reduces child poverty, children must be placed expressly at the centre of the national agenda, and this is exactly what a human rights approach compels states to do.

2. HUMAN RIGHTS APPROACH TO PUBLIC POLICY REGARDING CHILDREN LIVING IN POVERTY

States have assumed several obligations in regard to human rights. Some of these obligations are assumed at the domestic level through, for example, constitutional commitments or a Bill of Rights. Some are assumed at the regional level through, for example, human rights treaties such as the African Charter on Human and People's Rights[1] or the African Charter on the Rights and Welfare of the Child.[2] Finally, some are assumed at the so-called universal level, for example, through treaties adopted under the auspices of the United Nations, such as the United Nations Conventions on the Rights of the Child[3] or the International Covenant on Economic, Social and Cultural Rights[4] (ICESCR), to which most African states are a party.

By accepting human rights obligations (domestic, regional and/or universal), states agree to restrict their discretion in regard to their public policies.

Let us discuss this point in some more detail:

1. Sometimes human rights obligations act as a constraint on the broad spectrum of policy decisions that states have to make. States must not adopt policies that are in conflict with their human rights obligations. For example, while population control may be permissible for reducing poverty, forced sterilisation would not be permitted under a human rights approach.

It should be noted that under the ICESCR (Article 13) and under the CRC (Article 28) governments assume the obligation to provide free and compulsory primary education. As has been noted, numerous studies have shown that the rate of return on public investment in primary education is higher than in post-primary schooling. This notwithstanding, as argued persuasively by UNDP, an "investment" approach to budget allocations in education is not consistent with international human rights law. Contrary to the logic of the market, even

---

[1] Adopted 27 June 1981, OAU Doc. CAB/LEG/67/3 rev. 5, 21 I.L.M. 58 (1982), entered into force 21 October 1986.
[2] Adopted 11 July 1990, OAU Doc. CAB/LEG/24.9/49 (1990), entered into force 29 November, 1999.
[3] Adopted and opened for signature, ratification and accession by General Assembly resolution 44/25 of 20 November 1989, entered into force 2 September,1990, in accordance with article 49.
[4] Adopted and opened for signature, ratification and accession by General Assembly resolution 2200A (XXI) of 16 December 1966, entered into force 3 January 1976, in accordance with article 27.

if post-primary education were to provide higher returns than primary education, this should not lead states to change their policy priorities in regard to primary education, because "primary education is a fundamental right and entitlement; the highest level of priority must continue to be primary education, even if the rate of return on public investment is lower than other areas".[5]

2. Some human rights obligations require states to take relatively precise policy measures. For example, under the ICESCR, states parties must take steps towards the progressive realisation of such economic, social and cultural rights (Article 2 ICESCR) as the right to education (Article 13 ICESCR and Article 28 CRC), the protection of children (Article 10 ICESCR), and an adequate standard of living (Article 11 ICESCR and Article 27 CRC). This means that states must, among other obligations, devote the maximum amount of available resources to the realisation of these rights, according a degree of priority to human rights in the allocation of resources; collect disaggregated data; monitor the realisation of these rights; and devise and adopt plans of action in response.

The term 'to the maximum of its available resources' does not require a state to devote all the resources at its disposal nor, obviously, does it require a state to devote resources that it does not have in order to fulfil these rights. Nevertheless, it does impose limitations on a state's freedom to allocate resources. The allocation of resources is not left to the complete discretion of a state.

The obligation actively to take continuous steps also applies, so that if the level of resources increases, so too must the level of commitment to the realisation of economic, social and cultural rights. The resources allocated to the realisation of these rights must increase in a manner proportional to the global increase in resources.

From a children's perspective, these duties are crucial to addressing the situation of children living in poverty. In order to tackle child poverty, states must identify who the children living in poverty are and where are they living, and put children (and their families) at the centre of their public policies. States must then establish monitoring systems to regularly track the impact of previous policies on children, and to ensure that what is being done is in the child's best interests.

3. Most important of all, in order to comply with their human rights obligations, the design, implementation and monitoring of public policies should be centred on several principles, such as the universality and interdependency of rights, participation, non-discrimination, transparency, empowerment and accountability.

---

[5] Poverty Reduction and Human Rights. A practice note, UNDP, 2003, p. 9.

Let me briefly underline HOW some of these principles should determine public policies regarding children living in poverty.

3. UNIVERSALITY AND INDIVISIBILITY

The principle of universality requires that no child be left out of the reach of public policies and development assistance.

Enjoyment of a right is indivisible from, and interrelated to, the enjoyment of other rights. For instance, for a child to enjoy the highest attainable standard of health (e.g. Article 12 ICESCR and Article 24 CRC), he or she requires enjoyment of the right to education (e.g. Article 13 ICESCR and Article 28 CRC) as well as the right to an adequate standard of living (e.g. Article 11 ICESCR and Article 27 CRC). The right to be registered at birth (e.g. Article 7 CRC) is also an essential right if children are to be enabled to enjoy other rights, such as health and education.

All human rights – civil and political or economic and social – should be treated with the same respect. Policies and programmes should not aim to implement one particular right or set of rights alone.

Firstly, some insist on the alleged positive and negative dichotomy between the two clusters of rights. It is considered that only obligations of non-interference (attributable to civil and political rights) are amenable to immediate application, while positive duties (attributable to economic, social and cultural rights) are necessarily of gradual implementation. This distinction is artificial. There is no clear-cut division between civil/political rights and social/economic rights. It is now well established that the notion of progressive realisation does not detract from the fact that economic, social and cultural rights also impose obligations of immediate effect.

Secondly, some argue that civil and political rights impose obligations that are cost-free while the obligations imposed by economic, social and cultural rights require government expenditure. This argument is counter-factual, as the implementation of all rights has resource implications. All human rights require that states, at the very least, establish institutional structures to secure an appropriate degree of compliance, and this will always entail expenditure of resources. Once we accept that the realisation of both clusters of rights entails positive and negative obligations, the alleged differences in nature as to the resources required for their realisation are rendered untenable. This is not to say that there is no difference in the level of resources required for the realisation of specific obligations: rather, while the realisation of different obligations may well require different levels of resources, in practice such differences in the resources required may exist independently of whether the obligations originate in one cluster of rights or another. All human rights impose a plurality of duties, and each of those duties potentially requires different degrees of state involvement, as well as different levels of resources. There is no watertight division between the obligations imposed by the two categories of rights. All human rights impose a continuum or spectrum of obligations of different types. Each obligation may require a different level of state involvement and a different level of resources for its implementation.

The fact that all human rights should be accorded the same degree of respect does not preclude prioritising certain forms of support. The scarcity of resources and institutional constraints often means establishing priorities. For example, states might focus on two areas of public expenditure that are particularly important for a child's development, and that can help advance the realisation of child rights and address inequalities. This would be the case, for example, if policies focussed on education and health.

4. EQUALITY AND NON-DISCRIMINATION

Human rights are for everyone. International law prohibits discrimination against children in the enjoyment of human rights on any ground, such as ethnicity, colour, sex, language, religion, political or other opinion, national or social origin, property, disability, birth or any other status (Article 2 CRC).

Equality also requires that all children within a society enjoy equal access to the available goods and services necessary to fulfil their basic human needs. It prohibits discrimination in law or in practice in any field regulated or protected by public authorities.

Thus, the principle of non-discrimination applies to all state policies and practices, including those concerning healthcare, education and access to services.

The principle of equality also requires states to take steps to narrow the disparities between different groups of children, such as children from minority groups or from rural areas. Great disparities within a country would imply that insufficient consideration is given to this principle. In this regard, it is important to remember that failure by governments to invest in children will prolong the intergenerational transfer of poverty, and contribute to the further consolidation of existing inequalities.

The principle of equality and non discrimination also requires states to take special protective measures and affirmative action in order to ensure that the most disadvantaged or excluded children, such as street children, child labourers, children who are sexually exploited, and children with disabilities, enjoy their rights. This requires taking specific measures directly designed to improve their situation, so as to place them in a situation equal to that of other more privileged children.

Therefore, particular consideration for the most disadvantaged children must be addressed in the design, implementation and monitoring of public policies. In order to enable the state to do so, states are required to collect disaggregated data to identify children at risk. States should also identify and monitor the different impact on girls and boys of their public policies.

In conclusion, a human rights approach places special emphasis on particularly disadvantaged or socially excluded individuals and groups.

5. TRANSPARENCY

Why should public policies promote transparency and stand against corruption?

Evidence shows that corruption has a negative impact on all human rights, and in particular on the implementation of economic, social and cultural rights. Corruption diverts funds aimed at the realisation of basic human rights – such as health care, education and access to clean water – into private pockets. In this regard, corruption has a disproportionate impact on the poor.

Children are particularly dependent on public social services, therefore they are disproportionately affected by corruption. Moreover, corruption is a direct violation of the principles of equality and non-discrimination. For example: when a child is denied access to education because his or her parents are not able to pay a bribe, his or her right to education is violated.

6. PARTICIPATION AND INCLUSION

Children's participation in public policies can improve the sensitivity of decision-making to the needs and issues of children. From a human rights perspective, child participation is a right. States and other actors are obliged to create an environment that encourages the participation of children. This means that participation is not simply something desirable from the point of view of giving ownership, but rather a right with profound consequences for the design and implementation of public policies.

This in turn necessitates a supportive environment to enable children to develop and express their full potential and creativity. Examples of child-led organisations and child parliaments around the world demonstrate the effectiveness of some policies that recognise children as agents of change.

7. FINAL OBSERVATIONS

As I stressed at the beginning of this paper, a human rights approach alone is obviously not enough to overcome child poverty. Economic growth and, in particular, international assistance and cooperation are crucial. We must also be realistic. The current international context seems sometimes to be a major obstacle to the progressive realisation of economic, social and cultural rights, in a manner that is certainly sometimes quite depressing.

Nevertheless, despite the obstacles, those of us who strongly believe in the power of human rights must stress that the human rights system refers to entitlements and obligations. We are no longer speaking in the realm of goals or aspirations. We are not talking about whether or not "children should go to school"; rather, we are referring to the "rights of children to free primary education". This is a right that means governments, according to the guidelines that we discussed, must identify how many children are out of primary school, devise a plan progressively and without delay to improve the access of those children to primary education, monitor the implementation of that policy, and be accountable for what has or has not been done in this regard. As such, respect for human rights is to be reflected in a state's norms, institutions, legal frameworks, and economic, political and policy environments.

By adopting national human rights legislation or ratifying relevant human rights treaties, states have agreed to put children at the centre of their public policies and to comply with several guidelines in regard to their design and implementation. And we must continuously remind them to do so! These guidelines are relatively precise and compulsory when they are included in domestic legislation or human rights treaties ratified by the state.

The human rights approach offers an explicit normative framework that has been universally accepted and codified in the international law of human rights, bringing more legitimacy and consistency to various processes already in course in this regard.

The quest to take children out of poverty requires a multidimensional approach and the work of all, from all of our different perspectives and disciplines. Child poverty in Africa, or anywhere in the world, is everybody's concern.

8. REFERENCES

International Save the Children Alliance (2005). *Practice Standards in Children's Participation*, Save the Children.
OHCHR (2004). *Guidelines on a human rights approach to poverty reduction*. OHCHR
Ray, P. and Carter, S. (2007). *Each and Every Child: Understanding and working with children in the poorest and most difficult situations*. Plan International.
Sepúlveda, M. (2003). *The nature of the obligations under the International Covenant on Economic, Social and Cultural Rights*. Intersentia.
UNDP (2003). *Poverty Reduction and Human Rights: a practice note*. UNDP.
UNICEF (2005). *The State of the World's Children in 2005*. UNICEF.
UNICEF (2006). *Innocenti Social Monitor 2006: Understanding Child Poverty in South-Eastern Europe and the Commonwealth of Independent States*. UNICEF.

CHILD RIGHTS AND ECONOMIC POLICY

Professor Sir Richard JOLLY
Deputy Executive Director, UNICEF (1982–1996)
Architect, Human Development Report (1996–2000)

1. INTRODUCTION

None of us need reminding of the grievous economic difficulties facing most African countries today. Many of these constraints are national, directly or indirectly related to weak leadership and poor governance, compounded in many cases by conflict and civil war. But there are also international factors which for at least two decades have set back Africa's economies and made Africa's situation today very serious indeed, even in countries which have demonstrated impressive national action. These international factors began with the world recession of the early 1980s, rising debt and declining commodity prices, all compounded by structural adjustment policies which focused too narrowly on economic goals and neglected the human, including the priority needs of children.

Instruments of human rights have from the earliest days recognised the necessity of a positive international context for achieving human rights. The Universal Declaration of Human Rights of 1948 stated in Article 28 that "everyone is entitled to a social and international order in which the rights and freedoms set forth in this Declaration can be fully realised". Over 40 years later, Article 4 of the Convention on the Rights of the Child stated more specifically that "States Parties shall undertake such measures to the maximum extent of their available resources and, where needed, within the framework of international co-operation". Articles 24 and 28, in dealing with health and education, emphasised that, "particular account shall be taken of the needs of developing countries". These themes were also considerably elaborated in 1986, in the Declaration on the Rights to Development. Most recently, they have been reinforced by commitments of the global community to develop a global partnership for development, commitments endorsed by 189 countries committed to achieving the Millennium Development Goals (MDGs).

2. RIGHTS, GOALS, POLICY AND PARTNERSHIPS

My first main point is that we now need to bring four things together – rights, goals, national economic policies and international partnerships. All four are needed in order to achieve progressive realisation of rights for children ("progressive realisation" is the phrase often referred to in the Conventions). The specific targets of the MDGs, all of which deal directly or indirectly with the needs of children, provide a practical focus for action over the next decade.

Before we become too pessimistic, let us note that a fair number of countries are already on track towards these goals. This has been analysed in the Human Development Reports in 2002 and 2003. Unfortunately, most countries in sub-Saharan Africa – and most of the other least developed countries – cannot claim to be on track. Progress in these cases will depend on a new level of commitment by governments, and a greatly enhanced level of support from the international community. Though international action is important, let me make several points about national action.

First, national action is always essential – and the starting point. Unless countries, regions, districts and communities take the lead, there is little that the international community can do. Almost always, this will require struggle and political commitment. It will not be easy but it remains the challenge.

Second, however, the record is not as pessimistic as many often think. Over the 1980s, even in the midst of the so called "lost decade", many African countries demonstrated the possibility of accelerated action for immunisation, oral rehydration and other priority measures to reduce child mortality. By 1990, in spite of the lost decade, child mortality had been reduced significantly in most countries of Africa. The same techniques of political commitment, social mobilisation and cost effective approaches that achieved this are now priorities for progress towards the MDGs.

Third, some national action is always possible. Communities, districts, regions all have some room for manoeuvre, even when national and international action is lagging or absent.

3. NEEDS, COUNTRY BY COUNTRY

My second point is that action and initiatives must be taken country by country. As mentioned already, some opportunities and possibilities are almost always open at local or national level – or somewhere in between. Vision is needed to set the challenge, but response to the challenge can come from many quarters.

The needs and challenges of children can be felt and responded to in wonderful and sometimes surprising ways – as mothers and fathers and many others all over the world demonstrate every day. Even economists are susceptible to the call of children, though their hard-nosed training may cause them to miss the obvious. Hans Singer, the pioneering UN economist, was asked in 1984 by Maurice Pate, then Executive Director of UNICEF, to prepare a booklet on children and Economic Policy. Singer, now in his 90s, confessed in an interview a few years ago that, when first approached, he did not understand the challenge. He said to Maurice Pate, "I don't see the connection between children and economic policy." A few weeks later, he found himself listening to a lecture on child nutrition in Guatemala given by Nevin Scrimshaw, then a young nutritionist. Singer described his reaction: "Suddenly it hit me, like a bolt of lightning from the sky". Nutrition was fundamental to child development; children were the foundations of human capital formation, and the accumulation of capital was at the core of economic development. Singer returned to New York and told Maurice Pate, "Now I see the connection. Of course, I will be glad to write the booklet."

In the 1980s, the same lack of economic imagination hindered economists from seeing the needs of children in the making of adjustment policy. Blinkered by neo-classical orthodoxy, the focus of the IMF and the World Bank was on putting the economy right: reducing inflation, cutting deficits, shrinking government in order to restore economic growth. The human side was grotesquely neglected. They were "balancing the economy by un-balancing human lives," as Mahbub ul Haq put it in the *Human Development Report.*

It was left to UNICEF and the Economic Commission for Africa (ECA) to set out the case for a different approach (the ILO started on this task, but was threatened with the withdrawal of US funding if it proceeded). ECA developed AAF-SAP: the African Alternative Framework for Structural Adjustment Policy. UNICEF promoted "Adjustment with a Human Face". One of my most exciting memories of the mid-1980s is of participating in the lively and creative meetings of the UN task force on structural adjustment, which campaigned for the specifics of an alternative approach. The task force was chaired by Professor Adebayo Adedeji, co-chaired by myself, and included most of the concerned UN agencies, with Stephen Lewis as the larger than life commentator and enthusiast, to egg us on if ever our energy and vision began to flag.

These efforts and our group certainly made an impact – though long term results were mixed. The results were by no means totally successful, but neither were they a total failure. Little by little, the message got through – that adjustment policy needs to give a central place to human concerns. Today, no-one in Bretton Woods would argue in public that human concerns could be neglected – even in the short run – as once they did. But equally, implementation is still far from consistent.

Economists might argue that a change in approach came largely as a result of more careful analysis, recognising the high rates of return on investment in children, health and education. Some of this explanation may be true, but I believe that the most important changes came, not through economic logic, but through human empathy. In the IMF, on the first occasion when we argued the case for adjustment with a human face, the young assistant to the IMF Managing Director took me aside as we were leaving the room. He said, "All the time you were talking of rising malnutrition through inappropriate adjustment in developing countries, I was thinking of my own two children, aged two and four. I was asking myself how I would react if malnutrition caused by adjustment cutbacks was happening to them."

I believe that all of us do well to think of children – our own or some others we know – in order to understand the human dimensions of situations we try to analyse, as well as to discover the passion and conviction needed in developing policies for human development more generally.

ECA and UNICEF set out the specifics of what an alternative approach would achieve. To implement Adjustment with a Human Face, UNICEF argued strongly that three major changes to the conventional approach to structural adjustment were needed. Adjustment with a Human Face would embrace:

- A broader range of goals and objectives – to bring in human goals and to make them a central objective
- A change in the content and direction of sector programmes – in order to ensure that the human goals and objectives were adequately supported
- New modalities – to include a broader range of expertise and representation in the making of adjustment policy, and a broader approach to monitoring the human dimension of progress in addition to monitoring economic variables. A focus on nutrition status, education enrolments and health is just as important as a focus on the conventional variables of economic performance; and this means that adjustment policies cannot be made only by the Ministry of Finance and Planning, nor can they be made solely by economists or by governments.

As indicated, these ideas made some headway, though they are still far from fully accepted. In principle, the Poverty Reduction Strategy Papers (PRSPs) incorporate the MDGs as core objectives and allow for these broader modalities; but too often they are not carried through into specific policies and practice. The result is that in many of the PRSPs, the core of economic policy too often slavishly follows the tracks of orthodox adjustment policy, failing to develop a comprehensive and consistent strategy towards all the MDGs and achieve an integrated approach to human development.

Constraints come from the failure to have created a supportive international environment as well as from weaknesses in national policy and commitment. But I believe that failure also reflects weaknesses of understanding and imagination among political leaders and policy makers. The famous economist John Maynard Keynes described the problem in the preface to his path-breaking book *The General Theory of Employment, Interest and Money*. "The ideas which are here expressed so laboriously are extremely simple and should be obvious. The difficulty lies not in the new ideas but in escaping from the old ones which ramify, for those brought up as most of us have been, into every corner of our minds."

Many policy-makers, especially economists, need a bolt of lightning to strike them regarding a new understanding of children's needs and the economic priorities required to respond to them.

I will end this section by underlining five priority actions which would help national and international action for children:

- first, the adoption of a human development approach to analysis and policy-making, country by country. This would provide a frame within which, at country level, issues of human rights, human development, the Millennium Development Goals and poverty reduction could be brought together. A human development approach would also provide a framework within which the contributions of different UN agencies could be brought together into a Poverty Reduction Strategy Paper;
- the World Bank and the IMF need formally to acknowledge and adopt human rights guidelines for their programmes and activities. At the moment this is rejected on the grounds that human rights are not included within the Articles of Association of these bodies. Yet when they were founded, the pursuit of full employment was incorporated as a key objective in their articles. The pursuit of human rights is the more general equivalent today;
- a broader range of statistics needs to be developed and used country-by-country for monitoring progress in human development and human rights.

Most countries at present have data on prices, trade, balance of payments, government budgets and GNP. Often such data is available within a few weeks or months of collection. In contrast, data on children and on other key areas of human development are missing, and when they are available, are often only produced a year or two late;
- these changes will only occur with the support of a wide group of people and processionals, locally, nationally and internationally. We cannot expect change if we leave the initiatives to economists and economic policy makers;
- The African Child Policy Forum might establish a group of economists to explore economic priorities and policies needed in Africa, to set a better frame for child progress.

4. MOBILISATION FOR ACTION

My third main point is the necessity for mobilisation – for building a movement for children to carry forward these priorities and ideas. There is always a risk that professionals will think mainly in terms of policy-making and detached professional analysis. Almost always more important is a political and social commitment to action. The MDGs and the National Human Development Reports have already set the basis of an agenda, nationally and internationally: we need to build a widespread understanding of and commitment to their achievement, country by country. Experience shows that if and when people are really engaged, progress is possible.

Jim Grant, the Executive Director of UNICEF (1980–1995), demonstrated the power of such mobilisation, country by country. The ten commandments of his approach have been set out in a little book, *Jim Grant: UNICEF Visionary*. The ten commandments for successful action for children are as follows:

- articulate your vision in terms of inspiring goals;
- break down goals into time-bound, doable propositions;
- demystify techniques and technologies;
- generate and sustain political commitment;
- mobilise a grand alliance;
- go to scale;
- select your priorities and stick to them;
- institute public monitoring and accountability;
- ensure relevance to the broader development agenda;
- unleash the potential of the whole of the UN system.

Gandhi said, "When you are uncertain what to do, think of the poorest person you know and ask how he or she will be affected by the actions you are considering". In our case, we can and should think of children – the reality of their needs but also their creativity, their joy, their vitality and the love they can inspire. Let children serve as the source of a bolt of lightning which can electrify our thinking and bring us to new commitments and new action, stirring our awareness of children's needs and the opportunities and possibilities for fulfilling them.

CHILD POVERTY:
THE GENDER DIMENSION

Professor Meredeth TURSHEN
E.J. Bloustein School of Planning and Public Policy
Rutgers, the State University of New Jersey

1. OPENING OBSERVATIONS

In looking at the gender dimension of child poverty it seems important to restate what many already know: that "gender" is not a synonym for women, it is not a term exclusive to a feminist vocabulary, and it is not an attack on men. It is an attempt to elaborate the differences between girls and boys, going beyond biological and physiological traits to social and behavioural characteristics and the dynamic cultural, social, economic, and legal systems that create and reinforce those characteristics. Gender is therefore a critical tool in understanding how poverty affects girls and boys differently – from infancy through to adolescence.

To use gender as a tool in projects to mitigate child poverty, policy makers need information about sex and gender: data disaggregated by sex and information about the different roles, social status, economic and political power of women and men in society. Although offices of national statistics are making progress on publishing disaggregated data in vital statistics, health and education, they do not publish data on child poverty disaggregated by sex since child poverty is a reflection of family circumstances. If we are to correlate poverty with sex, age, and race or ethnicity, then we need a gendered definition of poverty that measures more than wealth and income of the family.[1]

---

[1] UNDP's introduction of the GDI (Gender Development Index) and GEM (Gender Empowerment Measure) allow comparisons of the status of women with that of men across countries. Neither index compares the status of the girl child with that of the boy child, although UNDP claims that the same methodologies can be applied at the national and sub-national levels through disaggregated GDIs and GEMs so as to compare differences between regions, ethnic groups, age groups, etc. and to assess inequalities between rich and poor, young and old, etc.

Secondly, for those of us oriented towards equity, our principal objective is the reduction of differences between rich and poor.[2] A concern with inequities is a concern with righting the injustice represented by inequalities or poor conditions among the disadvantaged (Gwatkin, 2002). When gender concerns lead policy makers to focus exclusively on disadvantaged girls, the services they provide may improve the lot of poor girls, but will do nothing to reduce differences between rich and poor. Policy makers tend to treat gender in isolation from structural analyses of inequality. An exclusive emphasis on gender roles leads to a focus on behavioural change at the individual level, rather than on policy change at the societal level.

Thirdly, clearly not all girls are alike, just as not all boys are alike; their circumstances vary in many ways – by poverty and wealth, by social class and caste, by ethnicity and religion, and by the social standing of the community into which they are born or marry. The United Nations Commission on Human Rights (since 2006, the United Nations Human Rights Council) refers to the experience of discrimination on more than one ground as *intersectionality,* the idea that racism, patriarchy, economic disadvantage, and other discriminatory systems create layers of inequality that structure the relative positions of females and males, racial and other groups. Intersectionality describes the way that specific acts and policies create burdens that flow along these intersecting axes, creating a dynamic of disempowerment (Coomaraswamy, 2001).

The Commission on Human Rights distinguishes three types of intersectional subordination: targeted discrimination (ethnically motivated gender-specific forms of violence; rape in civil conflicts is an example); compound discrimination (discrimination against girls and women who are also members of a subordinate racial or ethnic group); and structural discrimination (where policies intersect with underlying structures of inequality to create a compound burden for particularly vulnerable girls and women) (Human Rights Council, 2008).

Although gross poverty data exist for North/South differences and for male/female income differences, the data on racial, ethnic, and religious numerical minorities within countries of the South are largely nonexistent. In an issue of the *Bulletin of the World Health Organization* devoted to the theme of inequality and health, a comparative study of child mortality in nine developing countries

---

[2] Gender equality means that women and men have equal conditions for realising their full rights, contributing to development, and benefiting from the results; gender inequity refers to those inequalities between men and women in status, services and work participation that are unjust, unnecessary and avoidable. Gender equity strategies lead eventually to equality. Equity is the means, equality is the result (PAHO 2005).

(Wagstaff, 2000) shows that the largest difference between poor and non-poor occurs in Brazil, which is a highly unequal society. Such comparative studies are rare, and unfortunately this one does not differentiate between boys and girls.[3] Another article on child mortality in the same issue of the World Health Organization (WHO) Bulletin observes "there has been no systematic examination of ethnic inequality in child survival chances across countries in the [sub-Saharan African] region" (Brockerhoff and Hewitt, 2000:30). The criteria for determining inequality were geographical location of ethnic groups (residence in the largest city), household economic conditions, educational attainment and nutritional status of the mothers, use of modern maternal and child health services including immunisation, and patterns of fertility and migration. The authors report no breakdown by sex. Racism, sexism, class prejudice, and discrimination – as either the legacies of colonial rule or as the result of internecine power struggles – were apparently not issues considered relevant to inequality.

Today, economic disadvantage (sometimes socioeconomic disadvantage) is a common explanation of mortality differentials. These accounts do not hold organisers, participants, and perpetuators of discriminatory institutions and systems of prejudice accountable. Caste systems clearly affect people's life chances, yet few studies quantify the impact of caste on health. The same is true of education. For example, Dalit women enjoy significantly lower levels of literacy than the general Indian population: 76 per cent of Dalit women are illiterate compared with 46 per cent of all Indian women, and 83 per cent of Dalit girls drop out of secondary school. Researchers tend to use economic arguments, like pressure to earn an income in poor households, to explain this discrepancy, ignoring discriminatory systems.[4]

Although statistical offices have documented the association of high levels of income inequality and poor health, researchers have not explained the uneven experiences of minority communities that do not have the same rates of sickness and death. Societies privilege some minorities, like whites in Namibia, and social cohesion mitigates risk in other minority communities. It is not enough, however,

---

[3] The best-known synergy is between measles and malnutrition, sometimes a consequence of diarrhoeal disease, in young children. Despite decades of research on this synergy, studies do not routinely disaggregate data by sex in order to look at the contribution of sexism. Does the synergy affect girls more than boys? Organisations like WHO don't routinely coordinate the research of their women's health unit, which carries out gender analyses, with units studying nutrition or tropical diseases. Although health scientists know that malnutrition is the biggest risk factor in disease worldwide, households and health care facilities often fail to recognise the different nutritional needs of girls and women. Biases against girls and women are widely institutionalised. Economic differentials in property and inheritance, as well as divisions of labour within households and communities, reproduce those biases.

[4] Women's Net, accessed 26 June 2006.

to trace disparities in health status to disparate treatment, or to show the different outcomes that result from the minimal and delayed care of disadvantaged minorities when we control for socioeconomic status and access to health care. Intersectionality promises a much richer and deeper understanding of girls' and boys' poverty and health.

Fourth, gender means more than male/female differences and the disaggregation of data by sex: gender implies the dynamics of discrimination and subordination between the sexes. Without the social and economic contexts that establish power differentials, gender is misused as a synonym for the female sex. These social and economic contexts are found within families and communities, within nations, and in global relations between North and South. In societies that prefer and privilege sons, we know that daughters may not survive pregnancy and childbirth, may suffer or die in infancy and childhood from malnutrition and lack of medical attention to childhood diseases, and will attend school irregularly and receive fewer years of education than their brothers. How does this information correlate with women's poverty in adulthood?[5]

An example of the impact of gender used in this sense is that of sexual abuse of girls within families. Researchers cite various reasons for the frequency of abuse: poverty, which makes it harder for parents to keep children safe or relocate to safer neighbourhoods; a legacy of violent, oppressed societies; and cultural mores that allow offenders to escape criminal punishment, often by marrying their victims or compensating their victims' families (Addario, 2006).[6]

Fifth, war dramatically and fundamentally alters life prospects for girls and boys, although it may provide new opportunities – a few boys may use the military to advance, and in time of war a few girls may take on roles previously denied them. Most girls face more constraints in wartime, not only because their families may be displaced or even broken up, but because their communities

---

[5] A conceptual problem associated with the life expectancy component of the UNDP Gender Development Index is that it ignores the issue of sex-selective abortions. In China, India, South Korea, and elsewhere, sex ratios at birth (defined as the ratio of males to females born) have risen as a result of sex-selective abortions of female foetuses. In some places the treatment of living female children has improved, and thus female life expectancy of those who are allowed to be born has risen. In the logic of the GDI, the gender gap in life expectancy has been reduced, as the girls that were never born are not considered (KLASEN, 2006).

[6] For example, Justin Betombo was arrested in Sambava, Madagascar, in 2003 after his 9-year-old niece, Kenia, said he had savagely assaulted her. The police obtained his confession, which he later recanted, and a doctor's certificate that Kenia had been sexually violated, rendering her incontinent and anorexic. Twice they sent the case file to the prosecutor. Betombo denied Kenia's accusation. He was freed after convincing a prosecutor that he had falsely confessed after a police beating (ADDARIO 2006).

often become more conservative and xenophobic during armed conflict, and because government protections falter or fail. Poverty in wartime takes on a different character; war reveals the stark nature of poverty shorn of the mitigating context of neighbourly solidarity and familial networks of mutual assistance. Therefore, mitigation of child poverty in the aftermath of war must adapt approaches used in peacetime, or create new ones appropriate to the situation, taking into account the gender dimension.[7]

Sixth, one assumes that the purpose of improving qualitative and quantitative data about child poverty is to target aid programmes better. Targeting is the approach that, unfortunately, is currently the norm, and an older style of universal programmes that had neither means tests to qualify for aid nor other limitations like age and group affiliation is out of favour. The objections to targeted programmes are that they are expensive to administer, not transformative, not redistributive (despite claims to the contrary), and do not lead to structural change.[8] At best, targeted programmes bring about incremental improvements in the lot of targeted groups, which are often defined as 'vulnerable' with little elaboration of the structures that create vulnerability.[9]

Feminists have criticised a false universalism that masks male-biased arrangements, yet they have found universalistic social policies effective in eliminating forms of inequality in social frameworks that assume that males are the breadwinners and heads of household. Policies friendly to women and girls are found in societies that base their social policies on notions of social citizenship and on universalism as an integral part of social policies (Mkandawire, 2005).

The point here is that the poverty of girls is not separate from the poverty of their brothers; there are no sex-segregated data for child poverty because the

---

[7] For example, a frequent obstacle to female recruitment into the police in post-conflict contexts is a lack of qualifications stemming from years of neglected schooling, which prevents women from entering the service or precludes them from qualifying for promotion. The Liberian National Police addresses this problem by providing free education at the high school level to girls who are willing to undergo specialised police training once they are awarded their high school diplomas.

[8] Structural adjustment programmes and PSRPs are driven by a targeting rationale (MKANDAWIRE 2005).

[9] UNICEF has produced a conceptual framework for analysing the impacts of policies on children that models state, civil society and community impacts and focuses on the interrelationship between the macro level of national policy making and the micro level of children's experiences and community life. However, it does not distinguish between girls and boys and fails to take into account systemic discrimination. System reform in the UNICEF model refers to bureaucratic changes. (Hoelscher, Petra. 2008. UNICEF Global Child Poverty Study, CE E/CIS Regional Meeting, Tashkent, 2–4 April 2008).

measurement is of the poverty of families and households in which they live. So the issue is to find a way to measure the impact of the discriminatory systems operating in childhood that lead women to become the majority of the world's poor.

Finally, evaluation is a key component of projects to abate child poverty, but apparently meaningful evaluation is too rarely built into plans. As a result, this paper, which surveys projects on one aspect of childhood poverty – problems of access to health and education for girls and boys – cannot comment on good practices or failed programmes, because too often the necessary information is lacking.

2. SOCIAL TRANSFERS TO REDUCE CHILD POVERTY

A frontal attack on child poverty entails programmes to reduce familial or household poverty. Cash transfers are a proven way to improve family income. The three models of cash transfers are: means-tested (income, score cards) or categorical transfers, which are targeted to poor or disadvantaged groups of the population (e.g. disabled children); conditional cash transfers that are linked to families' behaviour change (that is, they are conditional on children's school attendance or health check ups, for example); and universal child benefits to ensure a minimum standard of living for all children (or specific age groups).

Targeted transfers are said to be cheaper than universal benefits but complicated procedures, high barriers to access, high administrative costs, and low coverage of target populations are drawbacks. The evidence of effectiveness of conditional cash transfers is mixed; they do not work where problems lie in the system rather than parents' behaviour. Universal child benefits are popular and not so easily subject to budget reductions as targeted or conditional programmes. It is rarely stated, but should be clear, that means-tested and conditional transfers are models for governmental and non-governmental programmes, but only governments can administer universal programmes.

The data from the European Union on reductions in child poverty after social transfers are stunning; most showed a dramatic drop in poverty, and only Turkey showed a modest rise (Hoelscher, 2008).

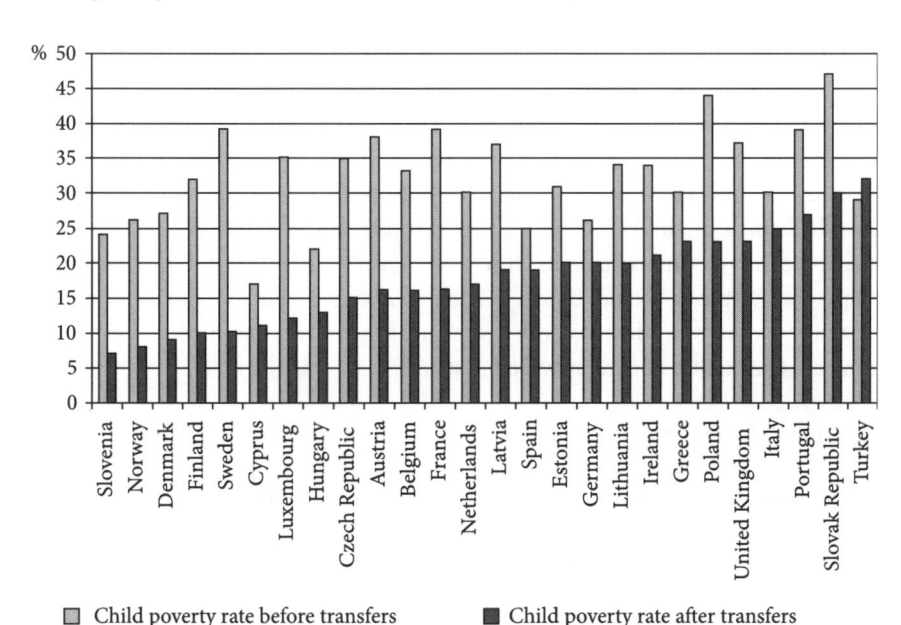

Child poverty rates before and after social transfers EU, 2003

□ Child poverty rate before transfers   ■ Child poverty rate after transfers

Source: Hoelscher, 2008.

3. HEALTH PROGRAMMES FOR CHILDREN AND YOUTH

Most of the examples of programming listed here are drawn from reports of intergovernmental and non-governmental organisations. Programmes that expressly target poverty in childhood tend not to differentiate between girls and boys, the assumption being that familial circumstances dictate the poverty of all siblings. Conversely, those programmes that address gender issues do not appear to target poverty directly, the assumption being that better health mitigates poverty. The intersectional approach recommended by the United Nations Human Rights Commission does not appear to be implemented as yet.

3.1. PROGRAMMES FOR REPRODUCTIVE HEALTH

A. *Pharmacies as a source for youth-friendly care*

A 1999 baseline survey conducted by Save the Children in Bolivia revealed that pharmacies are among adolescents' preferred sources of contraceptives, but that service quality is generally poor. To improve the quality and 'youth-friendliness' of services and information provided by pharmacies, Save the Children, in collaboration with the Population Council, conducted an operations research project in 2000–2001. Project interventions included training pharmacy staff in youth-friendly services and adolescent reproductive and sexual health issues; developing and disseminating information and educational materials; raising adolescents' awareness of their sexual and reproductive rights; and facilitating 'youth defined quality[10]' dialogues between pharmacy staff and adolescents to negotiate service improvements. The research objective was to study whether these interventions would increase adolescents' demand for and thus use of pharmacies for reproductive and sexual health information and services, and improve the quality of care provided to youth.[11]

B. Games for reproductive health

Direct research – as well as established theories of educational design, health and sexuality education, and communication – supports the educational effectiveness of games. For example, the Programme for Appropriate Technology in Health (PATH) conducted qualitative research on the educational value of two sexuality education board games (Safari of Life and Young Man's Journey) with 560 players in 11 countries. They found overwhelming enthusiasm for the games on the part of players and teachers, as well as indications of meaningful engagement and increased understanding of the subject matter.[12]

C. Facing the challenges of new reproductive technologies

According to The Association for Women's Rights in Development (AWID), without critical interrogation of new reproductive technologies (NRTs), young women remain passive recipients, the pawns of multi-billion dollar NRT industries. As debates emerge around these new technologies and their potential for misuse, and as young women become more aware of their reproductive rights, women can be a crucial force in critiquing and ensuring just and safe production and marketing of these technologies. The Association for Women's Rights in Development suggests that young women should consider the following questions:

---

[10] "Youth defined quality" is a means to engage young people and health providers in a process of exploring and sharing perceptions of quality health services, and it emphasises mutual responsibility for problem identification and problem solving.
[11] Source: Save the Children, 2004.
[12] Source: Programme for Appropriate Technology in Health [PATH], 2002, Washington, D.C., www.path.org.

- What are the impacts of new reproductive technologies for/on me?
- How are these new technologies being tested, marketed, and promoted in my community?
- Are we becoming more accustomed to turning to techno-fixes for solving problems or meeting challenges?
- Have we become more likely to accept new reproductive technologies without critical investigation of side effects or potential dangers?
- Who makes the decisions about the creation and control of NRTs?

AWID points out that one of the problems faced in Latin American countries is that prenatal testing is available, but abortion is not. Why are new technologies being brought into countries that do not guarantee full reproductive rights? In order to promote women's health and rights everywhere, women must be aware of new and changing debates, and must ensure that critical analysis takes into account the real effects of new reproductive technologies on women's lives throughout the world.

Young women benefit from frameworks already in place (international human rights treaties and programmes of action) that take into account sexual and reproductive rights. They can use these frameworks (such as the outcome documents of the International Conference on Population Development (ICPD) Cairo conference in 1994, the Beijing women's conference in 1995, and General Comment No. 4 of the CRC Committee on Adolescent Health and Development, in the context of the Convention on the Rights of the Child), as entry points for mobilising around new reproductive technologies. This generation can ask: Who is developing these new technologies and for whom? How can young women be pro-active in their activism and advocacy in order to use existing mechanisms, as well as create their own means by which to ensure the protection of all women's health and rights?

Debates and policies about the new reproductive technologies have not adequately contextualised the forces of globalisation, capitalism, patriarchy, scientific and medical establishments, and their impact on the creation, dissemination, and uptake of these new technologies. Corporations create and market new technologies in a global context like never before. Given women's experiences with reproductive technologies and their past struggles for reproductive rights, it is crucial that women's movements and gender equality advocates take notice of the radical changes and act together. Regulation and the protection of women's rights before profits is our number one priority.[13]

---

13   Source: Young Women and Leadership, Gender Equality and New Technologies no. 8, AWID, 2004.

D. Programmes to combat AIDS

Thirty years into the AIDS pandemic, the lack of information about which jobs pose greater risk, which work settings are especially hazardous, and how status – whether the high status of women in politics or the low status of girls in factories – affects risk, is egregious. Almost everywhere, economic restructuring and global transformation are reinforcing pre-existing inequalities and exclusions, such as sexism, racism, ethnic discrimination, and religious conflict (Parker and Aggleton 2003); yet the impact of these forces on women at work is poorly understood, and the relation of restructured economies to AIDS rarely investigated.

Poverty and gender discrimination often combine to deny access to drugs and services that can alleviate the effects of AIDS. Debate over the distribution of antiretroviral drugs continues to take place among drug manufacturers and international agencies, as does work to reduce the biases that discourage women from seeking male and female condoms and AIDS medications.

The negative attitudes of health providers, as well as discriminatory laws and policies, prevent young people from accessing services. Because youth-friendly health services are not widely available, both young women and young men are often excluded from reproductive health services. Youth responses to AIDS do not take into account the needs of young women when, for example, the initiative is a youth centre or other venue in which girls do not feel comfortable. To participate in decision-making, young women need safe spaces in which to voice their concerns, aspirations, and ideas. For more information on measures to address this need and other aspects of HIV/AIDS prevention and intervention programmes, see the recommendations of the CRC Committee in its General Comment No. 3 on HIV/AIDS and the rights of the child.[14]

E. Using games to reach children and youth

Instituto de Investigación y Desarrollo (IDES) is a small Uruguayan NGO with a tradition of promoting social and human rights. Juan José Meré of IDES explains how the use of games can turn AIDS prevention information from cold knowledge into feelings and action:

> "Since 1989, the Health Team of IDES has promoted the community prevention of AIDS through games – using them in training courses, workshops, seminars and advisory groups, in Uruguay and the border areas of Brazil and Argentina. The games are based on cards, ludo, dominoes, table or board games. This interactive strategy is a result of years of joint learning with community groups. It is also a never ending

---

[14] CRC/GC/2003/3, March 2003.

process – the games are based on the experience of the participants, who always have the last word about themselves."

According to IDES, games touch the emotions. People do not change their behaviour because of information or reason alone. Feelings and everyday life must be brought into the picture. That's why prevention strategies based on the use of an innovative didactic tool – the Open Game – work.

The Open Game has three main features: it adapts to the socio-cultural situation of each social group; it is flexible enough to stress different themes (for instance, using a condom or living with an HIV-positive person); and above all, it reflects and incorporates the many voices, thoughts, and experiences of the participants. The game provides a mask. Each participant faces different situations that might one day become their reality. They act out their part, but consider, talk to, confront, and negotiate with others.

One game is 'smart dominoes'. In the traditional game of dominoes, players match pieces strictly according to numbers of dots: their moves and thought processes are channelled through a single logic. In the 'smart domino' game, pieces show pictures of situations and statements about AIDS. There are multiple ways to match the pieces, and persons can argue for their own matching logic according to their view of the world.[15]

F. Peer education: not a cheap fix

On January 11–12, 2006, the US Agency for International Development (USAID) and Family Health International (FHI)/YouthNet sponsored an international consultation in Washington, DC, called *Taking Stock of Youth Reproductive Health and HIV Peer Education: Progress, Process, and Programming for the Future*. An overarching theme of the consultation was that peer education as an approach to reach young people is here to stay, that large investments are currently being made in this approach, and that serious efforts should be made to maximise these investments. Key findings from the 1999 international consultation on peer education should be integrated with reproductive health and HIV services, and, where possible, with community health and development initiatives. Another finding was that programmes must take into account gender inequalities and related community context issues.[16]

---

[15] Source: Programa Sida, Instituto de Investigación y Desarrollo, IDES, San José 1238, Montevideo 11100, Uruguay.

[16] For example, in societies where gender discrimination and stigma about HIV underlie the reproductive and sexual choices of young people, organisations supporting the peer education programme may need to focus on changes in social norms in order to change unhealthy behaviours among youth.

Participants found that clear selection criteria are needed to identify peer educators, and that some type of compensation should be offered to them. Opportunities for increased responsibility and personal and professional growth are needed to improve satisfaction, retention, and sustainability. Training must focus on how to convey information and on participatory techniques to engage the audience. Technically competent and supportive staff must conduct regular field supervision. Programmes must take into account gender inequalities and related community context issues. Peer education programmes need to set realistic behaviour change goals that take into account challenges faced by the intended audience, including where an audience member currently is on the behaviour change continuum. Generating financial resources and support for peer education is essential to ensure sustainability. Despite being considered by some as an inexpensive intervention (due to reliance on volunteers), good quality peer education can be costly.

Peer education can be an effective strategy, even with little research evidence to substantiate this: additional resources are needed for monitoring and evaluation and strengthening local research capacity. Stakeholders can play a key role in the success and sustainability of programmes, and they should be included from early stages of programme development.[17]

G. *Men as partners programme*

Many family planning and preventive health programmes focus exclusively on women, forcing them to take disproportionate responsibility for reproductive health and family size. The result is not only an extra burden on women, but also a closed door to the health system for men. EngenderHealth undertakes to involve men in reproductive health and to address their needs through its Men as Partners Programme. The programme has run in Tanzania, Uganda, India, and Indonesia, and has helped to create policy support and successful models for integrating men's services into existing health systems. In Nepal, Kyrgyzstan, Russia, Ukraine, South Africa, and the United States, EngenderHealth works with local partners to match services to needs while raising awareness about gender equity and rights. Local partners conduct workshops in a variety of settings, such as workplaces, trade unions, prisons, and faith-based organisations, to improve male involvement in reproductive health. The programme has impacted the men and women who have participated and those who run the programmes by making them more aware of the links between their own lives and social change. Evaluations of the

---

[17] Sources: Susan E. Adamchak, Youth Peer Education in Reproductive Health and HIV/AIDS: *Progress, Process, and Programming for the Future*, AWID Youth issues paper 7, 2006.

programme have indicated that older men tend to respond better to in-depth sessions of longer duration. On the other hand, adolescent boys are more amenable to accepting alternate views that challenge traditional constructs of masculinity. Many of the local partners run consecutive women-only empowerment programmes, and on occasion the two groups are brought together for dialogues on gender equality.[18]

H. *Exploring the intersections between youth, gender and AIDS*

The Association for Women's Rights in Development (AWID) and the United Nations Development Fund for Women (UNIFEM) co-hosted a three-week email discussion on young women and AIDS to explore the intersections between youth, gender and AIDS; the emerging challenges and successes in AIDS for young people (particularly young women); and the ways in which youth can participate in addressing gender and youth issues in AIDS programmes.[19]

I. *Newspaper for young people*

a. *Straight Talk*, Uganda

Straight Talk is a newspaper targeted at young people. With a circulation of around 100,000 per month, it has broken new boundaries in its explicit discussion of sex, and has won a large and involved audience. The paper is targeted at 14–19 year-olds, and is sent to all Ugandan high schools. It is also distributed in *New Vision*, one of the main Ugandan newspapers. *Straight Talk* is filled with comments and questions from readers, and the advice given is forthright. *Straight Talk* has contributed to openness about sexuality and AIDS prevention in Ugandan society.[20]

J. *Multimedia soap opera*

a. *Soul City*, South Africa

Health and media organisations in South Africa joined forces to produce a highly successful multimedia soap opera called *Soul City*. The soap opera is set in a South African township, and is broadcast on prime-time television and radio. Additional information and storylines are emphasised through newspaper booklets and publicity and advertising campaigns. Each week the programme deals with issues

---

18 Source: EngenderHealth, www.engenderhealth.org.
19 Source: www.unescobkk.org/ips/arhweb/arhnews/newstiles/declaration_nepal.htm.
20 Source: http//:excellent.com.utk.edu/greenlee.html.

such as domestic violence, AIDS, mental health, gender equity in male and female relationships, and immunisation. Programmes have used dramatic storylines to get listeners and viewers engaged in the lives of their characters, and have reached up to 11 million people.[21]

K. Creating participatory radio with children

The use of radio drama can be an important tool for any individual, group, or community, for telling stories, helping preserve culture, and for use as an educational tool to address issues as diverse as health, rights, community development, and the environment. *Creating Participatory Radio with Children: A Facilitator's Guide* is a South African resource that explores working with children in a participatory process to create radio dramas that spark young imaginations, explore social issues related to children, and help young people to express their views, thoughts, and feelings about the world around them. When involving children in creating radio dramas, it is important that the facilitator help guide them through the process of developing a good radio drama, while being sure that children are active in every part of the process. This also means being flexible and adapting the programme to suit the children and the working environment.[22] Both girls and boys have been equally involved in the radio programmes created in South African projects so far.

4. CONCLUDING COMMENTS

If we are to address the gender dimension of child poverty, it seems that a different sort of research design – leading perhaps to other kinds of projects – is needed. Research could be designed to gather data on girls' and boys' pathways from poverty in childhood and adolescence to an impoverished or better life in adulthood. Examination of these trajectories might reveal the points of divergence in girls' and boys' lives that lead to more poverty in adulthood for women. Such research should be both qualitative and quantitative, tracing children's life chances and setbacks in gendered settings.

The young lives research project on childhood poverty in Ethiopia suggests some elements of what we might expect to find:

---

[21] Source: www.soulcity.org.za.
[22] Source: Deborah Walter and Daniel Walter, 2004. *Creating Participatory Radio with Children: A Facilitator's Guide*, Community Media for Development/CMFD Productions, Johannesburg, South Africa.

Gender differentials: School enrolment is lower among girls than boys; similarly dropout and educational failure are more common among girls. Current efforts by the government to improve girls' education – including enforcement of the early marriage ban and affirmative action measures such as tutoring for girls – are narrowing this gap, as is public education expenditure at the primary school level, especially for rural and poorer children.[23]

What could be usefully added to this study is intersectional information on the discriminatory systems leading to fewer years of schooling and earlier marriage for girls; such information might suggest projects that address the discriminatory systems at work.

The young lives research project reveals the many contradictions involved in current poverty reduction programmes: for example, the conflict between labour intensive development approaches and child welfare (labour intensity undermines child welfare by increasing children's work burden). If boys are typically pulled out of school to work in family enterprises or earn wages, and girls drop out to work at home substituting for mothers, why is the outcome of their lack of education different? Do boys require less education to get out of poverty, or do they learn skills on the job that help them in adulthood? Do girls require more education to overcome gender stereotypes and discriminatory systems, or do domestic chores deprive them of the practical knowledge and experience they will need to take advantage of occupational opportunities?

Only a combination of qualitative and quantitative field research will yield answers to these questions, and only operations research will provide the designs for projects that help overcome the obstacles to elimination of child poverty.

5. REFERENCES

Addario, L. (2006). "Sex Abuse of Girls Is Stubborn Scourge in Africa". *The New York Times,* Friday 1 December.
Brockerhoff, M. and Hewitt, P. (2000). "Inequality of child mortality among ethnic groups in sub-Saharan Africa". *Bulletin of the World Health Organization* 78(1):30–41.
Coomaraswamy, R. (2001). *Contribution on the subject of race, gender and violence against women.* World Conference against Racism, Racial Discrimination, Xenophobia and Related Intolerance. A/CONF. 189/PC.3/5 27 July.
Gwatkin, D.R. (2002). *Reducing health inequalities in developing countries.* www.worldbank.org accessed 3 August 2005.

---

[23] Source: Young Lives Research Project: *Childhood Poverty in Ethiopia,* www.idrc.ca/en/ev-73382-201-1DO_TOPIC.html.

Hoelscher, P. (2008). *Assessing the impacts of policies on children*. UNICEF Global Child Poverty Study, CEE/CIS Regional Meeting, Tashkent, 2–4 April 2008.

Human Rights Council (2008). *Report of the Special Rapporteur on violence against women, its causes and consequences, Yakin Ertürk Addendum. The Next Step: Developing Transnational Indicators on Violence Against Women* A/HRC/7/6/Add.5, 25 February 2008.

Klasen, S. (2006). UNDP's "Gender-Related Measures: Some Conceptual Problems and Possible Solutions". *Journal of Human Development* Vol. 7, No.2, July.

Mkandawire, T. (2005). *Targeting and Universalism in Poverty Reduction*. UNRISD Social Policy and Development Programme Paper Number 23.

PAHO (2005). *Gender equality policy*. Washington, DC: Pan American Health Organization.

Save the Children (2004). *'Youth-Friendly' Pharmacies in Bolivia*. www.savethechildren.org.

Wagstaff, A. (2000). "Socioeconomic inequalities in child mortality: comparisons across nine developing countries". *Bulletin of the World Health Organization* 78(1):19–29.

CHILD MALNUTRITION: CHANGING PERCEPTIONS AND POLICY IMPLICATIONS

Urban JONSSON
The Owls
International Consultant on Human Rights and Development

> "It is quite obvious that we cannot even approach the question of what can and ought to be done, if we do not see and understand the problems of malnutrition against the background of a thoroughly mapped and analysed environment."
>
> Karl-Eric Knutsson, 1971

1. INTRODUCTION

Over the last five decades, development theory has gradually moved from a predominantly positivistic base towards an increased acceptance of normative thinking. This has been the result of the increasing awareness and acceptance that in the construction of 'reality', it is values as well as scientific facts that determine the meaning of the 'reality'.

The problem of young child malnutrition in developing countries is a good example of how changes in development theory have resulted in dramatic changes in approaches to solve a problem. The problem of malnutrition has been redefined several times, with each new approach reflecting broader and increasingly normative content.

A most useful idea in the theory of science is the concept of *paradigm*, introduced by Thomas Kuhn in his famous book *The Structure of Scientific Revolutions*.[1] His main point is that most scientists work and stay within a particular paradigm representing what they see as 'normal science', defined as "...research firmly based upon one or more past scientific achievements, achievements that some particular

---

[1] KUHN (1996).

scientific community acknowledges for a time as supplying the foundation for further practice".

More often than not, one paradigm dominates a specific research field for a certain period of time (the 'mainstream' paradigm), with one or several competing parallel paradigms used by much smaller research communities ('counterpoint' paradigms).[2] A *paradigm shift* takes place when the mainstream paradigm is replaced by one of the counterpoint paradigms. Such a shift occurs when the old paradigm increasingly fails to explain phenomena or causes of a problem in that particular research field. A paradigm shift means "to enlarge, renew, and give new meaning to what is already known".[3]

In this paper, a brief description is made of the changing conceptualisations or paradigms of the nutrition problem over the last five decades, and relates these changes to changes in the relative influence of science and ethics, as well as relationships between theory and practice.

An approximate periodisation of the mainstream paradigms in nutrition is listed below:

1. The period before 1950;
2. The era of the protein deficiency paradigm (1950–1973);
3. The era of multi-sectoral nutrition planning (1973–1980);
4. National nutrition policies (1975–1985);
5. Primary health care (PHC) and community-based nutrition (1978–1990);
6. An emerging consensus (1990–1995);
7. The period of micro-nutrient malnutrition (1995–2005);
8. Renewed interest in Protein-energy malnutrition (PEM) (2005-present) (but which approach?).

2. SCIENCE AND ETHICS – THEORY AND PRACTICE[4]

Almost any issue, problem or phenomenon in society has both a scientific and an ethical aspect. Science deals with what *can* be done, while ethics deals with what *should* or *ought to* be done.[5] Science is descriptive, while ethics is normative. Science is normally advanced through observation and logical deduction. Ethics is mostly advanced through dialogue, reflection, enquiry, struggle, and,

---

[2] HETTNE (2008).
[3] FLECK (1981).
[4] JONSSON (1995a).
[5] RESCHER (1987).

sometimes, confrontation. Most decisions that individuals make are based on a mental construction of 'reality', a construction influenced by both scientific facts and ethical values.

Both science and ethics are advanced through the interaction between theory and practice. Theory and practice are dialectically related. One lacks full meaning without the other. Statements like, "you find what you look for"[6] reflect this fact. Practice without accompanying reflection on the nature of that practice is both dangerous and common, as pointed out by Hechter: "without explicit theories, there is no way to decide on the relative importance of facts."[7]

In science, theories explain causality and the consequences can often be predicted. Theories of ethics, in contrast, are normally derived from moral axioms that cannot be proven right or wrong. There are many competing ethical theories.

The 'space for social action' can be defined by the science/ethics and theory/practice dimensions, as illustrated in Figure 1, below. The same dimensions can be used to structure Knutsson's 'reality room'[8]; Knutsson repeatedly warned against any type of reductionism, emphasising that the meaning of what we observe is influenced both by scientific facts and values (ethics), and that theory and practice are not enemies of each other, but rather that they must be understood together.

Figure 1. A space for social action

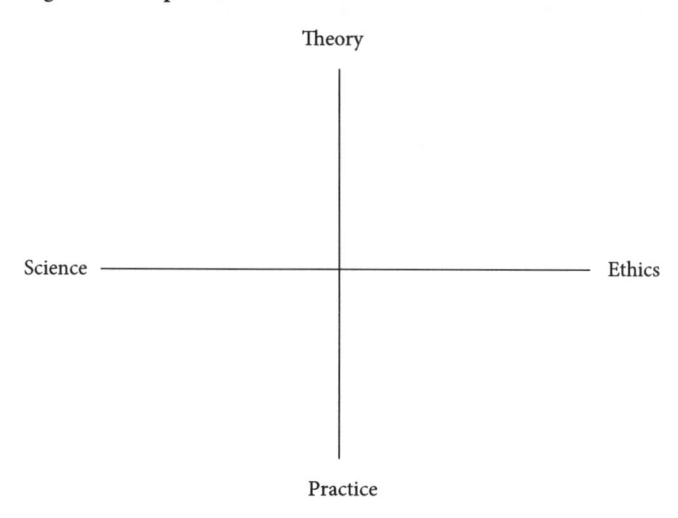

```
                    Theory
                      │
                      │
                      │
   Science ───────────┼─────────── Ethics
                      │
                      │
                      │
                   Practice
```

---

[6] KUHN (1970).
[7] HECHTER (1987).
[8] KNUTSSON (1997).

The gap between theory and practice manifests itself most dramatically in a gap between rhetoric and action. The process of moving from theory to practice is driven or constrained by science and ethics, as understood by those who have the power to decide. It is often said that good plans (i.e. good theories) are not implemented because of a 'lack of political will'. That is a very polite way of describing what in fact amounts to wrong political choices. The rhetoric/action gap exists because those who decide the process either fail to take a decision, or take the wrong decision, because of their misunderstanding of science or their particular ethical positions. The fact that current economic globalisation contributes to increasing inequalities in the world is not because globalisation is non-ethical; it is a result of the particular ethical base of the dominating free-market paradigm.[9]

3. EARLY PARADIGMS

3.1 THE PERIOD BEFORE 1950

People throughout history have had ideas about why hunger existed. Most descriptions prior to the nineteenth century reflect a deterministic and fatalistic perspective. Christianity, for example, promoted the ethical position that people who were poor and hungry were lucky, because they would be the first to enter Heaven – or, as Thomas of Aquinas stated, "naked follow naked Christ". Centuries later, Mahatma Gandhi promoted a similar position when he re-defined the lowest and most deprived social caste in India as 'Harijan', or 'children of God'.

The development of science during the 18th and 19th century resulted in an increased degree of specialisation. New discoveries in chemistry, biochemistry and biology provided new knowledge and a base for a new scientific discipline – *nutrition*.[10]

The fact that certain foods had a remedying effect on disease had been known since ancient times. By 1915, several vitamins had been isolated, and the first real 'paradigm' for nutrition had been created: *malnutrition in society is caused by lack of certain vitamins in the diet*. This was a scientific fact. The solution to the problem was straightforward; provide vitamins to people who are lacking them. This approach became the 'mainstream' paradigm for several decades.

---

[9] JONSSON (2006).
[10] LUSK (1909).

A 'counterpoint' position was promoted by those who saw the great importance of amino acids (building blocks of proteins) to the human metabolism. It had become known that certain amino acids are essential because they cannot be synthesised by humans, and must therefore be provided through the diet.[11] Soon, reports from new studies would change the picture in a way that emphasised this argument.

3.2 THE ERA OF THE PROTEIN DEFICIENCY PARADIGM (1950–1973)

Work with vitamins had convinced nutritionists that malnutrition was a result of something lacking from the diet. Certain research in human nutrition therefore focused on finding out what exactly was missing in the food intake of children who developed kwashiorkor.

From 1952 to 1955, an incredible amount of human nutrition research took place, with the results published in the most prestigious scientific journals and presented in big conferences.[12] It was agreed that kwashiorkor was a result of protein deficiency at the cellular level, and in 1952 it was agreed to replace the name 'kwashiorkor' with the description *protein malnutrition*. By 1954, the problem of protein malnutrition had been rephrased as the problem of a *lack of protein-rich foods;* the *protein deficiency paradigm* was now well established. The period that followed (1955–70) was characterised by 'puzzle-solving' as part of normal science, within which the protein deficiency paradigm was the dominant mainstream approach to nutrition. Several of the scientists and practitioners who raised alternative ideas were ruthlessly marginalised – they were not invited to important conferences, their papers were rejected by mainstream scientific journals, and their research careers floundered. Kuhn's 'hidden faculty' became a reality.[13]

Since the early 1950s, however, individual scientists had consistently criticised the protein deficiency paradigm as too narrow and too simple.[14] In an article in *The Lancet* in June 1973, Harper, Payne and Waterlow criticised the paradigm very strongly, stating that "the most likely effect of such statements is simply to distract attention from the need for a broad-based attack on the social and

---

[11] CATHCART (1940).
[12] Protein Conference, Rutgers University (Jan. 1951), Inter-African Conference on Nutrition, The Gambia (April 1951), FAO Regional Conference on Nutrition, Bandung June 1953), International Congress on Nutrition (June 1955), FAO/WHO/Macy Conference, Princeton (June 1955) and FAO Expert Committee on Protein Requirements, Rome (Oct. 1955).
[13] KUHN, T. *o.c.* No. 27.
[14] A good summary of the criticism can be found in WATERLOW and PAYNE (1975).

economic deprivation of which ill-health and malnutrition are but symptoms."[15] In August 1974, McLaren initiated the 'final' debate with a letter to *The Lancet* entitled "The great protein fiasco".[16]

In summary, discoveries in human nutrition first created, then weakened, the scientific basis of the protein deficiency paradigm. At the same time, many practitioners and researchers in the social sciences started to criticise the paradigm for reducing the problem of child malnutrition from a social and political problem to a technical, more specifically a medical, problem.[17] It was increasingly argued that it is un-ethical to continue to spend resources producing protein-rich foods when most malnourished children are denied their 'normal' diet anyway, as a result of poverty and exploitation.

4. FROM MONO-CAUSALITY TO MULTI-CAUSALITY (1973–1980)

Long before the 'protein era' had ended, an increasing number of nutrition scholars, many with practical experience from developing countries, had realised that the problem of child malnutrition could not be solved by limited medical interventions, or simply by providing proteins. Instead, a much broader approach was required, which would have to include social, economic, cultural and political aspects.[18] The science of nutrition was too narrow; a *science of nutrition problems in society* was required.[19] This new position formed the intellectual basis for the explosive development and acceptance of "multisectoral nutrition planning"[20] as the new mainstream approach. This theory was a very ambitious attempt to address the structural causes of malnutrition. As John Osgood Field summarised:

> "…the early proponents of multisectoral nutrition planning clearly defined protein-energy malnutrition as a structural problem embedded in poverty and underdevelopment: they recognised that multiple changes to socioeconomic conditions would be necessary to alleviate malnutrition… Multisectoral nutrition planning sought to go beyond technical fixes in favour of going to the heart of a country's development effort."[21]

---

[15] HARPER *et al.* (1973).
[16] MCLAREN (1974).
[17] BERG (1973).
[18] BERG *et al.* (1973).
[19] JONSSON (1983).
[20] JOY and PAYNE (1975).
[21] FIELD (1987).

This dramatic paradigm shift coincided with, or was probably a result of, changes in development theory in general, as it moved towards a stronger emphasis on political factors. It also coincided with increased interest in using systems theory for modelling development: multisectoral nutrition planning immediately adopted systems theory as the default planning framework.

During this period of dominance for the multisectoral nutrition planning paradigm, there were many who criticised it[22], but no single clear counterpoint theory had emerged. The consensus was primarily on what was wrong with this approach, and criticism resulted in a dramatic fall in the popularity of this theory before the end of the decade. Many were of the opinion that the approach had become too technical – or, as James Pines put it, "multisectoral nutrition planning, oversold and under-politicized from the start, stands discredited for failure to bring about nutrition improvement."[23]

By the end of the 1970s, most nutrition scholars had moved away from multisectoral nutrition planning, but this movement was not accompanied by a return to the 'old thinking'. Most researchers agreed that child malnutrition was a result of social, economic, political and cultural processes in society, and that efforts to solve the problem of malnutrition would have to address all levels of society, from national policy level to the community and household levels. Even if multisectoral nutrition planning had failed to mobilise political leaders, the problem of malnutrition had been put on the political agenda.

From the mid-1970s to the mid-1990s, many countries and agencies strongly promoted and supported the preparation of national nutrition policies and strategies.[24] As almost everything could affect nutrition, the need for high level monitoring and coordination were emphasised. Accompanying efforts to establish national nutrition policies was the idea of *national nutrition surveillance*.

A strong theoretical counterpoint to multisectoral nutrition planning had now emerged: firstly, too much emphasis had been given to rehabilitating already malnourished children; instead, emphasis should be given to *preventing children from becoming malnourished*. Secondly, individual children were affected by malnutrition, and they all lived in communities: preventive actions should therefore be *community-based*. As a result of this thinking, community-based nutrition programmes within a generalised primary health care (PHC) approach took over the 'mainstream' position.

---

[22] See, for example, FIELD (1977).
[23] PINES (1982).
[24] HAKIM and SOLIMANO (1976).

5. A FOCUS ON THE COMMUNITY (1978–1990)

After the 1974 World Food Conference (WFC) in Rome, the nutrition problem was no longer conceptualised as a global protein problem, but rather as a global food supply problem, and poverty was singled out as the major cause of child malnutrition.[25] This position was based on new research showing that the link between poverty and *young* child malnutrition was not a simple cause-effect relationship.[26] Instead, the idea was promoted that malnutrition should be addressed by all relevant sectoral policies and strategies. Interventions in different sectors should be *coordinated*, but not integrated, as had been promoted under the multisectoral nutrition planning approach. This approach soon became the 'mainstream' macro-level approach.[27]

Initially introduced by ILO, the World Bank adopted the new 'basic needs approach' in the late 1970s, as did many development agencies, including UNICEF. The need to be well nourished was immediately recognised as a 'basic need', and a 'basic services concept' was proposed as the key nutrition strategy, which was later endorsed by the UN General Assembly in 1976. The idea was to use a holistic approach to promote and respond to *community* initiatives by providing training for community workers, appropriate technology, effective support and referral services.

Very similar ideas were included in the 'primary health care' (PHC) approach, launched in the Alma Ata Declaration in 1978.[28] PHC was defined in the Declaration as follows:

> "Primary Health Care is essential health care made universally accessible to individuals and families in the community by means acceptable to them, through their full participation and at a cost that the community and country can afford. It forms an integral part of both the country's health system of which it is the nucleus and of the overall social and economic development of the community."

Under this approach, priority is given to the community level, where people actually live.

---

[25] REUTLINGER and SELOWSKY (1976).
[26] A recent review, see HADDAD *et al.* (2002).
[27] BERG and AUSTIN (1984).
[28] WHO and UNICEF (1978).

6. TOWARDS A CONSENSUS (1990–1995)

The year 1990 was an important year for the world's children. In September that year, the World Summit for Children (WSC) was held in New York: it was the largest ever meeting at that time of heads of states and governments, with 169 countries represented. The Summit agreed on a Declaration that included seven major goals and 20 supportive goals for women and children.[29] Eight of these goals were aimed at reducing child malnutrition by the year 2000.[30] Secondly, that same September, the Convention on the Rights of the Child entered into force,[31] wherein the right of children to good nutrition is enshrined. Both these events explain the great interest in child nutrition during the following years.

During the same year, 1990, Dreze and Sen published their findings about hunger, in which they argued that hunger is most frequently not the result of inadequate aggregate supply of food, but rather the result of a breakdown in people's entitlements. People are affected by hunger because they do not have the resources to produce, barter or buy the food they require.[32] There was an increasing consensus among many scholars and practitioners that hunger and malnutrition should be analysed and understood in the context of society.[33]

Also in 1990, the UNICEF Board approved a new strategy for improved nutrition of children and women.[34] Based on the experience of the successful Iringa Nutrition Support Programme in Tanzania,[35] the new strategy reflected the position that people who are poor should be recognised as the key actors in their own development. They should be supported to empower themselves through a 'learning by doing' process of assessment, analysis, action, re-assessment, improved action, and so on (named the 'triple A' approach).

The triple A strategy proposed a new conceptual framework for the causes of young child malnutrition. In this framework, malnutrition was seen as the final outcome or manifestation of three underlying causes:

---

[29] UNITED NATIONS (1990).
[30] These are: reducing severe and moderate malnutrition by half; reducing low birth weight to less than 10 per cent; reducing iron deficiency anaemia in women to one third; virtual elimination of iodine deficiency disorders; virtual elimination of vitamin A deficiency; empowerment of all women to breastfeed exclusively to 4–6 months; institutionalisation of growth promotion; dissemination of knowledge on household food security.
[31] *The convention on the rights of the child (CRC) was* adopted by the General Assembly by the resolution 44/25 on 20 November 1989; and entered into force on 2 September 1990 (UNITED NATIONS, 1989).
[32] WORLD BANK (1990); UNDP (1990); DREZE and SEN (1990a); DREZE and SEN (1990b).
[33] LATHAM *et al.* (1988).
[34] UNICEF (1990).
[35] JONSSON *et al.* (1993).

1. household food insecurity;
2. inadequate access to basic health services;
3. inadequate care of children (including lack of breastfeeding).

Each of these three needs – food, health and care – must be met to ensure good nutrition; each condition is necessary, and meeting one condition alone is insufficient. The degree to which any of these conditions is not met in a society will determine the appropriate mix of interventions.

This approach was fully endorsed at the 1992 International Conference on Nutrition (ICN) in Rome, the final report of which stated:

> "Although poverty is the root cause of malnutrition, nutritional status is affected by a wide range of factors which can be categorized into three main categories – food, health and care."[36]

The triple A approach became the mainstream approach during most of the 1990s, and at time of writing is still the dominant strategy for prevention of protein energy malnutrition.

In the early 1980s, USAID had already evaluated a number of community-based nutrition programmes with the aim of identifying 'success factors'. During the first half of the 1990s, the United Nations' Administrative Committee on Coordination/Sub-Committee on Nutrition (ACC/SCN) managed to achieve an unprecedented consensus on both the causes of malnutrition and strategies to prevent malnutrition in society. Several studies were carried out, by universities and by the ACC/SCN Secretariat, with the goal of examining 'success factors' in nutrition policies, programmes and projects.[37] Scholars and practitioners reached a reasonable consensus on 'lessons learnt' and 'best programming practices'.[38] The most important are summarised below:

1. people who are poor should be recognised as the key actors in their own development, rather than passive 'beneficiaries';
2. development means both the achievement of desirable outcomes *and* a process that ensures sustainability;
3. local ownership of programmes is essential;
4. development programmes should contribute both to poverty reduction and to disparity reduction;

---

[36]   FAO/WHO (1992a); FAO/WHO (1992b).
[37]   JENNINGS et al. (1991; GILLESPIE and MASON (1991); GILLESPIE et al. (1996); JONSSON (1995b); LEVINSON (1991).
[38]   See for example MASON et al. (1995); SANDERS (1999).

5. pure 'top-down' approaches and 'bottom-up' approaches should be avoided. The dynamic is not 'either/or'; it is a synergy of both;
6. all possible partnerships should be explored to establish a 'movement' for improved nutrition;
7. people who are poor live in 'communities'. As key actors of their development they need to be *empowered* and to be able to monitor their own development. They can learn from their own experiences.

7. BACK TO MONO-CAUSALITY – A PERIOD OF MICRONUTRIENT MALNUTRITION PROGRAMMES (1995–2005)

The key role of micronutrients (vitamins and minerals) in nutrition was well known 50–70 years ago. Control of vitamin deficiency was the mainstream approach until it was replaced by the protein deficiency paradigm in the early 1950s. Subsequently, the micronutrient strategy has played the mainstream role.

In 1991, a first meeting to pursue the WSC goals was held in Montreal, Canada. The title of the meeting, "Ending Hidden Hunger" referred to invisible but frequently-occurring forms of mild and moderate micronutrient malnutrition.[39] The conference managed successfully to mobilise the international nutrition community to allocate more resources to this rapidly growing field of nutrition. By the mid 1990s, control of micronutrient malnutrition, particularly deficiencies in iodine, vitamin A and iron, became the absolute mainstream paradigm in nutrition research and development.[40] At the same time the interest in protein-energy malnutrition dramatically decreased. Apart from the new interest in micronutrients, the nutrition field in general was given much less public attention after around 1995. In many agencies and developing country governments, nutrition departments or sections were closed or merged with health departments; fewer and less competent staff were hired, and scholarships for international nutrition training dried up.

It is difficult to explain the dramatic shift in priorities from protein-energy malnutrition (PEM) to micronutrient malnutrition. Several contributory reasons can, however, be mentioned. Firstly, results from research had over time conclusively demonstrated the health impact of deficiencies in iodine, vitamin A, and iron (anaemia). Secondly, technologies for providing these micronutrients to

---

[39] WHO *et al.* (1991).
[40] BEATON *et al.* (1993); ACC/SCN (1991).

individuals on a large scale had been developed at a low cost (e.g. salt iodisation). Thirdly, the World Bank and others had convincingly estimated that control of micronutrient malnutrition was one of the most cost-effective interventions in the whole area of health and nutrition.[41] Fourthly, in spite of the consensus regarding the problem of protein-energy malnutrition (PEM) and many large-scale efforts to prevent it, the impact of this work had been much less positive than expected. The fact that most of these failures were not the result of failing to apply the 'lessons learnt' did not make any difference. Fifthly, and perhaps most importantly, was the fact that micronutrient control programmes can easily be implemented in a 'top-down' fashion, and therefore rarely require any change in social and political power structures.

8. RENEWED INTEREST IN PEM AND MULTI-CAUSALITY (2005 – PRESENT)

Around 2005, interest in preventing protein-energy malnutrition (PEM) began to increase rapidly, not replacing, but rather adding to the great interest in micronutrient malnutrition control. There were several reasons for this change. First among these was a general increased commitment to reducing young child mortality rates, combined with the increased evidence and awareness of the fact that PEM significantly increases the risk of dying of childhood diseases. Secondly, the results and effectiveness of many micronutrient control programmes had come under increased questioning. Thirdly – as had been the case in earlier periods – the World Bank had decided to give much higher priority to PEM than before, which influenced many countries to change their priorities, at least on paper. In addition, more recently (January 2008), *The Lancet* published a series of review articles promoting the importance of preventing young child malnutrition.[42]

The new consensus – that much more needs to be done in order to reduce malnutrition – is not, however, accompanied by any consensus on which strategies should be used. There is an obvious conflict between the *investment in nutrition* paradigm and the *human rights-based approach to nutrition* paradigm. The first is strongly supported by the World Bank and the authors in the aforementioned *Lancet* series of articles; the second is supported by UN agencies and several international and national NGOs. These paradigms are different in several ways, and sometimes even contradictory. They definitely have different policy

---

[41] BEHRMAN et al. (2004).
[42] "The Lancet Series on Maternal and Child Undernutrition No. 1–5", *The Lancet*, January 17, 2008.

implications. In order to be able to describe these differences, a particular mental construct of *development* will be used, as outlined below.

9. DEVELOPMENT AS OUTCOME AND PROCESS

'Development' requires the satisfaction of at least two conditions: the achievement of a desirable *outcome* and the establishment of an adequate *process* to achieve and sustain that outcome. Most of the health, education, and nutrition goals set al the World Summit for Children or reflected in the Millennium Development Goals (MDGs), for example, represent specific, desirable outcomes. Effective human development demands a high-quality process to achieve such outcomes. Participation, local ownership, empowerment, cost-effectiveness and sustainability are essential characteristics of a high-quality process for achieving human development goals.

Level of outcome and quality of process define a two-dimensional space for social action, as illustrated below.

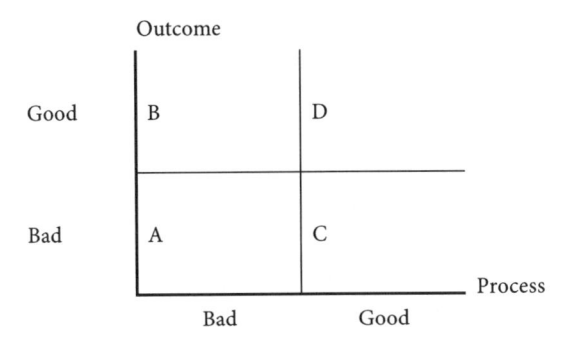

```
              Outcome
                 |
                 |
      Good    B  |  D
                 |
              ___|_____
                 |
      Bad     A  |  C
                 |_____ Process
              Bad    Good
```

Most development starts at A, and the ideal, final stage is D. Unfortunately, many development programmes move into one of the two areas represented by B or C.

B represents a good outcome at the expense of, for example, sustainability (sustainability is an accepted aspect of a good process), and is as ineffective as C – which represents a good process without a significant outcome. Some UNICEF-supported immunisation programmes in the 1980s rapidly moved into the B space, but subsequently proved to be unsustainable; while some local, community-oriented programmes moved into C but proved impossible to scale up.

While monitoring of the achievement of human development outcomes has improved considerably during the past ten years, far less progress has been achieved in monitoring the quality of *processes* – largely because the importance of process had not been recognised, and therefore very few process indicators had been defined.

Outcome-focused approaches are preferred by many economists and development agencies. The focus on achieving WSC goals had sometimes made UNICEF-supported programmes and projects relatively outcome-focused. One evaluation of UNICEF's work strongly recommended a reorientation that would place more stress on the quality of process, along with sustainability and empowerment.[43] The current 'blind' focus on the achievement of the MDGs is an even more dramatic example of the type of reductionism.[44] That can result from excessive and exclusive focus on goals.

Process-oriented approaches are often favoured by NGOs. Many small, local programmes have established high quality processes, but at a relatively high cost per person. Few have expanded to a markedly larger scale and achieved significant outcomes.

The difference between the investment in nutrition paradigm and the human rights-based paradigm can now best be explained using the Outcome/Process construct.

10. THE INVESTMENT IN NUTRITION APPROACH

The economic rationale for 'investing in nutrition in developing countries' has been supported by many scholars and practitioners over the years, and in particular by the development banks.[45] As part of the *Millennium Project* a number of task forces were established, including a Task Force on Reducing Hunger and Malnutrition. The final report of this task force strongly promotes an 'investment in nutrition' approach.[46]

More recently, the World Bank published a paper launching a new "Nutrition Initiative', based on the old argument to 'invest in nutrition',[47] and identifying

---

[43] UNICEF, "Multi-Donor Evaluation of Unicef".
[44] ALSTON (2005).
[45] BEHRMAN (1993); HUNT (2005); MASON *et al.* (1999).
[46] MILLENNIUM PROJECT (2003).
[47] WORLD BANK (2006).

three reasons for intervening to reduce malnutrition. These reasons are as follows:

1. high economic returns and high impact on economic growth and poverty reduction;
2. the alarming shape and scale of the malnutrition problem;
3. the fact that markets are failing to address the malnutrition problem in poor households.

In the same paper, three common myths are criticised:

1. malnutrition is primarily a matter of inadequate food supply;
2. improved nutrition is a by-product of other measures of poverty reduction and economic advances;
3. given the scarce resources, action on nutrition is hardly feasible on a mass scale, especially in poor countries.

The overall argument for preventing child malnutrition is that it is one of the best possible investments in human capital.

This new World Bank initiative was picked up by the global mass media, and is likely to result renewed international interest in nutrition.

At the same time as the new initiative was launched, the World Bank published a second report, arguing that the key challenge in mobilizing strong and lasting investment in nutrition is a *lack of commitment*,[48] and that there are three new opportunities currently available for strengthening commitment to nutrition. These are as follows:

1. using the unprecedented current interest in achieving the MDGs, of which almost all are related to child nutrition;
2. integrating nutrition-relevant interventions in countries' poverty reduction strategic papers (PRSPs) and using nutritional status as an overall outcome indicator;
3. building community capacity to choose interventions that are more cost-effective and therefore affordable at scale.

Seen in the perspective of the Outcome/Process construct, the investment in nutrition paradigm is definitely outcome-focused, in the sense that priority is given to the achievement of the MDGs. Process criteria are limited to sustainability

---

[48] HEAVER (2005).

(although this is given less importance than before), cost-effectiveness, and cost-efficiency. The lack of more ethically-derived criteria in development planning and implementation was acknowledged by UNDP in their *Human Development Report 2000*, in which they admitted that:

> "...although human development thinking has always insisted on the importance of the process of development, many of the tools developed by the human development approach measure the outcome of social arrangements in such a way that it is not sensitive to how these outcomes were brought about."[49]

The major reason that the investment in nutrition approach is likely to become the next mainstream paradigm in nutrition is because it was launched, and will be promoted and supported, by the World Bank. The second key reason, to some extent following on from the first, is the fact that this paradigm, by focusing on investment, avoids the sensitive social and political causes and consequences of malnutrition. Thirdly, and finally, this paradigm is a good reflection of the currently dominant free-market economy and ideology.

11. THE HUMAN RIGHTS-BASED APPROACH TO NUTRITION PARADIGM

In a human rights-based approach to nutrition, children are recognised as possessors of rights, with valid claims on others, who have correlative duties. This means that children have valid claims against their parents to be provided with adequate food, health and care – i.e. to be well nourished. The parents are therefore the first line duty-bearers.

Often, however, parents cannot meet their duties because they do not have access to cultivable land, salaries or other resources required for providing food, health and care for their children. In other words, they cannot meet their duty to their children, because as claim-holders some of the rights they have against the State have not been realised. This shows how the State becomes the *ultimate* or *final duty-bearer*. This is important, because it is the State that has ratified the relevant legal covenants and conventions that make it legally bound to meet its obligations.

In human rights treaties (covenants and conventions) human rights standards and human rights *principles* are explicitly codified. Seen in the perspective of the Outcome/Process construct, human rights *standards* define benchmarks for desirable outcomes, while human rights *principles* represent conditions for the

---

[49] UNDP (2000).

process. Human rights standards include desirable outcomes such as access to food, basic health care and basic education, adequate nutrition, water, and so on. All MDGs represent important desirable outcomes. Human rights principles are normally seen as including equality and non-discrimination, participation and inclusion, and accountability and the rule of law. The most important characteristics of the human rights-based paradigm are as follows:

Firstly, in a human rights-based approach to nutrition, children are recognised as holders of rights to adequate nutrition, and are no longer seen as 'beneficiaries' or 'targets' of interventions. Preventing young child malnutrition can no longer be a voluntary act of charity or benevolence, but must be an obligation. In a human rights-based approach to nutrition there cannot exist any level of malnutrition that is 'acceptable' – all children have the right to be equally well-nourished.

Secondly, a human rights-based approach aims at empowering rights-holders to claim their rights. Often people who are poor have valid claims on people who are less poor and more powerful, who are the duty-bearers. This is why in a human rights-based approach, power can be challenged, impunity rejected, corruption exposed and access to justice ensured much more effectively than in other development approaches.

Thirdly, a human rights-based approach rules out some trade-offs that have been accepted by many other development approaches, including the needs, equality and liberty trade-offs:

- the needs trade-off: relatively high levels of poverty should be accepted in order to maximise investment and future economic growth;
- the equality trade-off: initially economic growth will create inequalities that should be accepted;
- the liberty trade-off: civil and political rights must be temporarily suspended in order to allow for economic growth.

These trade-offs are rejected by the human rights-based approach.

Fourthly, a human rights-based approach pays more attention to exclusion, discrimination, disparities and injustice in society than most other approaches. Equality through reduction of disparities allows for actions to redistribute resources from the rich to the poor, something that most economics-based development approaches reject. A human rights-based approach aims at empowering people as claim-holders individually and collectively in civil society organisations. The strengthening of civil society is seen as a prerequisite for democratisation.

Reasons why the human rights-based approach could become the next mainstream paradigm in nutrition include the following:

Firstly, in such an approach, clear accountabilities are explicitly identified and monitored. Over the last several decades, governments have regularly agreed and committed themselves to achieving nutrition goals and targets – in the World Food Conference (1974), the World Summit for Children (1990), the FAO/WHO International Conference on Nutrition (1992), the World Food Summit (1994), the Millennium Summit (2000), and in an endless number of regional declarations. These commitments have been nothing more than promises, with absolutely no accountability or penalty for non-performers. The voluntary ratification of a UN Human Rights Covenant or Convention is dramatically different, in the sense that countries in principle are legally bound to act.

A second reason is the trend towards increasingly normative development thinking, which leads naturally to the position that continued high prevalence of young child malnutrition is simply morally unacceptable in a rapidly richer world. Human rights provide both moral and legal arguments for such a position.

12. DIFFERENT POLICY IMPLICATIONS

The major differences in the policy implications of the two competing paradigms are results of different levels of attention that each paradigm gives to Outcome and Process respectively. While the investment in nutrition approach is very outcome-focussed, the human rights-based paradigm gives equal attention to both outcome and process. The differences in policy implications are summarised below.

Investment in nutrition	Human rights-based approach
Interventions most often in the form of 'packages' to be 'delivered'. This is the standard method of the World Bank, and increasingly of UNICEF and UNDP.	Interventions mainly aim at building capacity for empowerment. Components of capacity include acceptance of responsibility, authority and power, access to resources, capability to take rational and informed decisions, and capability to communicate.
Often very 'top-down'. Most multilateral and bilateral development agencies use very top-down planning practices. The planning of poverty reduction programmes very seldom includes people who are poor.	Always a combination of *both* 'bottom-up' and 'top-down'. It is the *synergy* between top-down advocacy and social mobilisation and the support of bottom-up initiatives that makes a difference.
Planning 'for' rather than planning 'with': top-down planning implies planning 'for'.	Planning 'with' rather than planning 'for': bottom-up planning implies planning 'with'.

Investment in nutrition	Human rights-based approach
Power structures seldom addressed. Often, actions that threaten existing exploitative power structures are deliberately avoided.	Addresses power structures, exclusion and injustice, through more 'activist'-type strategies.
Accepts many trade-offs – for example the acceptance of increased income disparities in the short term, in order to achieve high economic growth in the longer term.	Accepts very few trade-offs, because from a human rights perspective it is not morally acceptable to sacrifice one child today in order that two may survive tomorrow.
Charity a most welcome contribution. Most money does not 'smell'.	"Charity is obscene in a human rights perspective" (Hegel). This is particularly true when charity is 'cold', i.e. reflects an eleemosynary practice.
Promotes the achievement of the MDGs without regard to the context of the Millennium Declaration (MD) – i.e. does not recognise that the MD stipulates that the MDGs must be achieved through a process characterised by democracy and human rights.	Promotes the achievement of the MDGs within the context of the Millennium Declaration – i.e. recognises the essential nature of a democratic and human rights-based process.
Promotes privatisation of health and education services, which always results in disparities between children in different socio-economic groups.	Promotes health and education services as a public good, which can ensure that *all* children receive the same level and quality of services.
Supports poverty reduction, but not necessarily disparity reduction – i.e. accepts the position that there is nothing wrong in some getting much better off as long as nobody gets worse off.	Promotes poverty reduction *through* disparity reduction – i.e. reflects the position that disparities are *per se* undesirable or even unacceptable. Resources should be transferred from people who are rich to people who are poor.

13. CONCLUSION

The investment in nutrition approach and the human rights-based approach to nutrition share the same scientific basis – a situation that differs from all previous paradigmatic conflicts in nutrition. The difference between the two paradigms, however, lies mainly in their very different ethical and moral perspectives, which are embedded in different, competing ideologies.

The investment in nutrition paradigm favours a more individualistically-oriented free-market ideology, while the human rights-based paradigm favours a more collectively-oriented social democratic ideology. This is the major explanation for why – for example – there are still many malnourished children in the very rich USA, whilst child malnutrition is hard to find in the less rich Scandinavian countries.

The conclusion must therefore be that the next mainstream paradigm in nutrition will be less determined by science than by ideology. In other words, the dominant approach will be decided by the global political power balance. The gap between rhetoric and action will continue to exist.

14. REFERENCES

ACC/SCN (1991). *Controlling Iron Deficiency*, Nutrition Policy discussion paper, February 1991.

Alston, P. (2005). "Ships Passing in the Night: The Current State of the Human Rights and Development Debate seen through the Lens of the Millennium Development Goals", *Human Rights Quarterly*, Vol. 27; Number 3; August 2005.

Beaton, G. et al (1993). *Effectiveness of Vitamin A Supplementation in the control of Young Child Morbidity and Mortality in Developing Countries*, ACC/SCN Nutrition Policy Discussion Paper No. 13, December 1993.

Behrman, J.B. (1993). "The Economic Rationale for Investing in Nutrition in Developing Countries", *World development*, Vol. 21, No. 11, 1749–1771.

Behrman, J., Alderman, H. and Hoddinott, J. (2004). "Nutrition and Hunger", in *Global Crises, Global Solutions*, Lomberg, B. (ed.), Cambridge, UK: Cambridge University Press.

Berg, A. and Austin, J. (1984). "Nutrition policies and programmes. A decade of redirection", *Food Policy*, November 1994, 304–312.

Berg, A. (1973). *The Nutrition Factor*, The Brookings Institution.

Berg, A., Scrimshaw, N.S. and Call, D. (1973). *Nutrition, National Development, and Planning*, MIT Press, Cambridge, MA.

Cathcart, E.P. (1940). "The Mystery of Alimentation", *The Lancet*, March 27, 1940, 531–537.

Dreze, J. and Sen, A. (1990a). *Hunger and Public Action*, Clarendon Press, Oxford.

Dreze, J. and Sen, A. (1990b). *The Political Economy of Hunger*, Volume I-III, Clarendon Press.

FAO/ WHO (1992a). *International Conference on Nutrition: Final report of the Conference*, December 1992.

FAO/WHO (1992b). *World Declaration and Plan of Action for Nutrition*, December 1992.

Field, J. O. (1987). "Multisectoral nutrition planning: a post-mortem", *Food Policy*, February 1987, 15–28.

Field J.O. (1977). "The soft underbelly of applied knowledge. Conceptual and operational problems in nutrition planning", *Food Policy*, August 1977, pp. 228–239).

Fleck, L. (1981). "Genesis and development of a scientific fact", in Trenn, T.J. and Merton, R.K. *"Genesis and Development of a Scientific Fact"*. Chicago; The University of Chicago Press. 1981.

Gillespie, S., Mason, J. and Martorell, R. (1996). *How nutrition improves*. ACC/SCN, Geneva. Switzerland.

Gillespie, S. and Mason, J. (1991). *Nutrition-Relevant Actions*, ACC/SCN Nutrition Policy Discussion Paper No. 10, September 2001.

Haddad, L., Alderman, H., Appleton, S., Song, L. and Yohannes, Y. (2002). *Reducing Child Malnutrition: How Far Does Income Growth Take Us?* International Food Policy Research Institute.

Hakim, P. and Solimano, G. (1976). "Nutrition and national development. Establishing the connection", *Food Policy*, May 1976, 249–259.

Harper, A. E., Payne, P. and Waterlow, J. (1973). *The Lancet*, June 1973.

Heaver, R. (2005). *Strengthening Country Commitment to human development: Lessons from Nutrition*, World Bank, Directions in Development, Washington, DC.

Hechter, M. (1987). *Principles of Group Solidarity*, Berkeley, CA: University of California Press. P. 2

Hettne, B. (2008). "Development Discourses in History", in B. Hettne (ed.) *Sustainable development in a Globalized World*, Palgrave Macmillan, 2008. p. 6–30.

Hunt, J. M. (2005). "The potential Impact of Reducing Global Malnutrition on poverty reduction and Economic development", *Asia Pac Clinical Nutrition* 14(S):10–38.

Jennings, J., Gillespie, S, Mason, J., Lofti, M. and Scialfa, T. (1991). *Managing Successful Nutrition Programmes*, ACC/SCN Nutrition Policy and Discussion Paper No. 8.

Jonsson, U., Ljungqvist, B. and Yambi, O. (1993). "Mobilisation for Nutrition in Tanzania", in Rohde, J., Chatterjee, M. and Morley, D (eds.), *Reaching Health for All*. Oxford University Press, 1993.

Jonsson, U. (1995a). "Ethics and Child Nutrition", *Food and Nutrition Bulletin* Vol. 16, No. 4, December 1995, pp. 293–298.

Jonsson, U. (1995b). *Success factors in community-based nutrition-oriented programmes and projects*. UNICEF, Kathmandu.

Jonsson, U. (2006). "MDGs and Other Good Intentions. How to translate rhetoric into action", in *Ethics, Globalisation and Hunger* (forthcoming book).

Jonsson, U. (1983). "A Conceptual Approach to the Understanding and Explanation of Hunger and Malnutrition in Society", Chapter 2 in *Hunger and Society*, Cornell International Nutrition Monograph Series, No. 17.

Joy, L. and Payne, P. (1975) *Food and Nutrition Planning*, FAO, Rome, 1975.

Joy, L. (1973) "Food and Nutrition planning", *Journal of Agricultural Economics*, Vol. 24, No 1, pp 1–22

Knutsson, K.-E. (1971). "Malnutrition and the Community", in B. Vahlquist (ed.), *Nutrition. A Priority in African Development*, The Dag Hammarskjöld Foundation, Uppsala, Sweden.

Knutsson, K. E. (1997). *Children: Noble Causes or Worthy Citizens?* UNICEF, International Child Development Centre, Florence, Italy, p. 96–101.

Kuhn, T.S. (1996). *The Structure of Scientific Revolutions*. 3rd ed. Chicago, Ill; University of Chicago Press, 1996. (First published in 1962).

Kuhn, T. (1970). *The Structure of Scientific Revolutions*, Second ed., University of Chicago Press.

Latham, M. (1969). "Starvation of Politics, or Politics of Starvation?" *The Lancet*, November 8, 1969, 999–1000.

Latham, M. C. (1984). "Strategies for Control of Malnutrition and the Influence of the Nutritional Sciences", *Food and Nutrition Bulletin*, Vol. 10, No. 1, 5–31.

Latham, M. C., Bondestam, L. and Jonsson, U. (1988). *Hunger and Society*, Vols. 1–3, Cornell International Nutrition Monograph Series Nos. 17–19, Ithaca, New York.

Levinson, J. (1991). *Addressing Malnutrition in Africa*, Social Dimension of Adjustment in Sub-Saharan Africa Working Paper No. 13, The World Ban, Washington.

Lusk, G. (1909). *The Elements of the Science of Nutrition*, W.B. Saunders company, Philadelphia and London.

Lynch, L. (1979). "Nutrition planning methodologies: a comparative view of types and applications", *Food and Nutrition Bulletin*, Vol. 1, No. 3, pp. 1–14.

Mason, J., Hunt, J., Parker, D. and Jonsson U. (1999), "Investing in Child Nutrition in Asia", *Asian Development Review* Vol. 17, No. 1, 2, Asian Development Bank.

Mason, J., Jonsson, U. and Csete, J. (1995). Is Malnutrition Overcome? Hunger Report, 1995, World hunger programme, Brown University.

McLaren, D.S. (1974). "The great protein fiasco", *The Lancet* July 13, 1974, pp. 93–96.

Millennium Project (2003). *Halving Hunger by 2015: A Framework for Action, Interim Report*, The Hunger Task Force, New York.

Pines, J.M. (1982). "National nutrition planning. Lessons of experience", *Food Policy*, November 1982, pp. 275–301.

Rescher, M. (1987). *Ethical Idealism: an Inquiry into the nature and Functions of Ideals*, University of California Press, CA.

Reutlinger, S. and Selowsky M. (1976). *Malnutrition and Poverty. Magnitude and Policy Options*. World Bank.

Sahn, D.E and Scrimshaw, N.S (1983). "Nutrition interventions and the process of economic development", *Food and Nutrition Bulletin*, Vol. 5, No. 1, pp. 2–15.

PART II
CHILD POVERTY IN AFRICA

CHILD POVERTY AND DEPRIVATION IN AFRICA

Shimelis TSEGAYE
Programme Coordinator, The African Child Policy Forum

1. BACKGROUND AND PURPOSE

Children account for a large percentage of the income-poor and the severely deprived worldwide. At least 600 million children under the age of 18 around the world are surviving on less than USD 1 a day; 40 per cent of these children live in developing countries.[1] Every second child in developing countries is deprived of even the minimum opportunities in life. As Assefa Bequele put it:

> "It is not too difficult to imagine the depth of desperation one feels in the face of the extensive and extreme poverty haemorrhaging the social fabric of African society... We all suffer from this pessimism at one time or another, but it is one we can ill afford."[2]

Growing up poor means being disadvantaged from before the start; it means shorter lives; it racks up social and economic cost for societies; and it wastes precious human potential. Social and economic change challenges African societies to improve material living standards for all children whilst at the same time ensuring that inequality does not lock poorer children out of the activities and opportunities that most can access.

There is thus a hugely credible moral, economic and social case for tackling child poverty.

> "When a country invests $1 in giving children a good start in life, it saves $7 in costs for health and other problems that arise when kids' basic needs are not met. Helping children out of poverty is therefore morally, socially and economically productive."[3]

---

[1] UNICEF (2000).
[2] ASSEFA BEQUELE (2006).
[3] Free The Children, Child Poverty, 2005, www.freethechildren.com/getinvolved/geteducated/childpoverty.htm#000.

It is an uphill struggle to try to tackle child poverty, or any other problem, without having researched evidence of the causes, extent and manifestations of the problem. Data and information influence policy, so having good information is an indispensable prelude to policy development, as is good access to relevant evidence of what works. Therefore, conducting studies to build the information and knowledge base on an issue and disseminating the results to as a wide a spectrum of audience as possible are pivotal in the policy advocacy arena.

The African Child Policy Forum (ACPF) undertook a study on the state of child poverty and deprivation in Africa in order to inform the third International Policy Conference on the African Child, held between 12 and 13 May 2009 in Addis Ababa, under the theme of child poverty. This chapter is an extract from that study, and gives an in-depth description of the extent and manifestations of child poverty and deprivation. It concludes with a set of possible steps to tackling child poverty in Africa.

2. WHAT WE MEAN BY CHILD POVERTY

In *State of the World's Children 2005,* UNICEF propose a working definition of child poverty:

> "Children living in poverty experience deprivation of the material, spiritual and emotional resources needed to survive, develop and thrive, leaving them unable to enjoy their rights, achieve their full potential or participate as full and equal members of society."[4]

The United Nations Convention on the Rights of the Child (UNCRC) and the African Charter on the Rights and Welfare of the Child (ACRWC) lend a rights-based dimension to the discussion of child poverty, seeing poverty as a denial of human rights. Both the UNCRC and the ACRWC place primary responsibility on the family for ensuring these rights, with governments responsible for supporting them ("in accordance with national conditions and within their means") and with particular regard to "nutrition, clothing and housing."

The rights-based approach to poverty is reinforced by the definition given by the Office of the UN High Commissioner for Human Rights, where poverty is regarded as:

> "...not only a matter of income, but also, more fundamentally, a matter of being able to live a life in dignity and enjoy human rights and freedoms. It describes a complex of

---

[4]   UNICEF (2004).

interrelated and mutual(ly) reinforcing deprivations, which impact on people's ability to claim and access their civil, cultural, economic, political and social rights."[5]

The Childhood Poverty Research and Policy Centre (CHIP) defines childhood poverty as referring to a child:

> "... growing up without an adequate livelihood; growing up without opportunities for human development; growing up without family and community structures that nurture and protect them; and growing up without opportunities for voice."[6]

One of the important features of child deprivation is the mutually-reinforcing nature of deprivations. A study by Gordon *et al.* (2003) showed that multiple deprivation of children has a self-reinforcing nature: deprivation in one aspect leads to or aggravates deprivation in another. Each exacerbates the other, and when two or more coincide, the effects on children can be catastrophic. For example, a lack of sanitation pollutes the water that children use, and poor nutrition makes them vulnerable to sickness and diarrhoea – which then go untreated, further reducing their body weight and resistance to disease. Children who are poorly fed, frequently ill or have no access to safe water, decent housing or adequate sanitation facilities are likely to encounter more problems in school.

A child severely deprived of shelter will be deprived of many basic services, such as health, education, protection from economic exploitation and abuse, and the right to a legal identity and citizenship.

3. WHAT WE KNOW ABOUT CHILD POVERTY IN AFRICA

There is growing appreciation of the gravity of the problem of child poverty in most parts of the world, and not least Africa; but most of the data available on the issue is anecdotal or outdated (making it hard to validate recent trends), and often of questionable quality. Child poverty is often overlooked in serious research because children have no 'voice' or because of the incorrect assumptions either that children respond in the same way as adults to development interventions, or that policies, as adult formulations, will always act in the best interests of their children.

Notwithstanding the complexity and difficulties involved in measuring child poverty, data commonly quoted and used about African countries is often focused

---

5   OHCHR (2006).
6   CHIP (Childhood Poverty Research and Policy Centre) (2004:1).

around survival – understandable but not in itself sufficient to understand the complex implications of inequality on child wellbeing. Even survival data is far from complete and sufficient, primarily due to the lack of vital registration services that leaves the birth and death of the majority of children invisible. About 66 per cent of children in sub-Saharan Africa are not registered at birth.[7] UNICEF estimates that in Zambia only 10 per cent of births are registered, while in Tanzania only 8 per cent are registered.[8] The same is true of child deaths: less than 10 per cent of deaths are registered in the African Region.[9] In Northern Ghana, only 13 per cent of neonatal deaths are in hospital, while in Ethiopia as few as five per cent die in hospital.[10]

Only a few of the 46 countries in WHO's African Region have some form of vital registration data, and only one country has complete current vital registration data. Others have reported incomplete data – including one where no mortality data has been collected since 1990 – and some have never reported such data.[11]

Uncounted and Unaccounted

Abena – her name means "girl born on a Tuesday" – was born in a dark hut. Abena's mother, Efua, had no money to go to hospital for the birth, and Efua's aunt helped her, cutting the cord with a dirty blade and covering Abena's cord with an old piece of cloth. Abena was able to suck well at first, but on the third day, Efua noticed that her sucking was weak. By the fourth day, Abena's muscles were stiff, she could not suck at all, and her body went into spasms at any disturbance. Her life only lasted five days. Efua's aunt buried the little body in the yam field and warned Efua not to cry, or the spirits would take away her next child, too. No one registered Abena's birth or her death.

Source: Lawn and Kerber (2006).

In addition to the above, data presented at aggregate level masks regional, local and sub-group differences. Finally, data from surveys typically treats family units as homogeneous; a child-focused measurement (for instance, capturing information around issues like happiness, feelings of security and access to play) is largely lacking.

---

[7] UNICEF (2003).
[8] UNICEF (2007b).
[9] WHO (2006a).
[10] Lawn and Kerber (2006).
[11] WHO (2006a).

As we can see, adequate researched data and statistics are lacking on child poverty, and the quality of available data is poor. Despite these issues, however, in the following pages we have made an attempt to look at the situation of household poverty and child deprivation from perspectives related to various issues, including nutrition, health, shelter, water and sanitation, and education.

3.1. HOUSEHOLD POVERTY AND DEPRIVATION

Although data on the number of children living in poverty in Africa is unavailable, overall poverty levels give us a good indicator of the number of poor or deprived children. The tendency to use overall poverty estimates as a proxy for child poverty is reinforced by the assumption that children represent at least half of the income-poor.[12] A study on child poverty in South Africa and Ghana and other countries outside of Africa conducted using the income poverty approach found that children made up a higher per cent of the income-poor than either adults or the elderly.[13]

Between 1987 and 1998, in the space of 11 years, the absolute number of people living in extreme poverty in sub-Saharan Africa grew from 217 million to more than 300 million.[14] Thirty-two of the 48 poorest countries in the world are located in sub-Saharan Africa.[15]

A similar trend is observed between 1990 and 2004. The proportion of the poor in Africa as a percentage of total population shows a decline since the mid-1990s; but the absolute number of poor people has increased. Moreover, in the same period, sub-Saharan Africa's share of the world's poor increased to 31 per cent, or by about 58 million people.

In 2004, the region was home to more than 298 million people living on below a dollar a day. In 2004, sub-Saharan Africa was home to three-quarters (76 per cent) of all the ultra poor (those living on less than USD 0.50 a day) in the world.[16] In 2005, 43 per cent of the population in sub-Saharan Africa lived on below USD 1 a day.[17]

Though there were encouraging statistical trends in countries such as Ethiopia, Tanzania, Uganda, Zambia, and Mozambique, which are home to between 5 and

---

12 VANDEMOORTELE (2000).
13 DEATON and PAXTON (1997).
14 Www.fightpoverty.mmbrico.com/facts/africa.html.
15 Http://library.thinkquest.org/05aug/00282/over_causes.htm.
16 AHMED et al. (2007).
17 UNICEF (2007b).

10 per cent of the continent's poorest, other countries, like Nigeria, have shown increases in rates of poverty.[18] Experts claim that this slow reduction in ultra-poverty rates suggests that the majority of those living in ultra poverty will continue to be in sub-Saharan Africa in the future.[19]

On the deprivation front, Gordon *et al.* (2003) found that more than half of the children in sub-Saharan Africa are severely shelter deprived (198 million) as well as water deprived (167 million). The region also suffers from the highest rates of deprivation with respect to education (30%) and health (27%).[20]

Africa is disproportionately affected by the dark blanket of deprivation when compared to any other continent in the world – as is clearly visible in the map below from Commission for Africa (2005).

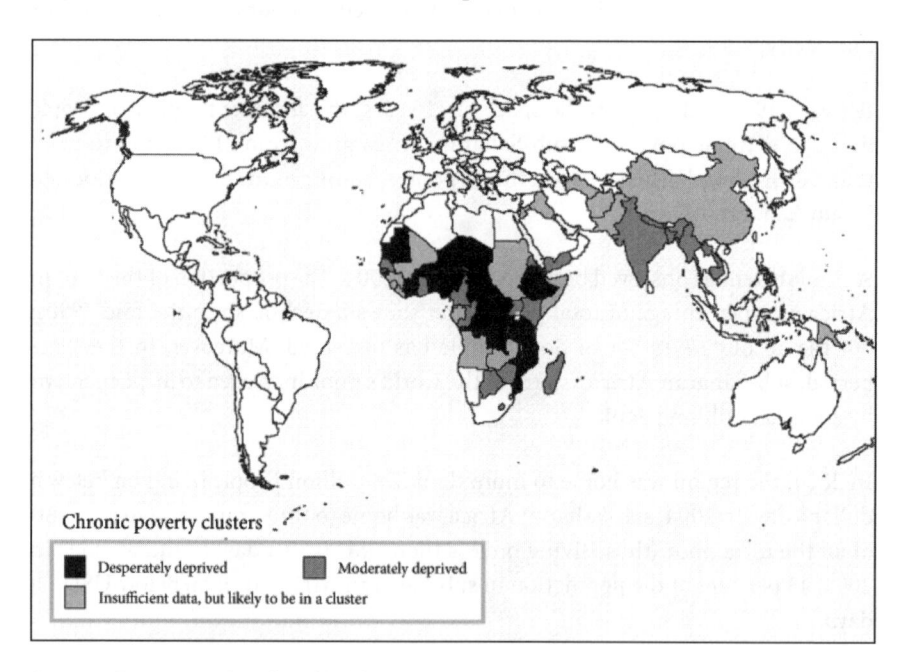

Map 3.1. Inter-continental variations in deprivation

Source: Commission for Africa (2005).

The African continent is not only affected by poverty and deprivation, but also by biting inequality among the various segments of the population. Inequality data

---

[18] AHMED *et al.* (2007).
[19] AHMED *et al.* (2007).
[20] GORDON *et al.* (2003).

is presented as the amount of income for the richest tenth of the population when compared to the poorest tenth (for instance, in Algeria, the richest 10 per cent have 9.6 times the income of the poorest 10 per cent). Inequality varies from a low of around 6.6 times (Ethiopia) to an astonishing 128.8 (Namibia).[21]

A study by UNECA describes Ethiopia, despite the relatively low level of inequality stated above, as "a typical case with very low initial income and high inequality". For instance, Ethiopia experienced economic growth between 1981 and 1995, which could have reduced the number of poor people by 31 per cent; but the fact that the benefits of this growth were unequally distributed instead led to a 37 per cent increase in poverty.[22] This shows that even the lowest inequality on the continent in relative terms is still significant.

As another example, in Burkina Faso, despite average annual economic growth rates of 5.6 per cent over the past decade, the share of people living below the poverty line rose from 44.5 per cent to 46.4 per cent.[23] Speaking of the scathing inequality in that country a commentator said, "Some take a plane to get treated for hay fever, while others die because they can't afford malaria treatment."[24]

Many countries do not report data, and given the potential for rich people to under-report incomes (for instance, for tax purposes), it is reasonable to assume income inequality at the national level is higher than reported.

The level of inequality between urban and rural populations is staggering in most countries of the African continent. As shown in Figure 3.1, below, the percentage of rural people living below the national poverty line in Uganda is more than three times higher than the percentage of poor people living in urban areas, while in Burkina Faso the number of the rural poor is just under three times higher than that of the urban poor. In Ghana, the incidence of poverty in Accra, the capital, is only 2 per cent; but in the dry savannah regions in the north, it is 70 per cent. In Accra, poverty has been declining, but in the savannah it has not shifted.[25]

Gordon *et al.* (2003) also showed that there may be significant differences between urban and rural areas in rates of severe deprivation among children. Table 3.1, below, shows their findings for African regions. These figures show that the gaps between urban and rural areas are wide – children born in the rural areas face nearly twice as much risk of being severely deprived and more than three times more risk of being multiply severely deprived than those born in towns.

---

[21] UNDP (2007); UNICEF (2007); UNICEF (2006); and Gordon *et al.* (2003).
[22] UNECA (2005a).
[23] HARSCH (2006).
[24] HARSCH (2006).
[25] COULOMBE and WODON (2007) cited in World Bank (2007a).

Figure 3.1. Percentage of population below the national poverty line in selected countries by place of residence

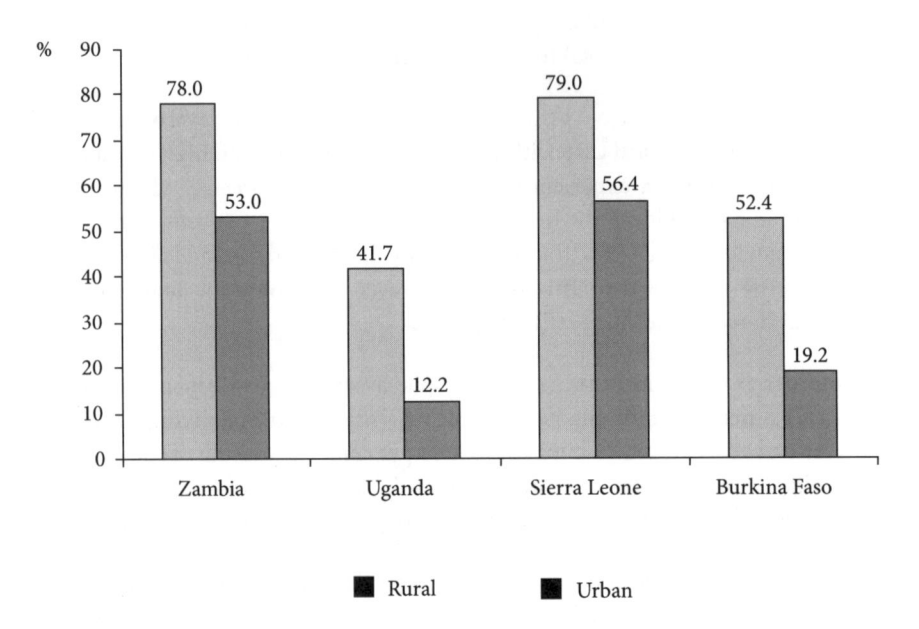

```
%   90
    80   78.0                          79.0
    70
    60            53.0                         56.4
    50                                                        52.4
    40                   41.7
    30
    20                                                               19.2
    10                          12.2
     0
          Zambia        Uganda       Sierra Leone      Burkina Faso

                   ■ Rural        ■ Urban
```

Source: Based on data from World Bank, World Development Indicators, 2007.

Children in rural areas face a risk of severe deprivation 2.8 times higher than urban children, and a risk of multiple severe deprivation that is a huge 6.3 times higher. Another study has shown that children in rural areas are more likely to die of easily preventable diseases than their urban counterparts. For 22 countries in Africa with Demographic and Health Survey data published between 2001 and 2006, neonatal mortality rate was, on average, 42 per cent higher among rural families than among urban families.[26]

Just as there is variation between urban and rural areas, it is extremely likely that variation also exists within groups – for instance, between different ethnic groups and across the geography of countries, and between slum (shanty town) dwellers and other urban dwellers.

The study by Gordon et al. (2003) also draws some conclusions about the differences between the circumstances of boys and girls, arguing that the starkest differences in severe deprivation centre around education (with 32 per cent of girls and 27 per cent of boys in sub-Saharan Africa suffering severe education deprivation). Regarding other deprivation (food and health), there are few known

---

[26] LAWN and KERBER (eds.) (2006).

differences in the circumstances of boys and girls, but since data is collected at household level, this may mask true variation.

Table 3.1. Urban and rural differences in severe deprivation and multiple severe deprivation (%)

		Rural	Urban	Ratio
Severe deprivation	Sub-Saharan Africa	93	53	1.8
	Middle East and North Africa	82	32	2.6
	Developing world	67	31	2.2
Multiple severe deprivation	Sub-Saharan Africa	78	25	3.1
	Middle East and North Africa	57	9	6.3
	Developing world	48	12	4.0

Note: The ratio shows the additional risk faced by children in the rural areas compared to those in urban areas.
Source: Gordon et al. (2003).

In the midst of this gloomy picture, some countries have made good progress in reducing inequality. Mauritius offers a good example of a country that was able to stimulate economic growth and at the same time reduce inequality, by ensuring access to basic services such as health, education, water, sanitation and housing.[27]

> **Mauritius' success in reducing inequality**
>
> Mauritius has had a stable democratic system for decades, with relatively smooth changes in government and a balanced distribution of political power. The authorities have taken into account the interests of the country's well-organised labour movement, while economic policies have encouraged a diversification from sugar production into manufacturing. The government resisted external pressures in the 1980s to make drastic cuts in public spending, and maintained relatively large budget allocations for health, education, water, sanitation, and housing assistance, drawing on taxes levied on sugar exporters. Then poverty fell significantly. After an initial rise, inequality has fallen, and social indicators have improved; they are now well above the average for Africa, and indeed for middle-income countries. According to the World Bank, Mauritius now has the lowest level of inequality among the 30 sub-Saharan countries for which data is available. The report released by the ACPF in 2008 ranked Mauritius as the most child-friendly government in Africa.
>
> Source: Harsch (2006)

---

[27] IMF (2007).

The glaring urban-rural disparities in both income poverty and deprivation are due to a lack of political will to provide services to the rural poor, and also to the fact that the construction of physical infrastructure in many remote areas can be technically very difficult. Sometimes, low population densities in rural areas may make it difficult to supply good quality services.[28] Some researchers also argue that demographic factors characteristic mainly of rural areas, such as high fertility, high prevalence of disability and rural-urban migration, contribute to high dependency ratios in rural areas[29] that may explain some of the persistence of chronic poverty in those areas. Fertility is high in rural areas due to, *inter alia*, low access to family planning services and low levels of education. Some 63 per cent of children in sub-Saharan Africa live in rural areas.[30]

In the long term, regardless of the level at which it manifests itself, income inequality is a barrier to tackling child poverty because it divides societies and puts social goods and opportunities out of reach of poorer children. Inequality affects child life chances because it mediates differences in power. Though inequality has been growing across the world, it does not automatically have to be so[31]: pro-poor economic growth can reduce inequality and make it easier to tackle child poverty.

3.2. THE EXTENT OF CHILD DEPRIVATION

A. Health and nutrition deprivation

Due to the lack of resources with which to provide health facilities and prevention services to its population, Africa accounts for the lion's share of the global disease burden and child mortality. Each year in Africa approximately 1 million babies are stillborn; about half a million die on their first day, and at least 1 million die in their first month of life.[32] The percentage of children dying before the age of five in Africa is more than six times higher than in other parts of the world minus Asia, as shown in the figure below.

A good indicator of deprivation in healthcare is limited access to immunisation services against measles, and the consequential death toll. In 2006, nearly four out of ten children aged 12–23 months in Nigeria, Ethiopia, and DRC, and more

---

[28] BIRD *et al.* (2002) cited in LYYTIKÄINEN *et al.* (2006).
[29] LYYTIKÄINEN *et al.* (2006).
[30] UNICEF (2006).
[31] ATKINSON (2002).
[32] LAWN and KERBER (eds.) (2006).

than two in four children in Angola, were not vaccinated against measles.[33] This lack of immunisation meant that in 2005 alone, about 316,000 infant deaths due to measles were reported in the sub-Saharan African region.[34]

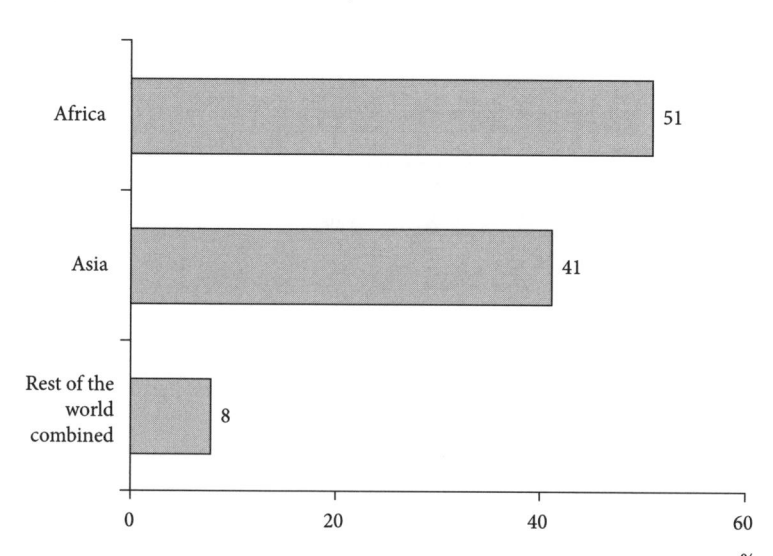

Figure 3.2.   Under-five mortality in Africa, 2007

Region	%
Africa	51
Asia	41
Rest of the world combined	8

Source: UNICEF (2008).

In Chad, Nigeria and Central African Republic, more than 65 per cent of children aged 12–23 months were not immunised against measles in 2005.[35]

The percentage of children suffering from Acute Respiratory Tract Infections (ARTI) rushed to a health centre (an accepted indicator of access to health services) is remarkably low in Africa. The percentage of children suffering from ARTI who were denied access to healthcare was 57 for the 23 African countries for which data was available in the 2000–2006 period.

---

[33]   WHO Regional Office for Africa, *Progress in routine immunisation in the African Region*, Presentation at the Annual Measles Partnership meeting, Washington, D.C., 2007, accessed in April 2008 at: http://a1881.g.akamai.net/7/1881/26640/v0001/ redcross.download.akamai.com/26640/measlesinitiative/ppt/meeting2007/11.ppt.
[34]   AREVSHATIAN *et al.* (2007).
[35]   UNICEF (2007b).

Figure 3.3. Percentage of children aged 12–23 months not immunised against Measles, 2005

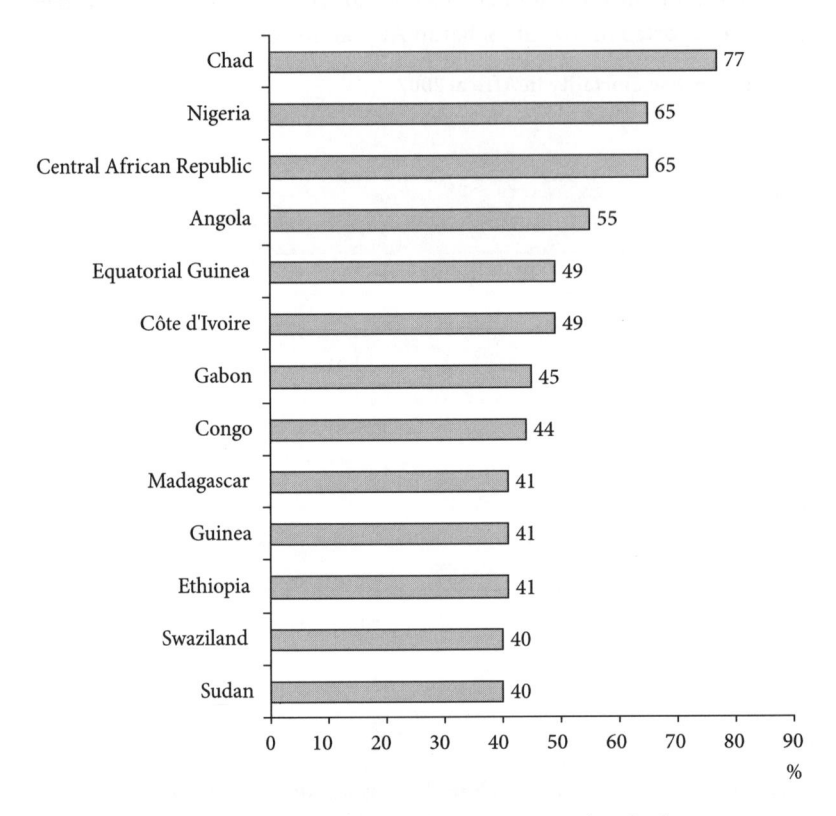

Country	%
Chad	77
Nigeria	65
Central African Republic	65
Angola	55
Equatorial Guinea	49
Côte d'Ivoire	49
Gabon	45
Congo	44
Madagascar	41
Guinea	41
Ethiopia	41
Swaziland	40
Sudan	40

Source: World Bank World Development Indicators 2007 – Online database.

The so-called the "big three" diseases – Malaria, HIV/AIDS and TB – alone claim the lives of an estimated 3 million Africans every year.[36]

According to WHO, there are an estimated 2.4 million new TB cases and half a million tuberculosis-related deaths every year in Africa.[37]

Malaria – dubbed "the disease of Africa" – is another major health challenge playing a part in the impoverishment of communities and nations. Africa accounts for over 90 per cent of an estimated 300–500 million clinical cases of malaria in the world each year,[38] and malaria accounts for twenty-five per cent of under-five deaths in sub-Saharan Africa.[39] More than 2,000 children die each day from the

---

[36] WHO (2006a).
[37] WHO (2006a).
[38] WHO (2006a).
[39] SAVE THE CHILDREN (2005).

disease.[40] Malaria contributes significantly to anaemia in pregnant women, and malaria-related anaemia is estimated to cause 10,000 maternal deaths each year. In addition, malaria also contributes to low birth weight in newborns.[41]

In 2007, about 2.2 million sub-Saharan African children under 15 were living with HIV,[42] and about 1,900 children are infected with the virus every day.[43] In 2007, more than 240,000 HIV-infected children younger than 15 died because of AIDS in sub-Saharan Africa.[44]

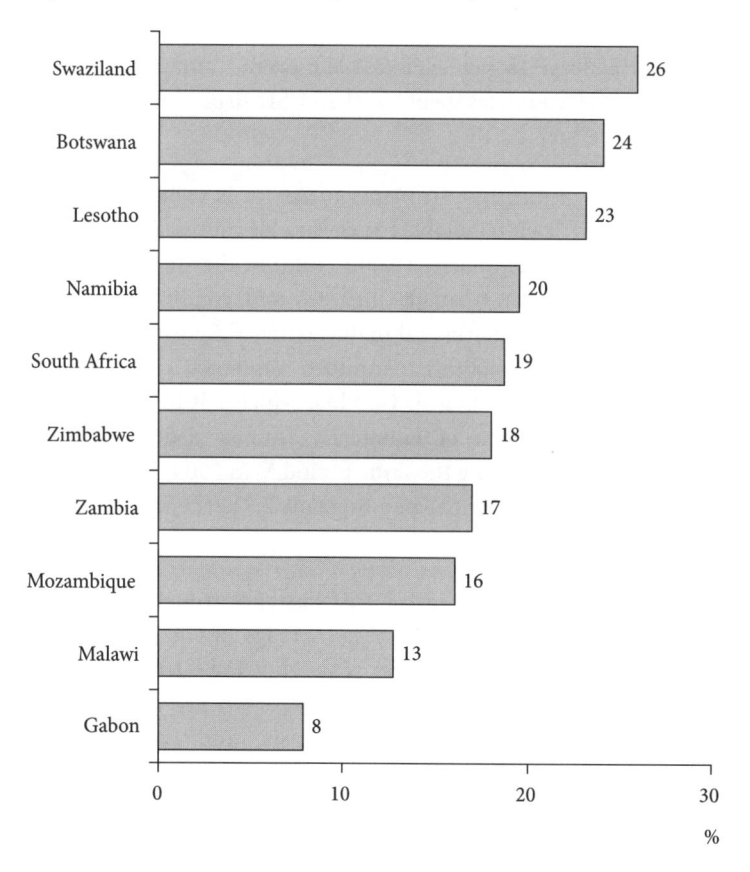

Figure 3.4. Countries with high HIV/AIDS prevalence, 2005–2006

Country	%
Swaziland	26
Botswana	24
Lesotho	23
Namibia	20
South Africa	19
Zimbabwe	18
Zambia	17
Mozambique	16
Malawi	13
Gabon	8

Source: Based on data from 2007 World Population Data Sheet.

---

[40] SAYAGUES (2006).
[41] WHO (2006a).
[42] UNAIDS (2006).
[43] DABIS et al. (2002) cited in SALAAM (2005).
[44] WHO (2006a).

The continent's disease burden is complicated by the lack of resources needed to tackle it, but this is not the only complication: further issues play a part, including limited government budgetary commitment and inadequate or ill-advised policies, such as the privatisation of healthcare services and the imposition of prohibitive user fees for healthcare services. These issues are further compounded by the incessant brain drain of health professionals to the West.

The political will to commit adequate resources for healthcare has been faltering in most countries of the continent, adding fuel to the existing disease burden. In 2004, only four countries – Burkina Faso, Liberia, Malawi and Rwanda – lived up to the pledge made by African governments in Abuja in 2001 to increase their spending on health to at least 15 per cent of their overall annual budgets.[45] According to WHO, about 29 countries spent less than USD 10 per person per year on health.[46]

The faltering commitment of most governments in Africa is seen in the large number of child deaths in Africa attributable to preventable causes. According to WHO estimates, every day an estimated 12,000 children die in sub-Saharan Africa from easily preventable or treatable illnesses and conditions such as pneumonia, diarrhoea, measles, malaria and malnutrition.[47] Between 2000 and 2004, a decrease in proportional health expenditure was noted in 19 African countries. The most significant was that of Gambia, which fell by 60 per cent within four years. The government of Equatorial Guinea also reduced its expenditure on health by a third during the same period.[48] In 2004, Burundi had the lowest expenditure on health in Africa, spending only 2.3 per cent of its overall expenditure for 2004 on this sector.[49]

The application of user fees is another factor that has effectively excluded the poorest segments of society from health services. Average public spending on health in Africa is about USD 10 per person per year, while the estimated cost of providing minimum health care is about USD 34 per person per year. Patients and their families must cover the remaining costs, and these can be substantial.[50]

The problem with user fees is that the poorest and most vulnerable people may not be able to pay them, and may not therefore have access to basic services. In many countries where user fees have been removed or where governments have

---

[45] AFRICAN CHILD POLICY FORUM (2008a).
[46] WHO (2007).
[47] WHO (2006a).
[48] AFRICAN CHILD POLICY FORUM (2008a).
[49] AFRICAN CHILD POLICY FORUM (2008a).
[50] WHO (2006a).

implemented exemption or waiver systems, public services have become more accessible for the poor.[51] When Uganda eliminated user fees at health facilities in 2001, public visits to those facilities increased by 80 per cent, with half of the increase occurring in the poorest fifth of the population.[52]

In Madagascar, once user fees were abolished, the numbers of people attending health centres increased.[53]

While Africa has 10 per cent of the world's population, it bears 25 per cent of the global disease burden and has only 3 per cent of the global health work force. Of the global shortage of health professionals, estimated at four million, one million are immediately required in Africa.[54] This lack of capacity is further complicated by the high level of emigration of the continent's health professionals to (mostly) western countries.

Africa's deadly shortage of health professionals

Among personnel trained in Africa, one in every four doctors and one in every 20 nurses are now working in the 30 most industrialised countries of the world. For example, 29 per cent of Ghanaian physicians are working abroad, as are 34 per cent of Zimbabwean nurses. Reportedly, there are more Sierra Leonean doctors living in the Chicago area of the United States than there are in Sierra Leone. At the same time, around 17 sub-Saharan countries have less than half of the WHO minimum standard of 100 nurses per 100,000 population (for example, Malawi has only 17 nurses per 100,000 people). In contrast, many western countries have more than 1,000 nurses per 100,000. The minimum standard set by WHO to ensure basic health care services is 20 physicians per 100,000 people: while Western countries boast an average of 222 physicians per 100,000, 38 countries in sub-Saharan Africa fall short of the minimum standard, and 13 countries have five or fewer physicians per 100,000 people.

Shinn (2002); WHO (2006b); New York Times (2004).

All of these situations have more pronounced effects among poor children than among their non-poor counterparts. Children who are poor are more likely fall sick, get no treatment and die than their rich counterparts. A study shows that the

---

[51] MINUJIN et al. (2005).
[52] UNDP cited in HARSCH (2006).
[53] FALCHAMPS and MINTEN (2003) cited in Save the Children (2005).
[54] AFRICAN UNION (2007).

mortality rate of the poorest 20 per cent of children in a given country is more than twice that of the richest 20 per cent in the same country.[55]

On top of the unbearable disease burden, armed conflicts pose a huge health challenge in Africa. According to *The Economist Magazine*, a typical civil war leaves a country 15 per cent poorer, with around 30 per cent more people living in absolute poverty.[56]

Even in times of peace, military expenditures have the potential to crowd out investment in social sectors. In 1999, South Africa agreed to buy armaments worth USD 6 billion, sufficient to provide combinations therapy treatment for five million AIDS patients for two years (Amnesty International and Oxfam (2003)).[57]

The toll on human lives inflicted by conflicts has been enormous: conflict causes as many deaths in Africa each year as epidemic diseases, and is responsible for more death and displacement than famine or flood.[58] Between 1998 and 2002, some four million people died in the civil war in the DRC alone.[59]

Countries with the highest infant and maternal mortality are those which have experienced war in their recent history. In a typical five-year war, the under-5 mortality rate in a country increases by 13 per cent, and adult mortality by even more.[60]

Sierra Leone is an example of a country devastated by a civil war, in this case one that lasted more than a decade, between 1991 and 2001. In 2006, the country had the highest under-5 mortality rate in the world: 270 deaths per 1,000 live births. The country also had the highest maternal mortality ratio in the world, with 2,000 deaths per 100,000 live births in 2002. It also had a stillborn rate of 50 per 1,000 births, and a neonatal mortality rate of between 42 and 56 per 1,000 live births. Since 2000, Sierra Leone has been at the top of the list of the 20 countries worldwide with the highest maternal mortality ratios.[61]

Even after the guns fall silent and the makeshift camps for the displaced are dismantled, the repercussions of war and conflict continue to undermine child survival. One study has shown that during the first five years of post-conflict

---

[55] GWATKIN *et al.* (2007) cited in Save the Children (2008).
[56] *The Economist* (2003), The global menace of local strife, 24 May 2003.
[57] AMNESTY INTERNATIONAL and OXFAM (2003).
[58] INTERNATIONAL RESCUE COMMITTEE (2003) cited in COMMISSION FOR AFRICA (2005).
[59] COMMISSION FOR AFRICA (2005).
[60] UNICEF (2004).
[61] WHO (2006a).

peace, the average under-5 mortality rate remains 11 per cent higher than its corresponding level before the conflict.[62]

Figure 3.5. Countries involved in conflict for at least four years and with highest child mortality rates

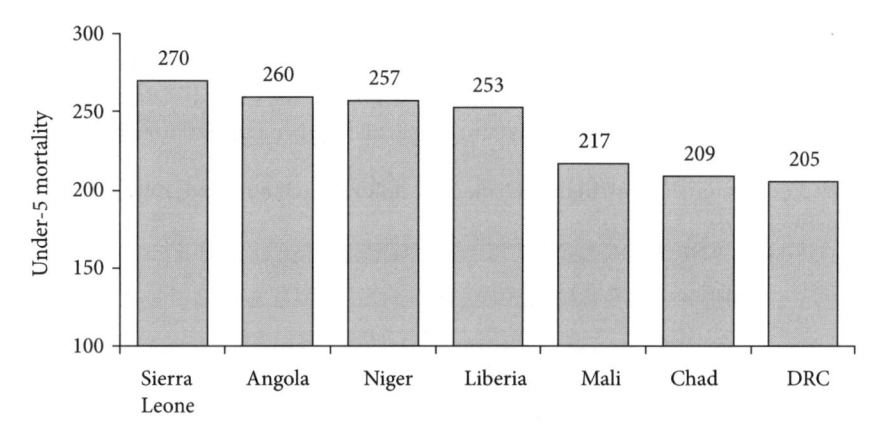

Country	Under-5 mortality
Sierra Leone	270
Angola	260
Niger	257
Liberia	253
Mali	217
Chad	209
DRC	205

Source: UNICEF (2007b); Uppsala Conflict Database.

The lingering legacies of war

The effect of the civil war in Angola continued to be felt years after it had finished. In April 1999, the country suffered one of the largest polio outbreaks ever recorded in Africa. The outbreak came after 30 years of war and destruction of health services, and massive population displacement that had resulted in overcrowding, poor sanitation, and inadequate water supply – an ideal environment for the spread of the poliovirus. In March 2005, an outbreak of Marburg haemorrhagic fever in Angola led to 329 deaths, the most deadly outbreak of Marburg fever to date. There is no cure or vaccine for Marburg. Neither the source of the outbreak nor the reservoir has been identified to date.

Source: WHO (2006a).

On the malnutrition front, in sub-Saharan Africa more than one-quarter of all children under five are underweight. Poor children are more likely to be underweight than non-poor children. A study by IFPRI showed a strong overlap between hunger and poverty in sub-Saharan Africa, where more than 80 per cent of the poor are food energy deficient. In Rwanda, a 2000 survey showed that the incidence of

---

[62] UNICEF (2004).

poverty among the hungry and the incidence of hunger among the poor both stood at 84 per cent, sharply underlining the overlap between poverty and hunger.[63]

Nutritional deficiencies during childhood lead to poorer learning outcomes, with consequent further inter-generational effects (the education of mothers has been shown to be particularly important for children's wellbeing). There is also a strong correlation between child poverty and malnutrition and stunting; malnourished girls are particularly affected, as they have a greater likelihood of later giving birth to low birth-weight babies, in turn jeopardising those babies' life chances.

Figure 3.6. Countries with high percentage of children malnourished, 2000–2006

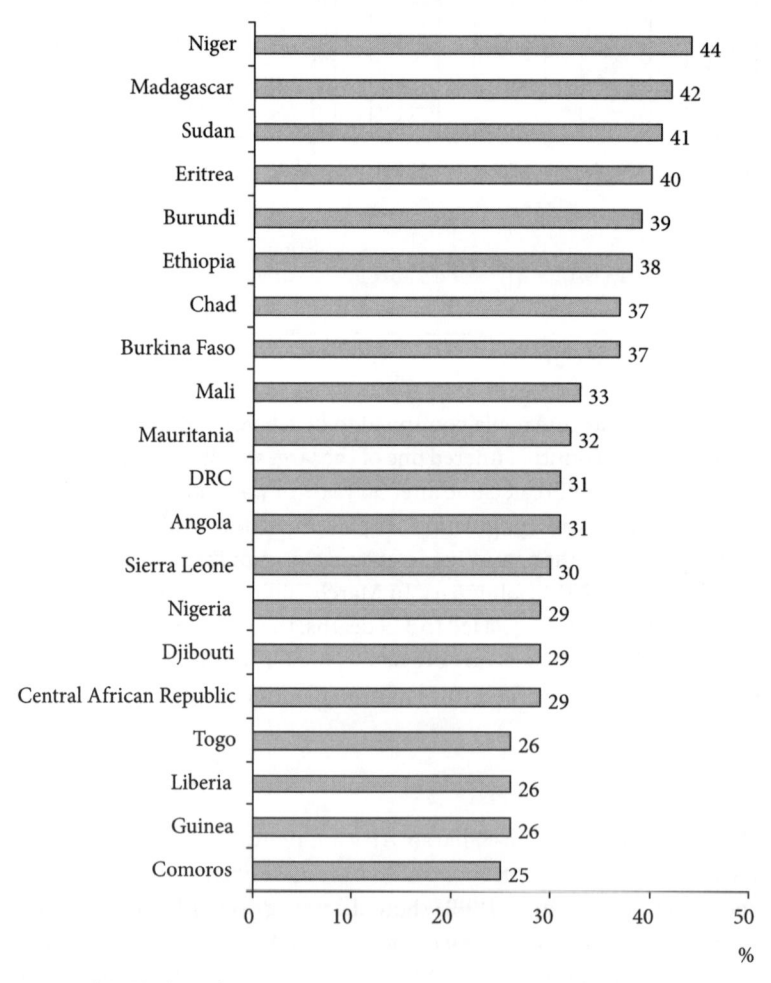

Country	%
Niger	44
Madagascar	42
Sudan	41
Eritrea	40
Burundi	39
Ethiopia	38
Chad	37
Burkina Faso	37
Mali	33
Mauritania	32
DRC	31
Angola	31
Sierra Leone	30
Nigeria	29
Djibouti	29
Central African Republic	29
Togo	26
Liberia	26
Guinea	26
Comoros	25

Source: UNICEF (2007c)

---

[63] AHMED et al. (2007).

In 2006 over a third of children in Africa under five were suffering from moderate to severe stunting[64]; Nigeria and Ethiopia alone account for more than a third of all underweight children in Africa.[65] In countries such as Niger, Madagascar, Sudan and Eritrea, two in every five children were malnourished in the 2000–2006 period.

Climate change, long spells of drought, increased demand for food, diminishing supply, changing consumption patterns in major developing countries like China, and the planting of crops for biofuel are all behind this poor state of nutrition and food security on the continent. The unprecedented recent surge in biofuel production has particularly contributed to the changing world food equation, and currently adversely affects the poor through price-level and price-volatility effects.[66]

B. *Deprivation in water and sanitation*

A child's level of access to safe drinking water is a function of her/his poverty status. A study in South Africa showed that in 2006, only 47.1 per cent of poor[67] and 41 per cent of ultra-poor children had access to "running water indoor or on site", compared with 82 per cent of the non-poor who had such access.[68]

Children without access to adequate water are exposed to substantial health risks, including diseases such as diarrhoea and cholera. Lack of access to adequate water is also closely related to poor sanitation and hygiene.

In 2004, only 58 per cent of the population in sub-Saharan Africa had access to safe water, the lowest rate in the world.[69] In this region, a baby's chance of dying from diarrhoea is almost 520 times the chance of a baby in Europe or the United States.[70] According to UNICEF, in countries such as Ethiopia, Rwanda and Uganda, four out of five children either use surface water or have to walk more than 15 minutes to find a protected water source, often at the expense of school time.[71] WHO estimates that every year African women and children spend 40 billion hours hauling water.[72]

---

[64] UNICEF (2007c).
[65] UNICEF, www.childinfo.org/areas/malnutrition.
[66] VON BRAUN (2007b).
[67] A child is defined as "poor" in the South African context if (s)he lives in a household in the bottom 4 deciles, and "ultra-poor" if (s)he lives in a household in the bottom 2 deciles.
[68] WOOLARD 2008.
[69] AHMED et al. (2007).
[70] WHO and UNICEF (2007).
[71] UNICEF (2004).
[72] WHO cited in COSGROVE and RIJSBERMAN (1998).

Figure 3.7. Countries where more than half of the population does not have access to safe drinking water, 2004

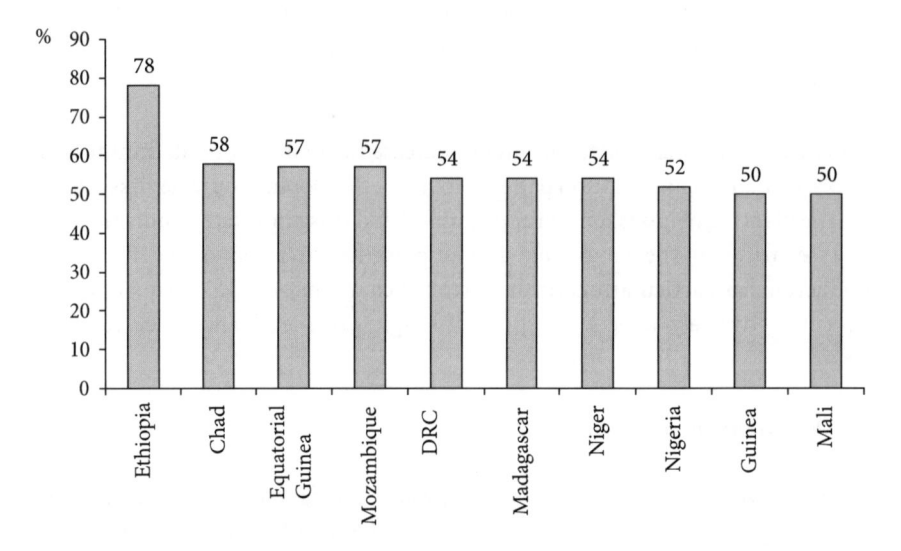

Country	%
Ethiopia	78
Chad	58
Equatorial Guinea	57
Mozambique	57
DRC	54
Madagascar	54
Niger	54
Nigeria	52
Guinea	50
Mali	50

Source: WHO and UNICEF Joint Monitoring for Water and Sanitation.

Studies across different countries show that sanitation is one of the major determinants of child survival: the transition from unimproved to improved sanitation combined with hygiene awareness and behaviour change reduces overall child mortality by about a third. Improved sanitation also brings advantages for public health, livelihoods and dignity – advantages that extend beyond households[73] to the general population.

Despite the benefits of access to sanitation services, Africa's sanitation coverage is lamentably low, with only about 36 per cent of the population having access to adequate facilities. A third of sub-Saharan African countries have coverage rates of 33 per cent or less.[74] In 2004, Eritrea had sanitation coverage of only 9 per cent, and only 13 per cent of Ethiopia's population accessed adequate sanitation facilities.[75]

---

[73]   WATERAID (2005).
[74]   WHO and UNICEF (2006).
[75]   UNICEF (2007d).

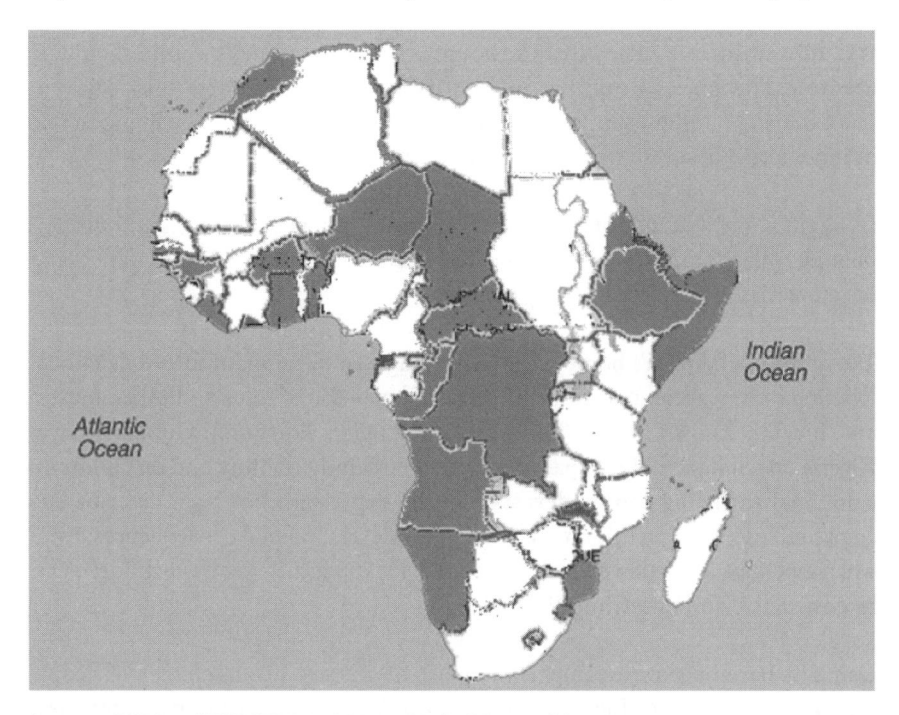

Map 3.2. Countries with less than 33 per cent sanitation coverage (in dark grey)

Source: WHO and UNICEF Joint Monitoring for Water and Sanitation, 2004.

In some areas, especially in urban slums where basic sanitation is lacking, people have to rise before dawn, making their way in the darkness to fields, railroad tracks and roadsides, where, due to the lack of access to toilets, they defecate in the open, or in plastic bags that are then thrown onto the streets. These bags – so-called "flying toilets", commonly used in Kibera, a slum in Nairobi, Kenya,[76] and in some parts of Addis Ababa, Ethiopia[77] – highlight what it means to be without sanitary services.

Considering present trends, unless appropriate steps are taken to increase the coverage of water and sanitation services, an additional 133 million African children will have died from diarrhoea by 2015.[78] Universal access to even the most basic water and sanitation facilities would reduce the financial burden on health systems in developing countries by about USD 1.6 billion annually – and by USD 610 million in sub-Saharan Africa, a saving that represents about 7 per cent of the region's health budget.[79]

---

[76] MULAMA (2006).
[77] DESTA (2006).
[78] WaterAid (2005).
[79] UNDP (2006).

C. Deprivation in shelter and clean living environment

It is universally recognised that the house is the place where the child should be able to eat, laugh, play and live in security and dignity. Despite this, however, more than 198 million sub-Saharan African children are said to be living in one or more forms of severe shelter deprivation.[80]

In Egypt alone, because of a dire urban housing problem, more than 5 million poor Egyptian families – equivalent to the entire population of Eritrea – are living in cemeteries in the populous city of Cairo.[81]

The number of Africa's homeless is increasing due to rampant forced evictions. Evictions, often accompanied by disproportionate use of force and other abuses, are currently known to have taken place in Angola, Equatorial Guinea, Kenya, Nigeria and Sudan.[82] The impact of eviction on family stability and on children's emotional wellbeing can be devastating; the experience has been described as comparable to war for children in terms of the developmental consequences. Even when evictions are followed by immediate relocation, the effects on children can be destructive and unsettling.[83]

Conflicts have become an important cause of massive displacements of people across the continent. Millions of people across Africa live in makeshift camps and tents because of war-driven internal displacements, without access even to rudimentary forms of water and sanitation services. In Darfur alone, at least 2.5 million people were internally displaced by the end of 2006,[84] and about 1.5 million people were displaced from their homes in Somalia because of ongoing conflict.[85] Some have transformed themselves into permanent settlements. The famous Ngara refugee camp in Tanzania, set up for people who escaped the terrible atrocities in the Rwandan genocide in the early 1990s, has become the second biggest city in the country (after Dar-es-Salaam).[86]

Regular moves from one emergency accommodation unit to another threaten familial, social and educational stability. Temporary accommodation can be totally unsuitable for a child's wellbeing; children living in such arrangements have histories of incomplete vaccinations, poor nutrition, retarded weight and height

---

[80] GORDON et al. (2003).
[81] BIZZARI (2005).
[82] CENTRE ON HOUSING RIGHTS AND EVICTIONS (2006).
[83] BARTLETT (2002).
[84] AMNESTY INTERNATIONAL (2007).
[85] YUSUF and SHEIKH (2007).
[86] ABDUL-RAHEEM (2007).

growth, and emotional and mental distress. These problems are not only the direct result of poverty, but are also factors that in turn reinforce that poverty.[87]

Rapid urbanisation and the accompanying proliferation of slum areas is the other major settlement challenge facing Africa today. Currently, 37 per cent of Africans live in cities, but by 2030 this proportion is expected to reach 53 per cent.[88] Rapidly expanding cities are often characterised by slum-dwelling, inadequate water and sanitation services, and wastewater problems; as always, children are on the frontline of the danger. Currently, 72 per cent of city-dwellers in sub-Saharan Africa live in slums.[89]

People living in Africa's urban slums inhabit actual dump-sites, where they expose themselves to a range of toxic risks, burns from explosions of built-up gases, and infections as a result of the mixing of medical waste with other types of waste.[90] Children are among the worst affected. Quoting WHO figures, UNEP has said that about 4.7 million children under five die each year from environmentally-related illnesses, and 25 per cent of deaths in developing countries are linked to environmental factors.[91] For instance, a study commissioned by UNEP found that half of 328 children tested near the notorious Dandora dumpsite in Nairobi, Kenya, had amounts of lead in their blood exceeding internationally accepted levels. Half of the children tested were also suffering respiratory diseases, including chronic bronchitis and asthma as a result of exposure to pollutants. Located near slums in east Nairobi, the Dandora dumpsite – 75 acres of fuming waste – receives about 2,000 tonnes of rubbish daily from a city of 4.5 million people, including plastic bags, used medical supplies, car batteries, dismantled printers and computers.[92]

D. *Education deprivation*

Access to education and low attendance in schools are directly linked to poverty. As poor families often rely on their children to help supplement their income, children are either pulled out of school for seasonal work, or simply cannot attend at all. Poor education is a key vehicle through which poverty is passed on from one generation to the next – while, conversely, good education can be one of the

---

[87] OLUSEYI (2008).
[88] UNEP (2002).
[89] WHO (2006a).
[90] WHO (2006a).
[91] UNEP News Release 2007.
[92] AFP (2007).

most effective means of helping to counteract the damaging effects of poverty and interrupting its intergenerational transmission.

Research has showed that at primary school, children in poverty are more likely to have negative experiences and feel criticised by teachers. While children from all backgrounds see the advantages of school, deprived children are more likely to feel anxious and unconfident about school. Children from poorer families are less likely to get help from parents than children with higher socio-economic status, as poorer parents may be under greater pressure, may lack confidence in their own abilities, and may themselves have bad memories of school.[93] It is educational deprivation that is the main vehicle of the intergenerational transmission so characteristic of child poverty. Poor children are likely to end up being poor parents who in turn beget children who inherit poverty. Without education, the future of children of poor parents will be a "distressing echo of their own".[94] But it should nonetheless be noted that the relationship between poverty and education is not immutable – some poor children excel in school.[95]

> In Nigeria and Ethiopia there were over 5 million out-of-school children, and another 1 million in Burkina Faso, Mali and Niger combined. More than two-thirds of Africa's out-of-school children have never been enrolled and may never go to school unless additional initiatives are taken. Partly due to poverty, about 94 per cent of children who don't attend school live in the developing world.

Poverty affects the school enrolment and completion of children. At age 16, for instance, 93 per cent of non-poor children in South Africa are enrolled in an educational institution, compared to 90 per cent of poor[96] and ultra-poor children.[97]

Similarly, there is a marked difference in grade progression depending on poverty status. As the same study from South Africa shows, even at age eight, there is a difference of 0.3 years in the number of years of schooling between non-poor and ultra-poor children. By age 15, this difference has increased to a full year.[98]

---

[93] JOSEPH ROWNTREE FOUNDATION (2007).
[94] AHMED et al. (2007).
[95] OLUSEYI (2008).
[96] A child is defined as "poor" in the South African context if (s)he lives in a household in the bottom 4 deciles and "ultra-poor" if (s)he lives in a household in the bottom 2 deciles.
[97] WOOLARD (2008).
[98] WOOLARD 2008.

There is, however, an exceptional condition known as the 'wealth paradox', where wealth itself may sometimes be a reason for children being denied education. Children in the families of land- and/or livestock-rich people have been shown to be more likely to be working instead of being in school – a situation that indicates that asset ownership and child schooling could be negatively related, depending on the household's economic circumstances.[99]

In one out of four African countries, half the children enrolled in the last year of primary school do not continue to the secondary level in the following year.[100] In the majority of countries with data, less than two-thirds of a cohort of pupils who had access to primary education reached the last grade. In some countries, the persistence rate to the last grade is lower than 40 per cent. In 2004, 38 million children in sub-Saharan Africa were out of school. In Nigeria and Ethiopia alone there were over 5 million out-of-school children, and more than 1 million in Burkina Faso, Mali and Niger combined. More than two-thirds of Africa's out-of-school children have never been enrolled and may never go to school unless additional initiatives are taken.[101]

African rates of enrolment and completion at the secondary level are even worse. Only 27 per cent and 23 per cent of children of secondary school age attend secondary school in west/central and eastern/southern Africa respectively.[102] Burkina Faso, Burundi, Chad, Mozambique, Madagascar, Niger and Rwanda stand out as having the lowest secondary gross enrolment rates, and only Mauritius, South Africa and Seychelles have gross secondary enrolment rates of more than 80 per cent.[103] Secondary school completion is lamentably low in sub-Saharan Africa, where, according to UNESCO, fewer than 20 per cent of children complete secondary schooling.[104] Additionally, there is a considerable gender disparity in schooling in Africa: for instance, in 2004, in Chad and Guinea-Bissau, the gross enrolment rate at primary level was only 56 per cent for girls for both countries, compared to rates for boys of 86 per cent and 84 per cent respectively. In 2004, in Djibouti and Niger, only three or four in ten school age girls were enrolled in school.

---

[99] BHALOTRA and HEADY (2003) cited in Woldehanna et al. (2005a).
[100] UNESCO INSTITUTE FOR STATISTICS (UIS) (2006).
[101] UNESCO (2007).
[102] UNICEF (2007a).
[103] WORLD BANK (2006).
[104] UNESCO (2007).

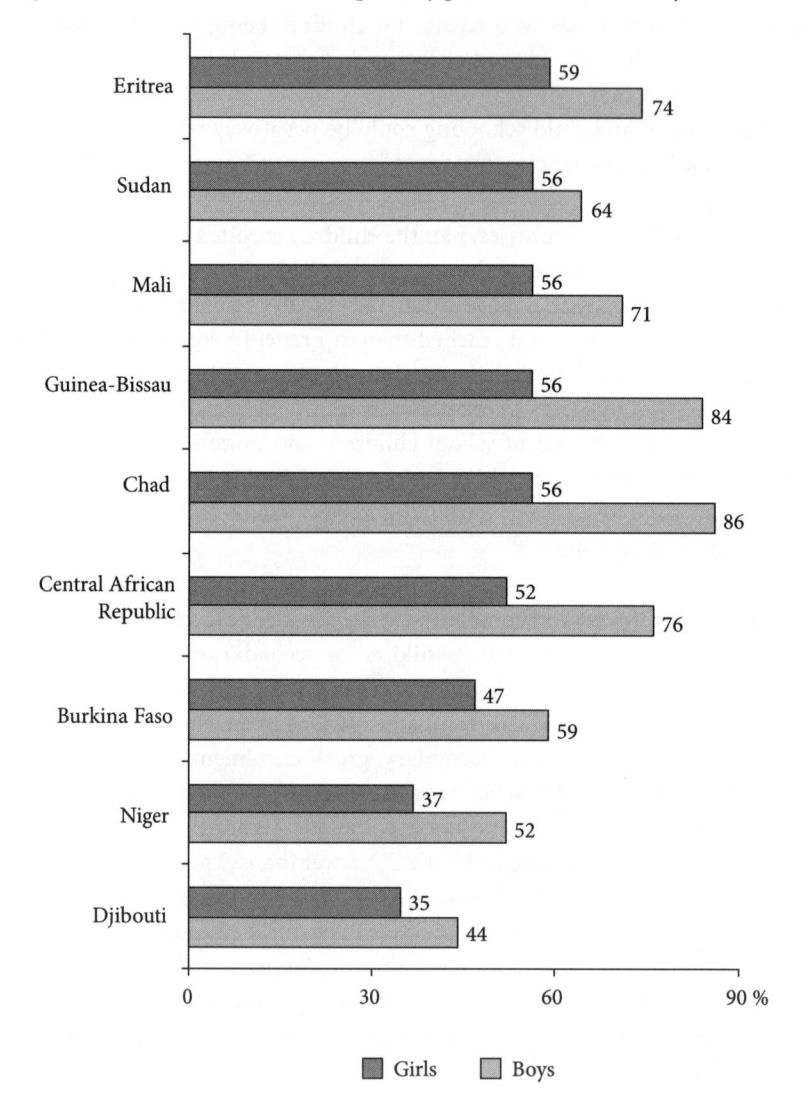

Figure 3.8. Countries with lowest primary gross enrolment rates by sex, 2004

Country	Girls	Boys
Eritrea	59	74
Sudan	56	64
Mali	56	71
Guinea-Bissau	56	84
Chad	56	86
Central African Republic	52	76
Burkina Faso	47	59
Niger	37	52
Djibouti	35	44

Source: World Bank African Development Indicators, 2004.

Gender-based factors are strongly at play in Africa in limiting girls' access to education. Early marriage, lack of proper sanitation facilities for girls in school, demand for girls' labour and the tendency to consider girls' education as a waste (since it benefits the family into which she marries rather than her own), are among such factors. Moreover, parents may object to sending their daughters to school, because they feel the facility is unsafe, or that the long journey to school exposes girls to risk of sexual assault or other forms of violence.[105]

Related to the issue of education is that of information deprivation. In a rapidly globalising world, access to information has increasingly become important in developing human capital – helping citizens to access opportunities and participate in society. Yet, in this respect as well, Africa remains far behind. About 39 per cent of children in sub-Saharan Africa do not have access to television, radio, telephone or newspapers.[106] Some rural communities have hardly been touched by such modern amenities as telephones, televisions or electricity. Some "have never made a phone call and do not live within easy walking distance of a telephone".[107] This situation is the result of several factors, including poor infrastructure, poverty, unreliable telephone systems, and poor energy supply.[108]

Mainly due to this lack of access to information outlets, a large number of children in Africa know little or nothing about such critical issues as child rights, HIV/AIDS and drugs. About half the children interviewed in a children's poll carried out in the eastern and southern African Region by ACPF and UNICEF said they know nothing or little about child rights. About 45 per cent said they know nothing about HIV/AIDS, while only 25 per cent said they know something about drugs and associated prevention methods.[109]

3.3. DEPRIVATION AMONG VULNERABLE GROUPS OF CHILDREN

A. Child labourers and child slaves

Driven by poverty, every year tens of millions of children make their way onto city streets and end up as victims of exploitation, violence and abuse; trafficked; and/or forced to work in prostitution or hard labour. Just as they make their desperate attempt at escaping poverty, these children are thereby received into the often lifelong embrace of poverty and exploitation. 71 per cent of working children interviewed in a study in Burkina Faso stated poverty and family breakup as the main reasons for their being engaged in child labour.[110] Grootaert (1998) also found a clear positive correlation between the degree of family

---

[105] UNICEF (2003).
[106] GORDON et al. (2003).
[107] Association for Progressive Communications (APC) & Communication Rights in the Information Society (CRIS) (2003).
[108] OTUKA (2003) in PILLAI (ed.). (2001).
[109] AFRICAN CHILD POLICY FORUM and UNICEF (2007).
[110] Some (2008).

poverty and the participation in labour of children aged 7–14 in Côte d'Ivoire in 1988.[111]

According to 2001 estimates, there are about 80 million child workers across Africa.[112] One in three children aged 5–14 in sub-Saharan Africa is engaged in labour,[113] and the number of child labourers is expected to rise to 100 million by 2015.[114] Even worse, slavery also still abounds: it is estimated that 90,000 African children are enslaved in Mauritania alone.[115] In Niger, the number of slaves is estimated at 43,000. In Sudan, violent genocide and the high number of those missing or assumed dead makes slavery statistics difficult to come by, but as of 2002, there were an estimated 5,000 to 10,000 child slaves[116] in the country.

> Research from Swaziland reveals how poverty contributes to the "sugar daddy" phenomenon rampant among rural schoolgirls, many of whom trade sexual favours for material goods beyond their reach, often the so-called "four Cs": cars, cell phones, cash and clothes. Some parents, unaware of the deadly health consequences of this lifestyle, silently enjoy the rare commodities their daughters bring home.
>
> Source: UNESCO and the Early Childhood Development Network for Africa (ECDNA) (2003).

Child labour and child slavery are made easier by the trafficking of children, which is on the increase because it profits traffickers as much as USD 800 per child.[117] Poor families, unable to support their children, may be induced to sell them or hire them out – girls and young women tend to be the first to be given away for such forms of exploitation and, thus, are very likely to be trafficked for this purpose. The labour of children sold in this manner is usually parent (or guardian)-controlled, whereby the employer pays the parents or the guardians for the child's labour, payment which may or may not be redistributed in turn to the children.

Major areas of potential economic exploitation of the labour of trafficked children include the demand for work in domestic settings; as commercial sex workers; in commercial agriculture and plantations; and in mining and other hazardous industries. Togolese boys who are smuggled to Nigeria and other countries to take up casual agricultural jobs – such as picking coffee on plantations – work excessively long hours, sometimes with dangerous equipment, often enduring beatings

---

[111] Cited in ANDVIG et al (2001).
[112] HARSCH (2001).
[113] UNICEF (2007c).
[114] HARSCH (2001).
[115] UN (2006).
[116] PENDLETON (2007).
[117] BBC (2007).

and other maltreatment. Many even work at night, with torches bound to their legs.[118] According to Global Witness, children as young as 8 or 10 work in and around copper and cobalt mines in the DRC, usually working in teams and together lifting bags weighing between 50 and 90 kg and loading them onto vehicles. Each child would receive 800 francs (equivalent to 1.2 euro) for loading a 20 tonne vehicle, or 1000 francs (equivalent to 1.50 euro) for loading a 40 tonne vehicle.[119]

A study in Burkina Faso found that most boys work on cotton farms and get a paltry fee, in the range of between 35 and 110 euros, for a year's work. In some cases, when the payment is in kind, the wage for a year's work is just a bicycle and/or clothing and a bus ticket home. The majority of children reported being paid less than what had been promised beforehand.[120]

The International Organization for Migration (IOM) estimates that 1,000 girls aged between 14 and 24 are taken from Mozambique each year to work as prostitutes in South Africa. Other cases are documented of girls being trafficked from Malawi to the Netherlands, to work in brothels run by Nigerian madams.[121] A study in Zambia in 2002 found that the average age of children engaged in prostitution was 15. The daily earnings of the child prostitutes ranged from 3,000 to 33,400 kwachas (about USD 0.63 to 7); the majority, especially younger ones, rarely made as much as 10,000 kwachas (USD 2.10). According to the report, on average, the children slept with three to four clients each day.[122]

Another form of child labour that is hard to follow up and report, because it is hidden from the public eye, is that of domestic child workers. Most such domestic workers are girls from extremely poor families: in some countries, child domestic workers tend to work very long hours – many as 10 to 15 hours a day.[123] Their pay is paltry, and often subject to delay or being withheld totally. Normal pay for a house girl is around USD 6 per month in Nairobi,[124] and was until recently as low as USD 3 in Addis Ababa. In 1995, in Burkina Faso, the monthly pay for child domestic workers was 4–8 times lower than the nationally defined poverty line.[125]

Regardless of the form it takes, child labour has many harmful effects. At first, the risks and dangers associated with these exit options (prostitution, child soldiering and violent gangs) may be deemed a fair trade-off by the child for a potentially exciting escape from a humdrum life of poverty and sibling responsibility; but

---

[118] DAVIES (2005).
[119] GLOBAL WITNESS (2006).
[120] DE LANGE (2006).
[121] IOM (2003).
[122] MUSHINGEH et al. (2002) cited in UNICEF (2003).
[123] Cited in AFRICAN CHILD POLICY FORUM and ILO (2006).
[124] ANDVIG et al. (2001).
[125] SOME (2008).

their long-term impacts may be devastating. All of them compound the risks of sexual exploitation and HIV infection, and, in the case of child soldiering, there is an added high risk of premature death in combat zones.

Along with low pay, long working hours, loss of educational opportunities and physical and sexual abuse come the additional brutal realties of the daily lives of child labourers and child slaves. Child labourers often suffer physical harm that includes increased risk of accidents, assault, violent theft, and risk of illness from poor hygiene and exposure to chemicals. For those children engaged in sex work, the stakes are even higher. Sex work in a situation where children are unable to negotiate safe sex and where there is a tempting financial reward for unprotected sex further increases exposure to HIV infection: a study in Zambia revealed that children made as little as K10,000 (USD 2.50) for protected sex, compared to over ten times as much for unprotected sex – between K100,000 and K150,000 (USD 22.50 to 33).[126] Naturally this makes these children extremely vulnerable to HIV/AIDS and premature death.

B. Orphans and street children

The combined onslaught of the HIV pandemic and armed conflicts on the African continent has left behind a staggering orphan population. UNICEF reports that the total number of children orphaned from all causes in sub-Saharan Africa reached 46.6 million at the end of 2005,[127] and in the same year, about 12 million sub-Saharan African children had lost one or both parents to AIDS.[128] South Africa, Tanzania, Kenya and Uganda were each home to more than a million children orphaned by AIDS in 2005.

Table 3.2. Number of orphans (in thousands) in selected African countries, 2005

Country	Orphans	
	Due to AIDS	Due to all causes
Nigeria	930	8,600
Congo (Brazzaville)	680	4,200
South Africa	1,200	2,500
Tanzania	1,100	2,400
Kenya	1,100	2,300
Uganda	1,000	2,300
Sub-Saharan Africa	12,000	46,600
World	15,200	132,700

Source: Based on data from UNICEF (2007c).

---

[126] ECPAT INTERNATIONAL (2007).
[127] UNICEF (2007c).
[128] UNICEF (2007c).

Orphaned children can be categorised as being generally poorer and more deprived than any other group of children. In a study in South Africa, it was found that whereas 88 per cent of non-poor children have both parents alive, this is only true for 75 per cent of poor[129] children and 73 per cent of ultra-poor children. Similarly, 2 per cent of non-poor children are double orphans, whereas 5 per cent of ultra-poor children have lost both their parents.[130] Orphans are also more likely to be malnourished and stunted than non-orphans. Research in Tanzania shows that the loss of either parent and the death of other adults in the household will increase a child's chance of stunting.[131] In a study of households in the poor suburbs of Dar-es-Salaam, it was found that orphans were more likely to go to bed hungry than non-orphans.[132]

Even among orphaned children, those who are orphaned by AIDS tend to be poorer and more deprived than those orphaned by other causes. They are less likely to get proper food, shelter and clothing, and more likely to have limited access to schooling. The preoccupation with the death of the parents and the undertaking of additional work that comes with supporting oneself after one's parents have died often make it difficult for orphaned children to concentrate in school, an issue compounded by the isolation and stigma experienced by many children orphaned by AIDS.[133]

Orphaned children are also more likely to be driven onto the streets and to engage in hazardous labour because of their impoverished circumstances. An ILO study to investigate the situation of working children found that orphaned children are much more likely than non-orphans to be working in commercial agriculture, domestic service, commercial sex, and as street vendors.[134] A 2002 rapid assessment in Addis Ababa showed that more than three quarters of domestic workers were orphans,[135] and another rapid assessment in four mining areas in Tanzania found that 7 per cent of children working part time and 38 per cent of children working full-time were orphans.[136]

Orphans swell the army of children with ragged clothes and worn-out shoes roaming African city streets, engaged in all sorts of activities ranging from begging and petty trade to sex work and manual labour. There are an estimated

---

[129] A child is defined as "poor" if (s)he lives in a household in the bottom 4 deciles and "ultra-poor" if (s)he lives in a household in the bottom 2 deciles.
[130] WOOLARD (2008).
[131] AINSWORTH and SEMALI (2000).
[132] MAKAME et al. (2002) cited in UNICEF (2006).
[133] SALAAM (2005).
[134] SEMKIWA et al. (2003).
[135] KIFLE (2000) cited in UNICEF (2003).
[136] MWAMI et al. (2002) cited in UNICEF (2003).

32 million such street children in Africa.[137] Although a good number among them are not, most are orphans. The majority of children living on the streets of Brazzaville, Congo and Lusaka, Zambia are orphans.[138]

> The street is not only the option to earn a subsistence income and find refuge, but also a temporary escape route from a traumatic past filled with sorrow and stigma.

> **The Talibés of Senegal**[139]
>
> In Senegal, there is a different group of street children, known as "talibés", who "belong" to Muslim leaders known as "marabouts". "Talibé" is an Arabic word meaning "one who seeks and asks". According to a recent report by UNICEF, there are between 50,000 and 100,000 talibés in Senegal. Traditionally, families contracted with marabouts to raise their children and provide them with a Koranic education; in exchange for this education, the families would provide compensation or gifts to the marabouts, and the children would be engaged in farming or other enterprises to support the marabouts. The children would go house to house in their villages reciting the Koran, receiving donations along the way; depending on his reputation, a single marabout might have between 20 and several hundred talibés in his "care," 85 per cent of whom will be from the poorest families.
>
> Talibés often live in appalling conditions, where hunger, thirst, and disease are rampant. During the daytime, marabouts send the talibés out into the streets to beg. They are readily recognisable throughout Dakar, the capital of Senegal, for the rags that they wear and the tomato paste cans hung around their necks for collecting alms. Many marabouts require that their talibés meet a certain begging quota for the day, and if the talibés do not meet their quota, they may be severely beaten.
>
> It is said that the talibés' begging is part of their Koranic education, designed to teach them humility, while at the same time offering the opportunity for other Muslims in the community to practice charity. Although the talibés do receive a minimal Koranic education, this education is insufficient to enable the talibés to find employment as adults. The result is that they usually become either unemployed homeless adults, or adult disciples of the marabouts.

---

[137] UNEP and UNESCO. Facts & figures STREET CHILDREN/BY COUNTRY. Available at www.youthxchange.net/main/b236_homeless-h.asp.
[138] Cited in UNICEF, Africa's orphaned generation.
[139] Arms of Love International (2007).

For orphaned children, working on the street becomes a survival imperative, both in terms of feeding oneself and of – for example – paying up gang leaders in order to guarantee a street space for night time refuge. This dynamic is even more pressing for children orphaned by AIDS, because of the limited household resources left them after depletion by their parents' medical and funeral expenses.

The street is not only an option for earning a subsistence income and finding refuge: it can also be a temporary – but perilous – escape route from a traumatic past filled with sorrow and stigma. Many reports exist of children orphaned by AIDS being utterly rejected and stigmatised by their communities, and eventually being driven out of their parents' property.[140]

While on the street, children can be exposed to police beatings,[141] rape, drug abuse and other forms of exploitation, making them more vulnerable to contracting HIV. The increasing misguided tendency to associate the deprived state of street children with criminal behaviour has resulted in their continuous abuse: thus these children, who have already lost a substantial part of their 'sweet' childhood, cannot even take refuge in the freezing cold of street corners or sewerage tunnels, as they are chased away, beaten, detained, or even killed. Street children regularly sniff glue and petrol to dissipate the pain of hunger, and as a shield from the cold. They also often say that the high from such chemicals makes them braver in facing beatings from the police, or when attempting to pick-pocket.[142]

In some countries, orphaned street children as young as nine years old have been found engaged in sex work.[143] There are reports of orphaned girls heading households trading sex for siblings' school fees, or to buy food and medicines.[144] A study in Ghana showed that girls living on the street resort to prostitution to top up income from other street activities, exchanging sex for food, shelter or protection from older men and street gangs.[145] Concern also exists that, given the fact that orphaned 'street' children are increasingly rootless, uneducated, under-nurtured, traumatised and lacking in food, shelter, safety and nurturing, they

---

[140] For instance, AIDS is considered by some communities in the DRC as an illness of the night – in other words, an illness of witchcraft. Children whose parents died of AIDS are accused of bewitching them to death, and are forcefully driven out of their dwellings ("Africa Feature: Around 20,000 street children wander in Kinshasa", *Peoples' Daily Online*).
[141] HUMAN RIGHTS WATCH (2006a).
[142] IRIN (2006).
[143] HUMAN RIGHTS WATCH (2001).
[144] HUMAN RIGHTS WATCH (2003); AFRICAN CHILD POLICY FORUM (2008b).
[145] AIDOO (2008).

> **One day in the life of a street child**[146]
>
> He was leaning on the wall. His head was too large for his emaciated neck to carry. His eyes were closed in an apparent concentration.
>
> On one of his skinny arms was wrapped a piece of cloth which might have once been white. His greasy shorts were tight on the waist and very wide on the thighs. His shirt, without a single button, was torn on his wrist. Apart from these, the only thing that covered his itching body was his-lice-riddled hair.
>
> His childish complexion had faded into the dull look of an old man. He seemed to care nothing about the deafening noise around him
>
> He opened his eyes to his surroundings. I looked at his wax-jammed ears and wondered if he could hear the noise at all.
>
> He turned his beautiful large eyes towards me, and, making sure that I was not 'looking', he unwrapped the piece of cloth from his arm and poured some liquid onto it from a small plastic bag. Bringing the cloth closer to his nostrils, he inhaled it with all his might. As he did, I saw his umbilical cord, which had apparently been cut sloppily, disappearing deep into his abdomen. Then, as he sneezed, the mass of mucus that dangled from his nostrils, still glued to his arm, burst out…
>
> He did not get time to rest his head on the wall. From his teat-sized mouth and his cigarette-charred lower lip came a glacier of dribble. From underneath his wide shorts and down his widely-opened legs rolled a thin string of yellow urine. His eyes were now crammed with flies.
>
> Staring at his desiccated eye pupils, I murmured to myself: "So it is possible for a child's glorious and wonderful gaze to be decimated by deprivation and neglect!!"

may fall into the embrace of crime gangs, military warlords and terrorists. An ILO survey found that along with refugees, male orphans are particularly vulnerable to recruitment, and may join armies or armed groups in hope of getting regular food and becoming accepted by a family of peers.[147] A rebel fighter in Congo reportedly claimed that his militia pays the school fees for the children

---

[146] SHIMELIS (2007).
[147] DUMAS (2003).

in his group, most of whom are orphans.[148] Children as young as seven years old are among the 300,000 children fighting in wars around the world today. Child soldiers are subject to ill treatment and sexual exploitation: they are often forced to commit terrible atrocities, and are beaten or killed if they try to escape.[149] They fight on the front lines, in danger of violent death, are forced to work as human mine detectors, and in the most extreme cases are coerced to take part in suicide missions.[150]

> Along with refugees, male orphans are particularly vulnerable to recruitment, and may join armies or armed groups in hope of getting regular food and becoming accepted by a family of peers

C. Child-headed households

Children in child-headed households are more likely to be poor and to experience morbidity and mortality at higher rates than their peers.[151, 152] For example, a study in Ethiopia has shown that children in child-headed households are very unlikely to receive treatment for illnesses, due to the limited capacity of children heading households to articulate their health problems and the fact that they there are often legally too young to claim the right to access public health services (it is customary in many countries to require that children present themselves with an accompanying adult in order to access public healthcare services). Even if young children do succeed in accessing health services, they are still subject to a higher risk of taking medications at wrong dosages or at the wrong time.[153]

The same study showed that many children in child-headed households can only access low quantities of food, and that they often survive on rotten and thrown-away foodstuffs. The study also found that, in most cases, these children engage in hazardous labour in exchange for food, or, in the case of girls, trade sex for food.[154]

Children in child-headed households find it hard to go to school because of a lack of money and scholastic materials; even if they do attend school, the majority do not attend regularly, because they feel tired because of household chores, do have not enough food to sustain them during school hours, or are frequently sick. Most

---

[148] WAX (2003) cited in SALAAM (2005).
[149] OCHA and IRIN (2003).
[150] HUMAN RIGHTS WATCH (2006b).
[151] World Bank. OVC Toolkit. OVC Core Definitions http://info.worldbank.org/etools/docs/library/237764/toolkiten/howknow/definitions.htm.
[152] UEYAMA (2007).
[153] AFRICAN CHILD POLICY FORUM (2008b).
[154] AFRICAN CHILD POLICY FORUM (2008b).

of those living in urban centres have to work late into the evening to make a living by selling cigarettes, roasted grain, lottery tickets, and so on. Most of these children score lower academically, especially in subjects that require extra time and help – a trend that can be traced to a lack of adult pedagogic support at home.[155]

Child-headed households are more likely to lose their right to a home through failure to secure inheritance rights, or because of property theft by opportunist relatives. Unlike adults, minors' property rights are actually future rights, and therefore are more susceptible to being usurped by relatives or neighbours. Moreover, unlike adults, children do not ordinarily have the mental maturity or the physical strength to resist such actions by relatives.[156] Such children, especially those orphaned by AIDS, are more likely to be forced out of their homes and onto the streets by relatives or guardians, for ostensible fear of contagion or on the basis of unfounded allegations of witchcraft.[157]

To complicate things further, customary practice and statutory law in most African countries dictate that children must make their claims to property and inheritance through adult guardians. This requirement is further complicated by the reluctance of many guardians, who may themselves be suffering the adverse effects of HIV/AIDS, to represent the children, or by their tendency to compete with the children for the same property rights that the children seek to protect.[158]

Children who are bereaved of their parents after their parents have suffered prolonged illness are likely to begin their new lives with very limited resources. Illness is often impoverishing, often requiring households to sell off land to raise money for hospital bills and medication. Resources badly needed for survival are depleted even before the parents die, raising the risk of chronic poverty for the children when they subsequently become child-headed households. Girls in such households often end up as prostitutes or get married at a very early age, frequently to much older men, while the boys join armed groups, or make their way to the streets to look for petty employment.

With limited education, external support or means of generating income to provide for their families and a sense of desperation, children in child-headed

---

[155] AFRICAN CHILD POLICY FORUM (2008b).
[156] PRENDERGAST et al. (2007).
[157] LUSK and O'GARA (2002).
[158] PRENDERGAST et al. (2007).

households have no choice but to engage in what is known as child-controlled labour.[159]

D. Conclusion

Despite Africa's encouraging economic outlook in recent years, millions of children still struggle on the margins of survival on the continent. Child poverty is exacerbated by the rising impoverishment of households: as of 2005, 43 per cent of the population in sub-Saharan Africa lived on incomes of below USD 1 a day. Three quarters of the world's ultra poor (122 million people) live in sub-Saharan Africa, and the number of poor people in the region living below the poverty line is also increasing in absolute terms, because of rising inequality.

The HIV pandemic, armed conflicts and population growth are all exacerbating Africa's poverty. These factors are eating away at scarce resources both at the household and national levels, leading to a rise in the number of children suffering deprivation. On top of this, due to climate change, long spells of drought, increased demand for food, slow-growing supply, changing consumption patterns in major developing countries like China and the planting of crops for biofuel, the world is in the midst of an unprecedented severe food crisis, and Africa is hard hit.

The costs of poverty for children are enormous and brutal. Too many poor children die from avoidable diseases, and millions die or fall sick for lack of food and safe drinking water. About 30,000 children every day succumb to preventable death for want of a glass of clean water and a meagre meal.

A huge and growing orphan population has been created by war and HIV. About 1,900 children are born with HIV every day on the continent; a million babies are stillborn every year and never see the light of day; still a child dies every minute for lack of a measles vaccine that costs as little as USD 1 per child; and 6 million more die of hunger every year. Nearly fifty per cent of Africa's children live in some form of housing deprivation. About 32 million sleep in tunnels, sniff glue and eat rotten food, largely forgotten and abused by the world around them. 240 million children defecate in open fields or come in contact with their faeces for lack of rudimentary sanitation facilities.

Poverty has continued to drive millions of children into slavery and onto the streets. About 50 million children work in slave-like conditions to survive each

---

[159] This is labour where the process as well as the returns from it are controlled entirely by the child himself/herself, unlike family-controlled labour, where both the process and the income are controlled by the family, or the trafficker in the case of trafficked children.

day. Others have to contend with the oft-unacknowledged yet ubiquitous phenomenon of gratuitous violence against children.

On the educational front, despite modest progress in education provision, a very large number of African children – especially girls – are still denied education.

4. THE WAY FORWARD

Social and economic change challenges African societies to improve material living standards for all children, while at the same time ensuring that inequality does not lock poorer children out of the activities and opportunities that most can access. Reducing child poverty as a short-term objective would thereby also reduce adult poverty in the long run. In addition to saving countless lives and reversing the desperation and misery of hundreds of millions of children, now and as parents in the future, there are hugely credible moral, economic and social cases for tackling child poverty.[160]

The problem of child poverty is complex, intertwined as it is with a large number of social, economic and structural factors. Policy identification in this area is therefore a particularly arduous task. It is in this context that we propose the following steps to tackle child poverty.

Recognise child poverty and count its cost:

- appreciate the fact that poverty affects children differently from adults, and recognise that it is an unacceptable situation. This implies improved data collection and research that includes relevant evidence of what works;
- counting the cost of poverty is not enough: governments, national and private media, NGOs and civil society organisations need to undertake sustained campaigns and public education on all aspects of child poverty, as it is known now and as it is elaborated further by new studies and research.

Pursue pro-poor economic policies and employment generation programmes:

- put in place and pursue economic policies that are pro-poor and conducive to human development, and which include scope for redistribution and increased equality; trade liberalisation preceded by investment in human development,

---

[160] Free The Children, Child Poverty, 2005, www.freethechildren.com/getinvolved/geteducated/childpoverty.htm#000.

especially education; attention to preventing exploitation of children; and macroeconomic strategies which consider potential social impacts;
- maximise the labour market participation and economic freedom of mothers: the role of mothers is an important element in tackling child poverty and promoting women's financial independence and protection from poverty. The disadvantaged labour market position and continued barriers that women continue to face mean that any anti-poverty strategy that relies on paid work as the main route out of poverty has to be an explicitly gendered strategy; micro-credit services that do not require prohibitive collateral, coupled with provision of proper training, may be needed to draw women into the labour market.

Introduce child benefit packages such as social transfers:

- develop social security – introduce child benefit, a key tool to address children's wellbeing. Social security is a key way of supporting vulnerable children and families. Progressive policies should redistribute payments targeted at children, either in cash or kind, through mothers. On a regular (weekly or monthly) basis, these can have a direct impact on reducing extreme poverty. Payments can be used to support child involvement in education, to improve nutrition, and to protect children from child labour.

Implement free universal access to health and education services:

- provide preventive and curative health services for all, with an emphasis on under-five and maternal health, complemented by user fee exemption on basic essential primary health care services. Provide better access to nutrition, toilets, cleaner water and adequate shelter, as these can make substantial improvements to child survival. Concrete steps have to be taken to address the current food crisis, which is taking a huge toll on Africans even as this is written;
- as a matter of critical health priority, take steps to ensure free universal access to anti-retroviral treatment to prolong the lives of children and parents infected with HIV, and to prevent the transmission of HIV from mothers to children;
- provide free universal access to education of at least 10 years, complemented by school feeding programmes and school fee exemptions. Equally importantly, ensure that the education provided is of adequate quality, and ensure that the factors that disrupt children's schooling are minimised.

Ensure enhanced protection and support for vulnerable groups of children:

- ensure enhanced protection and support for vulnerable groups of children, including child-headed households, street children, child labourers, child domestic workers and children with disabilities. These children tend to be poorer than other groups of children, and may easily fall between the cracks of public programmes.

5. REFERENCES

Abdul-Raheem, T. (2007). *Foreign NGOs: Are they the right answer for Africa?* Available at http://newint.org/easier-english/Africa/africango.html.
ACORD (Agency for Cooperation and Research in Development) (2001). *Research into the living conditions of children who are heads of household in Rwanda*. London.
AFP (2007). *Nairobi e-waste dump threatens lives of hundreds of children.*
African Child Policy Forum (2008a). *The Africa Report on Child Wellbeing*. Addis Ababa: African Child Policy Forum.
African Child Policy Forum (2008b). *Reversed Roles and Stressed Souls: Child-Headed Households in Ethiopia*. The African Child Policy Forum.
African Child Policy Forum (2008c). *HIV/AIDS, Orphans and Child-Headed Households in sub-Saharan Africa*. The African Child Policy Forum. Forthcoming.
African Child Policy Forum and ILO (2006). *Violence Against Girls at Work in Africa*. The Second International Policy conference on the African Child. Violence Against Girls in Africa.
African Child Policy Forum and UNICEF (2007). *Children and Youth Polls Country Report, AFRICA REGION*.
African Development Bank (2007). *African Development Report 2007: Natural Resources for Sustainable Development in Africa*: Oxford University Press.
African Union (2007). Third Session of the African Union Conference of Ministers of Health, Johannesburg, South Africa 9–13 APRIL 2007. CAMH/MIN/5(III) Theme: Strengthening of Health Systems for Equity and Development in Africa DRAFT Rev 2 Africa Health Strategy: 2007 – 2015.
African Union (2004). *Declaration on Employment and Poverty Alleviation in Africa*. Assembly of the African Union Third Extraordinary Session on Employment and Poverty Alleviation, September 8–9, Ouagadougou. EXT/ASSEMBLY/AU/3 (III).
Ahmed, A.U., Hill, R.V., Smith, L.C., Wiesmann, D.M. and Frankenberger, T. (2007). *The World's Most Deprived: Characteristics and Causes of Extreme Poverty and Hunger*. International Food Policy Research Institute. 2020 Discussion Paper 43. October 2007.
Agüero, J., Carter, M. and Woolard, I. (2007). *The Impact of Unconditional Cash Transfers on Nutrition: the case of the South African Child Support Grant*. IPC Working Paper No. 39. Brasilia: International Poverty Center.
Aidoo, A. (208). *Child Poverty in Ghana*. Addis Ababa: African Child Policy Forum.

Ainger, K (2004). "The Scramble for Africa". *New Internationalist Magazine*, May 2004. *Third World Traveler.* www.thirdworldtraveler.com/Africa/Scramble_Africa.html

Ainsworth, M. and Filmer, D. (2002). *Poverty, children, schooling and HIV/AIDS: A targeting dilemma.* World Bank Policy Working Paper No. 2885. Washington, D.C.: World Bank.

Amnesty International Report (2007). *The state of the world's human rights.* Amnesty International.

Amnesty International and Oxfam (2003). Shattered Lives: the case for tough international arms control.

Andvig, J.C., Canagarajah, S. and Keilland, A. (2001). *Issues in child labour in Africa.* Africa Region Human Development. Working group paper series.

Arevshatian, L., Clements, C.J. Lwanga, S.K., Misore, A.O., Ndumbe, P., Seward, J.F. and Taylor, P. (2007). "An evaluation of infant immunisation in Africa: is a transformation in progress?" *Bulletin of the World Health Organization,* June 2007, 85 (6).

Arms of Love International (2007). *Where We Work: Dakar, Senegal.* www.armsoflove.org/where_senegal_talibe.htm

Assefa Bequele (2006). *Ideals without illusions: Promoting child rights in the context of poverty.* Keynote Speech prepared for the XVIth ISPCAN International Congress. York University. September 2006.

Association for Progressive Communications (APC) and Communication Rights in the Information Society (CRIS) (2003). *Involving civil society in ICT policy: The World Support on the Information Society.* Johannesburg, South Africa: STE Publishers.

Atkinson, T. (2002). "Is rising income inequality inevitable? A critique of the 'Transatlantic Consensus.'" In Townsend, P. and Gordon, D. (2002), *World Poverty: new policies to defeat an old enemy.*

AU and NEPAD (2005). *Comprehensive Africa Agriculture Development Programme.* www.nepad.org/2005/files/documents/caadp.pdf

AU and UNFPA (2004). *The African Family in the New Millennium: Challenges and Prospects.* Social Affairs Department. AU.

Barrientos, A. and DeJong, J. (2004). *Child Poverty and Cash Transfers.* CHIP (Childhood Poverty Research and Policy Centre) Report No. 4.

Bartlett, S. (2002). *Urban children and the physical environment,* paper presented at children and the City Conference held by Arab Urban Development Institute in Amman, Jordan, on 11–13 December 2002. www.araburban.org/childcity/Papers/English/Sheridan%20Bartlett.pdf

Baynham, S. (1994). *Eternal Sentinels – The Legacy of Landmines in Africa.* African Defence Review. Issue No 18. Africa Institute of South Africa. www.iss.co.za/ASR/ADR18/Baynham.html.

BBC (2007). *Child Trafficking in Ethiopia. Fighting Africa's child trafficking boom.* 12 November 2007.

BBC (2005). *Guides: Poverty in Africa: Population Growth.*

Bloom, D., Canning, D. and Sevilla, J. (2002). *The Demographic Dividend: A New Perspective on the Economic Consequences of Population Change.* RAND.

Boler, T. and Timæus, I. (2006). *Father figures: why fathers and cash grants matter in responding to the impact of AIDS on education*. Centre for Population Studies, London School of Hygiene and Tropical Medicine. Powerpoint presentation.

Braithwaite, J. and Mont, D. (2008) *Disability and Poverty: A Survey of World Bank Poverty Assessments and Implications*. SP DISCUSSION PAPER NO. 0805. The World Bank. http://siteresources.worldbank.org/DISABILITY/Resources/280658-1172608138489/WBPovertyAssessments.pdf

von Braun, J., Rosegrant, M.W., Pandya-Lorch, R., Cohen, M.J., Cline, S.A., Brown, M.A. and Bos, M.S. (2005). *New Risks and Opportunities for Food Security Scenario Analyses for 2015 and 2050*. IFPRI.

von Braun, J. (2007a). "Focus on the World's Poorest and Hungry People". In IFPRI (2007) *Eliminating Hunger and Reducing Poverty. Three Perspectives*.

von Braun, J. (2007b). *The world food situation: new driving forces and required actions*. IFPRI's Biannual Overview of the World Food Situation presented to the CGIAR Annual General Meeting, Beijing, December 4, 2007.

Breman, J.G., Egan, A. and Keusch, G.T. (2001). "Introduction and Summary: The Intolerable Burden Of Malaria: A New Look At The Numbers". *American Journal of Tropical Medicine and Hygiene*. 2001. Vol. 64.

Budlender, D. and Woolard, I. (2006). *The impact of the South African child support and old age grants on children's schooling and work*. International Labour Organisation Programme on the Elimination of Child Labour: Geneva.

Case, A., Hosegood, V. and Lund, F. (2005). "The reach and impact of Child Support Grants: evidence from KwaZulu-Natal". *Development Southern Africa* 22(4): 467–482. October 2005.

Central Statistics Authority (Ethiopia) (2007). *Statistical Abstract 2006*.

Central Statistics Authority (Ethiopia) (2006). *Ethiopian Demographic Health Survey 2005*.

Centre on Housing Rights and Evictions (2006). *Defending the Housing Rights of Children*. Geneva.

Chant, S. (2003). *Female Household Headship and the Feminisation of Poverty: Facts, Fictions and Forward Strategies*. Issue 9, May 2003.

Charities Aid Foundation (2008). *Poverty and Environment in Africa: An Overview*. Available at www.conserveafrica.org.uk/index.html

CHIP (Childhood Poverty Research and Policy Centre) (2004). "Children and poverty – some questions answered". In CHIP *Briefing 1: Children and Poverty*, London. P.1. www.childhoodpoverty.org/index.php/action=documentfeed/doctype=pdf/id=46/

Commission for Africa (2005). *Our common interest: Report of the Commission for Africa*.

Cosgrove, W.J. and Rijsberman, F R. (1998). "Creating a vision for water, life and the environment". In *Water Policy* 1 (1998), pp. 115–122.

Davies, W. (2005). *For the price of a bike. Child trafficking in Togo*. Plan International.

Deaton, A. and Paxton, C. (1997): *Poverty among children and the elderly in developing countries*, Princeton.
www.wws.princeton.edu/%7Erpds/downloads/deaton_paxson_poverty_children_paper.pdf

Desta, T. (2006). "Of flying 'toilets' and Addis slum life." *Capital*. www.capitalethiopia.com/archive/2007/july/week4/feature.htm

Economist (The) (2003).The global menace of local strife. 24 May 2003.

Fajth, G. and Holland, K. (2007). *Poverty and Children: A Perspective*. UNICEF DPP Working Paper. 2007.

Feeny, T. and Boyden, J. (2003). *Children and Poverty: A Review of Contemporary Literature and Thought on Children and Poverty*. Children and Poverty Series, Part I. Christian Children's Fund, CCF.

Finfacts Business News Centre (2008). *Global Food Crisis Summit: FAO says world only needs $30 billion a year to eradicate the scourge of hunger; OECD countries spent $372 billion in 2006 alone to support their agriculture*. June 3, 2008. Available at www.finfacts.ie/irishfinancenews/article_1013783.shtml

Global Witness (2006). *Digging in corruption: Fraud, abuse and exploitation in Katanga's copper and cobalt mines*. A Report by Global Witness. July 2006.

Gordon, D., Nandy, S., Pantazis, C., Pemberton, S. and Townsend, P. (2003). *Child poverty in the developing world*.

Groce, N.E. (1999). *An Overview of Young People Living with Disabilities: Their needs and their rights*, UNICEF Programme Division (Working Paper Series), New York, 1999.

Harsch, E. (2001). "Child labour rooted in Africa's poverty: Campaigns launched against traffickers and abusive work". *Africa Recovery*, Vol.15 #3, October 2001, page 14. United Nations.

Harsch, E. (2006). "Combating Inequality in Africa". *In* Africa Recovery, United Nations Department of Public Information. Vol. 20, No. 2. July 2006.

Hazell, P. and Pachauri, R.K. (eds.) (2006). *Bioenergy and Agriculture: Promises and Challenges: Overview Focus 14*. Brief 1 of 12. December 2006.

Hulme, D., Moore, K. and Shepherd, A. (2001). *Chronic poverty: meanings and analytical frameworks*. Chronic Poverty Research Centre Working Paper 2.

ILO (2004). *Global Employment Trends for Youth 2004*. Geneva.

IMF (2007). *World Economic and Financial Surveys Regional Economic Outlook: Sub-Saharan Africa*.

IOM (2003). *The Trafficking of Women and Children in the Southern Africa Region*. IOM.

IRIN (2006). *Sudan: Living on the Streets*. IRIN News. www.irinnews.org

Jones, N., Tefera, B. and Woldehanna, T. (2005). *Research, Policy Engagement and Practice: Reflections on efforts to mainstream children into Ethiopia's second national poverty reduction strategy*. Young Lives Working Paper No 21.

Joseph Rowntree Foundation (2007). *Young children see poverty holding them back at school*. www.jrf.org.uk/pressroom/releases/070907.asp

de Lange, A (2006). "Going to Kompienga": *A Study on Child Labour Migration and Trafficking in Burkina Faso's South-Eastern Cotton Sector*. IREWOC (International Research on Working Children).

Lawn, J. and Kerber, K. (eds.) (2006). *Opportunities for Africa's Newborns – Practical data, policy and programmatic support for newborn care in Africa*. Cape Town: The Partnership for Maternal, Newborn and Child Health.

Leatt, A. (2006). *Child poverty – its meaning and extent*. Children's Institute.

Lister (2005). *The links between women's and children's poverty.* ww.cpag.org.uk/info/Povertyarticles/Poverty121/links.htm#note3

Lyytikäinen, M., Jones, N., Huttly, S. and Abramsky, T. (2006). *Childhood poverty, basic services and cumulative disadvantage: an international comparative analysis.* Young Lives Working Paper No 33. London: Young Lives.

Makonnen, A., Tefera, B., Woldehanna, T., Jones, N., Seager, J. Alemu, T. and Asgedom, G. (2005). *Child Nutrition Status in Poor Ethiopian Households: The role of gender, assets and location.* Young Lives Working Paper No 26. London: Young Lives.

Manda, N. and Mohamed-Katerer, J. (2006). "Section 3: Emerging Challenges: CHAPTER 11 Chemicals" in *Africa Environment Outlook 2: Our environment, our wealth.*

Mehrotra, S. (2004) *Improving Child Wellbeing in Developing Countries. What Do We Know? What Can Be Done?* CHIP Report No. 9, London: Childhood Poverty Research and Policy Centre.

Mikkelsen, J. (2008). *The World Food Crisis: Impact on Children requiring food assistance in Ethiopia.* Paper prepared based on the presentation made to the Third International Policy Conference on The African Child organised by The African Child Policy Forum, in Addis Ababa in 12–13 May 2008.

Minujin, A., Delamonica, E., Gonzalez, E.D. and Davidziuk, A. (2005). *Children Living in Poverty. A review of child poverty definitions, measurements, and policies.* Desk Review paper for UNICEF's Conference on "Children & Poverty: Global Context, Local Solutions" Graduate Programme in International Affairs. New School University. April 25–27, 2005. New York.

Montague, D. and Berrigan, F. (2002). "The Business of War in the Democratic Republic of Congo". *Dollars and Sense Magazine.* July/August, 2002.

Moore, K (2005). *Thinking about youth poverty through the lenses of chronic poverty, life-course poverty and intergenerational poverty.* University of Manchester.

de Morais, R. (2007). *Private security companies and a parallel State in Angola.* www.africafiles.org/article.asp?ID=16918

Mulama, J. (2006). "Menace of the flying toilets". *Mail and Guardian Online.* www.mg.co.za/articlePage.aspx?articleid=287858&area=/insight/insight__africa/

Narayan, D. with Patel, R., Schafft, K., Rademacher, A. and Koch-Schulte, S. 1999. *Can Anyone Hear Us?* Washington DC: World Bank.

Nations Unies (2003). *Population, éducation et développement.* Rapport concis. Département des affaires économiques et sociales. Division de la population.

NEPAD (2003). *Action Plan for the Environment Initiative.* New Partnership for Africa's Development, Midrand.
http://nepad.org/2005/files/reports/action_plan/action_plan_english2.pdf

New York Times (2004). "Africa's Health Care Brain Drain". 13 August 2004.

Noble, M., Wright G. and Cluver, L. (2006). "Developing a child-focused and multidimensional model of child poverty for South Africa". *Journal of Children and Poverty,* 12 (1): 39–53.

Nuwagaba, A., Bantebya, G., Ssekiwanuka, J. and Tamwesigire, C. (2008) *Child Poverty and National Budgetary Responses.* Background paper prepared for The African Child Policy Forum.

OHCHR (2006). *Principles and Guidelines for a Human Rights Approach to Poverty Reduction Strategies.*

Oluseyi, O.B. (2008). *The State of Child Poverty in Nigeria.* Addis Ababa: African Child Policy Forum.

O'Neill, T. (2007). *Curse of Black Gold: Hope and Betrayal in the Niger Delta.* National Geographic Society. Nigerian Oil @National Geographic Magazine.

Ongwen, O. (2006). "For Life or Profit? GATS and the Externalization of Africa's Resources". In Burnett, P. and Manji, F. (eds.). (2007): *From the slave trade to 'free' trade: How trade undermines democracy and justice in Africa.* Fahamu.

Otuka, J.O. E. (2003). "Innovative ideas and techniques for science, technology and mathematics education in Africa". In Pillai, R.S. (ed.) (2001), *Strategies for introducing new curricula in West Africa:* Final report of the seminar/Workshop held in Lagos, Nigeria, 12–16 November 2001, pp. 13–18, Geneva: UNESCO International Bureau of Education.

Oxfam and Safer World (2007). *Africa's Missing Billions.* IANSA. Oxfam and Safer World.

Pendleton, L. (2007). *Slavery Continues in Africa.* IIJD, Inc. www.iijd.org/110907Slavery.html.

Sarraf, M. and Jiwanji, M. (2001). *Beating the Resource Curse: The Case of Botswana.* Paper No. 83. Environmental Economics Series. The World Bank Environment Department.

Save the Children Sweden (2007). *First Introduction to work for child rights from a budget perspective. Studies and Experiences from different Countries.*

Save the Children (2008). *Saving Children's Lives: Why equity matters.*

Save the Children (2007) *State of the World's Mothers 2007. Saving the Lives of Children Under 5.*

Save the Children (2005). *One in Two: Children are the Key to Africa's Future.*

Sayagues, M. (2006). *Writing for Our Lives. How the Maisha Yetu Project Changed Health Coverage in Africa.* International Women's Media Foundation.

Selva, M. (2006). *Toxic Shock: How Western Rubbish is Destroying Africa.* Independent News and Media Limited.

Semkiwa, H., *et al.* (2003). *HIV/AIDS and Child Labour in the United Republic of Tanzania: A rapid assessment,* Paper No. 3, International Labour Organization, International Programme on the Elimination of Child Labour, Geneva.

Sen, A. (1999). *Development as freedom.* Oxford.

Shimelis, T. (2007). "Does Anyone Care? The plight of street children in Ethiopia." *Metropolitan.* Vol. 1, No. 17. October 12–13, 2007.

Silverstein, K (2001). "Diamonds of Death", *The Nation Magazine,* April 23, 2001. *Third World Traveler:* www.thirdworldtraveler.com/Africa/Diamonds_Death.html

Smith, N. (2008). The Wonga Coup: Transparency and Conspiracy in Equatorial Guinea. http://forums.csis.org/africa/?p=84. Centre for Strategic and International Studies.

Some, P.A. (2008). *Situation de la pauvreté des enfants au Burkina Faso.* Addis Ababa: African Child Policy Forum.

Sommers, M. (2002). *Children, Education and War: Reaching Education For All (EFA) Objectives in Countries Affected by Conflict*. Conflict Prevention and Reconstruction Unit. Working Paper No. 1. June 2002.

Tomlinson, M. (2007) *School feeding in East and Southern Africa: Improving food sovereignty or photo opportunity?* EQUINET/MRC working paper on nutrition response. EQUINET: Harare.

Townsend, P. (1979). *Poverty in the United Kingdom: a survey of household resources and standards of living*, Penguin, 1979.

Tryon, J. (2002). *Cocoa made with sweat of child labour: study.* CTV News.

UN (2005). *The 2005 Report on the World Social Situation: The Inequality Predicament.* UN Department of Economic and Social affairs.

UN (1996). *Promotion and Protection of the Rights of Children. Impact of armed conflict on children.* Note by the Secretary-General. Distr. GENERAL A/51/306 26 August 1996. Fifty-first session Item 108 of the provisional agenda A/51/150.

UN (2007). *Africa and the Millennium Development Goals*, 2007 update.

UN (2006). *World Report on Violence against Children.* Geneva.

UNAIDS (2008). "The global HIV challenge: assessing progress, identifying obstacles, renewing commitment". *Report on the Global AIDS Epidemic 2008.*

UNAIDS (2007). *AIDS Epidemic Update 2007; UNAIDS Fact sheet: Sub-Saharan Africa, 2006.*
http://data.unaids.org/pub/GlobalReport/2006/200605-FS_SubSaharanAfrica_en.pdf

UNDP (2000). *Overcoming human poverty.* Poverty Report, 2000.

UNDP (2006). *Human Development Report 2006. Beyond scarcity: Power, poverty and the global water crisis.*

UNDP (2007). *Human Development Report 2007/2008. Fighting climate change: Human solidarity in a divided world.*

UNECA (2005a). *MDGs in Africa: A challenge for change. Tackling income inequality could help Africa quash extreme poverty.* www.uneca.org/mdgs/Story31October06.asp

UNECA (2005b). *Striving for Good Governance in Africa. Synopsis of the 2005 African Governance report.* www.uneca.org/agr/

UNECA (2005c). *Meeting the Challenges of Unemployment and Poverty in Africa: Overview.* Available at: www.uneca.org/era2005/overview.pdf

UNEP (2002). *Global Environment Outlook.* "Chapter Two: state of the environment and policy retrospective: 1972–2002."

UNEP News Release (2007). *Africa Rubbish Tip Major Hazard to Children and the Environment: UNEP report links lead and other heavy metals pollution to degrading health of children living around Dandora waste dump in Nairobi, Kenya.* Nairobi, 5 October 2007. News Release 2007/30.

UNEP News Release (2002). *The State of Africa's Environment Chronicled in Ground-Breaking Report: Hard Facts Tough Choices.* UNEP News Release 2002/50. July 2002.
www.unep.org/Documents.Multilingual/Default.asp?DocumentID=255&ArticleID=3086&l=en

UNEP/FAO (2003). *Global IPM Facility Expert Group on Termite Biology and Management 2003.*

UNESCO and the Early Childhood Development Network for Africa (ECDNA) (2003). *Protecting the rights of young children affected and infected by HIV/AIDS in Africa: Updating strategies and reinforcing existing networks.* Report of the International Workshop co-organized by (Paris, 13-17 May 2002) UNESCO Action Research in Family and Early Childhood June 2003.

UNESCO Fact Sheet, *Sub-Saharan Africa: Strong foundations: Early childhood care and education,* Education For All Global Monitoring Report, accessed in April 2007 at: www.unesco.org/education/GMR/2007/fact_sheet_ssa.pdf.

UNESCO (2007). *Global Education Digest 2007: Comparing Education Statistics Across the World.* Institute for Statistics.

UNESCO Institute for Statistics (UIS), accessed in April 2008 at: www.uis.unesco.org/TEMPLATE/pdf/EducGeneral/UIS_Fact%20 Sheet_2006_02_SecAfr_EN.pdf.

UNICEF (1987). *State of the World's Children 1988.*

UNICEF (2000). *Poverty Reduction Begins with Children.* Report, New York: UNICEF.

UNICEF (2003). *Africa's orphaned and vulnerable generations.*

UNICEF (2004). *The State of the World's Children, 2005. Childhood under Threat.*

UNICEF (2006). *The State of the World's children 2007. Women and Children: The Double Dividend of Gender Equality.*

UNICEF (2007a). *Global Study on Child Poverty and disparities 2007-2008.* Guide. New York.

UNICEF (2007b). *The State of the World's Children, 2008. Child Survival.*

UNICEF (2007c). *Progress For Children. A World Fit for Children.* Statistical Review Number 6, December 2007.

UNICEF (2007d). *Monitoring the Situation of Children and Women 2007.*

UNICEF (2007e). *Promoting the Rights of Children with Disabilities.* Innocenti Digest No. 13.

UNICEF (2008) *State of the World's Children, 2009. Maternal and Newborn Health.*

UN Population Division (2001). *World Population Prospects - the 2000 Revision Highlights.*

USAID (2005). Democracy and Governance in Africa. Available at: www.usaid.gov/our_work/democracy_and_governance/regions/afr/

USAID (2001). *Report to Congress: USAID Efforts to Address the Needs of Children Affected by HIV/AIDS.* An Overview of US Agency for International Development Programmes and Approaches. The Synergy Project.

Vandemoortele, J. (2000). *Absorbing Social Shocks, Protecting Children and Reducing Poverty,* UNICEF, New York, NY. pg. 3. www.unicef.org/evaldatabase/files/Global_2000_Absorbing_Social_Shocks.pdf.

Verner, D. (2005). *What Factors Influence World Literacy? Is Africa Different?* World Bank Policy Research Working Paper No 3496.

WaterAid (2005). *Dying for the toilet: The cost of missing the sanitation Millennium Development Goal? An extra 10 million children's lives.* WaterAid Report. www.wateraid.org.

WHO and UNICEF (2006). *WHO and UNICEF Joint Monitoring Programme for Water and Sanitation.*

WHO (2006a). *The Health of the People: The African Regional Health report*. AFRO Publications.
WHO (2006b). *The global shortage of health workers and its impact,* WHO Fact sheet No. 301, April 2006.
WHO (2007). *Health Financing: A Strategy for the African Region.* WHO Regional Office for Africa.
Woldehanna, T., Mekonnen, A., Jones, N., Tefera, B., Seager, J., Alemu, T. and Asgedom, G. (2005a). *Education Choices in Ethiopia: What determines whether poor households send their children to school.* Young Lives Working Paper No 15. London: Young Lives.
Woldehanna, T., Tefera, B., Jones, N. and Bayrau, A. (2005b). *Child Labour, Gender Inequality and Rural/Urban Disparities: how can Ethiopia's national development strategies be revised to address negative spill-over impacts on education and wellbeing?* Young Lives Working Paper No 20. London: Young Lives.
Woolard, I. (2008). *A description of child poverty in South Africa.* Addis Ababa: African Child Policy Forum.
World Bank (2008). *Food Crisis. World Bank $ 1.2 Billion Funding Programme.*
World Bank (2007a). *World Development Report 2008. Agriculture for Development.*
World Bank (2007b). *World Development Indicators 2007.*
World Bank (2006) Africa Development Indicators 2006. Washington D.C., USA.
Yusuf, A. and Sheikh, A. (2007). "Mogadishu violence kills 6,500 in past year". December 31, 2007. Reuters.

WHICH AFRICAN GOVERNMENTS ARE CHILD-FRIENDLY? WHICH ONES ARE NOT AND WHY?[*]

ASSEFA BEQUELE
Executive Director, The African Child Policy Forum (ACPF)

1. INTRODUCTION

African governments have an impressive record in their formal accession to the relevant international treaties on children, including the African Charter on the Rights and Welfare of the Child. However, the extent of their commitment varies widely, and the gap between promises and reality remains wide in many countries. Why? Which governments are doing well and which ones are not? How do African governments rank in relation to each other? What accounts for differences in government performance? To what extent are differences in government performance due to disparities in levels of development or levels of poverty?

These were some of the questions that were addressed in a recent report published by ACPF, *The African Report on Child Wellbeing 2008: How child-friendly are African governments?* This report uses the concept of child-friendliness and a child-friendliness index (CFI) to assess, score and rank the performance of all 52 African governments (those not covered being Somalia and Saharawi Arab Republic). Finally, it spells out the specific policies that account for differences in child wellbeing outcomes among countries, and the good practices that concerned governments may adopt. This paper highlights the approach and the major findings of that report.

---

[*] Paper based on AFRICAN CHILD POLICY FORUM (2008). *The African Report on Child Wellbeing 2008: How Child-friendly are African Governments?* Addis Ababa: The African Child Policy Forum.
Earlier versions of this paper were presented at the meeting of the African Committee of Experts on the Rights and Welfare of the Child (20 April 2009), and the Sixth African Conference on Child Abuse and Neglect (4 May 2009), held in Addis Ababa.

2. THE CHILD-FRIENDLINESS OF AFRICAN GOVERNMENTS

The child-friendliness index developed by ACPF assesses the extent to which African governments are committed to child wellbeing. Child-friendliness is a manifestation of the political will of governments to make the maximum effort to realise children's rights and wellbeing.

Three dimensions of child-friendliness were identified: namely, the extent to which a government is committed to the principles of:

1. full *protection* of children, through appropriate legal and policy frameworks;
2. adequate *provision* for the basic needs of children, assessed in terms of budgetary allocation and wellbeing outcomes;
3. *participation* of children in decisions that affect their wellbeing.

Though child participation is important, it was not possible to obtain sufficient data on participation to include this in the development of the CFI. At present, therefore, the CFI only covers the *Protection* and *Provision* components of child wellbeing.

The CFI uses a common framework for the organisation and analysis of information and data for all the 52 countries. It is based on 40 policy and wellbeing indicators, and assesses the individual and relative performances of all the 52 governments at a point in time (2004–2005) and over time (i.e. between the periods 1999–2001 and 2004–2005).

3. HOW PROTECTIVE ARE AFRICAN GOVERNMENTS OF THEIR CHILDREN?

The first question is: how committed are governments to protecting children against harm, abuse and exploitation, through the effective provision of appropriate laws and policies? The report assesses government performance in terms of protection by looking at such indicators as:

1. ratification of international and regional legal instruments relating to children;
2. existence of provisions in national laws to protect children against harm and exploitation;
3. existence of a juvenile justice system, National Plan of Action (NPA), and coordinating bodies for the implementation of children's rights;
4. existence of a national policy for free primary education.

The ranking based on the index values for the above indicators shows how African governments performed in laying the legal and policy frameworks for protecting children against harm and exploitation. As can be seen in Table 1, below, the ranking puts the Governments of Kenya, Madagascar, Burundi, Morocco, Namibia, Rwanda, Mali, Burkina Faso, Nigeria, and Libya on top, indicating that that they have performed well in laying appropriate legal and policy foundations for the protection of children. The bottom three governments in the ranking are those of Guinea-Bissau, Swaziland and Gambia. It is remarkable that some of the countries that scored at the top 10 – namely Kenya, Madagascar, Burundi, Rwanda, Mali, and Burkina Faso – are among the poorest in the world, while the list of countries that scored at the bottom includes countries such as Gabon, Seychelles, and Swaziland, which enjoy among the highest per capita incomes in Africa.

Table 1. Index values and ranking for protection of children

Country	Score	Rank
Kenya	0.855	1
Madagascar	0.849	2
Burundi	0.821	3
Morocco	0.821	4
Namibia	0.821	5
Rwanda	0.810	6
Mali	0.798	7
Burkina Faso	0.774	8
Nigeria	0.768	9
Libya	0.766	10
Mauritius	0.762	11
Uganda	0.762	12
Senegal	0.756	13
Tanzania	0.750	14
South Africa	0.738	15
Tunisia	0.738	16
Lesotho	0.726	17
Angola	0.714	18
Cape Verde	0.714	19
Mozambique	0.714	20
Togo	0.702	21
Zambia	0.700	22
Ethiopia	0.698	23

Country	Score	Rank
Algeria	0.690	24
Dem. Rep. Congo	0.685	25
Malawi	0.679	26
Sierra Leone	0.671	27
Guinea	0.671	28
Comoros	0.667	29
Equatorial Guinea	0.667	30
Mauritania	0.667	31
Niger	0.667	32
Botswana	0.664	33
Côte d'Ivoire	0.656	34
Egypt	0.655	35
Chad	0.643	36
Congo	0.643	37
Eritrea	0.643	38
Sudan	0.643	39
Benin	0.631	40
Cameroon	0.624	41
Ghana	0.619	42
Gabon	0.595	43
Seychelles	0.595	44
Zimbabwe	0.595	45
Djibouti	0.587	46
Liberia	0.583	47
Central African Republic	0.576	48
Sao Tome and Principe	0.548	49
Gambia	0.488	50
Swaziland	0.440	51
Guinea-Bissau	0.369	52

Source: The African Child Policy Forum, 2008.

4. RANKING OF GOVERNMENTS FOR CHILD PROVISION

The other dimension identified for the measurement of governments' child-friendliness was provision to meet the basic needs of children. Provision for children is measured based on two elements, each composed of distinct sets of indicators. The first element relates to budgetary expenditure that measures governments' resource commitment to provide for the basic needs of children and ensure their wellbeing. The other element measures the outcomes achieved in terms of actual access to various services (health, education, nutrition, water and sanitation). In the interest of brevity, we shall report here only the *ranking of governments for budgetary commitment*.

Among the indicators used to measure governments' budgetary commitment are:

1. government expenditure on health as a percentage of total government expenditure;
2. total public expenditure on education as a percentage of GDP;
3. percentage of the budget for routine EPI vaccines financed by government;
4. military expenditure as a percentage of GDP;
5. percentage change in governments' expenditure on health since the year 2000.

The score values for these indicators show that the Government of Malawi came out as the most committed to using the maximum amount of available resources for children. A close look at the five indicators shows that the Government of Malawi spent higher proportions of its resources for health and education; most importantly, its expenditure, particularly for health, increased four-fold since 2000, indicating enhanced commitment to supporting the sector. At the same time, Malawi's military expenditure was found to be one of the lowest in the continent. Following Malawi, the governments of Botswana, Burkina Faso, Seychelles and Namibia were found to be among the most committed. These countries also dedicated higher percentages of their resources to financing the health and education sectors, have considerably increased their budgetary allocations to these sectors since 2000, and have fully self-financed their national immunisation programmes.

At the other end of the scale, the group of least committed countries in budgetary terms includes Eritrea, Comoros, São Tomé and Principe, Guinea, Sudan, Central African Republic, Benin, Guinea-Bissau, Equatorial Guinea and Sierra Leone. Among these, the Government of Eritrea was found to be the least committed, having spent a relatively low proportion of its resources on health and education. Though Eritrea has shown an increase in the percentage of its budget allocated for education, health allocation showed a decline over the four-year period, and military expenditure remained high, contributing to the low overall score for budgetary commitment.

Table 2. Index values and ranking for budgetary commitment, 2004–2005

Country	Index value	Rank
Malawi	0.717	1
Botswana	0.643	2
Burkina Faso	0.613	3
Seychelles	0.600	4
Namibia	0.595	5
Tunisia	0.591	6
Swaziland	0.584	7
Cape Verde	0.571	8
Mauritius	0.571	9
South Africa	0.561	10
Djibouti	0.560	11
Algeria	0.560	12
Gabon	0.559	13
Lesotho	0.534	14
Morocco	0.532	15
Nigeria	0.531	16
Mali	0.529	17
Egypt	0.521	18
Niger	0.519	19
Kenya	0.510	20
Senegal	0.499	21
Rwanda	0.492	22
Togo	0.481	23
Libya	0.478	24
Ghana	0.475	25
Mauritania	0.473	26
Burundi	0.456	27
DRC	0.445	28
Chad	0.441	29
Mozambique	0.419	30
United Republic of Tanzania	0.401	31
Cameroon	0.400	32
Côte d'Ivoire	0.399	33
Congo	0.391	34
Madagascar	0.389	35

Country	Index value	Rank
Gambia	0.366	36
Uganda	0.365	37
Zambia	0.356	38
Angola	0.344	39
Ethiopia	0.344	40
Liberia	0.334	41
Zimbabwe	0.327	42
Sierra Leone	0.317	43
Equatorial Guinea	0.311	44
Guinea-Bissau	0.311	45
Benin	0.306	46
Central African Republic	0.306	47
Sudan	0.298	48
Guinea	0.276	49
São Tomé and Principe	0.226	50
Comoros	0.187	51
Eritrea	0.075	52

Source: The African Child Policy Forum, 2008.

5. HOW DO RICH AND POOR AFRICAN COUNTRIES SCORE IN BUDGETARY COMMITMENT?

The usual excuse offered by African governments for failing to enact pro-children policies is poverty. How far is this true? In order to answer this question, we compared governments' budgetary commitments with economic status as measured by GDP per capita. The comparison produced some interesting results. Policy problems concerning children seem often to be the result of lethargy and neglect rather than poverty. A number of countries with low GDP per capita were found to spend far more significant proportions of their limited resources on the education and health sectors than certain other countries with higher GDP per capita.

Table 3, below, presents countries that have performed both well and poorly in budget expenditure in comparison with their economic status. Exemplary governments in this regard are those of Malawi, Burkina Faso, Niger, Burundi, DRC and Mali. The Government of Malawi, for instance, ranked first in budgetary commitment, but has the 45th lowest GDP per capita in Africa. Conversely, Equatorial Guinea ranked 44th (one of the least committed) in terms of budgetary commitment, but had the highest GDP per capita in Africa in 2005.

The conclusion is simple, and perhaps not surprising: child-friendliness of governments is not necessarily related to economic status or availability of resources. It has to do with political will and political enlightenment. There are many poor countries that are committed to children despite economic difficulties. On the other hand, there are countries that are doing well in the economic sphere, but are not investing proportionally in their children. Most notable among such nations is Equatorial Guinea, which lies on opposite extremes of the respective rankings for budgetary commitment and GDP per capita. The governments of Sudan, Comoros, Angola and Libya also performed poorly, moving down 26, 24, 23 and 22 places respectively in their rankings for budgetary commitment when compared to their positions for economic status.

Table 3. List of countries by difference in their ranking for budgetary commitment from GDP per capita rank, 2004–2005

Countries which moved up in ranking for budgetary commitment		Countries which moved down in ranking for budgetary commitment	
Country	Number of places	Country	Number of places
Malawi	+45	Congo (Brazzaville)	–19
Burkina Faso	+34	Guinea	–21
Niger	+26	Libya	–22
Burundi	+23	Angola	–23
DRC	+23	Comoros	–24
Mali	+22	Sudan	–26
Togo	+17	Equatorial Guinea	–43

Source: The African Child Policy Forum, 2008 and World Bank's World Development Indicators, 2007.

6. MOST AND LEAST CHILD-FRIENDLY GOVERNMENTS

We now combine the results of these partial rankings and look at the overall picture. According to the composite CFI, Mauritius and Namibia emerged as the first and second most child-friendly governments respectively in the whole of Africa, followed by Tunisia, Libya, Morocco, Kenya, South Africa, Malawi, Algeria and Cape Verde. Rwanda and Burkina Faso have also done very well, coming 11th and 12th respectively in the CFI ranking despite their low economic status.

Table 4. Child-friendliness index values and ranking of African governments

Country	Index value	Rank	Category
Mauritius	0.711	1	Most child friendly
Namibia	0.705	2	
Tunisia	0.701	3	
Libya	0.694	4	
Morocco	0.693	5	
Kenya	0.680	6	
South Africa	0.672	7	
Malawi	0.663	8	
Algeria	0.654	9	
Cape Verde	0.651	10	
Rwanda	0.649	11	Child friendly
Burkina Faso	0.648	12	
Madagascar	0.637	13	
Botswana	0.635	14	
Senegal	0.634	15	
Seychelles	0.634	16	
Egypt	0.632	17	
Mali	0.629	18	
Lesotho	0.624	19	
Burundi	0.622	20	
Uganda	0.611	21	Fairly child friendly
Nigeria	0.609	22	
United Republic of Tanzania	0.602	23	
Gabon	0.579	24	
Mozambique	0.571	25	
Togo	0.569	26	
Zambia	0.567	27	
Mauritania	0.564	28	
Ghana	0.557	29	
Djibouti	0.552	30	
DRC	0.551	31	
Niger	0.545	32	

Country	Index value	Rank	Category
Cameroon	0.537	33	Less child friendly
Congo	0.534	34	
Angola	0.530	35	
Côte d'Ivoire	0.525	36	
Zimbabwe	0.518	37	
Equatorial Guinea	0.518	38	
Sudan	0.508	39	
Sierra Leone	0.507	40	
Benin	0.506	41	
Ethiopia	0.503	42	
Comoros	0.501	43	Least child friendly
Guinea	0.500	44	
Swaziland	0.494	45	
Chad	0.482	46	
Liberia	0.478	47	
São Tomé and Principe	0.476	48	
Gambia	0.461	49	
Central African Republic	0.445	50	
Eritrea	0.442	51	
Guinea-Bissau	0.366	52	

Source: The African Child Policy Forum, 2008.

These and the other countries that emerged in the top ten or twenty did so mainly for three reasons. Firstly, they put in place appropriate legal provisions to protect children against abuse and exploitation. Secondly, they allocated a relatively higher share of their budgets to provide for the basic needs of children. Finally, they used resources effectively and were able to achieve favourable wellbeing outcomes as reflected on children themselves.

At the other extreme are the ten least child-friendly governments in Africa: Guinea-Bissau, Eritrea, Central African Republic, Gambia, São Tomé and Principe, Liberia, Chad, Swaziland, Guinea and Comoros. Of course, the political and economic situation and the underlying causes for low CFI rankings vary from one country to another; but, by and large, the poor performance of these governments is the result of the actions they failed to take. More specifically, low rankings were caused by their failure to institute protective legal and policy instruments, the absence of child-sensitive juvenile justice systems, and the very low budgets they allocated to children. Government expenditure on health as a percentage of total government expenditure was only 3.5 per cent in Guinea-Bissau, compared with a median average of 9 per cent for Africa. Central African Republic also spent only 1.4 per cent of its GDP on education in 2006, compared to the regional average of 4.3 per cent around that time. Eritrea, the country with the second lowest CFI score of all, scored the lowest in terms of budgetary allocation, while military spending was extremely high, at 19.3 per cent of GDP in 2004–2005 – proportionally, the highest on the continent. At the same time, overall provision for the basic needs of children was correspondingly low.

7. ECONOMIC STATUS AND CHILD-FRIENDLINESS

Once again, recurring explanations or excuses provided by governments for inadequate action include their limited financial capacity, the poor performance of their economies, and a lack of resources. To what extent are these true?

In order to answer this question, we compared CFI rankings with rankings for economic status as measured by per capita GDP. An interesting finding thereby revealed was the fact that a number of governments with relatively low GDP have still managed to score highly for child-friendliness (see Table 5, below).

The child-friendliness rankings of the governments of Malawi and Burundi are 38 and 30 places higher respectively than their GDP per capita rankings. Such a relationship between low GDP and high CFI scores was also observed for the governments of Madagascar, Rwanda, Burkina Faso, Mali and DRC: for example, the child-friendliness rankings for Madagascar and Rwanda were 28 and 27 places higher respectively than their GDP per capita rankings.

Our analysis therefore shows that the child-friendliness of a government does not necessarily relate to its economic status. A country can be child-friendly by making effective use of its available resources and laying appropriate legal and policy foundations for the realisation of children's rights and child wellbeing.

Table 5. List of countries by the difference in their CFI and GDP per capita rankings, 2004–2005

Countries with higher CFI than GDP ranking		Countries with lower CFI than GDP ranking	
Country	Number of places	Country	Number of places
Malawi	+38	Guinea	–16
Burundi	+30	Côte d'Ivoire	–17
Madagascar	+28	Sudan	–17
Rwanda	+27	Gabon	–18
Burkina Faso	+25	Angola	–19
Mali	+21	Congo	–19
DRC	+20	Gambia	–19
Kenya	+18	Swaziland	–33
Uganda	+15	Equatorial Guinea	–37

Source: The African Child Policy Forum, 2008.

Conversely, some governments with relatively high GDP scores were found to be in the least child-friendly category, as they had failed to put in place appropriate legal and policy frameworks to protect children against exploitation and use their resources to bring about changes in children's wellbeing. Equatorial Guinea ranks first in terms of GDP per capita, but its CFI ranking is 37 places lower, indicating that its high economic performance is not benefiting children. The governments of Swaziland, Gambia, Congo (Brazzaville) and Angola could also have done better in utilising their resources for improving the wellbeing of children. The analysis showed that sixteen countries are ten or more places lower in their CFI ranking than their GDP per capita ranking. This indicates an ample, unutilised potential for improvement in utilisation of resources, and for investment in programmes that primarily target children.

Chart 6, below, summarises the comparison of child-friendliness and GDP per capita by positioning governments in accordance with their performance in these two areas. The upper left quadrant shows the governments that have performed well and are child-friendly, despite their low economic status. Governments in the upper right quadrant are those with higher economic performance that also did well in their degree of child-friendliness.

The lower right quadrant shows the worst scenario. Governments in this particular quadrant are those with high GDP per capita and poor performance in relation to the realisation of child wellbeing. The lower left includes governments with low rankings both economically and in terms of child-friendliness.

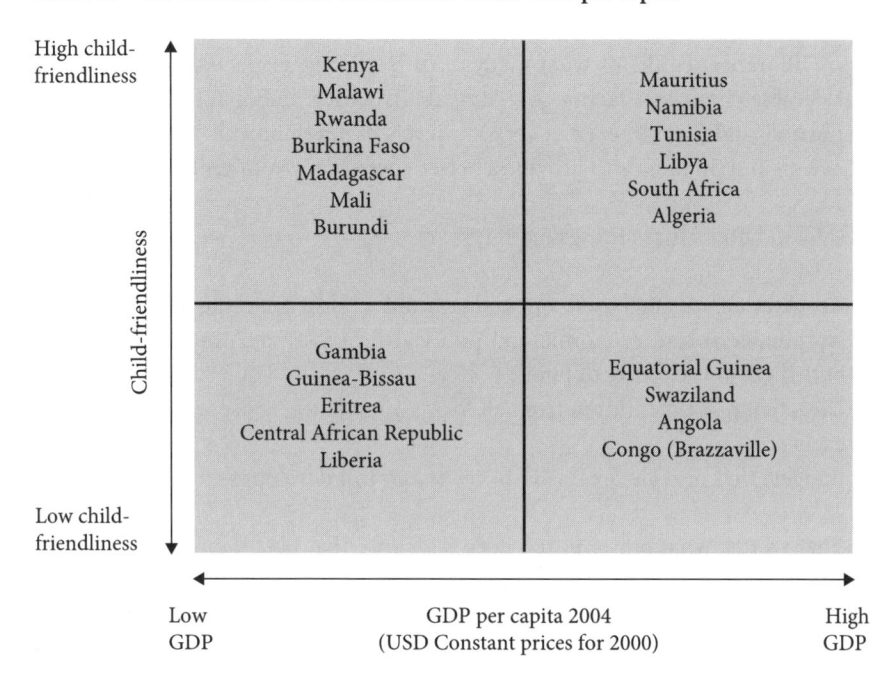

Chart 6. Governments' child-friendliness versus GDP per capita

	Low GDP		High GDP
High child-friendliness	Kenya, Malawi, Rwanda, Burkina Faso, Madagascar, Mali, Burundi		Mauritius, Namibia, Tunisia, Libya, South Africa, Algeria
Low child-friendliness	Gambia, Guinea-Bissau, Eritrea, Central African Republic, Liberia		Equatorial Guinea, Swaziland, Angola, Congo (Brazzaville)

GDP per capita 2004 (USD Constant prices for 2000)

The chart shows that, despite relatively low GDPs, Kenya, Malawi, Rwanda and Burkina Faso are among the best performers in Africa: they are among the twelve countries that have made the greatest effort to put in place an adequate legal foundation for the protection of their children, and for meeting their basic needs.

On the other hand, relatively wealthy countries, with relatively high GDPs – Equatorial Guinea and Angola, for example – are not investing sufficient budgetary resources in children, and so have not scored well in the CFI ranking, coming out 38th and 35th respectively.

The CFI data strongly confirms the fact that governments with relatively low GDPs can still do well in realising child rights and wellbeing. The missing factor is political will, reflected in misplaced priorities and the clouded vision of governments as to what constitutes the long-term interest of their countries.

8. CONCLUSION

The ACPF report confirms what many of us have long suspected. Yes, there are considerable challenges facing governments in Africa, but change and progress are possible and feasible, even at very low levels of development. You do not have to have oil and diamonds to provide a better country for your children.

All said and done, three things matter:

1. An African vision based on and around children as the foundation of sustainable social, economic and political progress, and therefore one that puts them at the centre of public policy
2. Laws that protect children from all forms of violence, abuse, exploitation and exclusion
3. Budgets that provide for the basic needs and full development of children.

In other words, what our children need is *politics* that puts them first, *laws* that protect them, and *budgets* that provide for them.

CLAIMING THE FUTURE:
AN INTERNATIONALIST PERSPECTIVE*

Stephen LEWIS
Co-director of AIDS-Free World

I am more than delighted to be here and feel very privileged to be a part of this excellent gathering. I regret missing much of what has gone before, because inevitably I will repeat numbers of things you have already heard. Although I think it is probably fair to say that the case for child poverty has been made explicitly in terms of enumerating its aspects on the continent of Africa and beyond. It is well established, you know the details, you understand many of the responses that are required; there is nothing that I can add to that particular area that would be more than an embellishment. I want, within the context of child poverty in Africa and beyond, to raise a number of issues, which will I think betray my impatience. I am 70 years old – I'm very irritated by being that old, because I have another 70 years of work to do and I feel that as I inch into my dotage, I'll never get there. But I feel a combination of rage on one hand and desperate concern on the other at the incremental nature of progress in this world and the way in particular we treat the children of the world. I don't mind meetings like this at all, if I may be so bold. I think they're filled with content, I think the Africa Child Policy Forum has that reputation and it's to Assefa's enduring credit that that's true, but you cannot imagine the number of conferences, meetings, seminars, reports... endless discussions over and over again of the same material – particularly under the auspices of the United Nations, I may say – *ad nauseum*, which always substitute for action on the ground. And it's terribly important I think to move from those endless discussions into a serious examination of issues on how we manage implementation. The self indulgent nonsense of the conference circuit is more than my frail psyche can endure.[1]

The context for what I want to say I think is fairly straightforward. Children are always at the bottom of the ladder of social and economic priorities. I know that at UNICEF, as much I loved my tenure at UNICEF, it was so difficult from the vantage point of the strongest children's agency in the world to get children

---

* This contribution is a transcription of a speech given at the Third International Policy Conference on the African Child (2008).

adequately onto the agenda, and that's true whether it's a developed country or a developing country. Take a look at my country – my country is Canada. It's a country that verges on angelic perfection, but when you set that nonsense aside, let me tell you a rather simple story. In 1989 in Canada, the House of Commons, the Parliament, agreed on a resolution to eradicate child poverty by the year 2000. It was a resolution which was voted on by every member of the house and there was not one dissenting voice. Along comes the year 2000, and the levels of child poverty are higher than they were in 1989 when the resolution was introduced. And now we are at 2008 and the levels of child poverty, according to the most recent statistics, are higher still. And Canada is the only G8 country with successive large budgetary surpluses – into the billions of dollars – and despite all of the rhetorical flimflam in the House of Commons, that we are going to do something about child poverty and despite having enormous sums of money to do it with, Canada has failed. And failed lamentably around children, as Marta Santos País's report of the Innocenti Centre indicated, and is true of so many other industrial countries. And obviously, if it's true of Canada, it's much more difficult and much more true in the developing world.

Three weeks ago, if memory serves me, the Secretary-General of the United Nations made a statement on the Millennium Development Goals for Africa, pointing out that no country in Africa would reach the Millennium Development Goals and that very few, if any, would reach even one of the goals and it was highly improbable the goal on halving hunger and poverty by 2015 would be reached. I went back to the State of World's Children Report of UNICEF in 2008 and found this quote: 'On balance, and despite many achievements' – and by that UNICEF means bringing the child mortality down below 10 million, for the first time, per year – 'the problem of child mortality is no less poignant today than it was 25 years ago, when the child survival revolution was launched by UNICEF. Every day, on average, more than 26,000 children under age five die around the world, mostly from preventable diseases.' (And everyone saw that in the narrative recitations of the earlier sessions today). I would like now to make the following points:

One: the African leaders themselves understand these issues completely. They had their famous OAU conference in the year 2001. They emerged with a programme, as you all know, called 'Africa fit for children'. They said in the statement which accompanied the programme, quote, 'Africa's children are in many ways the most disadvantaged in the world, facing a future affected by violence and poverty, and all too often foreshortened by HIV/AIDS, malaria and other pandemics.' So they made a solemn commitment and they then failed to honour the commitment. And in Cairo last September and October, there was a mid-term review of the 2001 document 'Fit for children' and a paper which was authored by a very good friend of Assefa's and a very, very close personal friend of mine, Dr Gerald Caplan (who, as it happens, is sitting at the back of this room); that document included the reference to the fact that since the commitments were made by the African leaders, 28,800,000 children have died, unnecessarily, from preventable diseases, on this continent (or a number slightly less than that, but still in the extraordinary millions). And that the new testament endorsed by the African leadership at Cairo last September and October restates what was true in 2001, but with no greater possibility or probability of implementing the necessary responses. And I want to emphasise the fact that one of the soul-destroying aspects of dealing with child poverty is the way in which we articulate the particulars; the way in which so many people understand the problem; the way in which the problem is confronted with thoughtful solutions; and after the rhetoric is over, we have a vacuum of response. I'll never understand it. I shake my head in wonder. I ask myself what has happened to the African leadership.

It leads me to the second point I wanted to make, which is quite simply what has happened to the international community? The way in which the international community compromises the continent of Africa of course speaks directly to the inability to resolve the problems. And I remind you, the international community has failed to write off all the debts of African countries that should be written off. And lest anyone think that it's not possible to do that, I ask you to notice the tens of billions of dollars that have been written off by the banks in the sub-prime mortgage crisis all over the world, vastly exceeding the needs in Africa, and that could easily be absorbed by western governments were they willing to do so.

Number two, the failure to reform the international trading arrangements, so that the agricultural subsidies which continue to be paid to the European Union and the United States of America make it impossible for Africa to maintain or achieve a reasonable degree of economic integrity and have the effect of keeping Africa poor. I remind you of the international community's failure to change the intellectual property rights laws, under the World Trade Organisation agreement, in order to make it possible to manufacture generic drugs and distribute them at prices that countries can afford, whether it's in response to AIDS, malaria, tuberculosis or other neglected diseases.

And I want to remind you, above all, of the astonishing and accelerating failure in official development assistance, in foreign aid, which was designated for Africa in particular, but for developing countries more broadly, and the discussions that have been had here, if I may be so presumptuous – I'm not an economist, I don't want to pretend to understand all of the detail, but the discussions you've had about cash transfers, about social welfare systems for poorer families and children, about building a safety net which holds; a safety net that isn't influenced by World Bank policy, but rises from the economic analysis of African governments themselves; if you want to have that kind of safety net put in place, it has to mean significant flow of official development assistance, because countries simply cannot bear the overriding cost even though that cost, we've learned, is relatively minimal. And I remind you of that incredible conference in Gleneagles in the United Kingdom in July of 2005, where such extraordinary promises were made to Africa, to double aid by the year 2010. Everybody had a spasm of triumph. It was considered a kind of jamboree of jubilation: Bob Geldof and Bono went berserk publicly at the excitement of what had been achieved. And incredibly enough, between 2005 and 2006, development assistance declined. And between 2006 and 2007, development assistance declined. And the people who pay the price for the decline in official development assistance are the children of Africa. The people who pay the price are the most impoverished and vulnerable groups on the continent. And the target we've had of achieving 0.7 per cent of gross national product for foreign aid has never even been closely approximated by any of the G8 countries. The only country that appears to be taking it seriously and moving determinedly to that target is the country of the United Kingdom. But no one else is even close – my country, Canada, that offered the target of 0.7 per cent is the only country in the G8 that's going backwards. We're actually reducing the percentage of GNP that's going to international aid. And the United States, in the last list of the development assistance countries under the OECD, stood second from the bottom: 0.18 per cent of gross domestic product for foreign aid. The United States is spending 3 billion dollars a week to fight the war in Iraq. Everyone has to understand the loss of the moral anchor here, and it's terribly important that African leaders seek out and be critical and not be hesitant. I watch Thabo Mbeki, I watch Obasanjo, I watch the people who went to their leaders in 2005 in what was undoubtedly a kind of neo-colonial exercise carefully orchestrated by Tony Blair, and I think to myself, the continent has to be tougher than that, has to be stronger than that, has to confront the industrial world when the industrial world engages in an almost instantaneous betrayal of the promises they make.

That leads me to the third general point, although I preface it with this thought. I've often asked myself – I've been going back and forth from this glorious continent since 1960, that's 48 years now – I've often asked myself, what is it about Africa and the western world? In a hundred days between April 6th 1994 and early July, 800,000 people were slaughtered in the genocide in Rwanda. And the world raised not a finger – everyone knew, and the world raised not a finger. And everyone said, 'never again', and along comes Darfur. Everyone says 'never again', and along comes Eastern Congo, which has a plague of sexual violence and rape, that makes it constitute the worst place in the world for women. And along comes

HIV and AIDS, carrying a scourge of nearly 25 years. Everyone says 'never again', and no one changes the policies so fundamentally. And I want to say what I admit is not often said from public platforms: there has to be a very strong aspect of subterranean racism at work, because there is no other way of fully accounting for the passivity, the indifference, the incrementalism, the contempt which is shown for a continent which will soon have a billion citizens. The third point I wanted to make, as of course everyone in this hall knows: AIDS complicates everything and it exacerbates the dimensions of poverty, as poverty exacerbates AIDS. And that is particularly true in the high prevalence countries of southern Africa and to some extent in eastern Africa. And I think many of you will not know that the Secretary-General of the United Nations has just released a report on the eve of yet another review of meetings that have gone before, which will be held at the United Nations in early June, reviewing the 2001 declaration of commitment on AIDS and reviewing the 2006 political declaration on AIDS. And in order to prepare for the meeting the Secretary-General gathered data from 147 countries and listen to what he says in his opening remarks – the data represents the most comprehensive body of evidence ever assembled regarding the response to HIV – *the most comprehensive body of evidence ever assembled regarding the response to HIV* – so let me tell you, if I may, while making appropriate comments *en route*, what the report shows, because every time AIDS is out of control; every time AIDS is inadequately addressed; every time AIDS sabotages the social and economic agenda of countries, poverty intensifies and everyone here understands the juxtaposition.

He begins; 'As of December 2007, an estimated 33.2 million people worldwide were living with HIV. Over 23 million are in Africa. In 2007, an estimated 2.5 million people were newly infected with HIV and 2.1 million AIDS deaths occurred. Sub-Saharan Africa accounted for 68 per cent of all adults living with HIV in the world; 90% of the world's HIV-infected children; and 76 per cent of all AIDS deaths in 2007.' The Secretary-General goes on, 'In 2007, national surveys found that 40 per cent of young males, ages 15 to 24, and 36 per cent of young females had accurate knowledge regarding HIV.' Look at the huge and vast domain of young men and young women who did not have accurate knowledge of HIV. My colleagues in UNICEF say, as part of this report, that they are doing preventive work in 100 countries or better, but something is missing somewhere if no more than 40 per cent of young men and 36 per cent of young women have accurate knowledge about HIV. Number three: the Secretary-General says that the percentage of HIV-infected pregnant women receiving anti-retrovirals to prevent mother-to-child transmission increased from 14 per cent in 2005 to 34 per cent in 2007. And then later in the report there is this astonishing quote: 'Although the cost-effectiveness of mother-to-child HIV transmission prevention programmes was demonstrated in the 1990s, children still accounted for 1 in 6 new HIV infections in 2007.' May I say to you what I think you all know? That the easiest preventive technology we have to counter HIV is to prevent transmission from mother to child during the birthing process or the subsequent breastfeeding. We know how to do it; we have the drugs to do it – we can use Nevirapine alone, we can use Nevirapine in combination with AZT, we can use a full course of anti-retroviral therapy over the bulk of the pregnancy – but the fact of the matter is that year after year we have been losing several hundred thousand infant lives for no reason whatsoever: none. And there is no reason in the world why the international agencies and the international community, working in concert with the governments of Africa, cannot save those lives. Last year alone, 420,000 children were born HIV-positive in Africa and 280,000 children died. How in God's name is that possible more than 25 years into the pandemic? Where have the responsible people been? Why do these things happen?

People sometimes used to say to me 'Stephen, was there a moment in your life as envoy that everything changed for you?' You bet there was. I was in the paediatric ward of the university teaching hospital in Lusaka, Zambia. I was touring the ward with the lovely superintendent of the hospital. There were five and six infants in every cot. They had this terrible siege of the virus on the one hand and malnutrition on the other. And as we were touring the ward, there was a sudden anguished cry, so intense, so otherworldly, that I remember swivelling around convulsively, and there in the corner of the room was a young mother on her knees beside a cot, crying inconsolably, while the nurse came in with a white sheet and covered up the infant babe and took the babe away. I'm not telling you anything you don't know as a sophisticated audience, but what surprised me at the time, and I've never been able to get over it, was that it happened every ten minutes I was in the ward. I remember turning to the superintendent and saying, 'How, how do you handle this?' He said, 'Mr Lewis, you just have to get used to it, it's a constant.' But those kids who die before the age of two – they don't have to die. And if there is a resolve in this group and in the United Nations agencies, it's got to be to bring an end to the transmission from mother to child, because there is not a single reason for it to continue except for the lassitude and passivity in the way in which we respond to the human drama.

And then the Secretary-General deals with the 80 per cent of countries, including 85 per cent in sub-Saharan Africa, who have policies in place to ensure the equal access of women to HIV prevention, treatment, care and support. Women in sub-Saharan Africa have equal or greater access to anti-retrovirals – well, of course they have equal or greater access to anti-retrovirals: women constitute 61 per cent of the number of cases in sub-Saharan Africa, and if you look at the age group 15 to 24, women constitute between 75 and 80 per cent of the cases of the people living with AIDS in Africa. So obviously they would be subject to equal or greater treatment, by the sheer numbers; not to mention the fact that they receive some measure of anti-retroviral treatment when they present themselves at antenatal clinics and are found to be HIV-positive.

And then the Secretary-General goes on to HIV treatment itself and he says, 'Anti-retroviral coverage rose by 42 per cent in 2007, reaching 3 million people in low-income and middle-income countries; approximately 30 per cent of those in need.' I beg you to think about it for a moment. Three million represents thirty per cent. Even for me, someone who is arithmetically challenged, that's not a difficult proposition to deal with. That means that seven million people who require treatment today are not receiving treatment. And those numbers will continue to accelerate. We are falling further and further behind. As things now stand on the present trajectory, there's not the slightest possibility of achieving universal access for treatment, prevention and care by the year 2010, as it has been promised. And again I have to say that we have the anti-retroviral drugs and if there was the appropriate flow of resources and the resources were directed towards replenishing human capacity, rebuilding infrastructure, maintaining most of the professionals by the kinds of schemes that are now being implemented in places like Malawi and Zambia, and rolling out the response, we could be saving millions more. And the poverty that is induced and the sheer wreckage for children when families and communities fall apart in the face of all of this, is predictably monumental.

And then the next observation of the Secretary-General, which frankly leaves me searching for comprehension, quote, 'According to recent household surveys conducted in 11 high-prevalence countries, an estimated 15 per cent of orphans live in households receiving some form of assistance, a modest increase over the estimated 10 per cent in 2005.' Fifteen per cent of the orphan population – over 12 million in sub-Saharan Africa – receiving some form of assistance: school fees, medicine, food, shelter; 85 per cent of the orphans do not receive any form of assistance – and this assistance encompasses not merely state assistance, it encompasses the assistance which comes from non-governmental organisations and community-based organisations and faith-based organisations. It tells you something about the damage that is being done to these children, and the tremendous and desperate lives they lead, and the intensification of poverty as they struggle through dealing with the loss of their anchor of life. It's heartbreaking. These little kids are incredibly traumatised. Most of them have stood in the hut and watched their parents die – you know that, I know that. If it weren't for the grandmothers of Africa, I'm not sure what would happen to the children who are orphaned as a result of the parents dying of AIDS. The grandmothers bury their adult children and then in their fifties, sixties, seventies and eighties they start to parent again. They struggle around food; they struggle around shelter; they struggle around healthcare. They don't have the money to pay for school fees. I spend a lot of my life these days ironically with African grandmothers. The African grandmothers are looking after 40 to 60 per cent of the orphaned grandchildren in a number of countries. It's really quite remarkable. It's as though we were redefining the human family. There has never been a situation like this where millions of grandmothers are looking after millions of orphaned grandchildren. Not even the Black Death in the Fourteenth Century approximated what is now happening. And I have to say to you that the impoverishment of these families as they desperately struggle for survival in their communities is something to witness. And it grinds everything down. And we need therefore for some kind of social security apparatus to sustain these families and to sustain the orphan children; it is desperately and urgently needed. And I'm not sure how it's going to happen, because governments are struggling so desperately. But I was talking to Peter Townsend earlier about these kids; they are so intensely traumatised by the experience of what's happened to them. It carries on week after week and month after month, and the pressure of simple survival is absolutely overwhelming. And the need to intervene, the need to take it more seriously, the need to engage in the support – I mean, the strength of the African continent, as everyone here understands, lies at the grassroots, it lies at community level, it lies with the sophistication and intelligence and generosity of spirit that suffuses the continent at the grassroots, particularly amongst the women of Africa. And there is no reason in the world, except for the indifference of the international community that these things continue to be sustained. I have never met with a group of grandmothers who asked for drugs or for dollars. They always ask for food. Everybody is hungry, and that's a situation which is clearly going to become more complicated, as Jeffrey Sachs told you a couple of days ago. And as the financing section of the Secretary-General's report, he simply says that USD 10 billion came in 2007 and everybody's engaged in an act of triumphalism, but the fact of the matter is that that's USD 8 billion short of what we need to deal with the pandemic. And the shortfall will continue to grow. And people may be concerned about the amount of money going to AIDS and vertical programmes and AIDS exceptionalism and the discussions that are taking place, but the reality is that if the industrial countries who had made a solemn commitment delivered on that commitment, then we would have enough resources to reach all of the Millennium Development Goals and to overcome child poverty in Africa in a way which made a qualitative difference to their lives. And then the Secretary-General in a kind of finale writes, 'In countries where HIV prevalence exceeds 15%, only an unprecedented national mobilisation involving every sector of

Claiming the Future: An Internationalist Perspective

society and making use of every available tool will meet the challenge posed by such catastrophic continued spread of HIV.' That's pretty tough language coming from the Secretary-General of the United Nations and I'd like to sit in his office one day and say, 'so where's your leadership Mr Secretary-General? When there's a food crisis internationally, you suddenly have a task force gathered together to do the ground work and meet in Rome with leaders of the international community. You've described a catastrophe. You've talked about the mobilisation of societies. Is that not worthy of the United Nations pulling together all of the heads of agencies and the Secretary-General of the United Nations effectively reading the riot act to the heads of agencies and saying, you are the major multilateral institution in this world – there has to be a more fervent and determined response.' It worries me, the way in which things are regarded as urgent, but not as an emergency.

And the final note I wanted to draw your attention to was where the Secretary-General ends his recommendations with the role of gender inequities in the HIV epidemic by saying, 'Countries should ensure a massive political and social mobilisation to address gender inequities, sexual norms and their roles in increasing HIV risk and vulnerability.' This pandemic is driven by gender inequality, and gender inequality lies at the heart of poverty, and gender inequality compromises the lives of children. And it doesn't matter whether you are talking about sexual trafficking or whether you are talking about an absence of economic empowerment, or whether you are talking about female genital mutilation, or child brides, or honour killings, or the absence of political representation, or laws against rape and sexual violence – the damage being done to women in the developing world is beyond belief. And it continues and it lies at the heart of the response. You have something very, very concrete – there is before the United Nations at this moment in time, a recommendation from a high-level panel (on which panel, by the way, sat the Prime Minister of Mozambique, and the former President of Tanzania, and the present Prime Minister of the United Kingdom, and the former President of Chile – it was a pretty high-level group) and they recommended the creation of an international agency for women, saying that the United Nations had an abysmal record on women. And it had to be changed, and there had to be some force that represented 52 per cent of the world's population, because you could never achieve a degree of social justice and equity by marginalising women forever. And now it's before the General Assembly of the United Nations, and on May the 16th there will be a consultation at the UN on the main recommendation for a new international women's agency. And the voices that are not being heard are the voices from Africa. Last Monday I visited the Ambassador for Kenya to the United Nations, because the former Minister of Health, Charity Ngilu, had spoken on behalf of the agency at the World Health

Assembly in Geneva last year. And I visited the Ambassador for Liberia to the United Nations, because the Ambassador for Liberia was the only person who had spoken in favour of the agency at the meeting of the commission on the status of women. But the other African voices as part of the G77 would make all the difference in the world, and I think the African Union as a group should be getting in touch with every single African Ambassador at the UN and asking them to participate in the consultation, and they will be at another consultation later in May, to make this objective reality, funded at a billion dollars a year, with an Under-Secretary General and with programmatic capacity on the ground, to influence and support the lives of women. I can't imagine anything that at the moment is more important in the response to child poverty, because the lives of women and children are so inextricably interlinked. And what a tremendous and dramatic impact it would have to have an organisation on the ground that spoke for the women of the world the way UNICEF speaks for the children of the world.

I was in Mozambique not very long ago. I was in Beira, the second largest city in the country. Mozambique is the one of the seven African countries where the prevalence rate of HIV/AIDS continues to rise. It is one of the countries where the prevalence rate among 15 to 24 year olds has neither stabilised nor declined. Beira is the port on the sea. When you have a port you have transportation corridors flowing outwards; when you have transportation corridors, you have truck drivers, traders, commercial sex workers. I went to the general hospital, as I do when I visit a city. I went up to the second floor, to the adult women's ward. There were 54 beds in the ward. There were between 80 and 90 women in the ward. They were lying on the concrete floor of the corridor; they were lying on the concrete floor under the beds; they were lying two and three to a bed. There was such a sense of incipient death and anguish, I couldn't get over it. The families were with them. And I stood at the door of the ward and realised that all of the women were in their twenties and thirties, and I thought to myself, has the world gone mad? How is it possible that, more than 25 years into the pandemic, well into the 21st century, we are still losing young women in such monumental numbers? And they all leave orphan children behind, and everything gets exacerbated, complicated and undermined. And I can't imagine a gathering more important than a gathering which addresses child poverty, but I beg you – you have so many concrete suggestions before you and there are so many useful interventions that can be made. Be strong and tough advocates! Gerald Caplan and I belong together to a new organisation in the United States called AIDS-Free World, and we created it in order to continue to do international advocacy, to make the powers that be understand that they have presided over a scourge that has taken a toll that is completely unnecessary and unwarranted. And what is done to children on the continent is almost beyond description.

PART III
TACKLING CHILD POVERTY: POLICY EXPERIENCES IN INDUSTRIALISED AND DEVELOPING COUNTRIES

CHILD POVERTY: AN INTEGRATED APPROACH

Professor Dharam GHAI
Executive Director
UN Research Institute for Social Development (UNRISD), 1987-1997

1. INTRODUCTION

The purpose of this paper is to highlight the key features of an integrated approach to the elimination of child poverty. The emphasis is on broad analytics of such an approach rather than on detailed empirical justification.

The paper begins with a discussion of the different concepts of poverty, including child poverty, before considering the various elements of an integrated approach to combating child poverty. It then sketches out the main features of a broad-based growth strategy with focus on equitable income distribution and employment generation. There is also a discussion of the crucial role of public services in overcoming material deprivations suffered by poverty groups.

The paper then considers some issues relating to the implementation of anti-poverty programmes and policies. It stresses the vital role of government leadership, accountability, transparency and capacity; and also the role of a dense network of community and civil society organisations and voluntary agencies, in devising and implementing an effective strategy for eliminating child poverty. It finally discusses the importance of generation, dissemination and utilisation of knowledge in an integrated approach to removing child poverty. The principal conclusions of the paper are summarised in the concluding section.

2. DIFFERENT WAYS OF MEASURING POVERTY

2.1. INCOMES, BASIC NEEDS AND HUMAN RIGHTS

There are several different ways of characterising poverty. The approach most commonly used by international agencies and the world media identifies poverty as an income or expenditure figure per head per day of a family. Thus families and individuals falling below the cut-off line are referred to as "poor". This measure also enables us to calculate not only the incidence of poverty but also its intensity, i.e. the shortfall between the actual and minimum expenditure needed to rise above poverty. Most African countries use this measure in their calculations of poverty, although South Africa generally employs a relative income and expenditure measure discussed below.

This absolute poverty line contrasts with another measure that uses relative income or expenditure per head. Such a measure is based upon some sort of average or median income or expenditure. For instance, the European Union countries define poor people as those whose incomes/expenditure fall below 60 per cent of the median. This measure is used mostly in developed countries.

An alternative way of defining poverty is through measures of deprivation of basic human needs. This approach is favoured by some UN agencies, researchers and civil society organisations. An individual or family is considered poor if their essential needs are not met. Typically these needs comprise food, basic health care, clothing, shelter, clean water, hygienic sanitation and primary education. Others add transportation and access to information to this core list of basic needs. These may be referred to as the core list of deprivations. Some go beyond the deprivation of material needs to include powerlessness, discrimination, exploitation, vulnerability, violence, sexual abuse, human trafficking, insecurity etc. This approach may be described as the expanded list of deprivations.

Another way to characterise these deprivations is in terms of human rights – an approach favoured by a growing number of multilateral agencies, development specialists and civil society organisations. For instance, deprivations, both material and non-material, may be described as violations of human rights. These rights have been enshrined in several international declarations and conventions, most notably in the Universal Declaration of Human Rights, the Conventions on Civil and Political and Social, Economic and Cultural Rights, the Convention on the Rights of the Child and the core conventions of ILO. There are also regional versions of some of these declarations and conventions and many countries have incorporated these rights in their constitutions.

While these two ways of portraying poverty as deprivations may appear to some to be a matter of semantics, there are in fact crucial substantive differences between them. The human rights language imbues the achievement of needs with a moral and legal imperative. Human beings have an entitlement to these rights that are universal in scope and are not dependent upon the favours of those in power nationally and internationally. Furthermore, the human rights conventions put the responsibility for the achievement of these rights on the families, states, the international community and other key actors at local and global levels.

There are of course other ways of describing human poverty and deprivation. Short descriptive portrayals of poverty, especially in the hands of good writers, are often a more powerful and moving way of showing what poverty means in the daily lives of the people than arid statistics or a litany of deprivations. Often the description of poverty by the people who live through their every day of their lives – women, men, girls, boys, widows and elderly – has a ring of reality that is lacking in other descriptions and measurements of poverty and it often yields surprising insights impossible to capture in quantitative data.

These alternative ways of portraying poverty have their distinctive uses and strengths and weaknesses as well. For a newspaper article, portrayals of poverty by the poor themselves may have a special appeal. Human rights specialists naturally prefer to couch poverty in terms of human rights violations. Development specialists and policy makers at national and global levels often prefer hard data on the nature and extent of poverty and the trends over time. Often these are complementary and mutually enriching ways of portraying poverty. But there are also some differences and commonalities among them, to which we now turn.

3. DIFFERENCES AND COMMONALITIES

We discuss first the differences between the absolute and relative income/expenditure approaches. The absolute income poverty cut-off point of USD 1 per day per person (purchasing power parity), first advocated by the World Bank, has perhaps become the best known measure of poverty. USD 2 a day has also been advocated as a measure of poverty that is less stringent than one dollar. The figure of USD 1 or 2 or a figure in between is supposed to measure the cost of absolute necessities that a family or individual must be able to purchase to escape poverty. The attraction of this measure is that it gives a single, simple measure valid across the world. It can give hard data on the number of households below the poverty line by countries, regions and the world as a whole and also help in monitoring the trends in poverty. It can also measure the intensity of poverty. Under this measure, it is possible, one day, to conceive of a country or the world without poverty.

The relative income (expenditure) measure reflects the notion that poverty is also a social phenomenon and that poverty in richer countries is of a different nature in relation to poor countries. People's perceptions of poverty are dependent upon how they fare in relation to more affluent groups. Thus under this measure, the higher the degree of income/consumption inequality in a country, the higher its rate of poverty, irrespective of its per capita income. Only an improvement in the distribution of disposable income can ameliorate the incidence of poverty. This implies that the basket of goods and services that define poverty must be different under the absolute and relative measures of poverty.

How are absolute income and core deprivations inter-related as measures of poverty? Everything depends upon what expenditure items are included in calculating the poverty line. At one extreme, the poverty line may be defined as the minimum income or expenditure needed for a family of a certain size to meet its caloric requirements plus other essential needs such as clothing, rent, water etc. Based on household income/expenditure surveys, poverty lines are sometimes calculated on the basis of the proportion of expenditure on food. There is no assurance under this sparse definition of poverty that even the core deprivations are met. The absolute poverty line may thus seriously underestimate the true incidence of poverty in a country.

In principle it is possible for the poverty line to incorporate in its calculation the expenditure or income needed to satisfy core basic needs. In practice, this is an extremely difficult and costly undertaking, especially given the problems of estimating the costs of such a range of services as access to clean water, adequate shelter, sanitation, basic health care, primary education, transport etc. in a context of mixed private and public provisioning of services at differential costs and of differential quality. We can, therefore, assume that most, if not all, poverty lines fail to take into consideration the core list of deprivations.

The advantage of the core deprivations approach is that it disaggregates poverty into its different components, thus revealing the pattern and extent of shortfalls in different households – something that stays hidden in a monetary approach to poverty measurement.

These calculations are based upon norms established for different basic needs such as food, access to water supply, hygienic sanitation, education, health, shelter etc. They also facilitate an evaluation of the progress made over time in removing poverty. On the other hand, it becomes difficult to convert different deprivations into a single poverty figure. The number of individuals or families living in poverty may refer to single or multiple deprivations.

It would be interesting to compare the estimates of the extent and severity of poverty in a given country or area based on the income/expenditure and core deprivation approaches. While few systematic attempts have been made to compare the results yielded by the two approaches, evidence from a few countries such as South Africa and Ethiopia indicates considerable overlapping; for instance, the lower income households also reveal greater shortfalls in meeting the core list of basic needs. But it would be useful to know how closely correlated are the two different ways of measuring poverty.

The expanded deprivations – *lack of power and participation, discrimination based on gender, race or ethnicity, exposure to exploitation, violence, sexual abuse etc* – are closely related to poverty. They are often both the cause and consequence of core deprivations. They have a profound effect on human wellbeing and their elimination is essential for the realisation of fundamental human rights and the achievement of poverty elimination goals. However, it is not necessary to include them in the definition of poverty. There are many issues that affect human and child wellbeing that go beyond the material deprivations constituted by poverty.

On the other hand, in many traditional societies the extended families and communities carry responsibility for the wellbeing of all their members. Thus poorer families may benefit from transfers and gifts in cash or kind from relatively better off members. This traditional system of redistribution of resources in favour of poorer members should work to lower overall and child poverty. Similarly, remittances from relatives in urban areas and those in the diaspora play an important role in many countries in reducing overall and child poverty. It is unlikely that such gifts and transfers in favour of the poorer households are captured fully in most household income and expenditure surveys. With the rapid social and economic change underway in most countries, it is not clear how important a role is played by intra-communal transfer of resources.

4. ADULT VERSUS CHILD POVERTY

Child poverty is different from adult poverty even when poverty is defined as core deprivations. Children's needs in terms of food and nutrition, clothing, health and education are different from those of adults. Estimates of child poverty are generally derived from figures for overall poverty measured by income and expenditure. Typically, the number and proportion of children in poverty are estimated from the child population in households below the poverty line. The proportion of children in poverty is almost always higher than the proportion of households below the poverty line. This is because the poorer households tend on average to have a higher number of children.

Even ignoring the specificities of poverty among children, this method tends to give a misleading picture of poverty for several cultural and demographic reasons. Household income and expenditure surveys ignore intra-household distribution of consumption and resources. While in some societies children get priority regarding food, clothing and health care, very often it is the reverse. Children and women rank lower in hierarchy and have to wait their turn until after the needs of the adult males have been met. Girls often suffer the greatest discrimination when it comes to access to food, health care and education. This will have the effect of understating child poverty.

Another issue concerns the definition of children. Most frequently children are defined as those below the age of 18. Yet material needs of youngsters of 15 to 18 years may differ as much, if not more, from the needs of infants and children below five years as the needs of children differ from those of adults. Estimates of child poverty based on household surveys clearly cannot take into account such fine distinctions. Intra-household distribution of consumption is also affected by the growing variety in the headship of households. The proportion of "atypical" households has grown rapidly in most countries as a result of changing economic and social structures and the spread of diseases like HIV/AIDS. Single parent households, especially female-headed households, have become increasingly important, accounting for a quarter to one-third of the total in many countries. The spread of AIDS has also brought in its wake the tragedy of grandmother- and even child-headed households.

An often-neglected dimension of poverty is child labour. A very high proportion of children in developing countries are expected to work in the household or the field or in other income-generating activities. Many labour for long hours at hazardous tasks that are a threat to their health and future potential. The worst cases involve slave-like conditions, child prostitution and trafficking. Child labour is both a cause and a consequence of child poverty. Abolition of child labour through legislation, income support for families and other programmes deserves the highest priority at global and national levels in the struggle against child poverty.

Most of these limitations do not apply to estimates of child poverty as core deprivations since these measures are generally based on direct observation. Measures such as weight and height for age, mortality and vaccination rates, school attendance, and access to/use of clean water, adequate shelter and sanitation already take into account the effects of demographic and household structures, as well as of other factors impacting on intra-household consumption.

5. STRATEGIES FOR POVERTY ELIMINATION

As noted above, the incidence and extent of poverty are affected by both the level and the distribution of income/expenditure and by the range and quality of public social and economic services. A strategy designed to combat overall and child poverty must therefore necessarily be comprehensive and integrated. Its various elements must mesh together and be as coherent and mutually reinforcing as possible, the more so as most core deprivations are interrelated. This section of the paper sketches out essential features of an integrated approach to eradication of poverty, while the next section dwells on some issues relating to strategy implementation.

First and foremost a strategy for quick reduction of poverty must combine elements of both rapid growth in output and incomes, and a substantial redistribution of resources to poorer households and children, both directly and through public services. Exclusive or dominant emphasis on one or the other of these approaches is likely to be sub-optimal. For instance, an approach focused largely on redistribution will soon run into resource constraints while negatively affecting growth through adverse effects on incentives to save, invest and take risks. A strategy focused on growth alone can take a long time before it begins to impact on poverty. An effective approach thus calls for a pro-poor growth pattern and a progressive structure of taxes and public expenditure.

The elements of a growth strategy of a country must be determined, *inter alia*, by that country's resource endowments, the structure of the economy, demographic characteristics, social and physical infrastructure, and the technical, managerial and entrepreneurial skills of the population. Everywhere, it is important to design appropriate macro- and micro-economic policies that ensure reasonable price stability, budgetary and foreign exchange balances, reliance on a market economy and incentives to farmers, informal sector operators and investors and savers. The central features of a pro-poor growth strategy for a "typical" African developing country with preponderance of the agricultural sector, a small industrial sector and limited human skills and poor social and physical infrastructure are briefly mentioned below.

In such countries, the emphasis should be placed on improving production and incomes in the rural and informal non-agricultural sectors, where the bulk of the poverty is located. This can be done through investments in rural roads and transport, expansion of electricity and other sources of energy to rural areas and urban slums, and enhancing productivity of small and medium size enterprises through improvement of production techniques and technical and vocational skills of producers and workers. The importance of the latter point cannot be over-emphasised for the crucial problem of poverty: not necessarily the creation of new employment opportunities, but rather enhancing the productivity of producers and workers who often work for long hours with abysmal incomes. This is especially the case with women and young girls who often put in 16 hours or so per day in working in the fields, at home or in child-rearing. Any innovations in technology that are labour-saving and productivity enhancing can make a powerful contribution to improving their wellbeing and reducing child poverty.

The second strand of an anti-poverty strategy comprises an appropriate level and pattern of public sector expenditure. A pro-poor growth strategy can help reduce poverty by enhancing productive employment and incomes of low-income households, while an effective public expenditure policy can reduce poverty by directly attacking core deprivations and by improving physical infrastructure. For it to be effective in this regard, the pattern of public expenditure must be designed carefully to focus on the most urgent unmet needs. The important services are good nutrition, health care, access to clean water and adequate sanitation, shelter and education.

The universalisation of the six services listed above can transform the social and economic situation in a country and bring about a drastic reduction in child poverty within a relatively short period of time. Universal social services of uniform quality can also do much to improve equity and provide equal opportunities for all children irrespective of the socio-economic background of their parents and communities. This in turn can be a major factor in spurring political stability, social mobility and economic growth. For most poor countries, lack of capacity and resources mean that universalisation of basic services can only be achieved gradually. But a resolute pursuit of this goal can bring about high levels of social development, as demonstrated by the experience of several low- and middle-income countries.

Dissemination of knowledge and information of good health practices and nutrition is an inexpensive way of avoiding numerous health hazards. Family planning, often overlooked, has also a critical role to play in this regard and may be included under health care. The latter comprises pre- and post-natal care of the mother and the child, vaccinations, medical care, and access to clinics and hospitals. Family planning can contribute to better spacing of children and the desired family size, thereby improving the health of infants and enhancing the rights and wellbeing of women. It should also lead to a reduction in the rate of population growth, the rapid expansion of which is one of the biggest obstacles to the achievement of child wellbeing as spelled out in the Convention on the Rights of the Child.

Experience in a number of countries has also shown the importance of certain specific programmes in rapid reduction of child poverty. These include cash transfers to poorer households, often tied to action on nutritional, health and education programmes for children; free school meals; abolition of school fees and health care charges; and the organisation of kindergarten facilities. The latter programmes are particularly beneficial for working mothers and can play an important role in levelling the playground for children from disadvantaged areas and households.

While moving towards the goal of universal provision of services, priority should be given to allocating scarce public resources to disadvantaged groups and areas. In most countries, the situation tends to be the reverse: limited public resources are typically allocated for services catering to urban areas and better-off groups. Political pressures and neglected infrastructure in poorer areas account for this state of affairs. But any serious effort to reduce child poverty quickly cannot succeed without a shift of resources towards deprived communities and areas.

Governments can also contribute to poverty reduction through an ambitious programme of labour-intensive public works geared to improving economic infrastructure in rural and less developed areas. The emphasis should be placed on feeder roads, expansion of electric and other sources of energy, clean water supplies, irrigation schemes, reforestation, land improvement, schools and dispensaries, low-cost housing, and communal buildings. A large-scale effort along these lines can yield rich dividends. It can contribute to higher incomes through creation of new employment opportunities, especially in rural areas, lowering costs and improving productivity of farmers and facilitating the provision of basic services.

It should be easier for resource-rich countries – exporters of petroleum and other high value minerals – to eliminate child poverty, because of the abundance of their wealth. Unfortunately, with some exceptions, such as Botswana, the opposite seems to have been the case with many African countries. Lack of effective capacity of the public sector is only part of the problem. The major reason for their failure to make much headway in reducing overall and child poverty lies in the waste and misappropriation of resources generated by mineral exports. We revert to the importance of governance for poverty reduction in the next section.

6. IMPLEMENTATION PROBLEMS

It is a relatively easy task to draw up an integrated and sound strategy for poverty elimination. It is immensely more difficult to implement the requisite programmes and policies. There are numerous political, institutional and capacity problems that constrain the implementation of well-conceived programmes and policies. The most decisive factor in successful growth and poverty reduction strategies is good leadership. Good leadership is needed to ensure the peace and stability without which development is not possible. It implies commitment, honesty and integrity, transparency, and accountability. Most development failures can be traced to poor leadership. This is not the place to dwell on the political systems that are likely to produce good leaders, but it is important to underline their importance for achievement of growth and poverty reduction objectives.

Even with good leadership, capacity constraints can severely limit the effectiveness of requisite programmes and policies. These constraints include limited managerial, technical and entrepreneurial skills as well as poor physical infrastructure. Accelerated programmes of higher education and training and of infrastructural development can go a long way in easing these constraints over time. Capacity can also be enhanced quickly through purposeful partnerships in carrying out development programmes and policies between government, the private sector, religious and community organisations, and voluntary development agencies, both national and global. It is the responsibility of the public sector to ensure coherence in the actions of different partners in delivering services and organising other development activities. In particular, government should ensure that the agencies can deliver good quality services to disadvantaged areas and groups.

Finally, it is necessary to underline the crucial importance of a sound system of generation, dissemination and utilisation of knowledge relating to child poverty. A sound system can contribute to poverty reduction in several ways. Data on the dimensions and characteristics of poverty is vital. Without information on the extent and pattern of child poverty, it is impossible to know the size of the problem. Such information, updated periodically, is also needed to evaluate the effectiveness of national programmes and policies for eliminating child poverty. It is further required to comply with the various regional and global conventions on the rights and wellbeing of children to which the country has subscribed.

Knowledge of good practices can often be an extremely cost-effective way of reducing child poverty. For instance, information on the harmful effects of polluted water, poor sanitation and inappropriate food can be an important tool in reducing infant mortality and sickness. It is essential that parents, and especially those with low levels of formal education living in disadvantaged areas, should have access to this knowledge. Similarly, the beneficial effects of family planning and the related services available should be brought to the knowledge of girls and women.

More generally, knowledge and information have a vital role to play in changing ancient customs and traditions that adversely affect the wellbeing of children and women. As examples, we might mention the division of labour between men and women, and forced and early marriages and genital mutilation of girls. The former has contributed to the massive overworking of women, with adverse effects on their wellbeing and that of their children. A fairer sharing of household and income generating activities can do much to enhance family wellbeing. Likewise, some traditional practices – such as genital mutilation – impose immense suffering on young girls, are hazardous to their health, and have long-term harmful effects. Dissemination of information and promotion of discussion among the community and religious leaders on the harmful effects of such traditional practices are necessary first steps for much-needed reforms in these areas.

7. CONCLUSION

This paper has attempted to lay out the broad contours of an integrated strategy for the elimination of child poverty. There is no one perfect measure of child poverty. The various definitions currently in use are often complementary, shedding light on the different facets of child poverty. Absolute poverty measured by income/expenditure and poverty as core deprivations are the two most widely used measures of child poverty, but both have their limitations. Child poverty is influenced by demographic and household structures as well as by the culture, beliefs and attitudes of families and communities. It differs from adult poverty in some crucial respects, as discussed earlier in this paper.

An integrated approach to elimination of overall and child poverty must take into account the multidimensionality of poverty. A broad-based growth strategy must be combined with redistribution of income and resources in favour of disadvantaged groups and households. A labour- and rural-intensive pattern of growth can make a quick dent in poverty. This must be complemented by a progressive pattern of public taxation and expenditure. Public expenditure must focus on the universal provision of some core services, including nutrition, heath care, family planning, clean water, hygienic sanitation, decent shelter and transportation. This should go hand-in-hand with expanded expenditure on economic and social infrastructure such as feeder and rural roads, electricity and other sources of energy, irrigation schemes, reforestation, land improvement, schools, clinics and community buildings. As far as possible, labour-intensive methods should be used in the construction of these facilities, which should be focussed on deprived areas and communities.

The real challenge of a strategy focused on poverty elimination lies in overcoming a variety of implementation bottlenecks. Good leadership is the most critical factor in the successful implementation of an integrated strategy. Good leadership implies commitment, honesty and integrity, and transparency and accountability, and is needed to ensure the stability and peace without which no development can take place. Management, technical and entrepreneurial skills must be developed to overcome capacity constraints. Capacity can also be enhanced through close and participatory collaboration with private sector, community and religious organisations and voluntary development agencies in organising and delivering programmes and policies for poverty eradication.

A sound system of generation, dissemination and utilisation of knowledge and information is an indispensable part of an integrated approach to poverty eradication. It helps map out the dimensions and characteristics of overall and child poverty, and assists in monitoring and evaluating the progress made in attaining poverty reduction goals. Dissemination of information on nutrition, the harmful effects of reliance on polluted water, and the existence of unsanitary conditions can be a highly cost-effective way of reducing infant mortality and child diseases. Knowledge combined with popular educational campaigns can also play a critical role in combating harmful traditional customs and practices through changes in beliefs, attitudes and behaviours.

THE ABOLITION OF CHILD POVERTY AND THE RIGHT TO SOCIAL SECURITY: A POSSIBLE UN MODEL FOR CHILD BENEFIT?[1]

Professor Peter TOWNSEND
Professor of International Social Policy, London School of Economics
Emeritus Professor of Social Policy, Bristol University

1. ACKNOWLEDGEMENTS BY THE AUTHOR

Less than two weeks following the launch of this report in the Houses of Parliament in London, I am indebted to The African Child Policy Forum for an opportunity to present the results in Africa.

An invitation in 2005 from Michael Cichon at the International Labour Office (ILO), Stephen Kidd at the Department for International Development (DfID) and Rüdiger Krech at the Deutsche Gesellschaft für Technische Zusammenarbeit (GTZ) was the starting point for new research on policies to reduce world poverty. I owe Michael Cichon, the Director of Social Security at the ILO and Christina Behrendt, also of the ILO, a lot for their expert sense of direction and priority, and also warmly thank Stephen Kidd for his enthusiastic encouragement and wise counsel. David Gordon and Shailen Nandy generously contributed in different ways to the report, and I am grateful to Tony Atkinson, Margot Salomon and Conor Gearty for shrewd comments on a draft. I thank Helen Gordon for her help in the production of this report, ahead of the planned collection of reports in one volume for the forthcoming ILO publication: *Social Security: Building Decent Societies*. Both LSE and the Centre for International Poverty Research in the University of Bristol have cradled my research in the last 10 years.

To Jean, my wife, and to our grandchildren, who sustained me through a difficult patch and who unwittingly contributed to the reflections in this report about the needs and rights of children, I owe my love.

---

[1] A report to DFID, GTZ and ILO.

2. INTRODUCTION

We live in a world where children are accorded priority emotionally and politically. Five of the eight Millennium Development Goals (MDGs) of the UN are directed at children: one is to eradicate extreme poverty and hunger, another to drastically reduce under-five mortality, a third to reverse the spread of HIV/AIDS, malaria and other diseases, and the fourth and fifth to ensure full and gender-equal schooling (see Appendix I for the goals as set out by the UN in 2000). However, those in authority at the UN have conceded that declared progress towards the goals cannot be made by 2015 (Brown and Wolfensohn, 2004).

The fact that these goals were announced at the start of the century shows that the policies designed over several decades to protect children's welfare have failed, and that failure is underscored by the admission that progress towards fulfilling the goals is small. The growing number of scarifying accounts of the hunger, exposure to conflict and abuse, extreme poverty and premature death still experienced by many millions of children across the world must concentrate the public mind (UNICEF, 2004; 2005). It is not enough to set new goals. Finding – and agreeing on – the necessary replacement policies is the top priority. New policies have to be devised to replace those that have failed. They have to have large-scale direct and positive effects. The time for elaborate pretence, with selectively helpful pilot projects for a very few children and for image-building by organisations at token cost, is over.

Children's living standards are often wrapped up in the living standards of their families or 'households'. Their social security, like their share of income and expenditure, is not defined precisely. Their entitlement to benefit is usually defined in relation to the entitlement of the family or household of which they are members. The scale of their right to income in developing countries has still to be defined, categorised for different age-groups in different locations, and endorsed by representative governments.

A number of reports, especially those from the International Labour Organisation (ILO) (for example, Cichon and Scholz, 2004; and see Townsend, 2007, pp. 15–17), have shown a continuing positive relationship between economic development and the expansion of social security systems. This has applied to the history of the industrialised world and is beginning to apply more strongly to middle and low income countries. In recent years, promising initiatives have been taken by some of their governments to accelerate the growth of social security systems and, in particular, protect those unable to obtain paid employment, including children, the elderly and disabled, from the worst poverty. This report aims to take the argument three steps further:

1. to focus on children, who have greater risk of being in poverty than adults and no opportunity to contribute to their own social security;
2. to pin down the nature and causes of child poverty to improve policy-effectiveness;
3. to demonstrate that international funds have to be found quickly to match national resources to meet child poverty directly.

I will discuss:

- the consequences of poverty and multiple deprivation for child survival and health;
- child rights as the appropriate framework for measurement, analysis and the construction of policy;
- the need to reveal the extent of international responsibility for funding anti-poverty strategies;
- the recent disappointing history of international finance; and, as the most practical alternative;
- the use of a currency transfer tax to build up a UN Investment Fund for child benefit.

3. CONSEQUENCES OF CHILD POVERTY AND MULTIPLE DEPRIVATION

A special investigation for UNICEF found that 56 per cent of children in developing countries – 1.2 billion children – experienced one or more forms of severe deprivation. Over half of these (674 million) suffered at least two forms of severe deprivation, such as the total absence of toilet facilities, lack of nearby clean water, malnutrition, extreme overcrowding and poor shelter (Gordon *et al.*, 2003; UNICEF, 2004). In sub-Saharan Africa 83 per cent suffered from at least one form of severe deprivation, including 65 per cent suffering from multiple severe deprivation. This is more potent evidence of child poverty than the (very crude, and unreliable) estimates by the World Bank of the numbers of children in households with less than USD 1 per capita per day.[2] Nevertheless, it is evident

---

[2] There is good reason to ask whether the World Bank had technically achieved accurate updating of its 1985 USD 1 per person per day poverty line (see for example, REDDY and POGGE, 2001; POGGE and REDDY, 2003; WADE, 2004; WADE, 2007; KAKWANI and SON, 2006) and why the failure to implement the original definition had not been made good in later research, as promised by the Bank in the early 1990s (see TOWNSEND and GORDON, 2002, Chapter 14).

that poverty and early child mortality are intertwined – whether that poverty is measured by household income or multiple material and social deprivation.

Ten million children in developing countries die each year, mainly from preventable causes, including malnutrition, pneumonia, diarrhoea, measles and malaria (UNICEF, 2007). The World Health Organisation (WHO) found that as many as seven out of every 10 childhood deaths can be attributed to these five causes or their combination. Three in every four children seen by health services are suffering from at least one of these conditions. Many of these deaths could be prevented using readily available medical technologies at comparatively little cost and many more by providing resources for shelter, clean water, sanitary facilities, food and fuel. Thus, the free issue of mosquito nets, as illustrated in one initiative in different areas of Kenya, can dramatically reduce rates of malaria among children (Rice, 2007). Again, public provision of shelter, food and sanitary facilities and basic income as well as access to services for those widowed or orphaned by HIV/AIDS can save many from a miserable existence and early painful death. The number of children in sub-Saharan Africa orphaned by HIV/AIDS is expected to rise to 15.7 million, or a quarter of all children, by 2010 (Akwanalo Maté, 2006, and UNICEF, 2007, p. 42). Globally, 1800 children are newly infected every day by HIV/AIDS (UNICEF, 2005, p. 16).

The accumulating studies of enforced child deprivation are calling sharp attention to mass violations of child rights that, for many children, maintain and, for some, increase the risks of survival (Pemberton *et al.*, 2007). For health professionals, this has led recently to fuller acknowledgement of the positive relationship between human rights and health.[3]

Until now, the WHO and other international agencies have been unable to distinguish rates of child mortality and malnutrition in richer and poorer households. The use, in representative country surveys,[4] of questions about assets owned by households has led to a breakthrough. Table 1 (below) gives figures from the WHO's report *World Health Statistics 2007* which, for the first time ever, measures ownership of assets and makes it possible to compare children in the poorest and richest 20 per cent of households in the country. In countries where there is mass poverty, it should be noted that asset impoverishment may still apply to some among the richest 20 per cent.

---

[3] See PEMBERTON *et al.*, 2005; GRUSKIN *et al.*, 2007; MACDONALD (R), 2007; MACDONALD (TH), 2007; SINGH *et al.*, 2007.

[4] There are now two principal sources of standardised cross-national survey data – Demographic Health Surveys (DHS) and Multiple Indicator Cluster Surveys (MICS), the latter sponsored by UNICEF.

Table 1 compares the poorest and richest under-fives and one-year olds in India, sub-Saharan Africa and Latin America, using three different measures. The poorest 20 per cent are around twice as likely to be physically stunted for their age in India and sub-Saharan Africa. This difference increases in Latin America, where the poorest are nine times more likely to be stunted. Mortality rates of under-fives in the poorest households in these three regions are also disproportionately high with India again at the bottom of the league with the poorest children almost three times more likely to die before their fifth birthday. Finally, the table shows the proportion of one-year olds not immunised against measles. Again, India has the worst record, with nearly three-quarters of the poorest children not immunised as compared with under 20 per cent of the richest children, a nearly four-fold discrepancy. In sub-Saharan Africa, around one half, and in Latin America, one third of the poorest children are not immunised.

Data for individual countries in the three regions are to be found in Appendix II. The highest percentages of children found to be stunted in sub-Saharan Africa (50 per cent or more) were in Rwanda, Malawi, Chad, Zambia and Madagascar. The highest percentage in Latin America was 65 per cent, in Guatemala. In India, this percentage must have been matched or even exceeded in some deprived areas.

Table 1. Child mortality and poor health conditions

Indicator	India (%)	Sub-Saharan Africa (25 countries) (%)	Latin America (8 countries) (%)
Under-fives stunted for age *Poorest 20%* *Richest 20%*	58 27	42 24	36 4
Mortality under five years *Poorest 20%* *Richest 20%*	14 5	16 10	9 4
One-year olds not immunised against measles *Poorest 20%* *Richest 20%*	72 19	46 22	34 16

Source: WHO (2007), *World Health Statistics 2007*, pp. 74–77.

4. USING CHILD RIGHTS TO DEFEAT CHILD POVERTY

Using human rights as a methodology to pin down major patterns of development and assess policy is of growing importance. For the first time, multiple deprivation – as reflected in numerous statements in different human rights treaties – can be expressed in precise statistical and empirical terms. Coordinated national surveys, namely the Demographic Health Surveys (DHS) and the Multiple Indicator Cluster Surveys (MICS) have been and are being conducted in countries covering more than 85 per cent of the developing world. Beginning in the last decade, a practicable method for constructing a comparable measure of the economic and social conditions of small and large populations has evolved. For example, during the five year period 2002/2007, one research team has been able to produce the first reliable global estimates for children, young people and all adults (Gordon *et al.*, 2003, UN Expert Group on Youth Development Indicators, 2006; Gordon et al, Report to DfID in 2007, 2008 forthcoming).

The methodology draws on the analytical framework of the human rights treaties. Human rights have come to play a central part in discussions about economic and social development and have been ratified by the great majority of governments in the world. There are rights to income and to social security enshrined in Articles 22 and 25 of the Universal Declaration of Human Rights; 9 and 11 of the International Covenant on Economic, Social and Cultural Rights; and 26 and 27 of the Convention on the Rights of the Child (UNCRC) (see Figure 1 below). Furthermore, the UNCRC contains elaborate injunctions to protect children from malnutrition, maltreatment, neglect, abuse and exploitation and ensure they are not deprived of access to clean water, sanitary facilities, shelter, health care services, education and information. Governments are enjoined to *"recognise the right of every child to a standard of living adequate for the child's physical, mental, spiritual, moral and social development."*[5]

---

[5] Article 27 and also see Articles 13, 17, 19, 20, 23, 24, 26, 28, 31, 32, 34, 37 and 39.

Figure 1. The rights to social security and an adequate standard of living

Authority	Social security	Adequate living standard
Universal Declaration of Human Rights (1948)	Article 22 – Everyone, as a member of society, has the right to social security and is entitled to realisation, through national effort and international co-operation and in accordance with the organisation and resources of each state, of the economic, social and cultural rights indispensable for their dignity and the free development of their personality.	Article 25(1) – Everyone has the right to a standard of living adequate for the health and wellbeing of their family, including food, clothing, housing and medical care and necessary social services, and the right to security in the event of unemployment, sickness, disability, widowhood, old age or other lack of livelihood in circumstances beyond their control.
International Covenant on Economic, Social and Cultural Rights (1966 – came into force 1976)	Article 9 – The States Parties to the present Covenant recognise the right of everyone to social security, including social insurance.	Article 11(1) – The States Parties to the present Covenant recognise the right of everyone to an adequate standard of living for himself and his family, including adequate food, clothing and housing, and to the continuous improvement of living conditions.
Convention on the Rights of the Child (1989)	Article 26(1) – States parties shall recognise for every child the right to benefit from social security, **including social insurance**, and shall take the necessary measures to achieve the full realisation of this right in accordance with their national law.	Article 27(1) – States parties recognise the right of every child to a standard of living adequate for the child's physical, mental, spiritual, moral and social development. Article 27(3) – ... and shall in case of need provide material assistance and support programmes, particularly with regard to nutrition, clothing and housing.

The statements, ratified by nearly all of the 193 nation states in the world, allow single but also multiple measures or indicators of the denial or fulfilment of the specified rights to be devised and tracked. Therefore, social science has a considerable role to play in coordinating the collection and analysis of such evidence and evaluating policy impact.

There are two particular arguments in favour of using this methodology in relation to poverty and social security. First, all the human rights treaties allow *multiple* indicators of violations of those rights to be constructed. The UNCRC, for example, does not contain an explicit human right to freedom from poverty. However, statements about the conditions of material and social deprivation underlying poverty and characterising ill health, as specified above, occur in a number of different Articles of the UNCRC and have become the subject of national and international survey investigation. The rights are interrelated and therefore deliberate action to fulfil a particular right is relevant to the realisation of other rights. I have argued that evidence allowing the development of an index of multiple deprivation can be used to justify the selection of a minimum threshold of specific income and/or value of assets (equivalent to income) to signal those who can be identified as being beneath – or on the margins of – an objective 'poverty line' (Townsend, 1993, p. 36 and 2006, p. 14). This will also provide empirical evidence for the analysis and fulfilment of the rights to an adequate standard of living and of social security.

This is an example of how scientific reasoning about new policies can be built on operational definitions of violations of singly described human rights and of multiple related rights. It is also an example of what has to be done in giving progressive realisation to human rights.

The second argument is that human conditions are rarely one thing or another – either good or bad. For example, there is under-nourishment but also extreme malnutrition. There is poverty but also extreme poverty. Empirical inquiry can trace a continuum from one extreme to the other and find thresholds of severity or absence of suffering. The advantage of empirical surveys of population conditions is that moderate needs can be distinguished from severe or extreme needs and doubts about over-generalised evidence removed. Another advantage is that, by measuring severity as well as multiplicity of condition, cause can be more exactly unravelled and priorities for remedial policy demonstrated. There is a gradient or continuum ranging from complete fulfilment to extreme violation of rights – for example, on the continuum ranging from 'good health' to 'poor health/death' (see Gordon *et al.*, 2003, pp. 7–8). Courts make judgments in individual cases about this gradient to establish the correct threshold at which rights have been either violated or fulfilled. Correspondingly, scientists and policy-analysts can demonstrate the point on the gradient at which there are severe or extreme violations, so that grey areas of the interpretation of mild or moderate violation can be set aside and governments and international agencies persuaded that there are unarguable grounds for institutional action.

The language of rights therefore changes the analysis of world conditions and the discussion of responsible policies. It shifts the focus of debate from the personal failures of the 'poor' to the failures to resolve poverty of macro-economic structures and the institutions and policies of nation states and international bodies (agencies such as the World Trade Organisation, World Bank, International Monetary Fund (IMF) and UN, but also the most powerful Trans National Corporations (TNCs) and alliances of groups of governments). Child poverty cannot then be considered as a parental problem or a local community problem, but a 'violation of rights' that nation states and international agencies, groups of governments and TNCs have a legal and institutional obligation to remedy (Chinkin, 2001). Violations of the rights of children to health, including problems like malaria and HIV/AIDS, would more easily be seen to be socio-structural problems and not only medical or health care problems.

Two 2007 examples may be given. The free issue of mosquito nets to selected populations (as in Kenya) can dramatically reduce rates of malaria among children (Rice, 2007). The problem is the scale of the issue – so that the children's needs are covered universally, rather than those of a small number of children covered by schemes piloted by NGOs or governments in a few selected areas. That means more money to enable purchase and/or free or subsidised availability of such facilities through government.

Second, public provision of shelter, food and sanitary facilities and basic income as well as access to services for those widowed or orphaned by HIV/AIDS children can save many from miserable existence and early painful death. The number of children in sub-Saharan Africa orphaned by HIV/AIDS is expected by UNICEF to be 15.7 million, or a quarter of all children, by 2010 (UNICEF, 2007, p. 42). Resources have to be mobilised for population care and especially material resources that directly reach children (Akwanalo Maté, 2006). Again, the problem is to ensure universal coverage so that children in extreme need do not slip through grudgingly-devised safety nets and have the universal right to the minimum resources required to cover multiple needs.

5. INTERNATIONAL RESPONSIBILITY FOR FUNDING: 1) TRANSNATIONAL CORPORATIONS (TNCs)

Who is responsible for ensuring these policies are universal? The argument developed here is that TNCs and the international agencies could work wonders by committing a tiny percentage of their growing resources to social security in the low income countries, and also by moving towards acceptance of minimum standards of monthly or weekly income on the part of wage-earners and those not in paid employment who are entitled to social security. Indirectly and directly, this will also strengthen their relationships with employees and their families and improve the public image of their corporation.

Both the OECD and ILO have issued guidelines on 'corporate social responsibility' (ILO, 1998; OECD, 2001). Both organisations have sought to fill a growing gap left upon the termination by the UN in the early 1990s of substantial monitoring and reporting of the trends in TNC practices. In 2003, the UN produced draft norms on the responsibilities of TNCs and other business enterprises with regard to human rights. It may be the first document to place human rights at the core of its mandate but it remains a generalised draft (UN, 2003; Vagts, 2003, p. 795; and see De Schutter, 2006). The guidelines issued by the OECD and ILO are not yet attracting vigorous debate. The desirability of universal rules of practice for TNCs and international agencies is absent from much current commentary and analysis.

The growing bargaining power of the TNCs in headquarter locations in the rich countries is creating social and economic disequilibrium. There is an 'institutional hierarchy of power' that has to be taken seriously. The triumvirate of the G8 countries, international agencies and TNCs wield the predominant economic power in the world. The power of the TNCs has been growing fast in relation to that wielded by middle and low income nation states. Within TNCs, the hierarchy of power is illustrated by elaborate stratification of wages, conditions of work and access to social security determined by Executive Boards in the US, Japan, Germany and the UK through to the 70 or 100 countries in which they operate. The biggest corporations have exceptional financial, political and legal leverage – more than all but the richest 20 nation states. The internal stratification of their power through corporation heads, divisional heads, national senior and lower-level staff, subsidiaries in one country or in several countries, subsidiary directors, managers and staff, sub-contractual heads, managers and lower-level employed and self-employed has many connected steps in pay and conditions.

Recent failures of privatisation schemes and of major trans-national corporations such as Enron, WorldCom, ImClone, Credit Suisse First Boston, Hollinger International, Adelphi Communications, Martha Stewart Living, Omnimedia and parts of the financial services industry, provide lessons that have to be learned and acted upon internationally to restore structural stability. In different ways their example calls attention to a general lack of information, accountability and regulation about the global operations of corporations. Recurring reports of instances of corporate corruption have paved the way for collective approaches to be made through law and regulation[6] that go a lot further than the minimal and highly variable expressions so far of the unenforceable appeals for the observance of 'corporate social responsibility' – as contained in the OECD and ILO guidelines or in the UN's Corporate Citizenship Initiative, *The Global Compact*, launched in June 2000.

Low income countries are heavily dependent on trade with corporations with far larger resources than they possess. Through subsidiaries and sub-contractors

---

[6] For example, SCOTT et al., 1985; LANG and HINES, 1993; HUDSON, 1996; KORTEN, 1996; KOZUL-WRIGHT and ROWTHORN, 1998; MADELEY, 1999; HERTZ, 2001; HELD, 2004; HINES, 2001; SKLAIR, 2001; WATKINS, 2002.

controlled from far away, they are restricted in the employment that can be found, the wages that can be charged, the taxes that can be raised and the conditions of life that have to be protected for national populations. Because of the scale of TNC operations, the scope they have for raising revenue from them is comparatively small. The poorest countries have too few resources to make swift headway in reducing poverty and creating real opportunities for enterprise on behalf of the great majority of their populations (see, for example, Watkins, 2002). There has been a huge upsurge in trans-national resources without corresponding modernisation of company law adapted to the new social conditions and responsibilities for economic and social development, which would impose particular obligations on corporations or invite them to build collective trust by agreeing to commit a small percentage of wage costs – the 'social wage' – to social security.

In its 1998 declaration, the ILO sought to encourage governments to reinforce corporate responsibility to pave the way for *"more specific potentially binding international standards"*, turning codes of conduct into *"the seed of customary rules of international law"* (ILO, 1998). The problem is that, as they stand, these guidelines have no teeth and are not routinely publicised and discussed. Observance is voluntary and not dependent on national or international sanctions or law. Some corporations and companies are concerned about their image and good name and are prepared to moderate their practices – and profits – in consideration of the rights of their workers. Others take advantage of non-existent or inconsistent law and weak forms of inspection and prosecution. One such example is in the area of child labour. Practices have sometimes dodged existing law or prosecution by removing production from factory to home, or across local state boundaries, as in India. New practices have been springing up – for example, cotton-picking in Kazakhstan brought about by the Government closing schools early in the summer term.

A starting point for TNCs and the UN would be to draw up an agreement about children. One serious and continuing embarrassment for many corporations is that children are involved in extreme forms of labour by sub-contractors and subsidiaries in locations remote from TNC headquarters (ILO, 2005). There is evidence of children as young as seven who are involved in producing paving stones to be sent to European garden centres, footballs, clothing and carpets, operating with dangerous pesticides and other chemicals, digging trenches, picking cotton and working in mines – often for 10 or more hours a day. A common corporation plea is that illegal practices, or violations of child rights, along the production line were unintended and unknown and abhorrence of such practices by headquarters would now be passed down the chain of command. The problem is that the conditions of payment and the standards expected of the finished product inevitably affect incentives and lead to extreme practices. Accountability for such practices could be ensured by legal and other means – particularly through monitored reports and statistics for which headquarter organisations must be held routinely responsible (in the same way as nation states) and that would have to be submitted for public scrutiny. Agreement reached by the UN and TNCs about their accountability for severe deprivation among children engaged in forms of bonded labour connected with their trade represents one useful future development.

A key step of greater magnitude would be to focus attention on company responsibility for social security. In the late 19th century and throughout the 20th century, employers came to accept provision of a 'social wage' as a condition of making profit. Laws were enacted to provide for temporary and long-term unemployment and contributions by employers for illness and disability and other dependencies of family members, especially children, were expected. There were insurance payments for specific contingencies and taxes to meet shifts in economic conditions that could not be predicted. The social wage was one of the rules of economic operation that became widely accepted. New global conditions in the 21st Century have transformed that responsibility and a new legal and social responsibility for impoverished conditions in low income countries has to be accepted throughout the hierarchy of power exerted by headquarters corporations. The income rights of children could lie at the core of discussions to make globalisation work socially.

In the early stages of the industrial revolution, employers in the OECD countries who were expected or compelled to make substantial contributions to social protection were national rather than trans-national employers. People with hard-earned professional skills built on minimum standards of living and universal access to public social services were not at that time tempted overseas from national service or careers in the national economy and neither were they given little or no alternative but to leave chosen countries of domicile. Cross-border social security is one burning question for the 21st century but only one example of the urgent need to develop basic universal social security.

Children have been placed at the centre of this analysis. Trans national employers could add one or two per cent of wage costs in different countries for a child benefit to help banish malnutrition, poverty and premature child death, and also encourage more schooling. The percentage could be further increased once all parties perceive the benefits of the system. That is a conclusion to be drawn from such evidence as that illustrated in Table 1 above from the World Health

Organisation. A child benefit would also have the effect of reducing extreme forms of child labour and the evasion of laws banning such labour. Standard contributions from employees as well as employers towards social insurance, or new taxes, to provide income entitlements during sickness, disability, bereavement and ageing, and the dependence of children in such families, could follow.

The question of social protection or social security in the national interest has become one of social protection in the *international* interest.

6. INTERNATIONAL RESPONSIBILITY FOR FUNDING: 2A) INTERNATIONAL AGENCIES: SAFETY NETS

The international financial agencies, especially the World Bank and the IMF, have not contributed as much to the diminution of the extreme poverty experienced by hundreds of millions of children as they would wish member governments of the UN to believe. The World Bank lends approximately USD 22 billion a year (the 2005 figure), USD 2.4 billion of which is estimated to be for social protection (Hall, 2007). However, this sum is less than five-hundredths of one per cent of world GDP and is dwarfed by the sum spent each year by rich countries on social protection (or social security) alone. Thus, the UK Department of Work and Pensions spent the equivalent of USD 210 billion in 2005, compared with the World Bank's total loans for social protection of USD 2.4 billion.

The responsibility of the UN and the international financial agencies in funding social security, especially child benefit, requires urgent review if the MDGs are to be successfully pursued. But what conclusions can be drawn from present international funding and how much of that funding actually reaches children in extreme poverty? One major part of the review would be to trace the outcome and potentialities of the 'safety-net' strategy. This is the third of the anti-poverty strategies favoured by the World Bank, the others being economic growth and investment in human capital. The problem about economic growth has been the difficulty of knowing how much of growth actually 'trickles down' to the poor (i.e. those with less than USD 1 a day). And the investment in primary education, bolstering human capacity to earn a subsistence living, can take many years to fulfil, and in any case does not deal with the immediate poverty of those incapable of earning a living, such as young children, disabled people and the elderly.

The World Bank has sponsored a series of 'safety-net' programmes for low income countries in agreeing loans for their economic development. Structural

Adjustment Programmes (SAPs), introduced in the 1980s, were extended to many countries in different regions of the world. At least 40 of the 54 countries of Africa were involved by 1993 (Donkor, 2002, p. 197). The declared intention was to stabilise national economies and promote growth by freeing imports from tariffs, general deregulation, reduced public expenditure and privatisation. However, in a short span of years serious criticisms were made of SAPs and by 1988 a Programme of Action to Mitigate the Social Cost of Adjustment (PAMSCAD), influenced in part by UNICEF, was introduced. The new programme quickly became difficult to discriminate from the SAP. In Ghana, for example, it was *"underfunded and lacked clear direction. ...It neither mitigated poverty nor did it indeed have the capacity to do so"* (Donkor, 2002, p. 227). Other programmes were substituted successively in the following years – such as the Poverty Reduction Strategy Programme (PRSP) and the Social Fund.

Many observers have come to believe that the Bank's frequent replacement of anti-poverty programmes has been to give an impression of major change and correction when the reality is different. The succession of differently described programmes has amounted to very little alteration in the strategy directed towards the entrenchment of free market policies, with small redistribution of resources in fact allowed to, or within, the low income countries, conditional loans being balanced by rates of repayable interest that largely reverse the flow of aid.[7]

The *"policy shift led to cutbacks in social investment, the privatisation of social programmes and the abandonment of social planning as an integral part of policy making"* (Mkandawire, 2004, p. 7). One analyst concluded that social policy had been condemned to a *"residual category of safety nets"* (Tendler, 2004, p. 119). This conclusion is borne out by illustrative statistics and by country case studies. Thus, public expenditure on social security (such as on child benefit, sickness and disability benefit and pensions for the elderly) amounts to nearly 14 per cent of GDP (2005) in the average OECD country compared with between 1 per cent and 3 per cent in most low income countries, for example, 1.5 per cent in India (Townsend, 2007, p. 9, and see also ILO, 2001). Because the redistributive mechanisms of social security are not in place, even for groups who cannot be expected to gain earnings through employment, there cannot be effective 'trickle-down' from economic growth.

---

[7] One give-away report, covering case-studies of seven African countries, scarcely mentions the safety-net strategy for incomes and basic social services, and the first sentence of its conclusion speaks volumes about the motives of the Bank. *"A common theme that emerges from the record of adjustment programmes in the seven case studies is that African governments are not yet much better at managing market economies than they were at managing economies through heavy intervention"* (HUSAIN and FARUQEE, 1994, p. 427).

Individual country instances of miserly aid can also be given. One report gives a graphic illustration of a village caught up in the HIV/AIDS crisis in Malawi. The population had been depleted of young adults. There was no clinic and no source of safe water. The Malawi Government was keen to begin treatment in the country of all 900,000 infected with the HIV virus but could not afford the cost of the low cost generic antiretroviral drugs supplied by India. With advice from the World Bank, political leaders were told by donor governments, including the US, to scale back their reasoned plan – first from 900,000 to 100,000 and then down to 40,000. Finally the meagre outside funds allowed as few as 25,000 patients to be treated over five years (Sachs, 2005).

7. INTERNATIONAL RESPONSIBILITY FOR FUNDING: 2B) INTERNATIONAL AGENCIES: GENERAL AID

When questions are asked about global funding of low income countries in general, as distinct from anti-poverty measures, international agencies emphasise three sources of aid: broad-based economic growth, debt relief and overseas aid. These measures have formed the funding strategy for a period of 40 years but can only be described as unsuccessful. Factors contributing to this lack of success include 'trickle-up' growth, conditionality policies for loans, cost-recovery policies in basic social services, cuts in public expenditure, lack of social security systems, excessive privatisation, unregulated globalisation, unequal terms of trade and enhancement of the power of the global 'triumvirate' – G8, TNCs and IFAs (International Financial Agencies).

Commentators have lately added a fourth element of international aid strategy – to bring about fairer trade through reform of the WTO. In practice, all four measures are principally dependent on generous decisions by the big economic powers, including TNCs, in the modern global economy. What this means for children cannot be worked out – because the four types of international funding are relatively indiscriminate and unpredictable in their distributional effect upon populations. Success depends on whether a sufficient share of additional cash income and income in kind from these sources happens to reach the poor and how quickly. Why are the results so difficult to define?

The absence of social security systems in many low income countries means that 'trickle-down' from economic growth, or indeed most forms of overseas aid and debt relief, does not arise. These forms of funding are 'indirect'. They are intended to reach the poorest in particular but this is difficult to demonstrate. Monetary aid generally reaches government in the form of repayable loans and not as payments to particular departments for, say, health and other social services and social protection. Therefore the division of loans or grants into amounts directed to particular purposes is hard to disentangle from variations already taking place in standard allocations of government resources. Measures of trends in extreme poverty, and not only the lack of any follow-up of aid from outside, cast doubt on the intended outcome of these international loans or grants. This over-generalised and indirect strategy by outside bodies has contributed to the failure to reduce poverty, especially child poverty. Joint funding by outside agencies and national governments to secure mutually satisfying results would require a completely different, and probably more successful, procedure. The chances of establishing a network of health and social security centres and schools would become a lot more immediate and practicable.

Have different forms of funding been considered? The problem of the scale of resources to be made available has become acute. In September 2000, the lack of significant progress in reducing poverty, together with severe delays in implementing funding agreements led the UN General Assembly to ask for *"a rigorous analysis of the advantages, disadvantages and other implications of proposals for developing new and innovative sources of funding"*. A panel was set up under the chairmanship of Ernesto Zedillo (UN, 2001).

On the question of scale, the Zedillo Panel estimated conservatively that an additional USD 50 billion was required annually to reach the MDGs. The World Bank estimated that additional overseas development aid (ODA) of USD 60 billion (over and above 2003 allocations) would be needed in 2006 and USD 83 billion by 2010 (World Bank, 2005, p. 162). These estimates were unrealistically low, since they depended on making up the incomes of population below USD 1 a day and not on the realistic estimates of what proportion of the relatively indiscriminate indirect funding provided by economic growth, overseas aid, debt relief and fairer trade was likely to reach the poor. Instead, the necessary increase in ODA projected was USD 20 billion for 2006 and USD 50 billion for 2010 – and even these gross underestimates leave a gap of more than USD 30 billion. By that year, the total is estimated to reach an average of 0.36 per cent GNI – Gross National Income (OECD, 2005) but *"it is not clear that this is realistic"* (Atkinson, 2005, p. 6). The Netherlands, Denmark, Sweden, Norway and Luxembourg are the only countries to have reached the UN target for ODA of 0.7 per cent of national income. In 2004, the UK stood at 0.36 per cent and the US at 0.16 per cent.

By 2003, the UN inquiry about alternative funding had lost momentum as well as focus. A parallel inquiry by the Helsinki-based World Institute for Development and Economic Research (WIDER) was mapping out alternative sources of development finance:

- global environment taxes;
- tax on currency flows (for example, Tobin);
- new 'Special Drawing Rights';
- international Finance Facility (UK Government);
- private development donations;
- global lottery or premium bonds;
- increased remittances from emigrants.

Because the UN process had offered little guidance, the alternatives were presented cautiously (Atkinson, 2004). The seven alternatives are of course different in scale as well as likely support. The International Finance Facility was planned to reach a flow of USD 50 billion for 2010 to 2015. Private donations, that is from NGOs, totalled USD 10 billion in 2003 and might be increased, however, on past evidence, they would be unlikely in the foreseeable future to provide the predominant share of the resources needed. They can be expected to fill only a small proportion of the funding gap. The creation by the IMF of Special Drawing Rights has been opposed by the US and, since any new issue has to be approved by an 85 per cent majority, the US alone can veto progress.

The two most promising alternatives for serious examination would appear to be a global environment tax and a currency transfer tax (CTT). The former is usually illustrated by a tax on hydrocarbon fuels with high carbon content – such as a tax on airline travel. The latter or 'Tobin' tax is an alternative tax on foreign currency transactions (covering different types of transaction – spot, forward, swaps, derivatives and so on).

Both these taxes have been vigorously opposed on economic grounds. As Atkinson has pointed out, both need not necessarily be of a scale to deserve hostility and could be scaled down to produce substantial funds without adverse reactions in different markets. A small-scale initiative could of course be criticised, on the one hand, for failing to reduce global warming or pollution, and on the other hand, for failing to reduce currency speculation. However, even small-scale taxes could produce substantial sums for international investment in development and the elimination of poverty. Such an investment could also be used to partially fund investments in a social security system by low income countries. Even a tiny CTT of 0.02 per cent has been estimated to raise USD 28 billion and a small energy tax twice this sum – giving figures from three to five times the value of all private donations.

The energies of international bodies were diverted from consideration of the CTT by two new issues which arose in 2003. First was the possible creation of an International Tax Organisation (ITO). After the United Nations International Conference on Financing for Development in Mexico in March 2003, the Zedillo Panel recommended creating such an agency within the UN and an *"adequate international tax source"* for global spending programmes (UN, 2001).

The second issue was to explore how multinational business might promote strong domestic private sectors in the developing world. In June 2003, a Commission on the Private Sector and Development, co-chaired by Ernesto Zedillo, was convened by UNDP at the request of Kofi Annan to recommend *"how to promote strong domestic private sectors in the developing world as a key strategy towards the achievement of the Millennium Development Goals."*[8] There was no reference back to the simplicity and affordability of a single form of international tax in relation to that aim. In particular, the commission looked at how multinational business could become a supportive partner for local entrepreneurs in the developing countries. The discussion of these issues at the world conference in Davos in 2004 was inconclusive. The case for a CTT was effectively kicked into touch.

8. A CURRENCY TRANSFER TAX: NEW RESOURCES FOR CHILD BENEFIT AND SOCIAL SECURITY

From the mid-1990s, there was a groundswell of support for the Tobin Tax, particularly in Europe,[9] as a source of international finance for aid and economic stabilisation.

James Tobin put forward the idea of such a tax first in 1972 and then it was resurrected in UNDP's Human Development Report for 1994. The rate of tax lately suggested is in the range 0.1 to 0.5 per cent of currency transactions. If applied universally, a tax of 0.1 per cent on all currency transactions, including the charge for changing different currencies for travellers, was estimated in 2002 to be likely to raise USD 400 billion a year (see Townsend and Gordon, 2002, p. 369) – or five times more than the low target of debt relief and aid advocated for low income countries by the international financial agencies and members of the G8.

---

[8] Mr Kofi Annan, Secretary-General of the United Nations: Address to the World Economic Forum, Davos, Switzerland, 23 January 2004.
[9] For example, a report commissioned by the Federal Ministry for Economic Cooperation and Development, Bonn, concluded that the Tobin Tax is feasible and does not need global ratification but could be started by OECD or EU countries (Federal Ministry for Economic Cooperation and Development, 2002).

Eighty per cent of exchange transactions currently involve only eight industrialised countries (with the UK and USA accounting for about half) and most offshore financial havens, which might require a small consequential extension of supervision, are conveniently close to these same countries. Eighty-eight per cent of transactions also take place between five currencies: the dollar, the pound sterling, the euro, the yen and the Swiss franc (Harribey, 2002). Thus, agreement among a bare majority of the G8 countries would be sufficient to ensure large-scale implementation at a first stage.

The key question is – taxation for what? In the first years of the new Millennium, progress in implementing international taxation to pump-prime social security systems has made very little progress. In 2002, the General Assembly of the UN considered a report prepared at the instigation of Kofi Annan. The Zedillo Panel (the UN High-Level Panel on Financing for Development) had been appointed in 2001, to *"recommend strategies for the mobilisation of resources required to accelerate equitable and sustainable growth in developing countries as well as economies in transition, and to fulfil the poverty and development commitments enshrined in the UN Millennium Declaration."* The Zedillo Panel reported an annual shortfall of USD 15 billion for the provision of global public goods, in addition to the extra USD 50 billion per year needed to meet the MDG targets. A number of governments had been pressing for consideration of the recommendation by James Tobin of a Currency Transfer Tax. Thus, a report from the Federal Ministry of Economic Cooperation and Development in Bonn explained that the tax was feasible and could even be introduced right away by the OECD or EC countries (Federal Ministry for Economic Cooperation and Development, 2002). The European Parliament carried out a feasibility study, with France, Germany and Belgium in favour, and the Vatican coming round to acceptance. Outside the European Union, Canada also offered its active consent. Poor countries saw the Tobin Tax as something which rich countries could implement straightaway,[10] a domestic taxation control that had very small financial drawbacks for the donors but large benefits for the potential recipients. In April 2002, at Monterrey, Mexico, at a UN conference on *Finance for Development,* a number of countries pressed for the Currency Transfer Tax. The report to be submitted to the General Assembly was signed by 113 countries but innovative mechanisms of financing were given only one paragraph and were left open for further consideration.

The Zedillo Report had described the merits of a CTT as *"highly controversial"* and concluded that *"further rigorous study would be needed to resolve the doubts*

---

[10] See AFRODAD (2002) for a really good overview of where African countries stand on the Tobin Tax.

about the feasibility of such a tax". The Zedillo authors claimed to have examined a range of proposed mechanisms including a carbon tax, a currency transactions tax and a new allocation of Special Drawing Rights (SDRs), concluding that *"new sources of finance should be considered without prejudice by all parties involved"*.

However, there is no evidence that the mechanisms were examined in any depth. Surprisingly, the Zedillo Panel made no attempt to consider alternative practicable models of the Tobin Tax and to compare them, nor to deal with the difficulties said to be involved in implementing such a tax. They did not compare its merits with other methods of raising funds for overseas development and give persuasive estimates of costs and outcome. The *uses* to which the tax might be put or what social benefits might be derived were not discussed. I believe that discussion of those uses is bound to improve the practicability of introducing the tax.

A CTT of 0.2 per cent, compared with a standard fee of 2 per cent or 3 per cent charged by firms for currency exchange at airports, would raise USD 280 billion. A start would be feasible for those OECD countries prepared to introduce a CTT for travellers. Compared with an existing charge of 2 or 3 per cent, it seems likely that the travelling public would accept an additional charge of 0.2 per cent if they were persuaded that the additional charge was going to be of public benefit. If all or a substantial part of it was known to be going directly to benefit the poorest children in the world, the public would accept the tax more readily.

Like a corporation 'tax' of 1 per cent of turnover, a CTT could directly benefit children. The potential use of the tax was not considered by Tobin when introducing his idea in 1972, nor in the 1990s when publicity was again attracted to his proposal and, despite the terms of reference agreed by the Zedillo Panel, the idea was not given serious attention in 2001 and subsequently. Interpreted and administered in the name of the world's impoverished children, the tax could have considerably more public appeal and therefore potential acceptance. The proceeds of a tax – introduced severally or collectively by the richest countries – could be used to set up an international investment fund for children. Following its initiative in introducing the MDGs, the United Nations would be the obvious international organisation to administer the fund. A universal benefit for children, in cash or in kind, would attract world-wide support. It could prove to be not just a salvation for the world's children, but could regain public respect for the work of the international agencies on world social development and the fulfilment of the MDGs.

Grants from that fund to governments could be made conditional on, say, payments by each government and by the UN of 50 per cent of the cost of the programme, as well as evidence of payment. The scheme would be monitored by a representative UN Committee as well as individual governments.

9. SOCIAL SECURITY AND CHILD BENEFIT IN DEVELOPING COUNTRIES

The schemes in developing countries present a diverse picture (see, for example, ILO reports by Van Genneken, 1999; 2003). A semblance of a system had been introduced by colonial authorities in most of Asia, Africa and the Caribbean. They were extended, in the first instance, to civil servants and employees of large enterprises. There were benefits for relatively small percentages of the population that included health care, maternity leave, disability allowances and pensions. In general, they neglected the poor, and especially the rural poor. After independence, this colonial-induced 'privilege' contributed to the perpetuation of internal inequalities.

In the last forty years, initiatives have been taken in developing countries themselves to establish social protection schemes. For example, in India, there are schemes in different states intended for large numbers as well as a range of schemes for small categories of the population such as middle and high ranking civil servants. Cash allowance schemes for children, disabled and the elderly are, however, few and far between (for example, Justino, 2007; ILO, 2001). Allowances for children seem likely to develop only as a by-product of other social protection schemes. In 1995, the Government of India introduced an all-India social protection scheme – the National Assistance Programme (NSAP). Social assistance benefits are intended to become gradually available to poor households in the case of old age, death of the breadwinner and maternity. Thus, there are three types of benefit: the National Old Age Pension Scheme, the National Family Benefit Scheme and the National Maternity Benefit Scheme.

One of these initiatives – relevant to children – is the National Rural Employment Guarantee Act of 2005 (NEGRA), launched by the Prime Minister Manmohan Singh, in February 2006. The Act seeks to guarantee employment for 100 days a year at the minimum wage to one person from every poor household to improve rural infrastructure – roads, school buildings and village water supply – and to regenerate the land while reducing soil erosion (Mehrotra, 2006, p. 13). A major problem in developing a social security system for those who cannot be employed (or are unlikely to be employed in the foreseeable future) and especially in considering child allowances, is that the Government collects only 8–9 per cent of GDP in taxes, compared with 22 per cent in China (2003) and 14 per cent generally in low income countries (1990–2001). In addition, tax revenues from the richest sections of the population have actually fallen in the last two decades (*ibid.*, p. 13).

In Latin America, some countries introduced social insurance and other schemes before the 1939 war and other countries followed suit after the war. A good start has been made by individual governments in the 21st Century, including Brazil, especially in schemes for children, for example, the *Bolsa Escola* programme. Relatively, local 'Conditional Cash Transfer' (CCT) schemes preceded this programme, which was launched in 2001. In less than a year, 5 million households with children between 6 and 15 years were receiving a cash benefit. Transfers were limited to USD 15 a month per family, conditional on school attendance. In 2003, the programme was absorbed with other federal CCTs into *Bolsa Familia* (Britto, 2006a, p. 15). Early research showed positive effects on schooling and nutrition but longer term effects on rates of poverty and child labour remained unclear (*ibid.*, pp. 15–16).[11] The enlarged *Bolsa Familia* programme now reaches more than 12 million households.

Mexico was the first country in Latin America to introduce, in 1997, a nationwide CCT programme – *Progresa*. In 2002, this was expanded and renamed *Oportunidades*. The scheme confers cash or in-kind allowances to the household (up to USD 60 a month) on condition the children attend school and health check-ups are arranged for all members of the household (*ibid.*, p. 15).

Less publicised than the *Bolsa Familia* programme in Brazil, has been the 'Continuous Cash Benefit Programme' or *Beneficio de Prestacao Continuada* (BPC). Since 1993, people aged 65 and over and people with a severe disability whose household per capita income is less than a quarter of the minimum wage (approximately USD 1 a day in March 2006) are eligible for a transfer equivalent to the monthly minimum wage (approximately USD 4 a month). In December 1996, after its first year of operation, as many as 346,000 benefited. At the end of 2005, over two million benefited, just over half being disabled and under 65 (Medeiros *et al.*, 2006, p. 15). There are other cash transfer mechanisms, including one of invalid pensions, which is a contributory scheme for workers in the formal market and benefited 2.6 million in 2005.

This illustration shows that programmes to gradually increase public expenditure so that categories of the extreme poor start to benefit offer a realistic, affordable and successful alternative. Under President Lula da Silva, the Brazilian

---

[11] "Initial evaluations have shown positive effects of CCTs on schooling and nutrition. The evidence regarding the impact on child labour is not conclusive since school attendance can be frequently combined with work and requires broader interventions. The impact on poverty is still not so clear. In the long run, the translation of higher educational attainment into higher earnings cannot be taken for granted. It depends on the quality of education, rates of employment, absorption of skilled labour in the economy and general rates of return to education." BRITTO, T. (2006a), pp. 15–16. See also BRITTO, T. (2006b).

Government's Zero Hunger Programme was planned to provide quantity, quality and regularity of food to all Brazilians in conjunction with accelerated Social Security reform (Suplicy, 2003). The Zero Hunger Programme includes food banks, popular restaurants, food cards, distribution of emergency food baskets, strengthening of family agriculture and a variety of other measures to fight malnutrition. The Social Security reform programme includes social assistance for low-income 15–17 year-olds, assistance for 7–14 year-olds who are enabled to go to school and avoid the exacting toll of the worst conditions of child labour, minimum income and food scholarships for pregnant and nursing mothers with incomes less than half the minimum age or who are HIV positive, benefits for elderly disabled with special needs, and a range of other transfer programmes for the elderly, widowed, sick and industrially-injured and unemployed that are being enlarged year by year (Suplicy, 2003).

The social security programmes being developed in Mexico, Chile, Costa Rica and especially Brazil are useful models for poorer countries in Africa and South Asia. They provide a parallel set of evidence to that for social security in the OECD countries, and can prevent governments and international finance agencies making mistakes in their plans to reduce poverty and improve social and economic wellbeing. However, extension of coverage to all the extreme poor is a fitful process and is slow in most middle and low income countries, especially because of little support, and sometimes strong opposition, from the big economic powers, international finance agencies and TNCs.

Africa presents a more varied picture of measures taken to counter poverty than is often appreciated. In some countries, new social insurance schemes have been introduced – for example, a maternity and sickness scheme in Namibia. Mauritius and the Seychelles have universal benefit programmes (and relatively low poverty rates). Means-tested cash benefits are found in Botswana and Mozambique. Zambia has successfully piloted a social cash transfer scheme targeted at the poorest tenth of households (Gassman and Behrendt, 2006). However, social security expenditure in countries like Burundi, Cameroon, Ethiopia, Ghana, Kenya, Madagascar, Mauritania and Nigeria, has declined or remains at a tiny level compared with GDP (ILO, 2001; Van Ginneken, 2003; and see Townsend, 2007, p. 9).

10. THE CHILD SUPPORT GRANT IN SOUTH AFRICA

South Africa has high rates of poverty, labour migration and unemployment, and the problem of HIV/AIDS has become acute. Nonetheless, since the fall of apartheid in 1994, strong attempts have been made to introduce a comprehensive social security system. In 1998, a Child Support Grant was started, worth R110 for each child below the age of seven whose carer had an income of less than twice this amount. By early 2003, there were 2.5 million beneficiaries. By late 2005, the age limit was being increased gradually to 13 years and the number of beneficiaries (Table 2 below) reached over five million (four million adults). A valuable account of the history and present dilemmas is to be found in Lund (2007). However, there are criticisms of coverage because, while there is good evidence that the grant reaches some of the poorest of children (Case et al., 2003), there are increasingly large numbers of orphans, street children and child-headed households, in many cases the consequence of the spread of HIV/AIDS, that remain largely ineligible (Barrientos and DeJong, 2004). Despite the difficulties, many South Africans regard the development as the 'road to universality' and give the example of the Child Support Grant when illustrating the significance of the incorporation by South Africa of the principle of the 'progressive realisation' of economic and social human rights into their common law jurisdiction. The idea of a staged programme towards comprehensive coverage was a feature of a major commissioned report (Committee of Inquiry into a Comprehensive System of Social Security for South Africa, 2002).

Some analysts believe progress could be faster, especially if universalism were to be embraced wholeheartedly. One calculation is that, if there were to be a universal income grant of R100 per month to all households, the incidence of household poverty would be cut by just over half and, for R200, nearly three-quarters. Although the costs would be large, it was argued that politicians should seriously examine different combinations of funding between hard cost and *"the obvious welfare-enhancing effects of a universal income grant"* (Bhorat, 2006, p. 10).

In South Africa, spending in households that receive social grants focuses more on basics like food, fuel, housing and household operations and less is spent on tobacco and debt. All major social grants – the Older Person's Pension, the Child Support Grant and the Disability Grant – are significantly and positively associated with a greater share of household expenditure being allocated to food. This increased spending on food is associated with better nutritional outcomes. Households that receive social grants have lower prevalence rates of hunger for young children as well as older children and adults, even compared with those households with similar income levels (Samson, 2008).

Regardless of estimation technique or model specification, the two key effects tested are corroborated by all the participation models: both receipt of the State Old Age Pension and receipt of the Disability Grant have a significant positive impact on both narrow and broad labour force participation (*ibid.*)

Table 2. Cash transfers in South Africa- numbers of beneficiaries (in thousands) and monthly level of grant

Type of grant	2003	2005	2007	Monthly grant
Child Support Grant	2631	5126	7880	R200
Foster Care Grant	139	249	381	R620
Care Dependency Grant	58	85	104	R870
Disability Grant	954	1292	1438	R870
Old Age Pension	2009	2067	2186	R870
War Veteran's Pension	5	3	2	R890
TOTAL	5796	8822	11991	

Source: National Treasury (table reproduced from Samson, 2008, forthcoming).

Provision for disabled children does not yet exist. The Disability Grant is for people over 18 years of age who are so disabled that they cannot work. It can be awarded on a permanent or a temporary basis. It has recently been extended to people with AIDS-related disabilities and this is likely to be one of the factors driving the growth in numbers of the permanent Disability Grant. Delaney *et al.* (2005) showed that there was a significant decrease in the average age of applicants between 2001 and 2004, from just over 46 to nearly 43 years. There was also an increase in the proportion of female applicants over the same period – from 45 per cent to 57 per cent in 2004. Both of these trends would be consistent with increasing applications from people with AIDS-related disabilities. It is not possible to estimate the numbers receiving as a proportion of those applying. It is certain that the amount of the Disability Grant covers only a small part of the overall financial needs of those with disabilities. There is a new cash grant in South Africa. But everywhere more substantial non-contributory schemes for children are urgently needed, preferably schemes that are categorical and not means-tested.

According to the ILO:

> "One of the key problems facing social security today is the fact that more than half of the world's population are excluded from any type of statutory social security protection. In South Asia and sub-Saharan Africa, those excluded number 90 per cent. In middle income countries, the number is between 20 per cent and 60 per cent. Social security had become more necessary than ever due to globalisation and structural adjustment policies... The challenge for governments, social partners and civil societies is to create such conditions that the large majority of the population contributes to basic social insurance schemes." (Van Ginneken, 2003, p. 7 and 71)

The ILO Convention 102 Social Security 1952 (which came into force in 1955) laid down minimum income requirements per child, of either 3 per cent of the ordinary manual labourer's wage, for the economically active, or 1.5 per cent of that wage for all other families. In families with four children, the benefit would amount to 12 per cent (or 6 per cent in the case of those not in work). The ILO Convention was signed by 40 countries – including Niger, Senegal and Mauritius. It became part of the European Code of Social Security and the blueprint for such instruments as the European Social Charter, the Treaty of Amsterdam of the European Union and regional agreements in Africa and Latin America (Kulke et al., 2006, p. 4). If the World Bank had sought policies to enforce this Convention rather than extend its neo-liberal anti-poverty strategy, there would have been a dramatic fall in world poverty.

A serious obstacle to social security schemes to reduce poverty has been a need to re-build and/or strengthen tax administration. Taxation and contributory insurance systems must be introduced or strengthened to raise national revenue to match international tax or aid revenues both for the protection of children and families, but also to be fully answerable to representatives of national electorates as well as participating overseas governments, with independent powers to monitor policies and outcomes. During the evolution of joint funding in the next years, monitoring by an independent international inspectorate will also become necessary.

11. CHILD BENEFIT IN THE UK

The northern and western countries that were first to industrialise have all developed substantial social security systems. Among their other functions, these systems have greatly reduced domestic poverty. In the 15 EEC countries, poverty (by European standards) is reduced on average from 45 per cent to 15 per cent if incomes are assessed before and after social transfers (Townsend, 2007, p. 10). Governments continue, however, to face strong pressure to do more for those in poverty, especially children.

In the UK, for example, serious concerns arose after the rapid increase of child poverty in the 1980s and early 1990s. In 1999, the Prime Minister, Tony Blair, gave a commitment to end child poverty in a generation. The aim was to eliminate poverty among children by 2020 and by a half, relative to 1999, by 2010. As in other OECD countries, there are in the UK a range of direct and indirect schemes affecting children, including child benefit, child tax credit, income support and allowances to families that are based on national insurance contributions.

Progress in reducing child poverty has been slower than necessary to meet the ultimate objectives since 1999, a fact admitted by Ministers.

One non-government commission on *Life Chances and Child Poverty* found that, in 2005, life chances remained very unequal.

> "Children from disadvantaged backgrounds have much worse chances in terms of their infant mortality rates; their subsequent physical and cognitive development; their experience of childhood; their outcomes at school; and later access to higher education and jobs. In many cases these inequalities are found to be as wide now as they were in 1997, and in some cases they are widening." (Fabian Commission, 2006, p. 201)

The Commission concluded that the strategy had become over-selective.[12]

> "Whilst universal Child Benefit and the means-tested Child Tax Credit should remain the twin pillars of income support for families with children, there should be a re-balancing of the system towards Child Benefit. One option would be to increase the rate of Child Benefit for second and subsequent children over the medium term so that it is closer to the rate for the first child. This would take some of the pressure off the Tax Credits system as well as achieving higher take-up rates and wider public buy-in." (Fabian Commission, 2006, pp. 187–188 and 204–5)

Among other key measures, the Commission called for an increased minimum wage relative to average earnings, a more progressive rate of income taxation and a review of the existing unequal distribution of income and wealth.

Other reports in the UK have provided evidence of the enhanced risk of poverty among children with disabilities. The latest example is for 2007 (Burchardt and Zaidi, 2008). The risk of poverty is greater once the extra costs of a disabled child are taken into account. Thus, 14.4 per cent of two-child families where there is a disabled child are in poverty, compared with 11.5 per cent of families not having

---

[12] In tracing the impact of policies for children before and after 1997, the Treasury was invited, in 2004, to answer particular questions in Parliament about total expenditure on child benefit, tax credits, and other income-related benefits for children. Total expenditure in 1997/8 was £8.41b, £1.33b and £2.94b, respectively – at 2004/5 prices (or 0.9%, 0.1% and 0.3% of GDP). In 2003/4, it was £9.66b, £9.14b and £3.95b – again at 2004/5 prices (or 0.9%, 0.9% and 0.4% of GDP). Since these schemes have a primary impact on the levels of child poverty, the trend in the years from 1997/8 to 2003/4 towards more selective or targeted but less efficient child benefits is clear. Child tax credit is relatively more difficult and much more costly to administer than universal child benefit. The intended precise relationship between actual income and eligible level of benefit is hard to achieve in practice and the mis-match provokes confusion and distrust. Child tax credits are therefore difficult to justify publicly and a substantial proportion of families who would be eligible for credits do not in practice receive them.

such a child. However, if extra costs are included, the number in poverty rises from 14.4 per cent to 15.8 per cent. This applies despite the range of allowances to which families are entitled, such as the care and mobility components of the Disability Living Allowance, the disabled child premium that contributes to housing costs and other benefits. The authors of the report show that the various allowances tend to be pitched too low in relation to costs, or for various reasons are not, or cannot be, claimed.

As in low income countries, developments in recent years in the rich countries, like this example from the UK, point towards wider acceptance of children's fundamental rights to social security and an adequate standard of living by means of emphatic endorsement of benefits that are universal or which cover social categories of the population, such as children under five, all children, or groups like the over-75s or disabled people.

One authority calls attention to the *"lamentable lack of a social justice literature which considers children"* (Gordon, 2008, p. 14). Making a deliberate link with human rights can strengthen anti-poverty measures constructed by governments and motivate action to be more consistent with commitments. Action to reduce poverty in rich and poor countries and needs and rights at the two extremes, can be better coordinated. Poverty is increasingly conceptualised as a denial of human rights, so that the links between equalities, human rights and the elimination of poverty can be a more automatic part of all governments' agenda. Since 1997, the UK has taken decisive action on economic and social rights in Europe and in the world. The Human Rights Act of 1998, coming into force in 2000, and the UK's signature to the Economic and Social Charter imply greater coordination of anti-poverty measures at home and overseas. The UK signed the Convention on the Rights of the Child in 1990 and ratified the Convention in 1991. In 2007, it stated that its commitment to the implementation of the rights of children *"remains unwavering"*. As declared by the Fabian Commission:

> "In 2003, the Joint Committee on Human Rights argued for a strategic, rights-based Commissioner for Children and Young People and also for an integrated Commission for Equality and Human Rights (CEHR) to work in a more concerted way than was proving possible with an assortment of bodies against discrimination in all its forms. The broad objective of the CEHR – to integrate action against discrimination and to end the arbitrary separation of types of discrimination and fragmentation of action is to be welcomed, though the difficulties entailed in achieving this ambitious goal in practice should not be underestimated." (Fabian Commission, 2006, pp. 12–13)

12. CONDITIONAL AND UNCONDITIONAL CHILD BENEFIT

Through unconditional child benefit and unconditional allowances for children dependent on parents who are sick, unemployed, widowed or disabled, many children in the rich industrialised countries gain rights to social security. This is rare in low income regions and countries. Most children have little or no income security. Conditional cash transfer schemes are being encouraged, as we have noted. However, in practice, as in the history of the rich countries, there are pressures to extend coverage and relax the discriminating conditions which are both difficult and costly to administer fairly. In one review, it was concluded:

> "Most governments tend to have a mixture of both universal and targeted social policies. However, in the more successful countries, overall social policy itself has been universalistic, and targeting has been used as simply one instrument for making universalism effective; such 'targeting within universalism' directs extra benefits to low-income groups within the context of a universal policy and involves the fine-tuning of what are fundamentally universalist policies." (Mkandawire, 2006, p. 5)

Another authority has argued that targeting and conditionalities for cash transfers are unnecessary and are counter-productive. Instead, he prefers a universal, non-conditional income grant. He maintains that this is better than commodity-based assistance, such as food aid, because poor families deserve the freedom to choose what they can spend their money on (Standing, 2007a; 2007b).

13. SUMMARY AND CONCLUSION: A UNIVERSAL CHILD BENEFIT

Children are at greater risk of being in poverty than women and men. At the turn of the 19th Century, the industrialising powers introduced laws against the employment of children and women in hazardous conditions, and also introduced universal social security schemes and social services to ensure stability during a period of economic upheaval and very rapid population growth. The market adapted its practices to meet these laws and poverty was greatly reduced.

However, in middle and low income countries, the scale of poverty among children is vast. The UNCRC contains elaborate injunctions to protect children from malnutrition, maltreatment, neglect, abuse and exploitation and ensure they are not deprived of access to clean water, sanitary facilities, shelter, health care services, education and information: governments are enjoined to "recognise the right of every child to a standard of living adequate for the child's physical, mental, spiritual, moral and social development". The statements, ratified by nearly all of the 193 nation states in the world, allow single but also multiple measures or indicators of the denial or fulfilment of the specified rights to be devised and tracked.

A special investigation for UNICEF found that 56 per cent of children in developing countries – 1.2 billion children – suffered one or more forms of severe deprivation, with over half of them (674 million) suffering at least two forms of severe multiple deprivation, such as total absence of toilet facilities, lack of nearby clean water, malnutrition and extreme overcrowding and poor shelter. Many children orphaned by HIV/AIDS face a miserable existence and early painful death. The number in sub-Saharan Africa is expected to rise to 16 million, or a quarter of all children, by 2010.

The poverty of children arises in part from the harsh working conditions in which they, and their parents, are placed. Children as young as seven years old are reliably reported to be producing paving stones, footballs, clothing and carpets, operating with dangerous pesticides and other chemicals, digging trenches, picking cotton and working in mines – often for 10 or more hours a day. The problem is that routine observance of children's needs and rights is neither widely proclaimed nor enforced. Responsibility extends beyond state laws.

Trans National Corporations have become a focus of attention. The largest have much greater powers than the governments of low income countries, and their responsibility for harsh conditions that may be created by sub-contractors and subsidiaries is not easy to assess accurately, even by the TNCs themselves. Information about the spread of wages, profits and taxes is also lacking. Agreement between the UN and TNCs, as well as between the UN and individual governments, about their accountability for severe forms of deprivation among children seems a long way off.

TNCs and international agencies can work wonders by committing a tiny percentage of their growing resources in particular to social security in the low income countries, and also by moving towards acceptance of minimum standards of monthly or weekly income on the part of wage-earners and those not in paid employment who are entitled to social security.

For example, Trans National employers could add one or two per cent of wage costs in different countries towards a child benefit to help banish malnutrition, poverty and premature child death, and also encourage more schooling. One practical possibility would be to extend existing employer contributions towards domestic social insurance schemes in the OECD countries to employer operations in the low-income countries. A small Currency Transfer Tax (CTT) (perhaps 0.2 per cent, raising a minimum of USD 280 billion) could produce even larger resources. James Tobin introduced the idea in 1972 and again in the 1990s. This could be the basis for a UN Investment Fund for child benefit to reduce child poverty.

Universal cash benefit schemes for children (together with other schemes for disabled and elderly people) can be introduced in low-income countries by stages. The administrative infrastructures would become one major source of economic and social stability to pit against the unravelling problems of conflict, AIDS, and competitive global avarice.

The priority recommendation is for an international child benefit that, once administratively in place, has a direct and immediate effect in lowering poverty.

Because the circumstances of countries differ widely, a new child benefit would necessarily take a variety of forms and be introduced progressively. It could be a weekly allowance in cash or kind for children under a given age – say 10 years, or five years, or infants under two. A low birthweight baby allowance is an example of a measure that could be applied in rich and poor countries alike. The scheme can be phased in, depending on available resources – maybe starting with infants – so long as it is introduced country- or district-wide. Precedents in parts of Latin America, like the conditional cash transfers and, in South Africa, the child support grant, could be copied and extended.

A second priority recommendation is a categorical child benefit for severely disabled children.

Whether parents are in paid employment or not, the costs of caring for a severely disabled child often account for family poverty and the market does not recognise this form of dependency. While some forms of congenital or disabling long-term illness may be declining, there are still the disabling conditions of the major problems of the last two decades, like HIV/AIDS, oil, nuclear and chemical pollution, and armed conflict, including landmines.

The use of a currency transfer tax for universal child benefit would immediately improve the life chances of hundreds of millions of children and pave the way for the emergence of social security systems in low income countries that would eventually compare with those in OECD countries and therefore radically reduce mass poverty.

14. REFERENCES

Afrodad, B.F.A. (2002). *The View from the South on the Tobin Tax*, REFERES, www.ppp.ch.

Akwanalo Maté, F. (2006). *Children's Property and Inheritance Rights: Experience of orphans affected by HIV/ AIDS and other vulnerable orphans in Africa*, LSE, Department of Social Policy (publication forthcoming).

Atkinson, A.B. (ed.) (2004). *New Sources of Development Finance*, UNU-WIDER, Oxford, OUP.

Atkinson, A.B. (2005). *Global Public Finance and Funding the Millennium Development Goals*, Jelle Zijlstra Lecture 4, Wassenaar, Netherlands Institute for Advanced Study in the Humanities and Social Sciences (NIAS).

Barrientos, A. and DeJong, J. (2004). *Child Poverty and Cash Transfers*, Childhood Poverty Research and Policy Centre (CHIP), Working Paper 2, available from the Institute for Development Policy and Management, University of Manchester – also available from www.childpoverty.org.

Bhorat, H. (2006). "An Income Grant to all South Africans?" in UNDP, International Poverty Centre, *Social Protection: The Role of Cash Transfers*, Poverty in Focus, Brasilia, International Poverty Centre.

Britto, T. (2006a). "Conditional Cash Transfers in Latin America", in UNDP, International Poverty Centre, *Social Protection: the Role of Cash Transfers*, Poverty in Focus, Brasilia, International Poverty Centre.

Britto, T. (2006b). *Recent Trends in the Development Agenda of Latin America: an analysis of conditional cash transfers* www.eldis.org/cf/search/disp/docdisplay.cfm?doc=DOC17797&resource=f1.

Brown, G. and Wolfensohn, J. (2004). "A New Deal for the World's Poor", *The Guardian*, 16 February.

Burchardt, T. and Zaidi, A. (2008). "Disabled children, poverty and extra costs", in Strelitz, J. and Lister, R. (eds.), *Why Money Matters: Family income, poverty and children's lives*, London, Save the Children.

Chinkin, C. (2001). "The United Nations Decade for the Elimination of Poverty: What Role for International Law?" *Current Legal Problems*, 54, 553–589.

Cichon, M. and Scholz, W. (2004). *Financing Social Protection*, Geneva, ILO.

Committee of Inquiry into a Comprehensive System of Social Security for South Africa (2002). *Transforming the Present. Protecting the Future*, Draft Consolidated report, Pretoria, Committee of Inquiry into a Comprehensive System of Social Security for South Africa.

Delany, A., Budlender, D., Moultrie, T., Schneider, M. and Kimmie, Z. (2005). *Investigation into the increase in uptake of Disability and Care Dependency Grants since December 2001*, Braamfontein: Community Agency for Social Enquiry (CASE).

De Schutter, O. (ed.) (2006). *Transnational Corporations and Human Rights*, Oxford, Hart.

Donkor, K. (2002). "Structural Adjustment and Mass Poverty in Ghana", in Townsend, P. and Gordon, D. (eds.), *World Poverty: New Policies to Defeat an Old Enemy*, Bristol, Policy Press.

Fabian Commission (2006). *Narrowing the Gap: The Fabian Commission on Life Chances and Child Poverty*, London, Fabian Society.

Federal Ministry for Economic Cooperation and Development, Germany (2002). *On the Feasibility of a Tax on Foreign Exchange Transactions*, Bonn, Federal Ministry.

Gassman, F. and Behrendt, C. (2006). *Cash Benefits in Low-Income Countries: Simulating the Effect on Poverty Reduction for Tanzania and Senegal*, Geneva, ILO.

Gordon, D. (2008 forthcoming). *Children, Policy and Social Justice*.

Gordon, D., Nandy, S., Pantazis, C., Pemberton, S. and Townsend, P. (2003). *Child Poverty in the Developing World*, Bristol, Policy Press.

Gruskin, S., Mills, E.J. and Tarantola, D. (2007). "History, principles and practice of health and human rights", *Lancet*, 370, 9585.

Hall, A. (2007). "Social Policies in the World Bank", *Global Social Policy*, 7, 2.

Haq Mul, Kaul, I. and Grunberg, I. (eds.) (1996). *The Tobin Tax*, Oxford, OUP.

Harribey, J.-M. (2002). *The Seven Mistakes of the Opponents to "The Tax"*, l'Université Montesquieu-Bordeaux IV, France, Scientific Committee of ATTAC.

Held, D. (2004). *Global Covenant: The social democratic alternative to the Washington Consensus*, Cambridge, Polity Press.

Hertz, N. (2001). *The Silent Takeover: Global Capitalism and the Death of Bureaucracy*, London, William Heinemann.

Hines, C. (2001). *Localization: A Global Manifesto*, London, Earthscan.

Hudson, E. (ed.) (1996). *Merchants of Misery: How Corporate America Profits from Poverty*, Maine, Courage.

Husain, I. and Faruqee, R. (1994). *Adjustment in Africa: Lessons from Country Case Studies*, World Bank Regional and Sectoral Studies, Washington D.C., World Bank.

International Labour Organisation (ILO) (1984). *Into the Twenty-First Century: The Development of Social Security*, Geneva, ILO.

International Labour Organisation (ILO) (1998). *The ILO Tripartite Declaration of Principles Concerning Multinational Enterprises and Social Policy – Ten Years After*, Geneva, ILO.

International Labour Organisation (ILO) (2001). *Social Security: A New Consensus*, Geneva, ILO.

Justino, P. (2003). *Social Security in Developing Countries: Myth or Necessity? Evidence from India*, Poverty Research Unit at Sussex Working Paper No. 20, Brighton, University of Sussex.

Kakwani, N. and Son H.H. (2006). *New Global Poverty Counts*, Working Paper No. 20, Brasilia, UNDP International Poverty Centre.

Korten, D.C. (1996). *When Corporations Rule the World*, London, Earthscan.

Kozul-Wright, R. and Rowthorn, R. (1998). *Transnational Corporations and the Global Economy*, Helsinki, Finland, UNU World Institute for Development Economic Research.

Kulke, U., Cichon, M. and Pal, K. (2006). *Changing Tides: A Revival of a Rights-Based Approach to Social Security*, Social Security Department, Geneva, ILO.

Lang, T. and Hines, C. (1993). *The New Protectionism*, London, Earthscan.

Lund, F. (2007). *Changing Social Policy: The Child Support Grant in South Africa*, Cape Town, HSRC Press.
MacDonald, R. (2007). "An inspirational defence of the right to health", *Lancet*, 370, 379-380.
MacDonald, T.H. (2007). *The Global Human Right to Health: Dream or Possibility?* Radcliffe Publishing.
Madeley, J. (1999). *Big Business, Poor Peoples: The Impact of Transnational Corporations on the World's Poor*, London and New York, Zed Books, 206 pp.
Medeiros, M., Diniz, D. and Squinca, F. (2006). *Cash Benefits to Disabled Persons in Brazil: An Analysis of the BPC - Continuous Cash Benefit Programme*, International Poverty Centre Working Paper 16.
Mehrotra, J. (2006). "Job Law with Right to Information can Cut Poverty in India", in UNDP, International Poverty Centre, *Social Protection: The Role of Cash Transfers*, Poverty in Focus, Brasilia, International Poverty Centre.
Mkandawire, T. (ed.) (2004). *Social Policy in a Development Context*, UNRISD, Basingstoke, Palgrave Macmillan.
Mkandawire, T. (2006). *Targeting and Universalism in Poverty Reduction*, Poverty in Focus, Brasilia, International Poverty Centre.
OECD (2001). *The OECD guidelines for multinational enterprises 2001: Focus: global instruments for corporate responsibility*, Paris, OECD (first adopted 1976 and amended 1991).
Pemberton. S., Gordon, D., Nandy, S., Pantazis, C. and Townsend, P. (2005). "The Relationship Between Child Poverty And Child Rights: The Role Of Indicators", in Minujin, A., Delamonica, E. and Komarecki, M. (eds.), *Human Rights and Social Policies for Children and Women: The MICS in Practice*. New York, UNICEF/New School University.
Pemberton, S., Gordon, D., Nandy, S., Pantazis, C. and Townsend, P. (2007). "Child Rights and Child Poverty: Can the International Framework of Children's Rights be Used to Improve Child Survival Rates?" *PLos Medicine*, 4, 10, e307 www.plosmedecine.org.
Pogge, T. and Reddy, S. (2003). *Unknown: The Extent, Distribution and Trend of Global Income Poverty*, www.socialanalysis.org.
Reddy, S.G. and Pogge, T.W. (2001). *How Not to Count the Poor*, Departments of Economics and Philosophy, University of Columbia.
Rice, X. (2007). "Net giveaway halves Kenya's child deaths from malaria", *Guardian*, 17 August.
Sachs, J. (2005). *The End of Poverty*, London, Penguin Books.
Samson, M. (2008 forthcoming). "The impact of social transfers on growth, development, poverty and inequality in developing countries", in Townsend, P. (ed), *Social Security: Building Decent Societies*, Geneva, ILO.
Scott, J., Stokman, F.N. and Ziegler, R. (1985). *Networks of Corporate Power*, London, Polity Press.
Singh, J.A., Govender, M. and Mills, E.J. (2007). "Do Human Rights matter to health?" *Lancet*, 370, 9586.
Sklair, L. (2001). *The Transnational Capitalist Class*, Oxford, Blackwell.

Standing, G. (2007a). *Conditional Cash Transfers: Why Targeting and Conditionalities Could Fail*, IPC One pager, 47, Brasilia, International Poverty Centre.
Standing, G. (2007b). *How Cash Transfers Boost Work and Economic Security*, UNDESA Working Paper 58.
Standing, G. and Samson, M. (2003). *A Basic Income Grant for South Africa*, Cape Town, UCT Press.
Suplicy, E.M. (2003) *President Lula's Zero Hunger Programme and the Trend Towards a Citizen's Basic Income in Brazil*, London, LSE.
Tendler, J. (2004). "Why Social Policy is Condemned to a Residual Category of Safety Nets and What to Do About it", in Mkandawire, T. (ed.) (2004), *Social Policy in a Development Context*, UNRISD, Basingstoke, Palgrave Macmillan.
Townsend, P. (1993). *The International Analysis of Poverty*, Hemel Hempstead, Harvester Wheatsheaf.
Townsend P. and Gordon D. (eds.) (2002). *World Poverty: New Policies to Defeat an Old Enemy*, Bristol, Policy Press.
Townsend, P. (2004). *Direct Policies to Fight Child Poverty*, In Focus, UNDP, Rio de Janeiro, International Poverty Centre.
Townsend, P. (2006). "Introduction", in *Rio Group, Compendium of Best Practices in Poverty Measurement*, Santiago, Chile, Rio Group.
Townsend, P. (2007). *The Right to Social Security and National Development: Lessons from OECD Experience for Low-Income Countries*, Discussion paper 18, Geneva, ILO.
UN (1988). *Transnational Corporations in World Development*, New York, UN.
UN (2001). *Report of the High-Level Panel on Financing for Development*, 28 June, New York, UN.
UNICEF (2004). *State of the World's Children 2005*, New York, UNICEF.
UNICEF (2005). *State of the World's Children 2006*, New York, UNICEF.
UNICEF (2007). *State of the World's Children 2008*, New York, UNICEF.
Vagts, D.F. (2003). "The UN Norms for Transnational Corporations", *Leiden Journal of International Law*, 16, 795–802.
Van Ginneken, W. (1999). *Social Security for the Excluded Majority: Case Studies of Developing Countries*, Geneva, ILO.
Van Ginneken, W. (2003). *Extending Social Security: Policies for Developing Countries*, ESS papers No. 13, Geneva, ILO.
Wade, R.H. (2004). "Is Globalisation Reducing Poverty and Inequality?" *International Journal of Health Services*, Vol. 34, No. 3, pp. 381–414.
Wade, R. H. (2007). "Globalisation, growth, poverty and inequality". In *Global political economy, 2nd edition*. Edited by Ravenhill, J. Oxford University Press.
Watkins, K. (2002). *Rigged Rules and Double Standards: trade, globalisation and the fight against poverty*, New York., Oxfam International, www.maketradefair.com and advocacy@oxfaminternational.org.
World Bank (2000). *Balancing Protection and Opportunity: A Strategy for Social Protection in the Transition Economies*, Washington D.C., World Bank.
World Bank (2000b). *Emerging Directions for a Social Protection Sector Strategy: From Safety Net to Spring Board*, Social Protection Sector, Washington D.C., World Bank.

World Bank (2005). *World Bank Development Report for 2005*, Washington D.C., World Bank.
World Health Organisation (2007). *World Health Statistics 2007*, Washington D.C., WHO.

APPENDIX I: THE MILLENNIUM DEVELOPMENT GOALS

1. Eradicate extreme poverty and hunger	Between 1990 and 2015: - Halve the proportion of people whose income is less than USD 1 a day - Halve the proportion of people who suffer from hunger
2. Achieve universal primary education	Ensure that by 2015 all children will be able to complete a full course of primary schooling
3. Promote gender equality and empower women	Eliminate gender disparity in all levels of education by 2015
4. Reduce child mortality	Reduce by two-thirds the under-five mortality rate between 1990 and 2015
5. Improve maternal health	Reduce by three-quarters the maternal mortality ratio between 1990 and 2015
6. Combat HIV/ AIDS, malaria and other diseases	By 2015 have halted, and begun to reverse - The spread of HIV/AIDS - The spread of malaria and other major diseases
7. Ensure environmental sustainability	- Integrate principles of sustainable development into country policies and reverse the loss of environmental resources - Halve the proportion of people without sustainable access to safe drinking water by 2015 - By 2020 have achieved a significant improvement in the lives of at least 100 million slum dwellers
8. Develop a global partnership for development	- Develop the world trading and financial system - Address the special needs of the least developed and landlocked and small island countries - Deal comprehensively with the debt problems of the developing countries

APPENDIX II: CHILD MORTALITY AND POOR CONDITIONS OF HEALTH

Table 3. Countries in sub-Saharan Africa

Country (year data collected)	Under-fives stunted for age (%)		Mortality under five years (%)		One year olds not immunised against measles (%)	
	Poorest 20%	*Richest 20%*	*Poorest 20%*	*Richest 20%*	*Poorest 20%*	*Richest 20%*
Benin (2001)	35	18	20	9	43	17
Burkina Faso (2003)	46	21	21	14	52	29
Central African Republic (1994/5)	42	25	19	10	69	20
Chad (2004)	51	32	18	19	92	62
Comoros (1996)	45	23	13	9	49	14
Eritrea (2002)	45	18	10	6	16	4
Ethiopia (2005)	48	35	13	9	75	48
Gabon (2000)	33	11	9	5	66	29
Ghana (2003)	42	13	13	9	25	11
Guinea (2005)	41	22	22	11	58	43
Kenya (2003)	38	19	15	9	45	12
Madagascar (2003/4)	50	38	14	5	62	16
Malawi (2004)	54	32	18	11	33	12
Mali (2001)	45	20	25	15	60	24
Mauritania (2000/1)	39	24	10	8	58	14
Mozambique (2003)	49	20	20	11	39	4
Namibia (2000)	27	15	5	3	24	14
Niger (1998)	42	32	28	18	77	34
Rwanda (2005)	55	30	21	12	15	12
South Africa (1998)	–	–	9	2	27	16
Togo (1998)	24	15	17	10	66	37
Uganda 2000/1)	40	26	19	11	51	36
United Republic of Tanzania (2004/5)	40	26	14	9	45	9
Zambia (2001/2)	51	37	19	9	19	12
Zimbabwe (1999)	29	21	10	6	20	14

Source: WHO, *World Health Statistics 2007*, pp. 74–77.

Table 4. Countries in Latin America

Country (year data collected)	Under-fives stunted for age (%)		Mortality under five years (%)		One-year olds not immunised against measles (%)	
	Poorest 20%	Richest 20%	Poorest 20%	Richest 20%	Poorest 20%	Richest 20%
Bolivia (2003)	42	5	10	3	38	26
Brazil (1996)	23	2	10	3	22	10
Columbia (2005)	20	3	4	2	36	10
Guatemala (1998/9)	65	7	8	4	21	9
Haiti (2000)	31	7	16	11	57	37
Nicaragua (2001)	35	4	6	2	24	6
Paraguay (1990)	22	3	2	2	52	31
Peru (2000)	47	4	9	2	19	8

Source: WHO, *World Health Statistics 2007*, pp. 74–77.

CHILD POVERTY AND SOCIAL INCLUSION IN COUNTRIES IN TRANSITION AND IN OECD COUNTRIES

Professor Marta SANTOS PAIS
Director, UNICEF Innocenti Research Centre

1. INTRODUCTION

There is still a long way to go before the fully-fledged citizenship of children is taken seriously and child poverty is recognised as a clear, urgent and lasting political priority.

Indeed, children growing up in poverty remain somewhat invisible. Child poverty is still largely envisaged in the broader context of the national population, the community or the family, under the assumption that children, all children, benefit evenly from economic growth, policy reforms and social support systems; and that children, all children, experience in a similar manner to adults the impact of economic recession or political crisis.

Children who grow up in poverty are at a marked and lasting disadvantage. They access basic social services less often and they suffer deprivation in the present, with strong implications for their survival, health, nutrition and overall development. As they get older, poverty has a cumulative impact on their evolving capacities with an increasing likelihood that their lives will be scarred by educational under-achievement, poor health, low employment opportunities and long term welfare dependence.

The circumstances that perpetuate these risks and challenges must be urgently addressed.

In rich and transition countries child poverty has failed to be given the priority attention it deserves. Children have not received a distinct and systematic visibility in economic and social policy formulation and in resource mobilisation; and social transfers to families with young children require a more decisive support by state authorities. This general pattern explains why child poverty figures so prominently in the programme of the UNICEF Innocenti Research Centre.

2. A REGION IN TRANSITION

The significant political transformation in Central and Eastern Europe (CEE) and the Commonwealth of Independent States (CIS), with the birth of new nations and the shift from a centrally planned to a market economy, have marked the reality of childhood in the region. To assess the impact of this process of transition on children, the Innocenti Centre has developed a close collaboration with National Statistical Offices, analysed regular child related information and produced a number of thematic studies that have contributed to giving children a higher stand in the policy agenda, at the national and international levels.

A key objective of the Innocenti research has been to draw attention to how children experience poverty, complementing the important analysis on growth promotion and governance conducted by partners in the region, including the World Bank and UNDP; placing the emphasis on children's enjoyment of an adequate standard of living; and promoting child-sensitive policy responses.

a) The CEE/CIS is an increasingly heterogeneous region – a region made of many countries, with different patterns of economic growth and social development, ranging from the extremely poor Central Asian Republics to Central Eastern European countries increasingly involved in the process of accession to the European Union.

This is also a region with important commonalities and with strong political and economic opportunities. In fact, all countries in the region are parties to the UN Convention on the Rights of the Child and have pledged to ensure its implementation. All countries have made commitments to the Millennium Agenda and to the achievement of the Millennium Development Goals, including poverty reduction. Several countries have formulated Poverty Reduction Strategy Plans, and some have developed national action plans to combat poverty and social exclusion in the context of their EU accession process. The value of these strategies and plans can be judged on the explicit visibility given to children, in particular those belonging to the most vulnerable groups. Across this wide region there is a significant opportunity to place children high on the policy and social agenda.

Since 1998 there have been clear signs of economic recovery, better opportunities for individuals, and a decline in the overall numbers of families living in poverty. But a key question remains: to what extent has this generally positive environment led to the improvement of children's lives, to their social inclusion, and to their development to their fullest potential? How far have overall poverty reduction efforts been translated into significant policy action for children?

To address these questions, our research has been guided by two important methodological dimensions.

Firstly, child poverty has been addressed through the lens of human rights. For this reason, our studies address the prevailing gap between states' commitments and accountability to the realisation of the rights of the child, and the effective progress achieved on the ground in promoting equity and non-discrimination, and monitoring progress through transparent processes and mechanisms. For this reason, our research gives particular attention to the situation of children belonging to the most vulnerable groups, and these children are envisaged as indicators of social progress as a whole.

Secondly, our work attempts to understand the distinct manner in which poverty affects children, and its detrimental effect on their survival, growth and development. We are committed to highlighting how different children's reality is when compared to adults' poverty and deprivation – most importantly, poverty not only impacts children's daily lives, but it also has a cumulative and lasting impact on their development and future; moreover, children are strongly dependent on their families for their care and protection, and on public policies to overcome marginalisation and social exclusion. This explains why well-targeted and child-sensitive policy interventions are so needed in our combined efforts to free children from poverty.

b) Between 1998 and 2003 there has been a significant decrease in the overall number of children below 15 years of age living in extreme poverty in the SEE/CIS region – from 32 to 18 million. At the same time, however, this decrease in absolute terms is partly explained by a dramatic demographic change and a sharp decline in the child population of 11 million.

In spite of a process of positive economic recovery, children who faced the highest risks at the start of the transition have not benefited evenly from economic growth and income poverty reduction. In fact:

- 1 in 4 children in the region still live in extreme poverty;
- regional children face higher risks of being poorer than adults – for example in Bulgaria and Romania, now members of the European Union, children are twice as likely to be poor as the rest of the population;
- disparities in child wellbeing have increased, both between countries and within countries, with widening gaps in access to and quality of social services.

c) Child poverty is also becoming more concentrated, and poor children are facing multiple deprivations. Indeed:

- child poverty is higher in the poorest countries in the region – in Central Asia, the Caucasus and in Moldova, more than 50 per cent of children live in poverty, a level up to 10 times higher than in some South Eastern European countries;
- child poverty is also higher in countries and regions where larger child populations live – in Tajikistan, children represent around half of the population, and the child poverty rate was 76 per cent in 2003;
- child poverty is more serious in rural areas,[1] where people's livelihoods are largely based on subsistence agriculture, there is limited access to social services of quality, and families can barely afford the costs of school materials, children's clothing and health services. In rural areas, children are less likely to attend pre-school or to benefit from access to water and clean fuel for cooking and heating, with dramatic consequences for the prevalence of children's respiratory diseases;
- child poverty is also more significant in large families; the risk of poverty increases according to the number of children in the household and particularly affects the younger children – in Russia this pattern is particularly steep, rising to 40 per cent or more among families with three or more children;
- closely linked with the family material poverty is the worrying level of child abandonment and the high number of children placed in institutions. In the Ukraine, for example, where more than 42,000 children were living in residential care at the end of 2006,[2] 80 per cent of the children in institutions are placed there as a result of their parents' poverty. This reality is linked to child stigmatisation and marginalisation, and has a dramatic damaging impact on child development;

---

[1] This is a pattern that also affects EU Member States: in Romania, extreme poverty rates are three times higher in rural areas (20%) than in urban areas (6%); in Lithuania, the rural population has a poverty risk 4 times higher than that experienced by people living in the capital city.

[2] At the end of 2006 in Ukraine, more than 42,000 children were living in residential care, constituting 0.5% of the child population; in Russia, children in residential care reached 1.3% of the child population.

- in some countries, poverty has also a dramatic impact on children belonging to ethnic minorities. In Bulgaria, although the Roma population constitutes less than 9 per cent of the total population, more than 60 per cent of children living in poverty are Roma. This group is over represented in residential care. The right to education for these children is also seriously compromised, with large numbers not attending compulsory school.[3] This group is further represented in high levels of repetition and dropouts.

d) Health and education are two essential dimensions of children's wellbeing and development, yet overall levels of public spending in health and education have remained low in the region. In some countries in Central Asia and the Caucasus, expenditure is less than 2 per cent of GDP on health. Despite recent economic growth, absolute levels of expenditure remain very low. These shortfalls have been compensated by rises in informal payments by households which further penalise the poorest and most disadvantaged families – in some cases, private expenditure amounts to 80 per cent of total health expenditure.

Cash support can play an important role in reducing income poverty and is particularly important in rural areas. Throughout the region, support to families with children is common. Unfortunately, however, this often happens in an indirect manner, through pensions. Moreover, social assistance schemes are often poorly targeted and levels of assistance are too low to offer children the protection from poverty they require.

Overcoming child poverty and reducing disadvantage and disparities are fundamental for advancing children's rights in this region. These strategies are also an investment towards meeting the development challenges ahead, to promote inclusive and democratic societies where every child can grow up to become all she or he can be.

3. CHILD POVERTY IN OECD COUNTRIES

During the 90s, child income relative poverty increased in the majority of OECD countries, and in a large number of EU Member States. This is shown by our research, and strongly confirmed by a very recent report issued by the European Union.[4]

---

[3] In Romania, in 2004, more than one fourth of Roma children were not attending compulsory schooling.
[4] Report issued by the Social Protection Committee on child poverty and wellbeing.

a) According to this EU report, not only are the numbers of children living in poverty high – at 19 million – but the percentage of those at risk of poverty is higher (at 19 per cent) than it is amongst the total population (at 16 per cent).[5]

The risk of poverty is particularly high for some groups of children, including those living in rural areas or placed in institutions, immigrant children, and children belonging to ethnic minorities, such as Roma children. These children access basic social services less often, and the services they access are of lower quality. They suffer deprivation in the present, and as they get older, it becomes increasingly likely that their lives will be marked by educational underachievement, poor health, low employment opportunities, and long-term welfare dependence.

b) There is wide variation of child poverty and deprivation within countries, as a result of the interplay of social, political, and market forces, but there are lessons to be learnt from policy approaches followed at the national level.

High government spending on family and social benefits has been clearly associated with low levels of child poverty. Indeed, no OECD country devoting 10 per cent or more of GDP to income transfers has a child poverty rate higher than 10 per cent. No country devoting less than 5 per cent of GDP to such benefits has a child poverty rate of less than 15 per cent.

But beyond the level of allocation, beyond the proportion of GDP, there is a difference in the way these allocations have been promoted. Indeed, the lowest levels of child poverty are to be found in countries where the highest support has been targeted at persons below the age of 18 – in particular those in low-income families – and in countries with the highest proportion of benefits allocated to pre-school children.

Government investment in early childhood services enables parents to take time off (up to a year) to be with their infants without drastically losing income or pension contributions, and allows mothers to go back to regular work with the certainty that their children are receiving quality care and education.

Early childhood services that stimulate the development of the child emotionally, socially, physically and verbally are particularly important to children in immigrant and other disadvantaged families. It enables these children to develop alongside their peers and to gain skills so that they benefit fully from schooling

---

[5] In almost half of the EU countries the risk of poverty for children is above 20%, in some close to 30%.

from day one. Investing in early childhood services helps to reduce the risk of discrimination, inequity and marginalisation, and, in turn, can help to break the intergenerational transmission of poverty. Early intervention contributes significantly to putting children from low income families on the path to development and success in school.

Internationally comparable data on government investment in early childhood services is instrumental in ensuring the best start in life for every child, and making sure that the opportunities of life are not determined by birth. Yet this data remains weak. For this reason, we are addressing this area, and we expect to release very soon a new Innocenti Study on countries' performance in the light of a proposed set of benchmarks on high quality early childhood education services.

c) These brief highlights are a clear indication of the importance of sound, reliable and accurate national and sub-national data systems for children.

To overcome child poverty, it is critical to promote transparent, regular and timely monitoring and analysis. This is also the call made by the Convention on the Rights of the Child, ratified by virtually all countries in the world.

The Convention advocates for the realisation of the human rights of all children at all ages, and promotes priority attention for those in greater need. Signatory governments made a commitment to promote the *progressive* improvement of children's living conditions and to mobilise *to their maximum extent* available resources for childhood policies.

This can only be achieved through effective national monitoring systems, required in order to acknowledge success, understand challenges, sharpen state accountability, mobilise public support, and inform the allocation of resources for children. Accurate data and strategic benchmarks are essential tools for this process.

Unfortunately, however, when child poverty is at stake, many challenges arise:

- on the one hand, monitoring and evaluation systems remain weak, hardly capturing the duration and persistence of social exclusion and its impact on child wellbeing. Data and analysis on vulnerable children is also limited and frequently unavailable, thus aggravating the invisibility of these children and reinforcing the likelihood of a persistent lack of sufficient attention paid to them in policy making. Available data is also insufficiently disaggregated by

age, gender or location, compromising opportunities to reduce disparities and overcome social exclusion;
- on the other hand, insufficient efforts have been made to assess the multi-dimensional facets of child deprivation. Child poverty is frequently considered through the lenses of income-related indicators only; no less importantly, children's experiences and perceptions of poverty, deprivation and exclusion are rarely taken into account. A child rights approach to child poverty will require a very different perspective.

d) Guided by these concerns, the Innocenti studies have attempted to capture the complexity of children's lives and relationships, and their evolving capacities and competencies, through the consideration of six dimensions:

- material wellbeing;
- health and safety;
- education;
- peer and family relations;
- behaviours and risks;
- young people's own subjective sense of wellbeing.

Anchored in the principle of the indivisibility and interrelationship of children's rights, this multi-dimensional approach considers areas where there is good data and information, such as health and education, together with innovative and qualitative dimensions of children's development, including parents' time and trust, friendship with peers, and children's own perception of satisfaction with life.

e) Guided by the principle of children's right to participation, our research is strongly informed by children's views and perspectives of poverty and exclusion. As a result, our Innocenti Report Card 2007 included a separate dimension on children's subjective assessments of wellbeing; and it also incorporated children's concerns and aspirations throughout the report, drawing upon qualitative and quantitative research and data sources informed by children's voices and experiences (e.g. reporting on low family affluence, relationships with family, and peers and bullying).

This is an area where priority efforts should be pursued. As we have confirmed through additional studies,[6] little is known about *what* poverty is experienced in the world of children and in their daily lives, *how* it is perceived, and *which* coping mechanisms are used to address it. Children are not simply passive victims

---

[6] E.g. in The Netherlands.

of the situations in which they grow up; nor are they a homogenous group. Only by listening to their voices and understanding their personal experiences and solutions through their own eyes will we be in a position to complement policies directed at reducing poverty and exclusion in improving the quality of lives of poor children.

4. LOOKING AHEAD

We are confident that the follow-up to these initiatives will inform future actions on child poverty, and that greater efforts will be made towards the utilisation of indicators on child wellbeing. With the work being done by a wide number of partners, there is a unique opportunity to promote a multi-dimensional approach to child poverty and acknowledge the critical relevance of children's views in the promotion of social inclusion.

We are also confident that the way forward will be shaped by important lessons we can draw from the overall process of implementation of the Convention on the Rights of the Child.

- firstly, no policy decision is neutral to children – indeed, each decision may have a negative impact on the enjoyment of children's rights, and at each and every occasion a positive difference can be made in their wellbeing;
- secondly, social progress can only be achieved when children's rights are high on the political agenda and addressed as a systematic and distinct concern;
- thirdly, improvements are only real when they affect the lives of the most vulnerable children – those at the bottom remain the real and most genuine indicators of social progress.

It is therefore, a question of accountability for children. Through our joint efforts, it can become a reality for all.

COMBATING CHILD POVERTY AND SOCIAL EXCLUSION IN EUROPEAN UNION COUNTRIES: LESSONS FOR POLICY AND PRACTICE

Professor Hugh FRAZER
Adjunct professor, National University of Ireland, Maynooth

1. INTRODUCTION

Reducing poverty and social exclusion and promoting greater social inclusion has been a key policy priority of the European Union (EU) since 2000. At the European Council in Lisbon in March 2000, the heads of state and government present established the EU Social Inclusion Process, the Open Method of Coordination (OMC) on poverty and social exclusion. The stated aim of this process was to make a decisive impact on the eradication of poverty by 2010.

The key elements of the EU's social inclusion OMC are:

- commonly agreed objectives;
- two yearly National Action Plans (NAPs/inclusion) prepared by each Member State as the means by which they work towards achieving the common objectives;
- a set of commonly agreed indicators on poverty and social exclusion to enable comparisons between member states and to support the exchange of learning;
- regular monitoring and reporting of progress.

The process has been supported by a community action programme on social exclusion which came into effect from January 2002,[1] and which, among other things, has funded the collection of data, the exchange of learning and good practice, thematic studies, conferences and seminars, networks of European organisations active in the fight against poverty, and awareness raising projects.[2]

---

[1] This has now been followed by a new Community action programme, The Community Programme for Employment and Social Solidarity, 2007–2013 (PROGRESS).
[2] For more information visit the European Commission's Social Protection and Social Inclusion website at http://ec.europa.eu/employment_social/spsi/the_process_en.htm. See also FRAZER (2007) and MARLIER et al. (2007).

Since 2001, consideration of child poverty and social exclusion has become an increasingly important part of the EU process. For instance, the issue has featured prominently in many member states' NAPs/inclusion and in the annual Joint Reports on Social Protection and Social Inclusion in the European Union. There has been a steadily growing number of thematic studies, transnational exchange projects, peer reviews, conferences and seminars which have focussed on the issue. Child poverty has been a key issue in the development of commonly agreed indicators for measuring poverty and social exclusion across the EU.

Several European poverty networks have focussed on the issue.[3]

The increasing importance of the issue of child poverty and social exclusion was reflected in the conclusions of the Spring 2006 European Council meeting of the Heads of State and Government. In endorsing new objectives and working arrangements for the OMC on Social Protection and Social Inclusion and in stressing the need to achieve a significant reduction in poverty and social exclusion by 2010, the Heads of State and Government asked *"the Member States to take necessary measures to rapidly and significantly reduce child poverty, giving all children equal opportunities, regardless of their social background"*.[4] The growing political importance of the issue received a further boost with the publication of a Commission Communication on the rights of the child, which gives particular attention to the issue of children's social inclusion and to the EU Social Inclusion Process.[5] The importance of the issue has been reiterated by the Council in 2007 and 2008.

In 2007 the issue of child poverty and social exclusion was made the special focus of the EU process for the year. This led to a series of important reports. Two in particular stand out. First, the report of a task-force on child poverty and child wellbeing which was established by the Social Protection Committee (SPC).[6] Secondly, the reports on child poverty and social inclusion for each member state and the overall synthesis report produced by the EU's Network of Independent Experts on Social Inclusion.[7]

---

[3] FRAZER (2006). Also visit the European Commission's Social Protection Social Inclusion website at http://ec.europa.eu/employment_social/spsi/child_poverty_en.htm.
[4] Council of the European Union, *Brussels European Council 23/24 March 2006, Presidency Conclusions.*
[5] EUROPEAN COMMISSION (2006).
[6] The SPC is the Committee made up of representatives of all Member States and the European Commission and is responsible for the EU's Social Protection and Social Inclusion process.
[7] FRAZER and MARLIER (2007).

This significant growth of interest in and concern about child poverty in the EU can be attributed to five main factors:

1. the data has shown that child poverty is a persistent and widely shared problem for the EU member states, with children being at greater risk of poverty than adults;
2. there has been a growing recognition that poverty is a threat to children's fundamental rights;
3. the ageing EU population has highlighted the need to maximise the EU's future human resources and thus to promote the wellbeing of children;
4. it is increasingly recognised that child poverty has long term negative consequences for economic and social development;
5. concern has grown that child poverty can impact negatively on long-term political and social solidarity.

The result of this increased interest in the issue of child poverty and social exclusion, and of all the work that has gone on since 2000, is that we now know a lot more about the issue of child poverty and social exclusion in the European Union, and in particular about the policies and programmes that work best to prevent and reduce the problem. This paper pulls together some of the key learning points from this experience.

2. EXTENT AND NATURE OF CHILD POVERTY

An important element in the EU's approach to preventing and tackling child poverty and social exclusion has been to try and better understand the nature of the problem, and who are the children most at risk. Child poverty emerges in the EU as a complex and multi-faceted issue. There are three main underlying elements. Firstly, there is inadequate income as result of lack of decent employment and inadequate income support systems. Secondly, poor children suffer from poor access to essential services and necessities such as decent housing, a safe environment, and access to health care, social services, childcare and transport. Thirdly, their opportunities for personal development are curtailed by inadequate educational opportunities and limited opportunities to participate in normal social, sporting, recreational and cultural activities.

These key underlying elements are often compounded by other factors, and this can lead to more extreme situations. For instance, discrimination against children from immigrant and ethnic minority backgrounds, especially Roma children, or children with disabilities, can deepen poverty and social exclusion. Gender inequalities can worsen the situation of some children. Violence and exploitation, such as domestic violence, trafficking, sexual exploitation and child labour, endanger some children. Children living in or leaving institutions are particularly vulnerable. Then there are children affected by crime and alcohol or drug abuse. Problems can also be compounded by social isolation, whether living in an isolated rural area with few facilities or living in an urban ghetto with multiple social problems and cut off from mainstream society.

Two other key features stand out from the EU experience. The first is that many of the problems described are interconnected and lead to multiple deprivation. Secondly, poverty is intergenerational – children who are poor tend to have poor parents and, they, in their turn, have a greater risk of having children who will grow up in poverty.

In the EU poverty is generally measured as a relative concept. Children (and adults) are considered to be at risk of poverty when they fall below a poverty line of 60 per cent of median income. However, the different value of that poverty line in different countries, the distance below the line that children fall (i.e. the intensity of poverty) and the length of time spent below the line all need to be taken into account. Increasingly there is also an effort to combine relative income poverty lines with the measurement of lack of basic necessities, known as "consistent" poverty. The risk of child poverty across the EU as a whole is 19 per cent, but this varies from 9 per cent to 29 per cent across the 27 member states. What is striking is that the countries where the problem is greatest numerically also tend to be those where the problem is most severe. For consistent poverty, the range is from 3 per cent to 25 per cent.[8]

The main groups of children at risk of poverty in the EU are children living in lone parent households (35% are at risk) and in large households of 3 or more children (25% are at risk). There is also a very strong correlation between child poverty and jobless households and, increasingly, a high risk of poverty when parents are in low paid and insecure employment. There is also evidence of high risk among children from an ethnic minority and immigrant background. EU evidence also suggests that some children are at risk of more extreme poverty. These include children living in and leaving institutions, children with a disability, victims of violence, abuse and trafficking, unaccompanied migrant children, Roma children, children forced into child labour, children with parents working abroad, and homeless/street children.

---

[8] EUROPEAN COMMISSION (2008).

3. SIX PRECONDITIONS FOR EFFECTIVE ACTION

Looking at experience across the EU and identifying the countries that are most successful in developing effective policies to prevent and reduce child poverty, one can identify six conditions for effective action.

3.1. POLITICAL PRIORITY AND PUBLIC SUPPORT

The first requirement is that there must be a high level of political priority and public support for policies to ensure the wellbeing of children. This means making children and families in general a central concern of government and making child poverty in particular a political priority. The countries that do best in the EU are those member states that have had long-term inclusive policies aimed at supporting all children and families. These are the countries which, in effect, have largely prevented child poverty and social exclusion arising, and in which child poverty levels are lowest. There is a growing body of evidence of effective arrangements used by member states to ensure that there is consistent political priority and leadership on the social inclusion of children. For instance:

- promoting the inclusion of children or the eradication of child poverty can be included as a specific goal or priority in a country's programme for government, or in key policy documents like National Development Plans;
- a minister can be appointed with particular responsibility for co-ordinating and developing policies in relation to children;
- a political commitment can be made to develop a strategy for children.

3.2. MOBILISATION OF ALL ACTORS

The second requirement is that all relevant actors need to be mobilised to participate in the efforts to improve the situation of children. Central and local government agencies have a key role to play. Non-governmental organisations (NGOs) working with children play a key role both in ensuring that experience on the ground and the voices of poor parents and children are taken into account in the development of policies and programmes and in delivering services. Social partners, both employers and trade unions, play an important role, particularly when it comes to increasing employment opportunities and ensuring decent income for parents. Academics contribute to analysis and better understanding and monitoring of policies. It is also important to develop partnership arrangements which enable the efforts of all these actors to be mutually reinforcing.

3.3. COMMITMENT TO CHILDREN'S RIGHTS

The third precondition is that there should be a commitment to children's rights and to non-discrimination. In this regard the UN Convention on the Rights of the Child provides a very important framework. There are several reasons for this:

- it puts the needs of the child at the centre of policy making;
- it puts the focus on addressing the specific needs of the child here and now, and not just on improving the position of their families and the communities in which they live;
- it provides a useful framework for developing a comprehensive strategy to prevent and reduce child poverty;
- it combines a mixture of survival rights, development rights, protection rights and participation rights;
- it puts the focus on the best interests of the child and on accountability and responsibility of both national authorities and families to ensure this;
- it puts a focus on the importance of adopting and enforcing strong legislation against discrimination as an essential element in preventing and reducing poverty and social exclusion;
- it recognises the role of the family in promoting the wellbeing of the child;
- it promotes respect for the views of children and their participation.

The EU countries that tend to do best on child poverty combine their efforts to tackle poverty and their efforts to promote children's rights.[9]

3.4. EFFECTIVE MAINSTREAMING AND COORDINATION

The fourth precondition is that arrangements should be in place to ensure that the goal of child wellbeing and social inclusion is mainstreamed and coordinated across government. This means, first, integrating a concern with the wellbeing and social inclusion of children into all relevant areas of policy-making including budgetary decision-making. Secondly it involves establishing arrangements to ensure political and administrative coordination across different policy domains and between different levels of governance (national, regional, local) and to avoid policy fragmentation. Thirdly, it means putting in place arrangements to coordinate the efforts of all stakeholders. Practical approaches to mainstreaming that can be identified from the EU experience include:

---

[9] FERNANDES (2007).

- requiring all ministries to include promoting social inclusion in general, or the social inclusion of children in particular, into the objectives of their ministry;
- appointing an official in each ministry who is responsible for social inclusion issues;
- requiring all policies to be proofed before they are adopted for their potential impact on the social inclusion of children and/or on children generally, and also monitoring their impact subsequently;
- creating a committee of the cabinet to ensure political coordination;
- creating a high-level committee of senior officials to regularly review progress and to link a strategy on child poverty or social inclusion with other key national strategies and programmes;
- making child poverty a key priority in the annual budgetary process;
- creating a committee or working group of officials from all ministries to meet regularly to prepare a strategic approach, oversee its implementation, and ensure that it is monitored and evaluated. In some countries this may also include representatives from regional and local government, social partners, NGOs and experts.

3.5. STRATEGIC APPROACH BASED ON CLEAR OBJECTIVES

The fifth requirement is that government must be committed to developing a strategic approach based on clear objectives. A consistent message emerging from the EU's social inclusion process in relation to all aspects of tackling poverty and social exclusion is the importance of member states setting clear objectives and priorities backed up by concrete quantified targets for its reduction. For instance, the European Commission's 2005 Report on Social Inclusion in the then 10 new member states concluded that strategic plans "need to be coherent and logically planned: they should move from a thorough analysis of the situation and identification of the key social inclusion challenges to the establishment of clear priorities with long and short term objectives." The report goes on to say that "concrete targets need to be set: effective strategic planning requires establishing clear targets that need to be achieved if significant progress is to be made towards the overall goal of eradicating poverty".[10]

A number of arguments can be identified for setting clear quantified targets for reducing child poverty and social exclusion. They provide a significant political statement of purpose and ambition in terms of eradicating child poverty that can lead to increased and sustained policy effort. They provide a goal against which to

---

[10] EUROPEAN COMMISSION (2005).

measure progress and thus a means of creating a dynamic process characterised by openness and accountability. They are a tool for promoting awareness of the strategy and thus for encouraging and mobilizing all actors to support it. They provide a focal point around which to concentrate the efforts of policy makers and practitioners.

3.6. GOOD DATA AND ANALYSIS

The final precondition is the availability of good quality data and in depth analysis of the situation of children in a country. This is essential for identifying problems, developing policy responses, and monitoring the impact of policies and programmes over time. Data must be multidimensional – that is to say it must cover more than just income and examine all the different facets of children's lives. As well as major national studies on the situation of children there is a need for specific studies of very vulnerable groups as they are often not covered (or are covered in insufficient detail) in large national surveys. It is very important to collect data on trends over time. Breaking down data on children by different age groups gives a more nuanced picture and is necessary for effective policy development. Taking into account children's own experience and perceptions is also important. The EU experience has also highlighted the value of trans-national comparisons, both in highlighting significant differences and in helping to understand better what policies work best.

4. A COMPREHENSIVE POLICY FRAMEWORK

It is clear from the nature of child poverty and social exclusion and from recent EU experience that there is no single solution to child poverty. A multidimensional, comprehensive, joined-up policy approach and coordinated delivery are necessary to address the complexity of the issue. The SPC's recent report concluded that:

> "Member states who are most successful at preventing child poverty and social exclusion are those who have developed policy frameworks which combine increasing access to adequately paid work for parents with ensuring effective income support for all families with children and increasing access to key enabling services (child care, education, housing, health and social services, etc.)."[11]

Overall, the EU experience suggests that a comprehensive approach should have four interrelated aspects: ensuring an adequate income; improving access to services; ensuring care and protection; and promoting participation of children.

---

[11] EUROPEAN COMMISSION (2008).

4.1. ADEQUATE INCOME

Ensuring an adequate income has three main aspects. First, there are policies to increase the access of parents (especially women) to employment, with particular emphasis on parents in jobless households and lone parents. There is a need for a comprehensive and well-developed policy package which aims at making work accessible through a broad range of policies which meet the differing needs of different families. In particular it is important to have a mix of policies which allows for effective family-work combination and which aims to increase employment of both parents. Special attention needs to be given to increasing and supporting the participation of mothers in paid work. This involves developing policies which facilitate the reconciliation of work and family life through more flexible working and the provision of accessible and affordable day care. It means developing training and activation measures which are particularly targeted at key groups such as parents in jobless households and lone parents. It can involve providing incentives to employers to encourage the employment of these parents.

The second aspect of ensuring an adequate income is making sure that work pays for parents and generates an income that is sufficient to lift them and their families out of poverty. Key policy approaches used by EU member states include minimum wages, allowing parents to retain benefits for a period on moving into work, providing in-work benefits, reducing employment traps, prioritising tax relief towards families with children, reducing costs associated with employment such as child care and transport, raising skill levels so that parents can aspire to better paid jobs, and reducing irregularity of employment.

The third dimension is providing adequate income support to families with children. The importance of social transfers in reducing child poverty in the EU is highlighted in the SPC's recent report.[12] On average in the EU, social transfers other than pensions reduce the risk of poverty for children by 44 per cent, which is a higher impact than for the overall population (38%). However, there is a very wide variation across countries. In Sweden, Finland and Denmark social transfers (other than pensions) reduce the risk of poverty for children by more than 60 per cent, whereas in Bulgaria, Greece and Spain this reduction is less than 20 per cent. It is clear from this report that in most cases the countries with the lowest child poverty rates are those who spend most on social benefits (excluding pensions).

---

[12] EUROPEAN COMMISSION (2008).

4.2. ACCESS TO SERVICES

Across the European Union, access to basic services emerges as a key element in the development of policies to promote the social inclusion of children. This is seen as particularly important in order to combat the negative consequences of poverty on the child's development, and to empower children. Key areas are housing, health care, education and transport.

Ensuring decent housing and a safe environment is seen as essential for the wellbeing and personal development of children. Among strategies highlighted by member states to improve the housing situation of families with children are the following: eradicating slum areas; subsidising more social housing; promoting more efficient use of land; developing measures to prevent the eviction of children from their homes; reducing the number of households in temporary accommodation; and providing temporary shelters for families with children who have lost their homes.

Given that children born into low-income families are more likely to experience unhealthy lifestyles and have poorer access to health services, it is not surprising that policies which aim to overcome health inequalities and increase access to health care are widely seen as an important aspect of tackling child poverty. Ways in which member states try to increase access to health services for children and their families include: developing preventive care such as prenatal and health care for young children; providing antenatal services for vulnerable pregnant mothers; ensuring regular check-ups of children and free maternity and child clinics; developing health-centres targeted at young children and their mothers; promoting health at schools (for example, by having health staff in schools who offer vaccinations, provide dental care, give advice on mental health, provide information on substance misuse, contribute to sexual education and health and promote healthy eating habits); providing more and better information on services available; training staff to work in multi-cultural environments; and taking special initiatives to assist immigrants and ethnic minorities to access health services.

Many member states prioritise developing inclusive education systems which counter and prevent educational disadvantage as key to reducing levels of child poverty and to breaking the intergenerational inheritance of poverty and disadvantage. Four themes emerge particularly strongly from the work of the social inclusion process. These are:

1. the importance of developing early childhood education and development services;
2. the need to develop strategies to tackle school dropout and educational disadvantage;
3. the importance of integrating minorities (i.e. ethnic minorities, migrants, children with a disability) in the school system;
4. reducing costs and financial barriers to participating in education.[13]

The importance of access to affordable transport is highlighted several times in the EU's annual Joint Reports on Social Protection and Social Inclusion. For instance, the 2005 report noted that access to affordable transport is often "critical to accessing jobs for people who are unemployed, to enable vulnerable people to access basic services and to facilitate participation in social and cultural life." Transport becomes especially important in the context of child poverty, as access to affordable and efficient transport is a key consideration both in making it economically worthwhile for parents to work, and in allowing flexible working and thus the reconciliation of work and family responsibilities. However, access to affordable transport is also seen as important in terms of enabling families with children to access essential services, enabling children to take part in social, sporting and cultural activities, and overcoming social isolation, especially in remote rural areas. A particular issue is also the availability of suitably adapted transport to enable children with disabilities to access services and social activities.

4.3. ENSURING CARE AND PROTECTION

The third group of policies necessary for a comprehensive approach is that of effective child protection systems and social services which protect children vulnerable as a result of adverse parenting practices, such as maltreatment, neglect, sexual abuse, drugs and alcohol, mental health problems or other reasons. There is a growing importance given in many Member States to developing social services so as to ensure high levels of social protection for vulnerable children, particularly at local level. In particular, there is an emphasis in many countries on ensuring better standards, improving local coordination, and increasing early intervention.

---

[13]   FRAZER and MARLIER (2007).

An important theme in the European process is the need to move away from institutionalised provision and to put more focus onto families and care in the community. This is especially, but not exclusively, evident in several of the newer central and eastern European member states. However, sometimes the best interests of a child make this impossible. In such situations it is important to have good systems for taking children into care. There is a clear recognition that wherever possible children should be placed with foster families rather than in institutions.

The key role played by social services in working for children's welfare and wellbeing, and empowering them and their families and carers to overcome poverty and marginalisation, is particularly well presented by one of the key European-level networks of organisations fighting against poverty and social exclusion. This is the European Social Network (ESN)[14], funded by the European Commission as part of the Social Inclusion Process.

4.4. PROMOTING PARTICIPATION

The fourth key element of a comprehensive approach to promoting the social inclusion and wellbeing of children is that they be given opportunities to participate in the same social, recreational, sporting and cultural activities as their peers. This is essential to ensure their personal development and their active inclusion in society.

Having access to sporting and recreational opportunities is increasingly being recognised as an essential element in anti-poverty strategies. It promotes participation in social life, personal development and better health.

The importance of increasing access to culture was highlighted in the findings of a thematic study on access to culture funded under the Commission's community action programme on social exclusion.[15] This noted that participation in cultural activities can contribute to the social inclusion of young people in several ways. For instance, it can help them to build their skills and self-confidence. It can enhance their self-esteem and identity. It can promote respect for cultural diversity and counter discrimination. Thus policies which increase the access of young people at high risk of poverty and social exclusion from such activities are particularly important.

---

[14] EUROPEAN SOCIAL NETWORK (2007).
[15] WOODS et al. (2005).

4.5. THREE CROSS-CUTTING THEMES

In developing a comprehensive policy framework there are three themes that recur regularly across EU member states. These are: the importance of early intervention; the need to balance universal and targeted approaches; and the need to balance prevention and alleviation.

The emphasis on early intervention stresses the importance of ensuring the best start in life for every child by combining early education with childcare, health and family support services, parental outreach, and employment advice for disadvantaged families. It also recognises that initiatives taken early in life are much more likely to be effective and have long lasting effects. They are thus a cost-effective investment.

A recurring theme in the EU process has been the need for a balanced approach. This involves: balancing a focus on prevention and on alleviation, and balancing universal provision for all children with some targeted measures for those at great risk. The 2007 national reports produced by the EU Network of National Experts on Social Inclusion demonstrated that most member states seem to combine both universal and preventative policies with more targeted policies aimed at alleviating poverty and the social exclusion of children. However, the balance between the two varies significantly across member states.

As regards balancing a universal and targeted approach, the evidence suggests that the most successful member states are those that adopt a predominantly universal approach based on a strong belief in preventing problems arising and ensuring equal opportunities for all children, backed up as necessary by targeted policies to address particular extreme situations – a sort of tailored universalism. While there may be pressure in member states with the most severe problems to focus on alleviation, it is nevertheless true that the structural nature of the phenomenon makes it urgent to combat poverty and social exclusion under a more preventative approach as well.

5. EFFECTIVE DELIVERY

The EU social inclusion process has mainly focussed on analysing and monitoring the extent and nature of child poverty and social exclusion, and identifying the main policy areas that impact on them. However, it has been increasingly recognised that having the right policies and programmes is not sufficient if they are not delivered effectively, and a growing body of learning is emerging about the effective delivery of policies. There is a growing body of experience from the various projects and studies supported as part of the EU process as to how best to ensure effective delivery. Six aspects of successful methods particularly stand out:

- promoting partnership and participation;
- emphasising the local dimension;
- ensuring continuity;
- being flexible and responsive;
- adopting a community development approach;
- undertaking regular monitoring and evaluation.

5.1. PARTNERSHIP, NETWORKING AND PARTICIPATION

Partnership, dialogue and participation at local levels are important as they help with the identification of problems and disadvantaged groups, lead to better targeting of social assistance, and help to activate and empower people experiencing poverty and social exclusion. One project supported as part of the EU process summarised the importance of a partnership and networking approach rather succinctly. It identified five levels of action in networking:

1. identification of problems;
2. participation of the people concerned (i.e. poor children and their parents);
3. need-oriented services that intervene early and involve committed volunteers;
4. identification with the community;
5. shaping public opinion.[16]

The development of partnership and networking structures can also be a key way of ensuring the participation of those experiencing poverty and social exclusion in the development and delivery of social inclusion policies and programmes.

5.2. THE LOCAL DIMENSION

Focussing on the local level is important because support needs to be close to where people are, and needs to be coordinated and integrated at point of delivery. For effective delivery, it is also vital to involve local actors in the preparation, implementation and monitoring of plans. It is also clear that if there are to be

---

[16] Report of a transnational exchange project: A Lobby for Children.

effective interventions, it is necessary to define clearly the roles and responsibilities of different levels of governance, and ensure that they are mutually reinforcing.

5.3. CONTINUITY

People's situations vary. Some families and children may only need particular help and assistance intermittently or in the short term, whereas others will need longer-term and consistent support which fosters their personal growth and development over time. Thus it is important to ensure that services are developed with a long-term perspective, and that, when necessary, they can provide support over time.

5.4. FLEXIBLE AND TAILORED RESPONSES

Services need to be delivered in ways that respond to the needs of each child and their family. In other words, they need to be flexible and delivered in a way that is tailored to meet their particular needs. They need to offer people real pathways for progressing out of poverty and towards greater social inclusion, in a manner and at a pace that is appropriate to their situation.

5.5. A COMMUNITY DEVELOPMENT APPROACH

A recurring theme is the importance of a community development approach which delivers policies and programmes in ways which empower people and avoid stigmatising them. The main arguments for a community development approach are that it can:

- contribute significantly to strengthening the quality of community life in disadvantaged communities, by promoting strong family, social and community networks and a healthy infrastructure of community and voluntary organisations;
- empower parents and children who are at risk of exclusion and isolation;
- help parents and children to act together to change their situation, and to work together with others to overcome such barriers to their active participation in society as poverty, lack of access to resources, rights, goods and services, and discrimination.

5.6. REGULAR MONITORING AND EVALUATION

The important contribution of monitoring and evaluation to effective delivery of policies and programmes has gained increasing prominence as the EU process has developed. This was particularly evident at the Luxembourg Presidency conference on *Taking Forward the EU Social Inclusion Process,* and in the subsequent publication by E. Marlier et al. (2007).[17] More particularly, the issue of monitoring and evaluation in relation to child poverty was a key subject for the SPC Task Force on child poverty and wellbeing.[18] Effective monitoring and evaluation are seen as key both to encouraging continuous improvement in performance, and to ensuring accountability.

Key elements of effective monitoring and evaluation that can be identified from the EU process include the following:

1. having clear objectives and targets;
2. setting appropriate and multi-dimensional indicators;
3. ensuring the availability of good quality data;
4. establishing good links between the policy and research communities;
5. involving all relevant actors, especially organisations working with children and children themselves;
6. establishing a focus on the link between specific policy measures and outcomes (i.e. impact assessments);
7. reporting regularly on findings.

6. CONCLUSION

In summing up all the learning that has emerged from the EU's social inclusion process, five essential actions stand out as critical if countries are to develop effective strategies to prevent and eradicate child poverty.

1. Firstly, make the social inclusion of all children and the reduction of child poverty a priority political goal, and establish institutional arrangements for mainstreaming and coordinating policy efforts to promote the social inclusion of children across all policy domains and in all key policy documents. In doing so, invest in building the capacity of national, regional and local administrations to deliver policies in a co-ordinated manner, on

---

[17] MARLIER et al. (2007).
[18] EUROPEAN UNION (2008).

the ground, in partnership with children living in poverty, their parents, and the organisations that work with them.
2. Secondly, develop effective income support schemes that will guarantee that all families with children have an income sufficient to live life with decency and that will ensure their personal development. In working towards this, first focus on raising the incomes of those who are in acute poverty and those at risk of being in long-term poverty.
3. Thirdly, assist the transition to work for unemployed parents with young children and those parenting alone, through a combination of education and employment measures, affordable and accessible childcare, and income support. Give especial attention to those experiencing extreme and long-term poverty.
4. Fourthly, increase the access of children living in poverty to essential services (especially housing, child care, health services, family and social services and education), so as to ensure their wellbeing and personal development. Give particular priority to intervening early to support children and families in acute poverty and at risk of living in persistent poverty.
5. Fifthly, ensure that there is effective legislation in place to promote children's rights and counter discrimination against children and families from ethnic minorities (especially the Roma), and promote their inclusion in mainstream society; and that appropriate institutional arrangements are in place to enforce anti-discrimination legislation.

At the end of the day, preventing and reducing child poverty is an essential task for all countries. It is an investment not only in the rights and wellbeing of children, but in the human and social capital of a nation and thus its future economic, social and cultural wellbeing. Child poverty and exclusion will not disappear without well-planned and coherent strategies to promote the inclusion of children. Progress involves making a conscious choice to prioritise and invest in children and their families.

7. REFERENCES

European Commission (2005). *Report on Social Inclusion 2005: An analysis of the National Action Plans on Social Inclusion (2004–2006) submitted by the 10 New Member States*, Brussels.

European Commission (2006). *Communication from the Commission: Towards an EU Strategy on the Rights of the Child*, July 2006.

European Commission (2008). *Social Protection Committee, Child Poverty and Wellbeing in the EU: current status and way forward.*

European Social Network (2007). *Child Poverty and Welfare in Europe: the message from Social Services*, ESN, Brighton.

Fernandes, R. (2007). *A child rights approach to child poverty*, Eurochild, Brussels.

Frazer, H. (2007). *Promoting Social Inclusion: the EU Dimension*, in *Administration*, Institute of Public Administration, Dublin, 2007.

Frazer, H. (2006). *Lessons learned on child poverty: Why and how to tackle child poverty*, UNICEF Regional Office for CEE/CIS/Baltics, Geneva.

Frazer, H. and Marlier, E. (2007). *Tackling child poverty and promoting the social inclusion of children in the EU: Key lessons*, European Commission.

Marlier, E., Atkinson, A., Cantillon, B. and Nolan, B. (2007). *The EU and Social Inclusion: Facing the Challenges*, The Policy Press, Bristol.

National University of Ireland (2008). *A comparative study of policies to tackle and prevent poverty and social exclusion among children*. An ongoing research project.

Woods, R., Dobbs, L., Gordon, C., Moore, C. and Simpson, G. (2005). *Report of a thematic study using transnational comparisons to analyse and identify cultural policies and programmes that contribute to preventing and reducing poverty and social exclusion*, European Commission, Brussels.

TACKLING CHILD POVERTY: LESSONS FROM INDIA

Professor A.K. Shiva Kumar
Development Economist and Adviser to UNICEF India

1. INTRODUCTION

India's growth story has become a topic of great interest across the world. The country's Gross Domestic Product (GDP) grew by 5.5 per cent per annum between 1997 and 2002, and by 7.2 per cent per annum between 2002 and 2007. Over the next five years, projections are that GDP growth rate will average between 8–10 per cent per annum.[1] There are rising expectations that these high rates of economic growth will soon catapult India into the orbit of developed nations. At the same time, there is increasing recognition that whether or not this happens will depend on the extent to which India's people – especially women, children and the poor – benefit from economic expansion.

The way we ought to view benefits or human progress has been greatly influenced by the idea of human development. In the human development framework, progress is evaluated by focusing not merely on an expansion of incomes, but on the widening of people's choices, an enhancement of freedoms, an expansion of capabilities, and an assurance of human rights.[2] A direct implication of adopting the human development framework is to redefine notions of equality and poverty. Human development is concerned not narrowly with inequalities in the distribution of incomes or assets, but more substantively with inequalities in the distribution of opportunities – economic, social, political and cultural – between regions, among women and men, and across communities. Similarly, human development is concerned not narrowly with poverty as income deprivation, but with human poverty or the poverty of opportunities. In other words, human poverty is multidimensional capability-deprivation, and so insufficient incomes, illiteracy, malnutrition, ill-health, lack of freedom to participate in public decision

---

[1] Planning Commission (2006).
[2] For a comprehensive set of readings on human development, see Fukuda-Parr and Kumar (2006).

making, discrimination and unequal treatment are seen as manifestations of human poverty. Human poverty is a denial of freedoms and a violation of rights. In the final analysis, therefore, tackling human poverty is a concern with human dignity.

The Constitution of India, like that of many other nations, embodies significant pledges to promote human rights. And this commitment has resulted in the formulation of several policies to promote the rights of children as well. India, for instance, ratified the Convention on the Rights of the Child in 1992, and formulated a new National Plan of Action for Children in 2005 that comprehensively commits itself to "ensure *all* rights to *all* children up to the age of 18 years".

India is home to the largest single population in the world of children under the age of 18 – nearly 450 million of them. Few nations in the world have such a youthful population. It is the demographic advantage of such a large young population on which India is gearing up to capitalise in the coming years.

In this paper, I begin by commenting on how far India has fulfilled its commitment to children. I then identify critical linkages that need to be strengthened if economic expansion is to translate better into improved conditions for children. And I conclude with some reflections and policy lessons that we can draw from the Indian experience.

2. INDIA AND SUB-SAHARAN AFRICA

Before commenting on India, it is worthwhile noting that there is much that India can share with and learn from Africa in matters of advancing child rights. There are many Indians, and I suspect a large number of Africans too, who, mesmerised by India's recent economic expansion, believe that India is doing much better than sub-Saharan Africa along most dimensions of development. After all, India has not been as badly affected in recent times by droughts and famines, HIV/AIDS, wars and conflicts – though we do have our fair share of these tragedies as well.

At first glance, India appears to do much better than sub-Saharan Africa, especially in matters of life and death. India's life expectancy (64 years) exceeds that of sub-Saharan Africa, where it has dropped to just 50 years, reflecting the tragic onslaught of the AIDS epidemic. India also does better when it comes to child survival. The infant mortality rate (IMR) in sub-Saharan Africa is 95 per 1000 live births; it is 58 in India.

If we look more closely, however, we find that India and sub-Saharan Africa have much in common as well.[3] The neonatal mortality rates are almost identical: 43 in India and 44 in sub-Saharan Africa. Sanitation coverage is similar. Some 33 per cent of India's population is using adequate sanitation facilities; the proportion is 37 per cent for sub-Saharan Africa. Women have similar access to maternal health care. Around 43 per cent of deliveries are attended to by a skilled birth attendant in sub-Saharan Africa; it is 47 per cent in India. The proportion of institutional deliveries is not very different: 41 per cent in India and 36 per cent in sub-Saharan Africa. And in 2006, India reported a per capita Gross National Income (GNI) of USD 820 – not very different from sub-Saharan Africa's GNI per capita of USD 851.

At the same time, there are critical dimensions in which India fares worse than sub-Saharan Africa. Let me point to three.

The first has to do with child malnutrition. Whereas 28 per cent of children under-five in sub-Saharan Africa are moderately and severely underweight, the proportion in India is 43 per cent.

The second has to do with the position of women in society. Strong anti-female biases persist in India, much more so than in sub-Saharan Africa. The systematic discrimination against Indian girls and women is reflected most acutely in the adverse female-to-male ratio: according to the Census of India 2001, there were just 933 women per 1,000 men in India's population. The situation was worse among children 0–6 years, in which group there were only 927 girls for 1,000 boys.

And third, it is worth noting that sub-Saharan Africa does better than India on some dimensions of public health affecting the lives of children. For instance, whereas 72 per cent of 1-year-old children are immunised against measles in sub-Saharan Africa, the proportion is much less – 59 per cent – in India.

It is true that looking at average accomplishments of sub-Saharan Africa masks the achievements and failures of individual countries – but a similar argument can be made for India as well, where national averages hide large inter-state differentials.

Indeed, there are many geographical, cultural, environmental, social and historical differences between India and Africa that impact on children's

---

[3] Comparative data on India and sub-Saharan Africa reported in this section have been taken from UNICEF (2007).

wellbeing. But circumstantially, the recent growth spurt places Africa in a position similar to what India faced a decade or so ago. And to that extent, examining how effectively India has translated growth into improved wellbeing of children can offer several valuable lessons for African and other nations.

3. THE INDIAN EXPERIENCE

India has been experiencing unprecedented vibrancy along many fronts, especially after the initiation of economic reforms in the early 1990s. Incomes have risen rapidly. The average per capita income of an Indian has nearly doubled since 1991. Parents are better educated and have better access to information, technology and facilities. Child survival has improved, and an Indian born today can expect to live 4 years longer than a child born in 1991. Primary school enrolment and attendance rates have been rising steadily for both boys and girls. Access to drinking water has improved. Unprecedented changes taking place in media and information technology are significantly improving awareness and public administration. Women have gained along many fronts, most notably in terms of their increased participation in the political process following the enactment of the Constitutional amendments in the early 1990s that reserved one-third of seats in local elections for women. Rapid transformation has occurred – and continues to occur – in centre-state relations, with the states enjoying greater fiscal autonomy and political decision making authority. Decentralisation has been further accelerated by local governments (called *Panchayats*), which have gradually assumed administrative responsibilities in most states. At the same time, vibrant women's groups, active non-governmental organisations and articulate community level groups are transforming power relations at the community level, within the household and in the public domain.

And yet we find that child rights in India are far from universal. Serious gaps exist. Take the case of child health and nutrition. The most recent data from the National Family Health Survey of 2005–06 reveal that, in India[4]:

- nearly 46 per cent of children under three years are underweight;
- close to 79 per cent of the children between 6 to 35 months of age are anaemic;
- only 43.5 per cent of children 12–23 months are fully immunised with BCG, measles, and three doses each of polio and DPT;

---

[4] Data are from Indian Institute of Population Sciences (2007).

- almost 45 per cent of women 20–24 years old were married before the legal age of 18 years;
- only 48 per cent of deliveries were attended by a skilled health worker.

Given India's large population size, these proportions translate into huge numbers. For instance, there are almost 11.5 million children in India who are not fully immunised, and 55 million children who are underweight. Over 1.5 million infants die every year from illnesses that are avoidable. In basic education too, there are large gaps to fill. Several millions of children can barely read and write, even after spending 5–8 years in school; and many girls in particular still lack equal opportunities to access good quality basic education.

At the same time, not easily captured in conventional statistics is the plight of several millions of children needing special protection: those needing early childhood care; adolescent girls; child labourers; children facing the threat of sexual exploitation, violence, HIV/AIDS and trafficking; and those affected by conflict and disasters. Similarly, fulfilling the rights of children with various disabilities has not received the priority it warrants.

Apart from the huge backlog of deprivations in the lives of children, many forms of inequalities persist. The Indian state of Kerala, for instance, reports an IMR of 14 – similar to that of many developed countries. On the other hand, Madhya Pradesh reports an IMR of 76. Similarly, whereas over 80 per cent of children are fully immunised in Tamil Nadu, the proportion is barely 25 per cent in Rajasthan and Uttar Pradesh. Again, large rural-urban differentials can be noticed across the country. For instance, while the urban IMR is 40, India's rural IMR, at 64 deaths per 1000 live births, is 60 per cent higher.[5] Girls also face several disadvantages: the death rate among girls aged 1–4 years, for example, exceeds by nearly 30 per cent that of boys in the same age group.

We can make three important observations based on the Indian experience.

Firstly, the Indian experience illustrates that economic growth and all-round prosperity do not automatically translate into improvements in the lives of children. India's progress in advancing the wellbeing of children has been extremely slow. For instance, over the most recent seven-year period, between

---

5   Office of the Registrar General (2006).

1998–99 and 2005–06 (coinciding with impressive economic expansion), we find, for instance, that:[6]

- the proportion of under-weight children under three years fell marginally from 47 to 46 per cent;
- the proportion of fully immunised children aged 12–23 months went up marginally from 42 to 44 per cent;
- the proportion of deliveries assisted by a health professional went up from 42 to 49 per cent.

In fact, the proportion of fully immunised children in urban India fell marginally from 61 per cent in 1998–1999 to 57 per cent in 2005–2006, suggesting once again that growing urban affluence is not sufficient for advancing child rights.

Secondly, the Indian experience suggests that reductions in income poverty do not also automatically translate into reductions in child poverty. Income poverty has fallen sharply in India. In 1973–74, more than half (55 per cent) of India's population lived below the poverty line. By 2000, the proportion had fallen to 26 per cent. In other words, from one out of every two being poor in the mid-1970s, the proportion came down to one in four; and in 2005, the proportion of poor was one in five.[7] Despite this impressive reduction in income poverty, we find, for instance, that 46 per cent of children under three are still underweight. To give another example, according to the Delhi Human Development Report 2006, Delhi is one of the richest Indian states in terms of per capita income, and only 8 per cent of Delhi's population lives below the poverty line. Despite this, nearly 35 per cent of children in the state are underweight.[8] These illustrations go to show that both income expansion and income poverty reduction do not automatically mean improved wellbeing of children.

Thirdly, economic progress and improved literacy have not necessarily resulted in better conditions for Indian girls. Greater freedoms and empowerment of women are well recognised for their positive impact on the wellbeing of children. There is strong evidence, for instance, of the beneficial impact of women's education and literacy on infant mortality, nutrition and health-seeking behaviour. However, we find that rapid economic expansion and improved literacy among both women and men have not necessarily had a favourable impact on discrimination against the girl child in India. This is reflected in the declining female-to-male ratio

---

[6] International Institute for Population Studies and ORC Macro (2000) and Indian Institute of Population Sciences (2007).
[7] The Planning Commission's most recent estimates indicate that the proportion of income poor fell to 22 per cent in 2004–05. See Planning Commission (2006).
[8] Government of Delhi (2006).

among children 0–6 years, which worsened from 947 girls per 1000 boys in 1991 to 927 in 2001. Particularly disturbing is the sharp decline in female-to-male ratios among children in the more affluent Indian states of Punjab, Haryana and Gujarat. Once again, the message is clear: there is no automatic linkage between increased opulence, improved standards of living, and the assurance of equal rights for children.

4. IDENTIFYING THE LINKAGES

Several factors and institutions intermediate between economic expansion, income poverty reduction, and the assurance of child rights. Public provisioning of basic services, for example, is one such critical factor. It is well known that markets, by ignoring the large positive externalities, will under-provide basic social services. And to that extent, the State has a central role to play in mobilising *public* action to ensure universal access to good quality basic social services. As a matter of fact, directly or indirectly, the State has a vital role to play in the assurance of virtually every right.

A review of the Indian experience points to five essential connections that must be established and strengthened if the benefits of economic growth are to be better translated into tangible improvements in the lives of children.

4.1. PUBLIC INVESTMENTS

Access to good quality basic services, such as health care, education, drinking water and sanitation, are far from universal in India. This is largely the consequence of insufficient public investment to ensure adequate reach and quality of basic social services. Take health for example: overall levels of health spending (public and private) in India, at 4.5–6 per cent of GDP, are higher than spending by countries like Malaysia, Singapore and Sri Lanka that report better health outcomes than India. However, *public* spending on health in India is abysmally low, at one per cent of GDP – among the lowest in the world. As a result, there is huge burden of out-of-pocket expenses on health care, borne especially by the poor. The consequences are not difficult to see. A single episode of hospitalisation almost inevitably drives poor families into debt and poverty. Today, private spending accounts for around 80 per cent of total expenditure on health, and public spending for 20 per cent.[9] This public-private mix of 20:80 in India is quite the opposite of what is found in many developed countries, where the public-

---

9   Commission on Macroeconomics and Health (2006).

private mix of spending on health is often around 80:20. Correcting the situation requires a massive step up in public expenditure on health. Similarly, such large increases in public investments are urgently required for ensuring universal access to basic services, especially for reducing poverty and insecurity in the lives of people.

4.2. PUBLIC MANAGEMENT

It is equally important, in addition to stepping up public investments, to ensure that resources, human and financial, are well deployed. And this brings us to another critical deficiency – namely good quality public management. Almost all evaluations identify several weaknesses in public management as a major reason for poor outcomes in human development. For instance, in Government of India's own analysis:

> "…the quality of care across the rural public health infrastructure is abysmal and marked by high rates of absenteeism, poor availability of skilled medical and paramedical professionals, callous attitudes, unavailable medicines and inadequate supervision and monitoring… The poor continue to avail of the costlier services provided by the private practitioner even when they have access to subsidised or free public health care, due to reasons of distance, but more significantly, on account of the unpredictable availability and very low quality of health services provided by the public sector."[10]

The state of schooling is not very different. Shortages of classrooms and teachers, teacher absenteeism, low accountability and little supervision make the system highly inefficient. As a consequence, children learn little in school. Clearly, improving public management is an area that deserves urgent attention. The reluctance to invest more in the public sector is often attributed to the high levels of inefficiency, leakage and wastage in the public sector. And so improving the efficiency of public management provides a vital link between public expenditures and human outcomes.

4.3. PUBLIC PARTICIPATION

Actively engaging NGOs and other local community groups is vital if the state wants to assure universal rights. The state, with the best of intentions, can reach some of the poor, not all. Many NGOs work with extremely poor and vulnerable groups across the country, and therefore engaging NGOs and other local

---

[10] Planning Commission (2006).

community groups is almost the only way for the state to ensure benefits to all, especially the poorest in society.

It is also reported that even if finances are available and public administration is efficient, sustainability of interventions is often threatened by the lack of ownership and effective community participation. Reports from the field suggest that chances of success and sustainability improve significantly with greater ownership by the community; this comes about if citizens and local agencies partner with the state in policy formulation, project design and programme implementation.

In addition to a large number of voluntary agencies and non-governmental organisations, India is witnessing the emergence of many new forms of community-based organisations, such as self-help groups of women at the village level. This definitely increases the potential for partnerships. There are, however, certain limitations of NGOs and community-based agencies that need to be addressed. Many NGOs have limited capacity and professional capabilities, and this prevents them even from documenting and building evidence in support of their interventions. They are also often severely constrained by finances and human resources. Given its critical role, the state needs to evolve a comprehensive strategy to expand opportunities for engaging non-state actors in public decision making.

4.4. PUBLIC VIGILANCE

Another important link is provided by public vigilance, monitoring and reporting on policy and programme implementation. Chances of success improve dramatically when interventions are monitored closely.

An important function of public vigilance is to be watchful of the unintended consequences of public policies. We find, for instance, that fierce international competition, particularly in exports, has led to a massive increase in sub-contracting of manufacturing to home-based women producers. These women workers are paid abysmally low piece-rates and nothing else. There is no consideration of any non-wage benefits, and no consideration of ensuring proper and safe working conditions. Reports from the field suggest that, especially in the export business, both earnings and conditions of such work appear to have deteriorated rather than improved.[11] A fall-out of such low-paid home-based work is the inevitable and unreported engagement of children in production activities. It is only a vigilant public that can alert policymakers to such situations, which would normally go unnoticed.

---

[11] GHOSH (2008).

Public vigilance is equally necessary to ensure accountability by the state. India has a monitoring system in place for government programmes, but there are several gaps in reporting. Apart from issues of reliability and timeliness, many data sets are not available at different levels of disaggregation. Maternal mortality estimates, for instance, are available for India as a whole, but not with any reliability for separate Indian states. Estimates of infant mortality are available at the national and state levels, but not at the district level. Similarly, gender-disaggregated data is not easy to access, and even today, we do not have specialised and systematic data on the learning achievements of Indian children.

Public vigilance and independent monitoring are also necessary to correct a basic flaw in most public systems. By and large, ministries responsible for programme implementation gather their own data and present it while reporting on performance. At best, they may commission an assessment, but they are the ones who commission and pay for such studies. This leads to obvious biases in reporting. To remedy the situation, the Indian state has been encouraging public hearings and social audits which are beginning to provide valuable insights into the functioning of government programmes. The media too has started playing an active role in promoting public vigilance. New private television channels and the press have, in recent years, drawn attention to many neglected concerns of children as well as to violations of rights. Encouraging all forms of public vigilance is therefore important for improving the linkages between programme implementation and outcomes for children.

4.5. PUBLIC VALUES

The last linkage in translating economic expansion into improved conditions for children has to do with public values, or more centrally with how society treats its children. It sometimes becomes difficult to explain why societies behave in ways that are extremely detrimental to children. For example, despite a law prohibiting the employment of children, we continue to see millions of children working in hotels and restaurants and as domestic servants in middle-class urban homes. Even though the benefits of schooling are well known, many parents do not encourage their daughters to study beyond Class V. Again, many young girls are married before the legally permissible age of 18 years. One wonders how these parents can deny girls the freedoms to enjoy childhood? Similarly, it is common to see many street children living under extremely dangerous and life-threatening conditions. How can any society tolerate such high levels of deprivation and injustice?

Clearly, this is a matter of societal values and norms. It raises the issue of a society's understanding of equality, fairness and justice. Unfortunately, public discussion on such societal norms and the universalism of human rights tends to be rather minimal and muted. There are still many who question the relevance of rights in a society when they cannot be assured. They hold the view that something cannot be called a right if it cannot be fulfilled. In this context, it is helpful to recall Nobel Laureate Amartya Sen, who makes a plea not to confuse an *unrealised right* (an acknowledged right that has not yet been fulfilled) with a *non-right*. In the case of children, many rights may remain unfulfilled – but that does not mean they cease to be rights. Similarly, there are many who question the relevance of child rights, because children are too young to exercise independent judgment and other adults have to perform this function for them. This makes no sense. Amartya Sen points out, for instance, that your freedom to fly safely is best fulfilled when you let the pilot take decisions rather than seizing control of the cockpit operations. So also child rights are not diluted or damaged just because children cannot decide for themselves and others have to decide for them. This is not a viable way of thinking about freedom.[12] There is certainly need for much more public debate and discussion on matters of societal norms in order to create a consensus on children's rights.

5. ESTABLISHING THE CONNECTIONS

Several efforts are being made by both state and non-state actors in India to step up public investments, improve public management, promote community participation, encourage public vigilance, and sharpen public debates around values. India's recent experience also points to certain shifts in policy thinking and environment that are needed for these connections to yield the best results for children.

Firstly, issues of child rights need to be more politicised. It is only then that they receive appropriate policy attention. This has happened in India in the past – as, for example, with child labour. But there are many more such examples today where sustained public advocacy and action have led to a greater focus on children's issues. For instance, concerns of food security for children have been brought to the centre-stage by the Right to Food campaign, which has systematically pushed for a better deal for children under six. Similar campaigns have been successfully launched to draw people's attention to issues of neonatal mortality, poor quality of education, child abuse, and so on.

---

[12] SEN (2007).

As a result, there is growing support for child rights among the top political leadership of the country. For instance, on assumption of office as President of India in July 2007, Mrs. Pratibha Patil said in her first address:

> "...We must banish malnutrition, social evils like infant mortality and female foeticide. I wish to express my full commitment to the protection of child rights. We must wage a relentless campaign against poverty, ignorance and disease to seek a better future for our children."

Prime Minister Manmohan Singh has drawn frequent attention to the plight of India's malnourished children. In a statement issued in December 2007, he pointed out that:

> "[The] challenges of malnutrition that India is facing need to be addressed on a war-footing. In this connection, it is important to focus on foetal under-nourishment and child rearing practices... It is important for mothers to understand the importance of breast milk as both a source of nutrition and for building immunity in the child."

In May 2008, over a hundred Members of Parliament, cutting across political parties, signed a resolution stating that:

> "...we will address the critical problem of child malnutrition in India... We resolve to take up this issue within Parliament and outside it, with Governments at the Centre and in states, and with civil society to tackle the alarming situation."

Building such a groundswell of political and public support for children's issues is a fundamental requirement for ensuring a better deal for children.

Secondly, the state must recognise the multi-dimensional nature of human poverty and initiate interventions that simultaneously address the many concerns of the poor, including insecure livelihoods, health, basic education, food security and children's nutrition. This, we find, is beginning to yield improved results for the poor in India. The National Rural Employment Guarantee Act, for instance, offers income security to the poor. This legislation assures one working member from every poor household 100 days of employment every year at the minimum wage. The National Rural Health Mission seeks to accelerate people's access to good quality health care. Hot cooked meals are now served in every school to all children. The revamped Sarva Shiksha Abhiyan (Education for All) Mission pays far greater attention to improving the quality of elementary education. More resources have been allocated to the Integrated Child Development Services to ensure proper growth and development of children under six years of age. Efforts at reducing human poverty are likely to succeed much more when the poor avail of the benefits of these different schemes and programmes all at the same time.

Thirdly, the State needs to pay much greater attention to inclusive programming. The approach paper to India's XI Five Year Plan (2002–07) recognises the growing inequalities within India as well as the serious shortfalls in social development, and identifies several measures to ensure 'faster and more inclusive growth'. Social sectors have started receiving much more attention, though no resources as yet. Special efforts are being made to focus on equity and accelerated progress for less privileged children. More flexibility and innovation are being built into all programming initiatives. It is only by recognising contextual differences and developing local strategies that child rights can be made universal.

Fourthly, society must pay more attention to improved accountability. Several steps are being taken in India to improve transparency in public decision-making processes. The newly enacted Right to Information Act is a major step forward in ensuring transparency and fairness in public decisions. Many civil society organisations have used the Act to get information and enforce and establish new norms of public accountability. E-governance and the use of information technology are also contributing to more openness in public systems. One can expect in the future that better outcomes for children will accrue as a result.

Fifthly, the state must set up new institutions that specifically promote child rights at different levels. The Government of India took a significant step in this direction when in 2007 it set up the National Commission for the Protection of Child Rights as a statutory body. The Commission has been active since its inception, and has introduced several measures to protect children's rights. For example, the Commission recently asked state governments to take immediate steps to check child labour and rehabilitate rescued children. The Commission was also asked to evolve a code of conduct for the employees of all public sector institutions, government undertakings, government funded institutions and government offices, which included the necessity not to engage children as domestic workers or encourage child labour in any form at their workplaces. It is expected that state governments may soon set up state commissions for the protection of child rights. Such institutions must begin to play a pro-active role in order to ensure that all Indian children get a better deal in the coming years.

6. CONCLUSION

Let me conclude by reiterating the main points I have attempted to make in this paper on the inter-connections between economic expansion and child rights.

The Indian experience, especially after the initiation of economic reforms in the early 1990s, reveals that high rates of economic growth and reductions in income poverty do not automatically translate into improvements in the wellbeing of children.

Five critical links need to be established and strengthened to better the situation for Indian children; and this requires focusing on public investments, public management, public participation, public vigilance and public values. In addition to establishing these linkages, it is equally important to politicise children's issues and ensure that they figure prominently on the agendas of political and other leaders. At the same time, public pressure is needed to ensure that the State intervenes not with one or two schemes, but with a range of programmes that address simultaneously the many dimensions of child poverty.

Lastly, it is important for the State to establish and nurture new institutions that will focus specifically on promoting child rights. It is only then that sustained economic growth can get converted in good measure into accelerated improvements in the wellbeing of children.

7. REFERENCES

Fukuda-Parr, S. and Kumar, A.K.S. (eds.) (2006). *Readings in human development*, Oxford University Press, New Delhi.

Ghosh, J. (2008). "The crisis of home-based work", *The Asian Age*, May 9, 2008, New Delhi accessible at www.asianage.com/presentation/columnisthome/jayati-ghosh.aspx

Government of Delhi (20006). *Delhi Human Development Report 2006*, Oxford University Press, New Delhi.

Government of India (2008). *Economic Survey 2007–08*, Ministry of Finance, Government of India, New Delhi.

International Institute for Population Studies and ORC Macro (2000). *National Family Health Survey (NFHS 2)*: 1998–99, Mumbai.

International Institute for Population Studies (2007). *NFHS-3 Fact Sheets: India and 29 States*, accessible at www.nfhsindia.org/factsheet.html

Kumar, A.K. S. (2007). *Why are children neglected?* Special issue on Children First, Seminar, June 2007, New Delhi.

Office of Registrar General of India (2006). *Sample Registration System Bulletin October 2006*, accessible at www.censusindia.net/vs/srs/bulletins/index.html.

Planning Commission (2006). *Towards Faster and More Inclusive Growth: An Approach Paper to the 11th Five Year Plan*, Government of India, New Delhi.

Sen, A. (2007). "Children and human rights", *Indian Journal of Human development*, Volume 1, Number 2, July-December 2007, Institute for Human development, New Delhi.

UNICEF (2007). *The State of the World's Children 2008*, UNICEF House, UNICEF, New York.

CASH TRANSFER PROGRAMME FOR VULNERABLE CHILDREN: A POLITICAL AND POLICY CHOICE FOR THE GOVERNMENT OF KENYA – 2002-2008

Roger PEARSON
*Senior Social Policy Specialist, UNICEF Ethiopia**

Carlos ALVIAR
*Cash Transfer Specialist, UNICEF Kenya**

1. INTRODUCTION

The Kenya cash transfer programme for vulnerable children was conceived in the run-up to the Kenyan parliamentary elections at the end of 2002. Conception stemmed from the realisation that some of the other elements of social protection in Kenyan society, especially family and communal mechanisms, were breaking down in the face of the growing HIV/AIDS pandemic (Csete, 2001). The 2002 publication of the *Children on the Brink* report (UNAIDS, UNICEF and USAID, 2002) pushed the debate on the consequences of the demographic momentum, highlighting increases in the numbers of orphans in Kenya as a consequence of HIV/AIDS. UNICEF further highlighted the issue in the course of the 2002/03 parliamentary elections through a media campaign that aimed to inform the public, stimulate discussion, and challenge parliamentary candidates to pledge to address the issue with seriousness if elected. Half of the members of the 2003–07 parliament signed that pledge.

One potential point of action that arose in the 2003 post-election discussions, notably in a parliamentary committee set up to address the Orphans and other Vulnerable Children (OVC) issue, and in a committee of the Ministry of Home Affairs charged with developing a national plan of action for OVC, was whether the time was ripe for the state to launch a cash transfer programme aimed at

---

* Any opinions expressed in this paper are the authors' alone and do not necessarily represent the opinions of UNICEF.

supporting very poor families with young children affected in some way by HIV/AIDS; these might be poor families that were fostering the young children of relatives or others that had passed away as a result of HIV/AIDS, or poor families themselves looking after people sick as a result of HIV/AIDS. By 2004 a first phase pilot programme was in place, targeting 500 households. It was a partnership between UNICEF (with partial funding from Sida) and the Government of Kenya, with funding from taxpayers. The aim was to implement such a programme on a small scale to see whether the concept would work before devising a larger pilot programme. If the results of the evaluation showed that the programme was efficient in terms of resource transfer, and if it improved outcomes for vulnerable children, then this could lead to an expansion of the programme.

By 2006, other partners, notably the World Bank and DfID, were keen to become supporters of the programme. By 2007 the second expanded pilot phase was under way, scaling up to over 40 districts by 2008, with 80,000 households likely to be enrolled by the end of the 2008/09 financial year, and with a well budgeted evaluation at the half way stage. The Ministry of Finance, happy with high expenditure rates from its previous allocations, doubled their allocation to the programme in the 2006/07 and 2007/08 budget years, and then tripled their allocation in the 2008/09 budget year. From an allocation of around USD 800,000 in 2005, over USD 9 million was budgeted as a contribution from Kenyan taxpayers in the 2008/09 budget year. How could such a programme, an initial innovation for Kenya in its design and ambition, grow so quickly?

This paper describes four key strategic elements that required action by the promoters of the programme, from its inception in 2002 to 2008. These will continue to receive attention as the programme further matures.

Firstly, of paramount importance, discussion was stimulated among a wide set of stakeholders on the pros and cons of such a programme, with a focus on forcing a political choice to either support or reject, in an informed way, the scaling-up of such a programme. The use of 'information rich' media campaigns at the time of the 2002 and the 2007 parliamentary elections were a key trigger for widespread debate about this type of programme among the public. Actions included providing information, calling for meetings, producing information notes and inviting the media and policy makers to witness the pilot programme in action.

Secondly, more detailed technical discussions were held on the costs and impact of the programme and how these might vary using alternative programme models, and to ensure that these alternatives were included in designing the evaluation work that would help to clarify the answers to these questions. The aim here was to ensure that policy makers had all the information they need to make an informed policy choice.

Thirdly, there was focus on the capacity to implement a programme design that could be taken to scale; this requires high levels of investments at the front end in terms of human, infrastructure and institutional resources required to maintain and expand the programme, even when outcomes, in terms of numbers of beneficiaries reached, are low at the beginning. This was a required risk in that heavy investments were made in capacity building for a programme (management information systems, payment mechanisms etc.) early on in its evolution when it was not at all clear that the programme would be maintained on the portfolio of poverty reduction programmes, and it might never have been scaled up to the point where the front end investments paid for themselves in terms of the efficiencies of scale.

Fourthly, intensive work took place at community level on a targeting mechanism that could be replicated across different communities and cultures and which was demonstrably efficient and fair to central level managers, programme funders, and communities themselves in reaching the intended target group. A key issue all cash transfer programmes have to address is who benefits and who does not: the borderline group of families who have just failed to qualify, and whose circumstances are usually not all that different from those successfully enrolled, is always an issue that requires sensitivity and community mechanisms where reviews of decisions can take place.

We argue that attention to all four of these strategic elements has been crucial to the evolution of this programme so far, and it continues to be a major programme that moves into an accelerated expansion phase.

2. CASH TRANSFER PROGRAMMES IN AFRICA COMPARED TO THE REST OF THE WORLD, AND THE ROLE OF INTERNATIONAL DEVELOPMENT PARTNERS IN HELPING TO BUILD SUCH PROGRAMMES

Why should the UN and other international development partners be helping the Kenya state develop a cash transfer programme for vulnerable children? One of the founding principles of membership of the United Nations is that member states should have in place a mechanism to transfer resources from the better off elements of society to the very poorest. The principle is articulated in the United

Nations Declaration of Human Rights (UNDHR). The covenants and conventions that follow this declaration are:

> UNDHR Article 22: Everyone as a member of society, has a right to social security, and is entitled to realisation of national effort and international cooperation and in accordance with the organisation and resources of each state, of the economic, social and cultural rights indispensable for his dignity and the free development of his personality

> UNDHR Article 25: Everyone has a right to a standard of living adequate for the health and wellbeing of himself and his family, including food, clothing, housing and medical care, and necessary social services, and the right to security in the event of unemployment, sickness, disability, widowhood, old age, or other lack of livelihood in circumstances beyond his control. Motherhood and childhood are entitled to special care and assistance.

Since the purpose of the funds and programmes of the UN is to help build member state capacity to work towards the fulfilment of the articles of the UNDHR and the associated covenants and conventions, it is clear that it is a core function of the UN to support such endeavours if it has the capacity and the state requests such assistance.

It is hard to explain why the funds and programmes of the UN and other international partners have done so little to build state capacity in Africa for social security systems, including an element of cash transfer, between 1950 and 2000. When the Kenya programme was being devised, one could only point to South Africa as an active large-scale programme anywhere else in Africa. This was a programme with deep roots stretching back to the 1950s, when it was targeted at poor white South Africans, which later opened up to all South Africans soon after the end of Apartheid. But we live in a world where cash transfers to the poorest are a cornerstone of social programmes outside of Africa, notably in Europe and the Americas, both north and south. The reason they have proved so popular is due to their demonstrable good value, efficiency and worth, not only in fulfilling the state's duty to reduce poverty, but in stimulating economic growth in often depressed pockets of the economies, creating jobs and more income, and hence ultimately improving tax collection. Some who read these words would not be doing so if their families in the past had not benefited from cash transfers provided by the state.

It is sometimes thought that African countries cannot afford simply to give cash to the poorest members of society. Table 1, below, presents the proportion of GDP and government expenditure if a sample of African countries developed a programme providing the equivalent of USD15 per month per household to the poorest 10 per cent of all people. The appropriate level of transfer, target group, size and type of programme will depend on local conditions and available resources. For Kenya, such a programme would represent 0.5 per cent of GDP and 1.7 per cent of the government yearly expenditure (using 2004 figures).

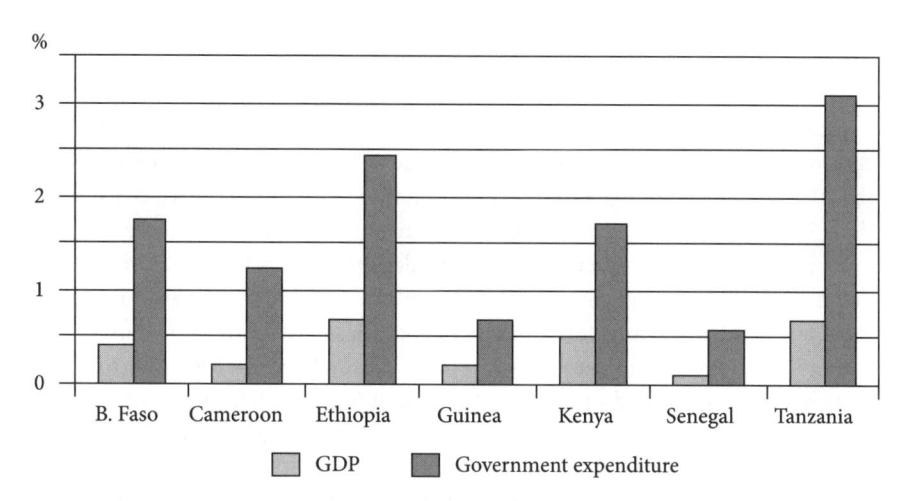

Table 1. Cost of transferring USD 15 per month to the poorest 10 per cent

Therefore the amounts required as a proportion of the overall economy or government expenditure are smaller than one might guess. Indeed, in countries with mature social security systems, far more is transferred to the poor than is shown in Table 1.

Why have international organisations, funded mainly from successful economies where cash transfers have been a core intervention for their own poor, not invested in cash transfer programmes in Africa? For decades international development partners have funded transfers to the poor in Africa, but only as long as it comes in the form of something other than cash, often delivered not by the state, but rather through civil society organisations contracted by international development partners. Since these resource flows are often not channelled through the Ministries of Finance, it is hard to capture exactly how much resources are transferred, and hence what proportion of the overall economy these transfers represent.

Typically this programme model has high overhead costs that are easily bettered in terms of efficiency by scaled-up cash transfer programmes. Free food is a well established form of resource transfer in Africa, for example, but, as has been well documented for thirty years, it is an inefficient way of transferring resources to the poor. Food as a vehicle for resource transfer requires an expensive logistical chain and, of course, free food potentially distorts incentives for local production, wholesale and retailing of food at the point of disbursement, especially if disbursements become routine over a period of years.[1] There are many other examples of programme strategies that aim to deliver resources to poor people but without actually putting cash in their hands – e.g. programmes that deliver school uniforms, supplies or a hot meal to poor families via contracted civil society organisations. Very few if any can claim the efficiency in terms of overhead or administrative costs that well managed cash transfer programmes can deliver. Typically, large-scale cash transfer programmes can be run with less than 20 per cent overheads. In Brazil, Colombia and Mexico, administrative costs are less than 10 per cent. Mexico's Progressa programme has administrative costs of less than 5 per cent (Caldes et al., 2004). In contrast, most civil society organisations operate in small subnational pockets, and despite all efforts to keep their costs down they cannot compete. Civil society administrative costs vary hugely but most fall within the range of 30–60 per cent. These are financial resources that end up in the towns and capital cities where the civil society organisations have their bases, and hence do not have the economic multiplier effects in terms of stimulating local economies that cash transfer programmes can generate.

Therefore, in Africa outside of South Africa, where cash transfers are a new concept and where many other resources transfer programmes of long standing are in place, it is natural that cash transfer programmes are sometimes perceived as a potential threat to business by long standing service providers who provide transfers using what might be termed more traditional delivery mechanisms. This constituency is large and must be serviced with information on the efficiency and impact of pilot cash transfer programmes as they grow to stimulate informed discussion about alternative ways of delivering resources to poor people. This has been a key element of the rationale for such a heavy investment in Kenya on political and policy dialogue around cash transfers – two of the four key strategic programme elements this paper describes.

3. POVERTY AND WEALTH IN KENYA

Kenya is a country of around 35 million people, half of whom are under eighteen. Fifteen million Kenyans are defined as ultra poor, meaning living below a poverty line of USD 1 per day. After a period of stagnation in the late 1990s, the economy

---

[1] This is not to say that free food distribution is always wrong. Where there is a shortage of food and a poorly developed cash economy, free food distribution is often the only way to support people living in food deficit areas.

is growing at a pace faster than population growth, even in 2008, with the post election violence in that year clearly causing contractions in some areas. However, even with a growing economy the proportion of Kenyans living in poverty has been increasing in absolute terms. Economic growth is driven by a relatively small portion of the people living in Kenya.

A recent report by the Centre for International Poverty Research (CIPR) (Centre for International Poverty Research, 2003) estimated the proportion of Kenyan children living in absolute poverty as 20 per cent of urban and 74 per cent of rural children. An analysis by the Central Bureau of Statistics (Kenyan Central Bureau of Statistics (2006) reported increasing geographic and socio-demographic disparities, with rural poverty ranging from 16 per cent to 84 per cent. Kenya's Poverty Reduction Strategy Paper (Government of Kenya, 2004) identifies the main correlates of poverty in Kenya as: location; household size; educational attainment of household head; sex of household head (female headed households are poorer); type of agricultural output (subsistence farmers versus cash crop farmers); and ownership of livestock and selected durable farm tools. To this must be added the debilitating and far-reaching effects of HIV and AIDS (6.2 per cent of Kenyan adults, or 1.15 million people, are estimated to be infected) and climate change in the Horn of Africa affecting pastoralists who live in the 80 per cent of Kenya categorised as arid or semi-arid.

There are three broad categories of the ultra poor in Kenya. One group lives in arid areas where the economy revolves around pastoralism, and, for various reasons, do not own an economically viable number of animals, and have no other economic assets. A second group comprises people who were otherwise poor anyway, but who have been affected by HIV and AIDS to the point whereby the economically active members of the household are either ailing due to HIV/AIDS or have died, leaving the older generation, if they are still alive, looking after orphans. This category can be found all over Kenya, but especially where poverty was greater anyway, and where HIV/AIDS has hit particularly hard, like in Nyanza and Western provinces (especially in those living close to Lake Victoria), and among communities living close to the Trans-African highway from Mombasa, through Nairobi and Nakuru, to the borders of Uganda. A third group is the poor communities living in urban slums around cities and towns, where transient populations of migrant labourers live together with people who have been in urban slums for several generations, and migrant labourers working in large agricultural businesses such as tea plantations and pineapple farms.

The numbers in the first category form a subsection of the 2 million plus people who have regularly been given free food handouts as part of humanitarian drought relief programmes in arid districts for the last 25 years. Funding for these programmes have come from the USA, Kenyan taxpayers (whose funds purchase food surpluses from large farms, mainly in Western Kenya), and cash grants, notably from bilateral and multilateral European aid programmes. Neither the second group nor the third enjoys support through a similarly coherent programme of long standing. They are supported by a large number of actors that aim to provide in-kind support for the second group through a myriad of funding sources, notably the U.S. government PEPFAR initiative.

Table 2. Trends in estimated numbers of orphans

	1985	1990	1995	2000	2005	2008
Maternal						
AIDS	0	1,196	72,965	362,539	635,208	655,358
Non-AIDS	583,738	595,451	577,670	533,335	481,997	460,692
Total	583,738	596,647	650,635	895,873	1,117,205	1,116,051
Paternal						
AIDS	0	2,394	71,893	263,755	416,777	430,300
Non-AIDS	908,512	896,738	829,476	776,433	736,198	727,110
Total	908,512	899,132	901,369	1,040,188	1,152,975	1,157,410
Dual Orphans						
AIDS	0	1,011	61,919	234,514	351,473	326,347
Non-AIDS	240,372	204,910	163,598	131,380	105,585	94,975
Total	240,372	205,921	225,517	365,894	457,058	421,322
Total Orphans	1,251,878	1,289,858	1,326,487	1,570,168	1,813,122	1,852,139
All AIDS Orphans	–	2,785	91,487	427,392	755,800	813,730

Sources: Takona and Stover, estimates based on ANC data and DHS 2003; National plan of action for orphans and other vulnerable children, Government of Kenya. 2005.

Within this context, the Children's Department of the Ministry of Home Affairs aimed to focus its support, whatever that may be, on helping ultra poor households to support their children so that they have access to health services and are able to attend school. As a result of many changes in society, the traditional support offered by households and communities was perceived when the programme was being planned as not being as strong as perhaps it was in times past: hence the rationale for the intervention of the state in expanding social protection for the poorest in society.

Actions were planned to start in those parts of Kenya where, due to HIV/AIDS, it was thought that poverty was increasing at a faster rate. Those areas of poverty served by the long-standing free food distribution programme would not be left out of scale-up plans, but would be focussed on after the programme had scaled up in HIV affected communities.

Another issue key to this decision of which the state was mindful was the mushrooming of private sector orphanages, driven by increasing numbers of orphans due to HIV/AIDS (Table 2, above). A key concern here was the often poor quality of these private sector services, their often tenuous funding base, and the fact that when the state has intervened in such institutions it has been found that many of the institutionalised children have had families after all. Indeed, recently the state has introduced legislation making it clear that unregistered orphanages are illegal institutions. From an economic and psychosocial point of view, while there will always be a necessity for some institutions to look after children who cannot be placed in a family environment directly or even after some time, it is far cheaper and beneficial for children to be fostered in a home environment.

4. THE CORE POVERTY PROGRAMMES IN KENYA IN 2004

In the case of Kenya it is not true that the state invests little in programmes with a social security objective: transfers from the state to the very poorest have been a feature of Kenya's state spending for many years. Allocations to core poverty programmes as defined by the Ministry of Finance were USD 390 million, USD 637.5 million, and USD 1.18 billion in the financial years 2002/03 to 2006/07 respectively. In the 2005/06 financial year, the allocation represented 4.9 per cent of GNP and total expenditures by government amounted to 27 per cent of GNP.

A key problem with these programmes, however, is that expenditure rates are often low. Well over a third of the resource allocations remained unspent early in the decade due to programme management capacity problems, especially at decentralised levels. Recently there has been a policy of decentralising management of core poverty programmes to the constituency level in an effort to improve efficiency. Several mechanisms now operate at this level, including, among other programmes, the Constituency Development Funds, School Bursary Funds, and Local Authority Transfer Funds, so the cash transfer programme needs to be seen in a programming environment where a number of changes are being implemented in the way the state manages its entire social protection portfolio.

A key question when adding a new programme to the list is how it would interact with existing programmes, and whether it would be able to demonstrate that it is at least as efficient as other existing programmes: hence the importance of ensuring that the cash transfer programme did not under-invest in the third of the four key strategic elements, capacity to implement.

5. POLICY DISCUSSIONS LEADING TO THE GENESIS OF THE KENYA PROGRAMME

The possibility that the state would start to develop a cash transfer programme from scratch, delivering cash direct to families affected by HIV/AIDS without going through civil society intermediaries, was discussed in Kenya in 2004 in a number of policy dialogue arenas, including around the development of the national action plan for orphans and other children made vulnerable by HIV/AIDS, an exercise sponsored by the Ministry of Home Affairs and well supported by many civil society organisations, World Bank, DfID, USAID and UNICEF (Ministry of Home Affairs, 2005).

The intended result of a cash transfer programme was to support poor families to support in turn their children, and other children they may be fostering, to grow within their families and communities instead of in institutions. The subsidy was intended to work as an incentive to providing continuous and adequate care to these children. By design, it would not be large enough to take beneficiary households out of poverty; it should also not lead to dependency, by virtue of the fact that it would only cover something like twenty per cent or less of minimal total household expenditures for very poor households. However, by allowing for a larger investment at the household level in children's human capital, through better nutrition and health in the early years and longer access to education, it would help to lift the next generation out of poverty.

The main mitigating factors against starting a cash transfer programme were:

1. that there was no previous experience in Kenya of a state-run cash transfer programme;
2. doubts expressed by several members of the national OVC national action plan steering committee about whether poor people could be trusted to make good use of cash handed to them.

The main arguments in favour were:

1. that the state did have the proven capability to send small amounts of cash on a regular basis to large numbers of people over a wide geographic area;

approximately 600,000 retired civil servants receive their pensions via the post office network with over 400 outlets in Kenya;
2. Kenya is a country where citizens pay a considerable sum in taxes. Over USD 5 billion was collected in taxes in fiscal year 2005/06, amounting to 22 per cent of GDP. Together with USD 1.5 billion in borrowing and USD 0.5 million contributed by international development partners, the Kenyan budget is in the region of USD 7 billion;
3. tax collection has been increasing due to an expanding economy and a more aggressive revenue authority, and this has continued despite the damage to the economy caused by post-election violence in early 2008;
4. the efficiency argument for cash transfers verses transfer of commodities via the NGO or private sector: if the administrative costs of the programme could be such that only 10–20 per cent of total resources went into overhead costs, this would beat contracting civil society organisations which cannot operate at that level of efficiency.

To move the political and policy dialogue forward, the Ministry of Home Affairs and UNICEF decided to launch a pilot programme to start learning some practical lessons about implementing such a programme, and to develop an information base on costs and impact on outcomes for children. Cash transfers were added to the overall Government of Kenya/UNICEF country programme learning district strategy (essentially a strategy of intensive support to building local and community capacity in three very different parts of the country, with an evaluation programme focussing on measuring impact and costs of expansion). The entire range of support that UNICEF provided to government programmes all converged in the early years of the millennium in three very different parts of the country: urban slums; an arid semi pastoral district; and a poor coastal area.

By December 2004, a targeting mechanism had been devised for the pilot, using a community driven mechanism with public participation in making the final decisions concerning which households should be enrolled. 500 households were enrolled in each of the three locations, and were being provided with KSh 500 (approximately USD 6.50) per child per month on a "pre-pilot" basis. By early 2005, workshops were being held with members of each of the communities involved, which totalled nine (three each in the four districts), to learn lessons and modify the programme design. Early results showed that the pre-pilot had a positive impact on the welfare of the beneficiaries, mainly in terms of access to education, health, and nutrition. It was learnt that funds were spent mainly on school uniforms, textbooks, food, and cooking oil.

That there was now a programme on the ground became a major boost to encouraging political discussion and policy debate on the merits and worth of such a programme. Politicians and policy makers in government could now travel to very diverse parts of the country to see a programme in action on the ground and decide for themselves whether the programme was capable of targeting the very poorest and whether the money was being well spent or not. The importance of targeting became clear as it was plain in the pilot that several very poor households had somehow not been enrolled, while several less deserving households were in the programme. It became clearer that the issue of capacity to implement was a key issue that would have to be addressed well if the programme was to have a hope of expanding to national scale. Indeed, it was crucial to have the programme in place, with all its problems, to serve as a benchmark against which a new improved programme could be designed that would eventually be capable of being scaled up to national scale.

The evaluation of the pilot highlighted the following lessons (Acaia Consult, 2007):

- access to health and education improved marginally;
- use of funds included rent, school uniform, food, and sometimes ARVs;
- there was little evidence of abuse in expenditures (see Table 3, below);
- traditional coping mechanisms (e.g. Zakat, or alms giving in the Islamic community) were not undermined.

Selling assets in times of stress is a fairly common coping mechanism, but also a destructive one when productive assets are sold, thereby depriving the seller of future income. The evaluation showed that the pilot seemed to have been effective in reducing beneficiary households' need to sell assets; just 9 per cent of beneficiary households compared with 15 per cent of control households (hh) reported selling assets in the six-month period since they received the first lump-sum transfer. Both groups sold assets mainly to provide food and medical care for families (72 per cent for beneficiaries and 62 per cent for non-beneficiaries). Beneficiary households were also more likely to have acquired assets over the six month period since receiving the lump sum (11 per cent of beneficiary hh compared to 7 per cent control group hh reported purchasing assets over the period). It was clear that the amount being disbursed was too small, and this led to discussions with the Ministry of Finance around what level of disbursement would be the most appropriate. Most community members were in favour of the idea that some sort of conditions should be imposed on the beneficiary families continuing to benefit from the grants. Exactly what conditions was not clear, and this issue became a point of debate between DfID partners (who were generally against conditions) and World Bank partners (who were generally in favour, based on their experiences in Latin America).

Table 3. Per cent of households in phase one reported spending cash on

Food	86
School fees	67
Clothes	54
Repayment of debts	41
Medical expenses	37
Paraffin/firewood	32
Income generation	24
Livestock	22
Home improvement	22
Saved/cash in hand	16
Transport	12

6. POLICY DISCUSSION, CAPACITY BUILDING AND TARGETING IN PHASE TWO

As experience with the programme increased, and early fears that poor people might not use the money wisely, or that no appreciable impact would be seen, began to diminish, confidence around scale-up grew. The greatest impetus to scale up the programme came from visits to beneficiary households by policy-makers, rather than through review of formal evaluation results. Simply through talking to a few households, it was made abundantly clear that the cash transfer made a huge difference in the lives of the beneficiaries, leaving senior officials with a keen desire to scale up the programme.

Work progressed on estimating to what extent it could be scaled-up. What were the cost estimates and what parameters might affect costs? Where would the resources come from? To what extent could the Kenyan taxpayer afford to contribute, and which international partners were willing to add their support to the programme and under what conditions? And would these be guaranteed or just promises? There were many uncertainties.

Estimates were produced, based on knowledge gained in phase one, of what the likely costs of the programme would be (Table 4, below) and what proportion of the government budget the programme would cost (Table 5, below) (Allen et al.,

2007). The absolute level of the transfer received intense discussion and review. One important factor was the information from the experiences of varying levels of transfer compared to poverty lines and impact in Latin America (Handa and Davies, 2006).

Table 4. Estimated cost (USD millions) of grant by number of children with varying operational costs

Operational overhead cost (%)	300,000 children	500,000 children	750,000 children
10	37.4	62.3	93.5
15	39.1	65.1	97.7
25	42.5	70.8	106.2
40	47.6	79.3	119.0

Table 5. Cost of a grant for 700,000 children using 2006 budget figures

Operational overhead costs	10%	25%	25%
Per cent of government expenditure	1.9	2.1	2.4
Per cent of GDP	0.4	0.5	0.6

Table 6, below, was produced for a technical note to inform discussions, led by the Ministry of Finance, to determine what the level of the transfer should be in the expanded second phase of the programme. The first part of the table showed the value of cash transfer schemes in Latin America against their national poverty lines. The key point made was that all but the Honduran programme had delivered significant impact on outcomes for children. The value of the transfer in Honduras was the lowest, and impact evaluations had shown little impact on outcomes for children, leading to the cancellation of the programme.

Two scenarios were presented for the case of rural Kenya, based on different assumptions about the potential benefit structure of the expanded programme:

- scenario 1: with a flat transfer of Ksh 1000 (and thus an average transfer per family of Ksh 1000), and an average family size of 5.5, the transfer was estimated to represent 8 per cent of the income of those on the national poverty line, and 16 per cent of the income of those on the ultra-poor line. This latter figure is more appropriate for the typical beneficiary of the Kenyan programme; they are virtually all from among the very poorest of society;
- scenario 2: if the transfer is based on the number of OVCs per household, with a cap of three, and assuming an average transfer of Ksh1500 per family, the

value of the transfer is about 25 per cent of the income of those on the ultra-poverty line.

Table 6. Comparison of average value of transfer in Latin America and the Caribbean and Kenya

	Monthly monetary benefit	Monthly transfer	Transfer % of poverty line
Brazil – Bolsa Familia	USD 18 per extremely poor family; USD 5 per child up to 3 kids	USD 24	12%
Colombia – Familias	USD 20 per family; USD 6 per child primary; USD 12 per child secondary	USD 50	
Honduras – PRAF II	USD 4 per family; USD 5 per child	USD 17	8%
Jamaica – PATH	USD 9 per eligible household member (child, elderly, disabled)	USD 45	16%
Mexico – PROGRESA/ OPORTUNIDADES	USD 13 per family; USD 8–17 per child primary; USD 25–32 per child secondary; one time grant USD 12–22 per child for supplies	USD 20	23%
Nicaragua – RPS	USD 18 per family; additional USD 9 per family with a school aged child; USD 20 once per year per child for mochila	USD 25	18%
Kenya (rural) scenario 1	Ksh 1000 flat transfer	Ksh1000	16% (ultra poverty-line)
Kenya (rural) scenario 2	Ksh 1000, 1500, 2000 depending on number of OVCs	Ksh 1500	24% (ultra-poverty line)

Assumptions for Kenya: Figures were given for rural poverty line only (Ksh2228 per capita). Average family size of 5.5 is assumed; ultra poverty line is half of full poverty line; scenario 2 assumes that the average transfer per family will be Ksh1500.

This value is still on the low end of the international rule-of-thumb. The decision on the transfer value involves a trade-off between ensuring the programme has a behavioural impact on recipients, while at the same time making sure that there is sufficient coverage across the country and among the very poorest.

Based on these calculations, a flat transfer of Ksh1,000 might have run the risk of not inducing behavioural change; even under Scenario 2, the average transfer value ends up at the low end of the 20–40 per cent range that is desirable for a scheme of this type, but might be more difficult to administer, since it requires different rates of payment to households based on the numbers of children defined as vulnerable according to the targeting methods.

After a series of discussions the decision was made to pay a flat rate of Ksh 1,500 per household whatever the number of eligible children (it turns out that on average, beneficiary households have just over three children). This was a pragmatic choice, leading to a simpler programme to administer than one with a variable scale depending on numbers of eligible children, and at a value of disbursement providing close to the 20 per cent of the national poverty line figure that Latin American experience had shown would lead to outcomes for children in sectors such as health care and education. Also, programme managers thought that this level of disbursement would be far too low to cause people to stop other efforts to find income and hence encourage dependency.

Negotiations took place with commercial banks and the state-owned Kenya Post Office on a contract for making transfers to poor households through them. Experts in setting up cash transfer programmes of national scale in Latin America were recruited to help refine targeting procedures, design management information systems, develop manuals for use at local level, and work intensively with the Ministry of Home Affairs to build a secretariat that could handle the programme management for scaling-up as capacity grew. Consequently, the secretariat has taken on the work of managing:

- the capacity building strategy;
- the management information system;
- the communication strategy;
- the monitoring systems (including spot checks and development of corruption control mechanisms, including fielding community level complaints, oversight and management of the evaluation);
- work on programme documentation and financing agreements to allow multiple international partners to contribute to the pool of resources required to reach programme targets before the full burden of the programme could be borne by the treasury.

Discussed at length was the issue of whether the programme should involve "conditionalities" other than the condition that beneficiaries be ultra poor. Some favoured the applying of conditionalities, a system that would only allow continuation of disbursements if certain conditions were met by families (including, for example, making sure that all children in the household regularly go to school); while others favoured a programme with no conditionalities. The case against conditionalities is that without them, certain overhead costs – especially those related to the development and management of computerised information systems to monitor compliance and other forms of checking that the conditionalities are being adhered to – are not required. This results in a simpler management system, and cost savings that can be applied to the front end of the programme, allowing more beneficiaries for the same overall cost. The argument against was that while these sorts of systems might work in more developed societies, they would be too complex to manage well in Kenya. The argument for conditionalities in Kenya was that the communities in the phase one pilot turned out to be in favour of some form of conditionalities themselves, as did the Ministry of Home Affairs programme managers.

There is a political element here, in that since government has recently made education in Kenya free, it is easier to argue with the Ministry of Finance for allocations to the programme if part of the argument is that it is helping to make state investments in other areas more efficient. Another argument in favour is that the management information systems required to monitor conditionality are in any case required as a tool to manage the quite complex payroll for the programme, which requires payments to be sent to many different post offices every two months; it is far less complex to rely on a computerised payroll than it is to rely on a manual pen and paper system. A robust household targeting system, including an element of central level oversight to supplement community based targeting, is also not realistic unless the oversight is computer-based. Central oversight helps to curb potential efforts to slip households into the beneficiary list that do not meet criteria for enrolment. Enrolment of families that should not be enrolled is an expensive error, given that families, once in, do not exit the programme for several years. Lastly, there is a difference between declaring that a programme will be managed with a conditionality element and actually following through on a large scale: the Brazilian programme is often pointed to as an example of a programme that declares conditionality, but with little follow-through.

The evaluation focuses on the following key issues.

Table 7. Estimated pace of programme expansion (households have on average three children)

Financial year	Households enrolled
2004–2005	500
2005–2006	3,000
2006–2007	8,000
2007–2008	22,500
2008–2009	60,000
2009–2010	80,000
2010–2011	100,000

Firstly, evaluation of the welfare and economic impacts of the programme amongst those who benefit from it against matched benchmark communities that are not benefiting from the programme. A key element here is the question of the precise fraction of total household costs in targeted households that is being covered by the cash transfer. Experience from Latin America shows that when the fraction dips much below 20 per cent of total household costs, then the programme runs the risk of having no discernable impact on outcomes for children such as improved educational and improved health outcomes. This was the case with a programme in Honduras, where the cash transfer hovered at around 10 per cent of total household expenditures: when the evaluation results showed that the programme was having little measurable impact on outcomes for children, it was cancelled. In contrast, programmes in Brazil, Mexico and other states that ran at closer to 20 per cent could demonstrate outcomes for children, and this resulted in greater political support for the programmes, and hence improved funding and scale-up.

Secondly, evaluation of the operational effectiveness of the pilot, including the very important fraction of costs required to administer the programme and being able to distinguish the extra costs in "conditional" communities versus programme areas where no conditions apply.

Thirdly, evaluation of the extent to which the programme reaches those in greatest need (targeting effectiveness).

Evidence on targeting effectiveness will shed light on the extent to which mechanisms in use are cost efficient, transparent and accountable in reaching those most in need, and most importantly which mechanisms minimise exclusion errors. Information on operational effectiveness will inform programme design with regard to effectiveness so that modifications can be made if and when scale-up occurs. For instance, the payment delivery mechanism needs to be tested for security, accessibility timeliness and value for money. The evaluation will use quantitative household surveys in a longitudinal/panel design; quantitative community surveys in a repeated cross-sectional design; qualitative focus group discussions with beneficiaries and other community members; in-depth interviews with beneficiaries and those responsible for programme implementation; an operational review; and a simple costing study. Household and community surveys will be carried out in locations selected at random for inclusion within the scheme.

The household survey will cover beneficiary and non beneficiary households in the selected areas and a sample of households in non-beneficiary areas. Having two survey groups (with and without conditionalities) and a comparison control group will allow the evaluation to provide information on the impact of the transfers in reference to the conditions, thus making it possible to test the conditions within the Kenyan context.

The evaluation design includes a baseline and a follow-up survey in the targeted communities. While the baseline survey has already taken place, the follow-up survey will take place in 2009. However, some results from the baseline are available and are being used to improve the rollout of the programme to new areas. Monthly expenditure per person among households enrolled in the programme in evaluation households was running at 51 Kenya shillings per person per day in programme households (March/April 2007 baseline survey), or 75 US cents per day. The transfers therefore cover around 20 per cent of household expenditure. This means that the 1,500 shillings transfer rate has been set just about right for the expected programme (as based on the Latin American experience). The rates were set based on an analysis of the poverty line derived from the 1997 household expenditure survey. More recent data was not available, so the result coming from the baseline was particularly reassuring for the programme managers.

With respect to household level targeting efficiency, in other words understanding to what extent the programme enrols truly poor households and excludes the not-so-poor, around 84 per cent of the beneficiary households were found to be living on less than USD 2 per day (38 per cent with less than USD 1) in the baseline survey[2]; this figure compares favourably with the large programmes in Latin America, quite an achievement given that the American programmes benefit from being implemented in an easier environment than Kenya. However, there is space for improvement and the targeting process is under adjustment based on the targeting analysis.

The targeting design has grown out of lessons learned from the first phase. First, districts are selected based on the capacity of government to expand the programme. Here there is tremendous pressure to expand, but it has to be balanced against the capacity of the Ministry of Home Affairs and budget availability. In 2007 expansion plans by district were determined mainly by ranking based on poverty rates, estimated levels of HIV, the numbers of orphans being generated by poor HIV-affected households, and information on the extent to which districts are being covered, mainly by the US government president's emergency programme for AIDS, which contracts NGOs to deliver resources to children

---

[2] Kenya OVC-CT programme operational and impact evaluation. Baseline Survey report. July 2008.

affected by HIV. Districts with a high coverage of such programmes were rated lower on the rollout schedule. The following table provides a current estimate of the rate of expansion in terms of numbers of children that will be enrolled in the programme.

Within a district the poorest locations are selected by a committee decision. Within the locations a committee is formed, and is informed of the budget allocation and approximately how many households can be enrolled in the scheme. A survey is carried out to determine which of the households are ultra poor, based on a combination of community knowledge and set criteria such as the quality of housing. Extra weight is given to households with no able bodied persons, with disabled children, with foster children, and so on. Second stage data is entered into a management information system to check on the criteria and to rank the households. The ranked list is then discussed in a community meeting to make a final determination of which households will be enrolled in the scheme.

Adjustments to the targeting process will give priority to those districts with the biggest numbers of ultra-poor OVC households (ensuring that minimum efficient coverage rates are defined), and will make more rigorous the poverty and vulnerability requirements to reduce errors. The adjustments take into account the baseline results from the Operational and Impact Evaluation, and are being done using the Kenya Integrated Budget Household Survey (KIBHS).

The post-election crisis in Kenya in 2007 affected more than 600,000 people all over the country. The cash transfer programme's response to this emergency was to double its coverage from 12,500 to 25,000 households. The response aimed at providing quick support to the most vulnerable households, often the most affected in periods of crisis, and frequently left out of social policy interventions. This initiative and the increasing of support to the programme within Government structures and international organisations, will enable the programme to reach around 70,000 households by the end of 2008. The initial target of 100,000 households will be reached before the end of the planned period. It will be possible to reach a total of 300,000 households by the year 2012. This is above the number of the total hardcore poor OVC households in the country, according to the latest KIHBS data, and translates to around 1 million children benefiting from the programme.

7. CONCLUSION

Four key strategic elements of programme management have guided the evolution of the Kenya cash transfer programme for vulnerable children:

1. the political element, underpinned by stimulation of dialogue on the value, merit and worth of the programme, is even more important in 2008 than it was five years ago. Government is allocating more resources now than in 2004, and hopes to allocate larger sums as the programme expands. The more resources allocated, the more intense political debate will become. The programme therefore needs to deliver the right kind of information, and this requires a well-executed evaluation with a substantive budgetary allocation made in the early stages of programme design;
2. the programme must be taken seriously as a potential policy option, with key actors such as the Ministry of Finance, the Ministry of Planning and parliamentarians understanding its financial implications and how financial estimates update as costs change with programme maturation;
3. managers must be forward-looking in terms of considering what human resources will be required as the programme expands, and must be willing to look at alternative business models. Should all work be carried out by civil servants, or might it be more efficient to limit the role of civil servants to contracting the private sector and civil society organisations to help manage the programme at local level, restricting civil servants to oversight over programme execution;
4. the programme must work towards an efficient, transparent targeting mechanism, and must have the monitoring elements in place to be able to read how efficiency is varying from place to place and between competing programme designs as they are tested.

Cash transfer programmes can only be one element of a broader social protection strategy involving many elements. Several of the other key programmes extant in Kenya today were briefly described in this paper. The government is currently looking at all of these programmes as part of an overall review of social protection in Kenya. In a number of Latin American countries, when such reviews have taken place, and where evaluative data on the impact and efficiency of cash transfers have been available, it has often been a policy response to scale back some of the older legacy programmes in order to provide more resources for cash transfers.

The Kenya cash transfer programme is too young and unproven for these kinds of changes: it has still to prove its worth. When the results start to come in from the impact evaluation in a year's time, the political and policy discussions around the programme will be enriched by the information gathered. Those results will depend on the hard work of all those associated with the programme, from community to senior management levels. In the meantime, anyone wanting to see for themselves the impact of the programme need only to visit some of the beneficiary households. It is an inspirational experience, especially knowing that the majority of the resources applied to the programme are derived from Kenyan taxpayers, with international partners playing very much a supportive role.

Activists march past Parliament in the course of the 2007 parliamentary election campaign. The 2007 parliamentary elections saw a renewed campaign by UNICEF modelled on the 2002 campaign. With respect to the cash transfer programme this was an opportunity to grab public attention – especially that of taxpayers that listen to the radio, watch TV and read papers – letting people know that the programme existed and make them aware of the early results on targeting efficiency and how the households use the money. In 2008 the Ministry of Finance tripled their allocation to the cash transfer programme over 2007 levels. [Photo: R. Pearson]

8. ACKNOWLEDGEMENTS

The cash transfer programme in Kenya is a result of cooperation between a large number of institutions and the people who work for them. This paper tells a story brought to life by a large number of people. Some of them are mentioned below.

First and foremost, the team at the Ministry of Home Affairs Children's Department, led by Mr. Ahmed Hussein at his headquarters and in several districts too numerous to mention here. The team has enjoyed the unswerving support of several permanent secretaries and the former Minister of Home Affairs and Vice President of the Republic of Kenya, Moody Awori, who took a personal interest and provided inspiration for the programme from the beginning. Several other members of parliament have also taken a keen interest, notably members of the parliamentary OVC steering committee.

Staff of the Ministry of Home Affairs have worked with enormous enthusiasm, as have members of the volunteer children's area advisory councils wherever the programme has been implemented.

Several international partners have supported the programme, notably Mike Mills of the World Bank, Marilyn McDonagh, Simon Bland, Rachel Lambert, Leigh Stubblefield and Ada Mwangola of DfID, Annika Nordin-Jayawardena, Josephine Mwangi of Sida, and DfID consultant Michael Sampson.

Three UNICEF Kenya representatives have encouraged UNICEF: Nicholas Alipui, Heimo Laakkonen and Olivia Yambi. Others that must be acknowledged include the UNICEF Kenya team working directly on the programme, notably Birgithe Lund-Henriksen, Joanne Dunn, Catherine Kimotho and the rest of the child protection team; Bonee Wasike, Sara Cameron and the rest of the communications team, Sumaira Chowdhury, and many staff from the operations group involved in accounting and logistics. The UNICEF regional office for East and Southern Africa supported the development of the programme, notably two Regional Directors, Urban Jonsson and Per Engebak, and among advisory staff, David Alnwick, Douglas Webb and Penelope Campbell of the HIV/AIDS team, and Karen Allen and Ashu Handa from the regional planning and programming section. Jimmy Kolker and Peter McDermott, current and former Directors of UNICEF's HIV/AIDS in New York, were very supportive from the very beginning, as was Mark Stirling of the Regional UNAIDS team based in South Africa. Other colleagues from the UN team must be acknowledged, in Kenya notably Kristan Shoultz and Jane Kalweo of the UNAIDS team. The experience brought to the development of the management information system by Francisco Ayala and his team from Ayala Consulting has also been crucial to the success of the second expansionary phase of the programme.

9. REFERENCES

Acaia Consult (2007). *Evaluation of cash transfer programme in Nairobi, Kwale and Gaissa Districts.* Report submitted by the independent consulting firm to the secretariat of the Ministry of Home Affairs cash transfer programme, January 2007.

Allen, K., Campbell, P., Chatterjee, S., Ismail, OCA, Pearson, R. and Renshaw, M. (2007). *Can the Kenyan State put the 300,000 most vulnerable children in the country on a Cash Transfer Programme by the end of 2010?* Division of Policy and Planning Working Paper, 2007, UNICEF.

Caldes, N., Coady, D. and Maluccio, J. (2004). *The cost of poverty alleviation transfer programmes; a comparative analysis of three programmes in Latin America.* Food Consumption and Nutrition Division, Discussion paper 174. February. IFPRI.

Central Bureau of Statistics (2006). Government of Kenya, *Geographic Dimension of Well being in Kenya: A Constituency Level Profile*, Volume II, 2006.

Centre for International Poverty research (2003). *The Distribution of Child Poverty in the Developing World.*

Csete, J. (2001). Kenya: "In the shadow of Death; HIV and children's rights in Kenya". *Human Rights Watch*, June 2001, Vol. 13. No. 4(A).

Government of Kenya (2004). *Investment Programme for the Economic Recovery Strategy for Wealth and Employment Creation, 2003-2007.*

Handa, S and Davis, B. (2006). "Conditional Cash Transfers in Latin America and the Caribbean: A Review of the Experience", *Development Policy Review* Vol. 24(5):513–536.

Ministry of Home Affairs (Kenya) (2005). *The national plan of action for orphans and other children made vulnerable by HIV/AIDS.* National OVC steering committee, Ministry of Home Affairs.

UNAIDS, UNICEF and USAID (2002). *Children on the Brink: A Joint Report on orphans estimates and programme strategies.*

PART IV
THE IMPACT ON CHILDREN OF THE GLOBAL FOOD, FINANCIAL AND ECONOMIC CRISES

THE GLOBAL FOOD CRISIS: OBSERVATIONS[*]

Professor Jeffrey D. SACHS
Director, The Earth Institute at Columbia University

I would like to discuss two things briefly. One is the fact that we are at the mid-point of the Millennium Development Goals and of course, we lag far behind where we need to be. This is mainly because the rich countries have failed so far to honour their commitments to scale-up the amount of financing needed for critical investments for success, but I believe there is still time to make up lost ground. And I have some confidence that this year we can cause a speeding up of these investments and the financial commitments that are needed. The second relates very closely to the current food crisis. Of course the food crisis is a huge shock for Africa, because Africa is a net food-importing region and grain prices have doubled or tripled in the last six months. Moreover, the price of fertiliser, which is a vital input for agriculture, has tripled, roughly, in the last six months because of soaring energy prices. So we face a very, very dire situation, on top of an already severe shortfall in achieving the Millennium Development Goals. These two phenomena are related.

Africa is a hungry continent chronically, made worse by the current crisis. The overwhelming reason why Africa is a hungry continent is that of food productivity. The production of food per farmer and the production of food per hectare of land, is the lowest on the world. If you take the yields of African farmers, they average, in a regular rainy season, about one ton of grain per hectare of land, whereas in other parts of the world, including other parts of the developing world, the yields are three or four or even five per hectare of land. Africa suffers from many inherent difficulties, the most important of which is that it has 96 per cent rain fed agriculture rather than irrigated agriculture. So Africa is at the mercy of the rains and the rains have become less stable, more unstable; so Africa has become more drought-prone in the last 25 years. Of course at the same time the population has continued to rise, the farm sizes have continued to fall, as

---

[*] This is the transcribed version of the speech delivered via video conferencing to the Third International Policy Conference on the African Child in May 2008.

the scarce land has been sub-divided within the communities. And so we have a kind of scissors of rising population and falling rainfall, which is cutting very hard and leading to chronic under-nourishment.

How does this relate to the current food crisis? The current global food crisis is a result of world demand for food rising faster than world supply. The world demand for food is rising especially rapidly in Asia, but it's rising everywhere because of population growth combined with rising incomes per person. Food supply, a phenomenon of the 1970s and 80s, has declined because of increased climate shocks even in food-exporting countries like Australia and Europe. The diversion of food crops into biofuel in Canada and the United States and Europe have further exacerbated the food crisis.

Now what could be done in the African continent? The main point is that Africa could grow a lot more food. The one ton per hectare could be increased, even with the difficulties of the rains, to between two or three tons per hectare on average, and in some places even more than three tons. This has won the support of many experts, but it has not yet won the support of the rich country governments. What they are focusing on is emergency food shipments; sending aid from Iowa farms to Africa, but we all know that this is very expensive, very unreliable, comes too late, does not empower the communities, and does not solve the larger problems of poverty.

So what we need is to speak out right now to say that the solution to the food crisis for Africa is to grow more food, not for food to be shipped from United States and Europe. It is very important that we speak out on behalf of Africa's farmers and to all the Finance Ministers and others wringing their hands in Washington and London and France, Paris and other places, to remind them that they sat on their hands for twenty years, giving no support to Africa's farmers and then they're surprised when a food crisis explodes like the way it has done. They've got to get off their hands, they've got to stop wringing their hands and they have to start funding the African green revolution. So this in my view is urgency number one – we don't want food aid year in and year out from the United States and Europe. It's too little, too late and it doesn't solve any problems. We want Africa to stand on its own by breaking the vicious circle of poverty and low food yields, so that Africa can grow more food.

We have done this in the Millennium Villages project, which I direct, together with UNDP and the NGO Millennium Promise, where food production has tripled or more because we have helped these small growers to get more inputs. Another complementary programme is the school feeding programme. This should be part of every country's comprehensive programme, but of course it depends on the communities growing more food and then having the finances that they need to establish kitchens and cooks at schools so that the children can get a midday meal. What a wonderful intervention this is! The kids are much more active, they're much more alert, they're better nourished, and the parents are sending them to school relieved that the children have something to eat. And this is a major way to not only combine increased food production locally, but increased school attendance and increased school performance.

Now, more generally, we are at the midpoint of the fifteen-year Millennium Development Goals. I think there is no longer any mystery about what to do. We need to increase access to healthcare – no user fees at the point of service, because we know that excludes the poor. We have to end the Bamako Initiative of charging user fees for school and health services. This was a bad idea back in 1987 and it's a terrible idea today, because it excludes the poor. We need free point-of-access health services. And of course we need basic roads, electricity, safe drinking water, sanitation and cell phone coverage. There's nothing magic in any of this. In fact there's nothing very expensive in any of this either. It fits within the amount of aid that the rich countries have promised. They promised 0.7 per cent of their gross national income as aid. They did that in the Monterey Consensus. That is about USD 250 billion a year – but they're only giving a hundred billion right now. This is the problem. The rich countries have so far defaulted on their commitments. It's time to stop blaming Africa. It's time to stop blaming African governments. It's time to stop blaming poor people.

The limiting factor for achieving the Millennium Development Goals are the rich countries. Their failure to follow through on aid; of course, the way they exacerbate the crisis by putting their food into the gas tanks in Europe, the US and Canada. We need solidarity in order to make the Millennium Development Goals succeed. There's no magic. Because we know the investments that are needed: an African green revolution, comprehensive malaria control, investments in community health workers, de-worming of all children, school feeding programmes, basic infrastructure (roads, power), safe water and sanitation, and connectivity. And the money is there – let me tell you ladies and gentlemen, that this year the United States will spend more on the Pentagon in one year than the entire world in all of history has given in aid for Africa. Let me say that again: in one year the United States will spend USD 700 billion on the military. This is more than all the aid that the entire world in all time has given to Africa. We are making choices – this is the point that people need to understand. Stop blaming the poor.

Let's understand that we've made bad choices in this world – military approaches, rather than peaceful approaches; failures to honour the commitments of the rich country governments. We need to put it all on the table and say 'here we are at the mid-point – let's be true to the process that we have started'. I call on all governments to be ready with comprehensive programmes of malaria control, education, healthcare in the villages – because we are going to get this financing. It would be too shocking for the rich world to simply renege on its promises and expect there could be security in the world after that. I don't believe they would do it because it's just fractions of one per cent of their income, and because they spend multiples of this on war, compared to what we are spending on peace.

What we are observing, basically, is a rapid world demand for all sorts of primary products pushing up against a rather inelastic supply for all types of primary commodities. It is not only food and energy; it is metals and many, many other commodities that are faced with very significant increases. You look at copper in a similar way. So copper is not affected by specifically biofuels or climate, like any other commodity it's affected by some supply shocks; for instance, instability in some mining regions. But basically world demand has been rapid relative to world supply.

I think it is a new phase for the world, because we are now 6.7 billion people. Back in the 1970s we were 4 billion people and we are at a world economy that was half the size, or less than half the size, of what it is today. The pressures on the physical environment were less and there were still unexploited resources that were easier to find at low cost. Indeed back in the 1970s the green revolution technologies were just beginning to diffuse, and so the doubling or tripling of crop yields was only then getting underway. I wish we could have confidence that there would be general doubling again of yields of crops as there were back in the 1970s onward, but the scientists don't believe that they have in hand such a doubling again easily. Maybe the science will be proved, but it's not something that's already sitting on the shelf, except in certain places like Africa, where the technology is there, but it isn't being used because of the poverty trap. But in other parts of the world the technologies are already being used, and in many cases the stresses are likely to become greater, because of the depletion of water. Especially think of the Gangetic Plains and the North China Plains, where groundwater is being depleted rapidly, in a place where hundreds of millions of people live. And so when you add on the climate change, the disappearance of glacier flows, the change of timing of snow melt, the depletion of groundwater, the rising of evapo-transpiration from warmer temperatures, and increased storm events, I think we have to say that we're in for a difficult period on the supply side.

Of course we have technology that can potentially break the traps. I believe, for example, that agro-bio technology – GMOs for drought-resistant varieties – may prove to be a critical breakthrough for food supply adequacy, but think of how controversial that is; most countries don't even accept the concept, much less the fact the technology is not yet developed. But I believe that we should not turn away any promising technologies beforehand, because this squeeze is serious. Consider also that the global population is continuing to rise, too fast. We are adding still 75 million people per year, in the poor countries. The rich countries are reaching population stabilisation, but the poor countries are still in a population increase and the poorest countries still in a population explosion. This is leading to mass environmental migration, such as the nomads moving from northern Darfur to southern Darfur, where it's a bit wetter, and helping to set off one of the disasters of conflict. And we're seeing this kind of environmental migration within India, in Bangladesh, in China, in other regions, in other parts of Africa; say from the Sahel to the coast of Guinea, such as Côte d'Ivoire. This is creating a lot of instability as well.

I've written a book recently called *Commonwealth: Economics for a crowded planet*, where I argue that we are being overtaken by this tremendous crowding of the earth in economic and demographic terms compared to the scarce resource supplies. Now it's not an original hypothesis of course, but I believe that the arithmetic scale of what we are facing, maybe I can say the geometric scale, is really pertinent right now. I also believe that technologies can help us find a way through. Solar power can replace a great deal of fossil fuel. High yield seeds can help expand Africa's food production, probably doubling it within the next few years, but we have to choose to invest in these improved technologies, and so far the rich countries have invested more in war than they have in sustainability. And this is the tragedy of our time, that we are missing the chances even as the situation becomes more and more difficult.

Now also remember that the price of food is now linked to the price of energy more directly and closely than ever before, because of this misguided policy of biofuels. I'm not sure that such a policy can easily be turned off entirely, and so the link of scarce oil with high prices of food is probably a feature of the coming years as well. So my answer is, we will not – we may have a year where the price comes down again in part, then we'll have an El Niño where the price will soar. We'll go back and forth, but I think on average, we're probably in for a period of high relative prices right now. And where we need to focus on what is called: RDD&D: Research, Development, Demonstration and Diffusion of sustainable technologies for food, water, energy and land use.

So here is where we are. We need help for basic investments. We need African governments ready to scale up these basic investments throughout the countryside to reach the poorest of the poor; to drop the user fees for health; to drop fees for schooling; to help more farmers get the inputs they need. To understand what it means to be in extreme poverty, means you cannot charge people money for these services; it will kill them if we charge them.

Finally let me say our Millennium Villages Project, which is now in a dozen countries in Africa: in Ethiopia, Ghana, Kenya, Madagascar, Malawi, Mali, Mozambique, Nigeria, Rwanda, Senegal, Tanzania and Uganda, and will soon spread to Benin and Cameroon as well. I want it to spread to every government that wants to be part of this. It is proving these basic truths, that investment in agriculture, health, education and infrastructure can be decisive in turning around extreme poverty. There's no excuse for failing to meet the Millennium Development Goals, either on the side of the African countries or the rich countries, as long as everybody does what they've promised to do. And right now, the promises are failing on the rich countries' side. That's why we have to spend special emphasis to get a fund for the African green revolution; to properly fund education for all; to properly fund the Global Fund to fight AIDS, TB and Malaria; to properly fund the infrastructure investments that Africa needs to participate in the world economy. There will be a General Assembly meeting of world leaders on September 22nd 2008 on Africa's Development Needs. This is one of our last chances, in essence, to break the deadlock and tell the rich world, 'you cannot renege on the promises that you made'. That will have to be the message, we'll have to get ready for it – the time is now.

WHAT WILL BE THE IMPACT OF THE GLOBAL ECONOMIC CRISIS ON CHILD POVERTY IN SUB-SAHARAN AFRICA?

Professor Andy SUMNER* and Ms. Sara WOLCOTT
Institute of Development Studies, University of Sussex

1. INTRODUCTION

The current global context for child poverty reduction is one of global recession, great uncertainty and many ongoing changes in policy and situations in response to unprecedented multiple and inter-linked crises, with potentially large adverse impacts on child poverty. How can we still find ways to meet the child-specific Millennium Development Goals (MDGs) amid this context?

In this paper we review the varied estimates of the impacts of the current global economic crisis on child poverty. We then turn our attention to previous economic crises, to see what we might learn from the evidence on the impacts of economic crises on child poverty. We focus on nine developing countries that have experienced a crisis episode since 1990. However, we find that our most recent evidence on the impacts of economic crises on child poverty are largely based on middle-income Asia and Latin America.

In light of this we discuss sub-Saharan Africa's macro-economic and child vulnerabilities in terms of the current crisis by identifying the different nature of likely macro-economic shocks in a set of sub-Saharan African countries, and levels of child vulnerability to the current crisis based on The African Child Policy Forum's (2008) *African Report on Child Wellbeing*.

We conclude by discussing tracking child poverty and vulnerability to poverty during crises. We link the MDGs with crisis child poverty indicators, indicators of vulnerability to child poverty, and indicators of the underlying causes of vulnerability to child poverty.

---

* Correspondence to a.sumner@ids.ac.uk.

The paper is structured as follows. Section 2 discusses the child poverty estimates of the current crisis. Sections 3 and 4 then review the research evidence on the transmission channels from an economic crisis to child poverty impacts, and the impacts of crises on child poverty, drawing on the literature from nine country crises. Section 5 then focuses on sub-Saharan Africa in the current crisis and both macroeconomic and child poverty vulnerabilities. Section 6 concludes.

2. IMPACT OF ECONOMIC CRISES ON CHILD POVERTY

Numerous studies are beginning to draw attention to the severe poverty impact of the current global crisis (see references in this section). While some examine the impact on child poverty, very few address the vulnerability of Africa's children.

Different studies have made different assumptions and specified different criteria for identifying countries at a high poverty risk. For example, Cord *et al.* (2009) identify 43 developing countries, a vast majority of them from sub-Saharan Africa, as being highly exposed to poverty effects given their decelerating growth and high poverty levels. World Bank (2009b) argues that women and girls in 33 countries – again a vast amount from sub-Saharan Africa – are at high risk of poverty based on low gender parity in schooling, high infant and child deaths and decelerating GDP growth. Others seek to estimate the actual number of new income-poor people by making assumptions on the poverty elasticity of growth and the deceleration in GDP growth. Of course these are income proxies, and of limited use in analysing the impact of the crisis on children. For example, DFID (2009) estimates the total number of newly poor at 90 million as a result of a 4.5 per cent deceleration in GDP growth in developing countries, based on the World Bank's assertion (2008b) that a one per cent decline in growth rates adds 20 million new poor people.

The World Bank itself (2008b; 2009) has revised upwards its estimates of the actual number of newly poor people as a result of the crisis, from 53 to 65 million based on the two-dollars a day poverty line, and from 46 to 53 million based on the US 1.25 a day poverty line (2007 versus 2008). These estimates are over and above the 130–155 million new poor people as a result of 2008 food and fuel price increases.

The IMF (2009:23) estimates that a one per cent fall in GDP growth raises income poverty by two per cent, citing this as the average across countries, as also noted by Ravallion (2004). The IMF has revised sub-Saharan African growth down to 3.5 per cent, which implies a 7 per cent increase in poverty in Africa. UNESCO (2009) has estimated a twenty per cent fall (around USD 46 per person) in the per capita incomes of 390 million poor people in sub-Saharan Africa. Related to income poverty, the ILO (2009) estimates a rise in global unemployment from 18 million in 2007 to 51 million in 2008.

Few studies focus specifically on children. A recent study by the World Bank estimates 200,000–400,000 additional infant deaths per year as, on average, a one per cent fall in GDP growth leads to an additional 1.5 boy infant deaths per 1,000 live births and 7.4 girl infant deaths per 1000 live births (World Bank, 2009a; 2009b).

Several questions arise with respect to assumptions for estimating elasticities and deceleration of GDP growth. For instance, it is not clear whether elasticities based on global averages and positive growth episodes are equally applicable during growth deceleration. Dollar and Kraay's *Growth is Good for the Poor* triggered a debate in the late 1990s by asserting that the poverty elasticity of growth was one-for-one (at least during positive growth episodes). Suffice to note here Ravallion's (2004) actual estimation that the IMF refers to is around 2 per cent, but the poverty elasticity of growth varies widely across countries from 0.6 to 4.3 using absolute poverty measures, and this elasticity depends on factors such as initial inequality, sectoral patterns of growth, the composition of public expenditure, labour markets, and social capital endowments.

Global estimates during the current crisis tend to be unreliable, as elasticities differ across countries and across time for the same countries. Further, reliable estimates of growth deceleration in developing countries are not easily available. A more fruitful exercise would be to review published literature on the impacts of financial crisis-related child poverty at the country level. This is what we seek to do in this paper.

3. TRACKING TRANSMISSION OF FINANCIAL CRISES TO CHILD POVERTY

3.1. METHODOLOGICAL ISSUES

Isolating the poverty impacts on children of a global crisis is problematic. Several issues arise while conducting such assessments on the impacts on child poverty. These would include, for instance, clarifying the definition of a 'crisis' episode, identifying criteria for choosing which crises to review and when to assess (the temporal nature of 'waves' of the crisis), addressing the absence of a counterfactual scenario, and delineating pre-crisis and during-crisis policies and factors contributing to the poverty impacts. It is, however, possible to describe what happened and identify indicators that demonstrate the visible dimensions of changes in childhood poverty during a crisis episode.

First, what is a financial crisis? As Jickling (2008:1) notes:

> "There is no precise definition of financial crisis, but a common view is that disruptions in financial markets rise to the level of a crisis when the flow of credit to households and businesses is constrained and the real economy of goods and services is adversely affected."

Typically, rapid falls in exchange rates followed by GDP contractions are commonly viewed as key indicators of a crisis.[1] The Frankel and Rose (1996:3) definition of a (currency) crisis is often cited in the literature on crises:

> "[A crisis is a situation whereby there is] a nominal depreciation of the currency of at least 25 per cent that is also a 10 per cent increase in the rate of depreciation."

Time is also an important dimension. There is generally a time lag from the start of a financial crisis to the various impacts on the real economy and on poverty. Changes in GDP growth can take 4–6 quarters from the onset of a financial crisis (Claessens, 2008) (Baldacci et al., 2008:7). A three-year window is usually taken for a crisis 'episode'. This might suggest that we need to compare data on poverty from the year of or prior to the crisis (pre-crisis) and two years later (for the peak impacts).

Financial crises historically have three crisis 'waves'. The first 'wave' is usually financial in nature, with visible changes in the exchange rate and stock market prices, interest rates, and so on. The second wave occurs with the transmission from the financial to the real sector, affecting, notably, construction and manufacturing sectors, and resulting in visible declines in investment and GDP. The third wave is the transmission of the crisis from the real economy (and finance) to noticeable impacts on poverty and children at the household and intra-household levels.

Conducting social impact assessments during turbulent times is tricky. We need to examine trends in poverty incidence or severity over time using time series

---

[1] See for review of definitions BALDACCI et al., (2008:7).

data (assuming available data is of good quality). Ideally we would need a peak-to-trough picture in terms of spikes and contractions in GDP. A socioeconomic survey may not have been conducted just before a crisis starts. However, many countries tend increasingly to conduct mini-surveys during crises using smaller sample sizes. And this raises issues of comparability of different data from different surveys conducted at different times during the crisis episode.

There is the issue of the counter-factual. What would have happened without a crisis? It is indeed difficult to isolate crisis impacts from other factors such as positive impacts of emergency programmes on mitigating child poverty. The current crisis has multiple linkages which includes the 'triple-f' crises: the food price hike of early-mid 2008; the fuel prices rises in mid 2008; and the financial crisis. This is particularly important for child poverty, given that a large proportion of household budgets of the poor is spent on food and fuel.

3.2. CONCEPTUAL LINKAGES

We have a reasonable understanding of childhood poverty transmission mechanisms during crises episodes, although much of the literature has an adult focus (Baldacci *et al.*, 2002; Lustig and Walton, 2009; Pernia and Knowles, 1998; Prennushi *et al.* 1998). We know that small losses of income make big differences to families living on or around a minimum income level. We know that many crisis-coping mechanisms entail household decisions that impact disproportionally on children.

A financial crisis is transmitted to children as follows.

Stock markets and exchange rates fall. Capital flows out. Rates of interest may rise to arrest outflows. Import inflation can result from the exchange rate fall as imported goods become more expensive. Inflation may also occur from scarcity of certain goods and increases in the money supply as central banks provide emergency credit to prevent the credit crunch. These inflation spikes could be short-lived. However, a trade shock via commodity prices may make matters worse in terms of import inflation. Indeed, some developing countries are at risk during the current crisis because they are primarily linked financially to the global economy by hot money (e.g. Nigeria, Brazil) and international banks (e.g. Ukraine, Pakistan). Other developing countries are at risk because they are primarily linked by their real economy to the global economy via non-oil exports, particularly so when commodity prices fall (e.g. Zambia where the Economist commodity prices index fell 40 per cent between July and December 2009). Other economies are at risk when manufacturers experience falling demand from western markets or are dependent on remittances from workers (e.g. India, Mexico) or are aid dependent (e.g. Uganda and Tanzania).

As exchange rates fall, the rush for dollars when firms try to service foreign debts triggers further declines in the value of the currency. As debts rise and credit and demand contract, investment and thus outputs slow or even fall as firms become insolvent or bankrupt. Central banks may try again to provide emergency liquidity to banks to ease the credit crunch. If output growth does slow or fall, redundancies may follow and household incomes may fall, leading to changes in consumption. For example, households may tend to replace meat with carbohydrates. Health and children's education expenditure may be cut. Depending on severity, migration back to rural areas may occur, and real rural incomes may fall as a result. Retrenched urban workers returning to their villages may depress rural wages.

In sum, financial crises have an impact on childhood poverty through several transmission mechanisms. Baldacci *et al.* (2002) argue that 60–70 per cent of the poverty impacts of a crisis are due to four factors: unemployment, inflation, reduced public expenditure and GDP contraction. Prennushi *et al.* (1998:1) identify five main types of transmission mechanisms between shocks and welfare: changes in relative prices which lead to changes in relative wages, consumption baskets and employment patterns; changes in aggregate labour demand which can reduce employment levels and/or wage rates; changes in the rates of return on assets; changes in levels of public transfers, in cash and kind; and changes in community environment, in terms of public health or safety. Lustig and Walton (2009) identify a similar set. We have made such analysis child-centric (see below).

How does a crisis transmit to child poverty?

A crisis may transmit to child poverty through the following:

- Changes in labour demand for adults (and children themselves)
- Changes in prices relating to child consumption, such as food, education and health prices
- Changes in public spending on child-specific public provision such as health, education and nutrition programmes
- Changes in the value of economic, human, social, environmental and financial assets owned by children or on which children can make claims
- Long-term impacts on children of constrained capabilities (i.e. effects of malnutrition, schooling dropouts, etc.).

The exact nature of child poverty impacts is likely to be, in particular, a function of the pre-crisis structure of child poverty and vulnerability (notably child poverty levels, inequality levels, clustering of people near the poverty line, education, health and economic asset levels, and so on). This is why, although there is evidence of the impact on children of economic crises largely for Asia and Latin America (see next section), we need to discuss the consequences of the current crisis on child poverty in sub-Saharan Africa.

Also of significance are the pre-crisis social and economic policy packages in place (social protection in particular); the differential nature or type of the financial crises as noted above (is it a capital account shock or a banking crisis or a current account shock via trade?); the economic and social policy response to the crisis (social safety nets in particular, but also fiscal stimuli and changes in public expenditures) and the health of the global economy. Countries can export their way out of crisis or receive large aid flows if global growth is strong and aid budgets buoyant. But what happens if there is a global recession?

Households adversely hit may respond by trying to increase income. They may do this via family members seeking new or additional work and drawing upon savings, credit (if available), selling assets, possibly with child labour increasing, and allowing children to drop out of school. Families may also try to reduce household expenditures via changes in quantity and quality of children's diets, or expenditure on health and children's education (see Gottschalk, 2008; Lustig and Walton, 2009).

4. CHILD POVERTY IMPACTS: EVIDENCE

4.1. CHILDREN AND HOUSEHOLD INCOME POVERTY IMPACTS

Income poverty is of course a weak proxy for child poverty. Nevertheless, declines in income significantly impact children when household monetary consumption falls. What will be the impact on income poverty of the global economic crisis? The total number of poor people is most likely to rise dramatically during a crisis if we look at poverty impacts of previous crises (see Table 1, below; World Bank, 2008a). The headcount poverty impact hides the heterogeneity of crisis impacts. Cline (2002) puts the average poverty impact of a crisis at a seven per cent increase in the poverty headcount per country.

Table 1. Impact on national poverty headcount of selected financial crises, 1990 – present

Country (date crisis began)	GDP contraction (year of crisis)	Proportional change in national poverty headcount (% increase)	Poverty headcount (% of population under *national* poverty line)	
			Pre-crisis (year prior to crisis)	Post-crisis (crisis + 2 years)
Mexico (December 1994)	–6.2	119.4	36.0 (1994)	43.0 (1996)
Thailand (July 1997)	–10.5	138.8	9.8 (1994)	13.6 (1998)
Indonesia (July 1997)	–13.1	172.6	15.7 (1996)	27.1 (1999)
Malaysia (September 1997)	–7.4	114.8	6.1 (1997)	7.0 (1998)
South Korea (October 1997)	–6.9	200.0	9.6 (1996)	19.2 (1998)
Russia (August 1998)	–6.4	149.3	21.9 (1996)	32.7 (1998)
Brazil (January 1999)	–4.3	na	22.0 (1998)	21.5 (2003)
Turkey (June 2001)	–6.2	na	28.3 (1994)	27.0 (2002)
Argentina (December 2001)	–10.9	147.2	35.8 (2001)	53.0 (2002)

Source: IMF International Financial Statistics Database; World Development Indicators (December 2008).

We find that, even after noting deficiencies in data, the reported increases in income poverty are significant. Further, poverty increases do not seem to be as closely tied to the magnitude of the GDP contraction as one might expect.

The rise in income poverty above reflects changes in real household per capita consumption, real wages, and unemployment (see Table 2, below). Again, this data is useful, but limited for an analysis of child poverty impacts.

Table 2. Changes in real household per capita consumption, real wages and unemployment

Country (date crisis began)	Change in real household per capita consumption	Change in real wages	Changes in unemployment
Mexico (December 1994)	25.0 (1994–1996)	13.5% (1995)	From 4.2% in 1994 to 5.7% in 1995.
Thailand (July 1997)	12.1 (1996–1998)	10% (1998)	From 1.5% in 1996 to 5.6% in 1998.
Indonesia (July 1997)	7.4 (1998)	30%–50% (1998)	From 4.7% in 1997 to 5.5% and 6.4% in 1998 and 1999, respectively.
Malaysia (September 1997)	12.3 (1998)	na	From 2.4% in 1997 to 3.0% in 1998.

Country (date crisis began)	Change in real household per capita consumption	Change in real wages	Changes in unemployment
South Korea (October 1997)	12.4 (1998)	4.2% (4th Q, 1997) and 8.9% (1st Q, 1998)	From 2% in 1997 to 6.7% in 1998.
Russia (August 1998)	25.0 (1996–1998)	16.8% (1998)	From 10.8% in 1997 to 11.9% and 13.7% in 1998 and 1999, respectively.
Brazil (January 1999)	na	na	From 7.8% in 1997 to 9.6% in 1999.
Turkey (June 2001)	10.3 (2001)	na	na
Argentina (December 2001)	23.8 (2001–2002)	na	21.4% in May 2002

Source: Adapted from Gottschalk (2004:11–12).

As noted, the extent of the rise depends at an aggregate level on changes in GDP and income inequality (see Baldacci *et al.*, 2002), and at the household level on household characteristics, education and location. Some of the poor could well be protected by their geographical isolation and poor connectivity with national and global markets (Ravallion, 2008; World Bank, 2008a).

4.2. CHILDREN, INEQUALITY AND DISTRIBUTION OF IMPACTS

The distributional impacts of crises are highly uneven. Income inequality often worsens during a crisis (see Table 3, below; Ravallion, 2008), and this adds to the pressure on child poverty. Furthermore, impacts on the existing poor and the severity of poverty can be more significant than what is captured by changes in the headcount ratio (Table 6, Dessus *et al.*, 2008).

Table 3. Selected inequality impacts of financial crises, 1990–present

Indicator	Gini co-efficient		Income share of bottom 20%	
Country (date crisis began)	Pre-crisis	Post-crisis	Pre-crisis	Post-crisis
Mexico (December 1994)	51.06 (1992)	48.54 (1996)	3.92 (1992)	4.3 (1996)
Thailand (July 1997)	43.39 (1996)	41.36 (1998)	5.9 (1996)	5.99 (1999)
Indonesia (July 1997)	36.55 (1996)	38.36 (1998)	7.81 (1996)	7.94 (1998)
Malaysia (September 1997)	49.15 (1997)	na	4.37 (1997)	na
South Korea (October 1997)	na	31.59 (1998)	na	7.90 (1998)

Indicator	Gini co-efficient		Income share of bottom 20%	
Russia (August 1998)	41.56 (1998)	45.62 (2000)	5.51 (1998)	4.92 (2000)
Brazil (January 1999)	59.19 (1999)	59.25 (2001)	2.52 (1999)	2.47 (2001)
Turkey (June 2001)	40.03 (2000)	43.638 (2003)	5.96 (2000)	5.5 (2002)
Argentina (December 2001)	52.24 (2001)	51.28 (2003)	3.15 (2001)	2.97 (2003)

Source: World Development Indicators (December 2008).

Gender plays a critical role in any assessment of the poverty impacts. Across the nine crises reviewed, gendered impacts are particularly evident via indicators of changes in labour markets (See Table 4, below; World Bank, 1999). Women are more likely to lose jobs than men as women dominate export sectors in sectors for garments, electronics and agriculture exports (Buvinic, 2009). Similarly, girls are often worse affected than boys. Girls are more likely to drop out of school in both low and middle income countries (Skoufias and Parker 2006; Schady 2004), and the infant mortality rates among girls exceed those among boys during a downturn (Baird et al., 2007).

Indeed, Elson (2009) identifies four gender biases during crises, as follows: a deflationary bias; a privatisation bias; a male breadwinner bias (protect male jobs if possible); and a reliance on women to provide safety net bias (through informal work, both paid and unpaid).

Table 4. Selected labour market impacts of financial crises, 1990–present, by gender

Indicator	Unemployment (%)				Labour force participation (%)			
Country (date crisis began)	Pre-crisis		Post-crisis		Pre-crisis		Post-crisis	
	Male	Female	Male	Female	Male	Female	Male	Female
Mexico (December 1994)	4.0 (1994)	4.8 (1994)	5.6 (1996)	6.1 (1996)	86.8 (1994)	38.4 (1994)	86.7 (1996)	39.3 (1996)
Thailand (July 1997)	0.8 (1997)	0.9 (1997)	3.0 (1999)	32.9 (1999)	86.6 (1997)	71.9 (1997)	85.1 (1999)	69.5 (1999)
Indonesia (July 1997)	3.8 (1997)	5.5 (1997)	5.0 (1999)	6.1 (1999)	85 (1997)	51 (1997)	86.8 (1999)	52.8 (1999)
Malaysia (September 1997)	2.3 (1997)	2.9 (1997)	3.5 (1999)	3.3 (1999)	83.4 (1997)	44.5 (1997)	83 (1999)	44.6 (1999)
South Korea (October 1997)	2.8 (1997)	2.3 (1997)	7.2 (1999)	5.1 (1999)	77.5 (1997)	53.2 (1997)	76 (1999)	51 (1999)
Russia (August 1998)	13.6 (1998)	13 (1998)	10.2 (2000)	9.4 (2000)	74.4 (1998)	64.2 (1998)	74.2 (2000)	64.7 (2000)
Brazil (January 1999)	7.8 (1999)	12.1 (1999)	7.5 (2001)	11.9 (2001)	86.1 (1999)	58.8 (1999)	85.1 (2001)	58.7 (2001)

Indicator	Unemployment (%)				Labour force participation (%)			
Country	Pre-crisis		Post-crisis		Pre-crisis		Post-crisis	
(date crisis began)	Male	Female	Male	Female	Male	Female	Male	Female
Turkey (June 2001)	8.7 (2001)	7.5 (2001)	10.7 (2003)	10.1 (2003)	76.3 (2001)	28.5 (2001)	74 (2003)	28.1 (2003)
Argentina (December 2001)	19.7 (2001)	18.4 (2001)	14.1 (2003)	18.7 (2003)	82.5 (2001)	56.1 (2001)	82.9 (2003)	59.3 (2003)

Source: World Development Indicators (Dec. 2008).

Unemployment refers to the share of the labour force that is without work but available for and seeking employment. Definitions of labour force and unemployment differ by country. Labour force participation rate is the proportion of the population aged 15 and older that is economically active: all people who supply labour for the production of goods and services during a specified period.

Furthermore, during crises, major rural and urban variations are often evident because of different impacts on different production and consumption patterns (World Bank, 2008a). However, poverty data from World Development Indicators is very limited (see Table 5, below). The rural poor may be hit harder during the ongoing global crisis, as falling agriculture and export commodity prices reduce rural employment and incomes (IMF, 2009:23). The impact depends upon whether or not the household is a net producer or consumer of food.

Table 5. Proportion of population under national poverty line, financial crises, 1990–present, by urban/rural (U/R)

Country (date crisis began)	Rural		Urban	
	Pre-crisis	Post-crisis	Pre-crisis	Post-crisis
Mexico (December 1994)	na	42.4 (2000)	na	12.6 (2000)
Thailand (July 1997)	na	na	na	na
Indonesia (July 1997)	na	34.4 (1999)	7.2 (1996)	16.3 (1996)
Malaysia (September 1997)	na	na	na	na
South Korea (October 1997)	na	na	na	na
Russia (August 1998)	na	na	na	na
Brazil (January 1999)	51.4 (1998)	41.0 (2003)	14.7 (1998)	17.5 (2003)
Turkey (June 2001)	na	34.5 (2002)	na	22.0 (2002)
Argentina (December 2001)	na	na	29.9 (1998)	na

Source: World Development Indicators (December 2008).

4.3. CHILD-SPECIFIC INDICATORS AND NON-INCOME POVERTY IMPACTS

Children are particularly vulnerable to financial crises, via the effects of those crises on many non-income dimensions, such as health, nutrition and education. Non-income poverty impacts are particularly child-specific. This is partly because many households adopt coping mechanisms that include decisions affecting children, such as expenditures on food, education and health (Bhutta et al., 2008; Mendoza, 2008). Indeed, there is strong evidence that crisis shocks impact the future wellbeing of children and can lead to decreased height, delayed school enrolment and reduced grade completion (Alderman et al., 2006; Yamano et al., 2005). Furthermore, children may be asked or forced into child labour, often of the worst kind (Mok, 2009). A particular concern is that crisis poverty impacts have long-term or inter-generational poverty effects. A negative shock of sufficient size can push households past a 'threshold' or 'tipping point,' while the same households can bounce back from smaller shocks (Ravallion, 2008).

Through our review of nine crises we can identify child-specific indicators. For example, child health and child nutrition indicators generally deteriorate during a crisis episode. These are not always dependent on government policies (see Tables 6 and 7, below). A one per cent contraction in per capita GDP raises infant mortality between 0.18 and 0.44 deaths per thousand children born (Baird et al., 2007).

Table 6. Changes in low birthweight babies as % of all births during selected financial crises, 1990–present

Country (date crisis began)	Pre-crisis	Post-crisis
Mexico (December 1994)	7.9 (1994)	9.0 (1999)
Thailand (July 1997)	7.3 (1995)	8.8 (2001)
Indonesia (July 1997)	15.0 (1996)	9.0 (2002)
Malaysia (September 1997)	8.3 (1994)	10.0 (1998)
South Korea (October 1997)	na	3.8 (2000)
Russia (August 1998)	na	6.3 (2001)
Brazil (January 1999)	10.0 (1996)	8.2 (2003)
Turkey (June 2001)	15.05 (1998)	na
Argentina (December 2001)	7.0 (1999)	8.0 (2003)

Source: World Development Indicators (December 2008).

Table 7. Changes in infant mortality in East Asian crisis, 1997–9

	GDP growth (%)	Infant mortality rate (per 1000 live births)	
		1995–1996	1997–1998
Severely affected countries	−22.8	50.6	58.6
Moderately affected countries	−11.8	52.5	52.9

Source: Bhutta *et al.*, (2008:7:23).

Additionally, during crises there is strong cross-country evidence of psychological distress and mental health problems (Das, 2008); elevated levels of community and intra-household conflict during and post-crisis (Friedman and Thomas, 2007; World Bank, 2008a); and negative environmental impacts as people are driven to exploit natural resources (often illegally) (Pernia & Knowles, 1999).

Regarding the child-related education MDGs, governments can and do successfully intervene to prevent severe crisis impacts. There is evidence that in some middle income country crises (but not all), education indicators may be unaffected or actually improve as a result of interventions and the changing opportunity cost of child labour (See Table 8, below; Ferreira and Schady, 2008).

Table 8.   Primary school completion rate (% of relevant age group) during selected financial crises, 1990–present

Country (date crisis began)	Pre-crisis	Post-crisis
Mexico (December 1994)	91.6 (1994)	97.2 (1996)
Thailand (July 1997)	na	96.0 (1999)
Indonesia (July 1997)	96.7 (1997)	95.3 (2001)
Malaysia (September 1997)	92.5 (1995)	94.0 (1999)
South Korea (October 1997)	98.2 (1996)	91.8 (1999)
Russia (August 1998)	91.4 (1995)	94.2 (2000)
Brazil (January 1999)	89.8 (1995)	100.0 (2001)
Turkey (June 2001)	na	na
Argentina (December 2001)	98.3 (2001)	100.0 (2003)

Source: World Development Indicators (December 2008).

In summary, a review of crises in nine countries reveals that child poverty increases along many dimensions. Children can and do face multiple impacts, including some of the worst. The distributional impacts of crises are highly uneven, and gendered. Experience also indicates that it is possible for governments to intervene successfully to mitigate some of these impacts.

Most recent evidence on the impacts on child poverty of financial crises since 1990 is drawn from the middle-income countries of Asia and Latin America. However, there is a significant gap in our understanding of the impacts of economic crises on children in sub-Saharan Africa. Of course, some lessons can be drawn from the structural adjustment literature of the early 1980s; but much has changed, both in Africa and beyond, over the past twenty-five years.

It is quite possible that the impacts of the current crisis on child poverty may be worse than in previous crises, for three reasons. Firstly, the financial crisis is only one of the crises faced; secondly, the financial crisis comes as a particularly significant 'shock' following a relatively benign period; and thirdly, this is a new kind of crisis.

First: Africa and the world face multiple systemic crises: food, fuel, finance, climate-change-induced natural disasters, and growing water scarcity. The current crisis comes on the tail of food and fuel prices spikes in 2008. Food and fuel account for the majority of poor and near-poor household consumptions. Households may respond to crises with coping mechanisms such as changes in children's diets and school enrolments, asset sales, and so on. Inadequate nutrition for new mothers and children greatly damages children's long-term health and wellbeing. This is bad enough, but multiple shocks are likely to be much harder to deal with.

Second: the current crisis follows a relatively good period for poverty reduction and thus is, perhaps, more of a 'shock'. Progress towards MDG 1 on income and food poverty is, of course, linked to economic growth and to food prices to some considerable extent.

Third: this is a new kind of crisis. It originates in the developed world. Countries cannot export their way out of this crisis as they have done in the past – at least, not by increasing exports to OECD countries. There is also likely to be the additional costs of bailouts, in terms of higher taxes and lower public expenditures in rich countries in the future, which might lead to a shrinking of aid budgets. All of this comes on top of what is the 'normal' crisis pattern within a given country: a crisis-induced squeezing of public expenditures in developing countries (as tax revenues fall). This is disturbing, as MDGs 2, 3, 4 and 5 (on children's education, health and gender equality in education) are all highly dependent on public expenditure, and often also on aid flows.

What, then, can we do? We ought to assess macro-economic and child vulnerabilities to the current crisis in sub-Saharan African countries by identifying the likely impact on children.

This is what we do in the next section of this paper.

5. SUB-SAHARAN AFRICA, CHILDREN AND THE CURRENT CRISIS

5.1. PRE-CRISIS MACRO-ECONOMIC VULNERABILITIES AND IMPACTS SO FAR

For the sake of this discussion, there are, broadly speaking, two groups of countries (some countries may be in both):

- those countries with macro-economic vulnerability via their capital (financial) account. These countries are primarily linked financially to the global economy by hot money and international banks, to remittances or aid flows, or a mix;
- those developing countries at risk because they are primarily linked by their current (trade) account. These countries are primarily linked via trade in commodity exports, many of which are falling in price (Zambia is one example, but there are many – see below).

Some countries fall into more than one category and thus could potentially experience multiple shocks. Private capital flows to developing countries are set to fall from USD 929 billion in 2007 to just USD 165 billion in 2009 (IMF, 2009). Similar declines are predicted by the IMF for Africa as well (see Table 9, below).

The changes in capital and trade earnings are significant. In 2008, Africa as a whole experienced a halving of total private capital inflows. This amounts to a reduction in total private capital inflows of USD 57.2 billion in 2008 and a further estimated reduction of USD 129 billion in 2009. Trade earnings remain positive, but only marginally so, and are likely to turn negative in 2009.

The net effect of this for Africa is an estimated financial loss of USD 62.3 billion, or 5.9 per cent of GDP, in 2008, and USD 130 billion, or 11 per cent of GDP, estimated for 2009. This implies the 2.7 per cent GDP growth rate of Africa in 2007 fell to 1 per cent in 2008, and will become a –2 per cent GDP growth rate in 2009.

Table 9. Estimated macro-economic impacts for Africa, 2007–2009

% change	2007	2008	2009
Total private capital	0.644	−0.498	−0.645
FDI	0.332	−0.412	0.119
Bank lending	0.936	−0.594	−1.364
Trade earnings	0.145	0.010	−0.022
Advanced GDP	0.027	0.010	−0.020

Source: IMF (January 2009).

Exchange rates in many developing countries have been falling rapidly (relative to the dollar) since January 2008. According to *the Economist's* "Slumpometer", there is a 40 per cent fall on a year-on-year (January 2008–09) basis in South Africa, and an equivalent 25 per cent fall in Zambia.

What does this all mean at country level? We can identify key country level vulnerability indicators for selected sub-Saharan African countries, such as portfolio flows, remittances, external debt, reserves, current account balances and primary commodities as percentage of export trade (see Table 10, below). For example, Kenya and Uganda are vulnerable to financial shocks resulting from falls in remittances. However, all countries are vulnerable to a trade shock based on current account deficits and primary commodity concentration.

Table 10. Pre-crisis macro-economic vulnerabilities in selected sub-Saharan African countries

	Vulnerability to capital (financial) account shock			Vulnerability to current (trade) account shock			Level of risk	
	Equity/ Portfolio Flows (% of GDP)	Remittances (% of GNI)	External debt, total (% of GNI)	Reserves 2008 (months of imports)	Current account balance (% of GDP) 2008	Primary Commodities as % of Export Trade	High (H) = 2+ Medium (M) = 1 Low (L) = 0	
							Capital Shock	Trade Shock
DRC	0.0	...	137.5	0.0	−1.9	96.0	M	H
Ethiopia	0.0	1.1	17.5	1.6	−5.0	93.9	L	H
Ghana	0.0	0.8	24.9	2.4	−6.3	79.2	L	H
Kenya	0.0	5.0	28.6	3.1	−6.1	64.6	M	H
Malawi	0.0	0.0	27.2	0.9	−8.2	86.1	L	H

	Vulnerability to capital (financial) account shock			Vulnerability to current (trade) account shock			Level of risk	
	Equity/ Portfolio Flows (% of GDP)	Remittances (% of GNI)	External debt, total (% of GNI)	Reserves 2008 (months of imports)	Current account balance (% of GDP) 2008	Primary Commodities as % of Export Trade	High (H) = 2+ Medium (M) = 1 Low (L) = 0	
							Capital Shock	Trade Shock
Mozambique	0.0	1.2	53.2	4.6	−13.6	93.9	M	H
Nigeria	0.0	2.3	7.6	12.7	6.2	98.6	L	H
Rwanda	0.0	0.7	16.9	4.8	−9.3	93.1	L	H
Sierra Leone	0.0	2.3	100.9	3.5	−6.3	90.5	M	H
South Africa	5.9	0.2	14.2	3.3	−8.0	52.5	M	H
Sudan	−0.1	3.2	55.5	1.4	−6.3	98.4	M	H
Tanzania	0.0	0.1	33.6	3.6	−9.0	90.2	L	H
Uganda	0.2	7.0	13.6	6.0	−3.4	81.5	M	M
Zambia	0.0	0.5	23.9	3.2	−7.1	90.9	L	M
Zimbabwe	0.0	...	...	n/a	−3.5	70.9	L	H

Sources: World Development Indicators (Dec. 2008); IMF World Economic Outlook database; World Bank Global Development Finance database.

If we can convert this into an overall macro-economic vulnerability rating (by assigning 1 to low, 2 to medium, and 3 to high vulnerability) we can say that some countries have higher macro-economic vulnerabilities (DRC, Kenya, Mozambique, Sierra Leone, South Africa, Sudan and Uganda) than the other countries listed. What does this all mean for the poverty and vulnerability of the African child in the current crisis?

5.2. POVERTY AND CHILD VULNERABILITIES

As noted earlier, UNESCO (2009) calculated that in sub-Saharan Africa the current growth reduction represents USD 72 billion, or USD 85 per capita (which represents a loss of 20 per cent of average income). The impact below the poverty line (390 million people) is a loss of USD 46 per capita. However, we do not yet have real time poverty data from Africa that allows us to say what the impact of the crisis will be on children. Nonetheless, we have two sources that do allow us to say something about the impacts of the current crisis in sub-Saharan Africa on child poverty: firstly, we can identify the macro-economic vulnerability of selected countries based on the data above, as we have done; and we can assess levels of child vulnerability based on The African Child Policy Forum's 2008 *African Report on Child Wellbeing*.

The ACPF report contains data on the child-friendliness of each African government based on child protection (by legal and policy frameworks); child provision (efforts to meet basic needs assessed by budgetary allocation and achievements of outcomes) and participation of children in consultations held to draft Poverty Reduction Strategy Papers (PRSPs) or other national plans. Here we make use of the child provision data as a proxy for children's vulnerability to the current crisis in the overall child provision index value (table 23, ACPF, 2008:158). A higher index value is better for children. For the set of 15 countries selected, the average is 0.457, enabling us to say that children are either living in higher risk or lesser risk countries. Of course, this approach is a rough and ready way of assessing vulnerability, and is only as good as the original data from official sources; but it does identify the priority needs of children where intervention is most urgent.

Table 11. The ACPF index on child provision in selected sub-Saharan African countries

	Index rank	Higher end of scale (> 0.457) Lower end of scale (> 0.457)
DRC	0.417	Lower
Ethiopia	0.309	Lower
Ghana	0.495	Higher
Kenya	0.505	Higher
Malawi	0.648	Higher
Mozambique	0.428	Lower
Nigeria	0.450	Lower
Rwanda	0.489	Higher
Sierra Leone	0.342	Lower
South Africa	0.605	Higher
Sudan	0.374	Lower
Tanzania	0.455	Lower
Uganda	0.461	Lower
Zambia	0.433	Lower
Zimbabwe	0.441	Lower

Once this is in place, we can then map high and medium macro-economic vulnerability with national child provision situations (see Table 12, below). The results of this process tentatively identify which children are most vulnerable in the current crisis based on what we know now. This would suggest policy intervention is a particularly urgent priority in DR Congo, Mozambique, Sierra Leone, Sudan, and Uganda.

Table 12. Mapping child vulnerabilities and macroeconomic vulnerabilities in selected sub-Saharan African countries

Child vulnerability to poverty	Macroeconomic vulnerability	
	Higher crisis macro-econ vulnerability: DRC, Kenya, Mozambique, Sierra Leone, South Africa, Sudan, Uganda	Medium crisis macro-econ vulnerability: Ethiopia, Ghana, Malawi, Nigeria, Rwanda, Zambia, Zimbabwe
Higher child vulnerability (lower end of ACPF Index) DRC, Ethiopia, Mozambique, Nigeria, Sierra Leone, Sudan, Tanzania, Uganda, Zambia, Zimbabwe	DRC, Mozambique, Sierra Leone, Sudan, Uganda	Ethiopia, Nigeria, Zambia, Zimbabwe
Lower child vulnerability (higher end of ACPF Index) Ghana, Kenya, Malawi, Rwanda, South Africa	Kenya, South Africa	Ghana, Malawi, Rwanda

This approach is useful, but what we actually need to do is track child poverty and vulnerability better. To this end, we can do two things:

A. *Invest in better child poverty and vulnerability early warning tracking systems*

Tracking child poverty alone is not enough during a crisis. For each child poverty indicator, we can propose a corresponding child vulnerability indicator. We also need rapid qualitative appraisals of poverty impacts.

B. *Explicitly link these new tracking systems to the following*

- planning of child-specific responses, and social protection and pro-child public expenditures;
- indicators of the underlying *causes* of child vulnerability, such as the indicator sets we have for food security and social protection;
- the Millennium Development Goal (MDG) framework. Policy responses should be integrated with the medium-term global poverty goals by developing corresponding vulnerability indicators for each MDG.

Ongoing tracking and evaluation becomes particularly important given that, in terms of child poverty, this is a fundamentally new crisis. This is because of the following: the global nature of the crisis (meaning that export-led poverty reduction will be difficult); the fact that the current crisis follows household shocks in food and fuel prices (already causing major poverty impacts); and the fact that aid and public expenditures are under threat (with major poverty implications). Child poverty and vulnerability must be carefully tracked, and interventions should be made using the results as an evidence base to mitigate the child poverty impacts of the current crisis.

6. CONCLUSIONS

The MDGs have been pursued to date in a relatively stable world, reasonably predictable in terms of planning, growth and aid.

However, the world is now a different place. The child poverty impacts of the current crisis are likely to be severe, depending on GDP contraction in particular, and highly uneven, with strong gendered and child-specific impacts. From the past, we know that the better our ability to track and understand shifts in poverty at a micro level, the better we are able to respond.

We need to expand the MDG lens in order to capture the increased child vulnerabilities and insecurities as a result of the current crisis, which are hindering progress on child poverty reduction. We can do this by drawing on what we know of the impact of previous crises, linking child vulnerabilities to poverty to their corresponding MDGs, and capturing the underlying enabling and disenabling processes that lead to those vulnerabilities and (in)securities. Fortunately, we can build on existing work quickly and develop better policy indicators – i.e. not only reduce vulnerability outcomes, but supply indicators to ensure underlying processes are supporting this. In a rapidly changing world, children in particular need voice and visibility in policy processes, either directly via participatory institutions for adaptation (i.e. voice) or in pro-child indicators (i.e. visibility) used by policy makers.

Alternatively, we could think about an MDG target board. The bull's-eye is the MDGs. The concentric circles around it are vulnerability to poverty indicators, then indicators of the underlying causes of vulnerability.

In summary, to plan for social policy/protection issues, we need to link the MDG radar to tracking indicators for vulnerability to poverty. Of course, tracking, monitoring and evaluating will not, in and of themselves, solve the problems of poverty. This needs to be done within a rapid-response context. 'Operation rooms' are needed to allow national- and local-level governments, civil society and aid agencies to respond efficiently and effectively with locally-appropriate responses. Furthermore, these processes need to be connected to long-term development plans. It is essential that, in responding in the short term, we do not forget about the long term. Previous financial crises have often been opportunities for advancing national and regional economic, political and social shifts: it is vital to steer the socio-economy towards a country's long-term development goals.

7. REFERENCES

African Child Policy Forum (2008). *The African Report on Child Wellbeing: How child-friendly are African governments?* Addis Ababa: The African Child Policy Forum.

Alderman H., Hoddinott, J. and Kinsey, B. (2006). *Long-term consequences of early childhood malnutrition.* Oxford Economic Papers. 58(3):450–74.

Altimir, O. (2002). *Poverty, income distribution and child welfare in Latin America: A comparison of pre- and post-recession data.* United Nations Economic Commission for Latin America: Santiago.

Baird, S., J. Friedman and N. Schady. (2007). *Aggregate Income Shocks and Infant Mortality in the Developing World.* World Bank Working Paper 4346. World Bank: Washington, DC.

Baldacci, C. et al. (2002). *Financial Crisis, Poverty and Income Distribution,* IMF Working Paper, 02/04, IMF: Washington, DC.

Barrientos, A. (2007). *Core Analytical Framework and Indicators for the Evaluation of DFID-supported Pilot Social Transfer Schemes.* DFID Evaluation Working Paper. DFID: London.

Bhutta, Z., Bawany, F., Feroze, A. and Rizvi, A. (2008). *The Impact of Food and Economic Crisis on Child Health and Nutrition.* Paper for UNICEF conference. UNICEF: New York.

Buvinic, M. (2009). *Impact of Financial Crisis on Women and Families.* Presentation. World Bank: Washington, DC.

Cameron, L. (2000). *The impact of the Indonesian Financial Crisis on children: an analysis using the 100 villages data.* UNICEF: New York.

Claessens, S., Kose, M. and Terrones, M. (2008). *What Happens During Recessions, Crunches and Busts?* IMF Working Paper 08/274. IMF: Washington, DC.

Cline, W. (2002). *Financial Crises and Poverty in Emerging Market Economics,* Working Paper No. 8, Center for Global Development: Washington, DC.

Cord, L., Verhoeven, M., Blomquist, C. and Rijkers, B. (2009). *The Global Economic Crisis: Assessing Vulnerability with a Poverty Lens.* World Bank: Washington, DC.

Das, J. (2008). *Mental health patterns and consequences: results from survey data in five developing countries.* World Bank Policy Working Paper 4495. World Bank: Washington, DC.

Devereux, S. (2006). *Strengthening Emergency Needs Assessment Capacity*. IDS: Brighton.

DFID (2009). *Crisis update – 90 million to be pushed into poverty by 2011*. DFID Press Release, 9 March. DFID: London. www.dfid.gov.uk/news/files/fin-crisis-update1.asp.

Diprose, R. (2007). *Safety and Security: A proposal for international comparable indicators of violence*. Oxford Development Studies. 35(4): 431–458.

Dollar, D. and Kraay, A. (2002). "Growth is Good for the Poor", *Journal of Economic Growth*, 7:195–225.

Duryea, S., Lam, D. and Levison, D. (2007). "Effects of Economic shocks on Children's employment and schooling in Brazil". *Journal of Development Economics*, 84, 188–214.

Elson, D. (2009). *Gender Equality and the Economic Crisis*. Presentation at IDRC/SID-OG meeting, Ottawa 27 November.

Eriksen, S. and Kelly, P. (2007). *Developing Credible Vulnerability Indicators for Climate Adaptation Policy Assessment. Mitigation and Adaptation Strategies for Global Change*. 12(4):495–524.

Fallon, P. and Lucas, R. (2002). "The Impact of Financial Crises on Labor Markets, Household Incomes and Poverty: A review of evidence". *World Bank Research Observer*. 17(1): 21–45.

Ferreira, F. and Schady, N. (2008). *Aggregate economic shocks: child schooling and child health*. World Bank Working Paper 4701. World Bank: Washington, DC.

Frankel, J. and Rose, A. (1996). *Currency crashes in emerging markets: Empirical indicators*. CEPR Discussion Paper 1349. CEPR: London.

Friedman, J. and Thomas, (2007). *Psychological health before, during and after an economic crisis: results from Indonesia 1993–2003*. Policy Research Working Paper 4386. World Bank: Washington, DC.

Gottschalk, R. (2004). *How Financial Crises Affect the Poor*, DFID: London.

Guarcello, L., Mealli, F. and Rosati, F. (2003). *Household vulnerability and child labour: the effects of shocks, credit rationing and insurance*. Understanding Children's Work working paper series at www.ucw-project.org

Holmes, R., Jones, N. and Wiggins, S. (2008). *Understanding the impact of food prices on children*. ODI: London.

ILO (2009). *Global Employment Trends January 2009*. ILO: Geneva.

IMF (2009). *The Implications of the Global Financial Crisis for Low-Income Countries*, IMF: Washington, DC.

Jickling, M. (2008). *Causes of the Financial Crisis*. Congressional Budget Research Service. US Congress: Washington, DC.

Justino, P. (2009, forthcoming). "Poverty and Violent Conflict: A Micro-Level Perspective on the Causes and Duration of Warfare". *Journal of Peace Research*, 46 (3), May 2009.

Lustig, N. and Walton, M. (2009). *Crises and The Poor: A template for Action*. World Bank: Washington, DC.

Mendoza, R. (2008). *Aggregate shocks, poor households and children: Transmission channels and policy responses*. UNICEF: New York.

Mok, K. (2009). *Impacts of the economic crisis on education*. UNICEF: New York.

Paxson, C. and Norbert, S. (2005). "Child Health and Economic Crisis in Peru". *World Bank Economic Review* 19(2): 203–223.

Pernia, E. and Knowles, J. (1998). *Assessing the Social Impact of the Financial Crisis in Asia.* EDRC briefing notes number 6, Asian Development Bank: Manila.

Phillips, D. (2008). *Social Quality: Indicators from Europe and their Implications for Asia.* Paper presented at national Taiwan University Workshop on Social Quality. April.

Prennushi, G., Ferreira, F. and Ravallion, M. (1998). *Macroeconomic Crises and Poverty: Transmission Mechanisms and Policy Responses.* World Bank Working Paper, Washington DC: World Bank.

Ravallion, M. (2004). *Pro-Poor Growth: A Primer.* World Bank Policy Research Working Paper No. 3242. World Bank: Washington, DC.

Ravallion, M. (2008). *Bailing out the World's Poorest.* World Bank Development Research Group. Policy Research Working Paper 4763. World Bank: Washington, DC.

Samman, E. (2007). "Psychological and Subjective Wellbeing: A proposal for international comparable indicators of violence". *Oxford Development Studies.* 35(4) 459–486.

Schady, N. (2008). *The Positive Effect of Macroeconomic crises on the schooling and employment decisions of children in a middle income country.* Working Paper Series, 2762. World Bank: Washington, DC.

Schady, N. (2004). "Do macroeconomic crises always slow human capital accumulation?" *World Bank Economic Review.* 18(2):131–54.

Skoufias, E. and Parker, S. (2006). *Labour market shocks and their impacts on work and schooling: evidence from urban Mexico.* IFPRI Discussion Paper 129. IFPRI: Washington, DC.

Sumner, A. (2002). *The Social Impact of the 1997/8 Economic Crisis in Indonesia 1997/8.* Unpublished PhD Thesis.

UNDP (2009). *Pro-Poor Governance and the Policy Process: A Framework.* Framework Paper 2. UNDP Oslo Governance Centre. Oslo.

UNESCO (2009). *Global crisis hits world's most vulnerable.* Press release, 3 March. UNESCO: Paris.

World Bank (2009a). *Swimming Against The Tide: How Developing Countries Are Coping With The Global Crisis.* World Bank: Washington, DC.

World Bank (2009b). *Women in 33 Countries Highly Vulnerable To Financial Crisis Effects.* World Bank Press Release 245/PREM, March 6. World Bank: Washington, DC.

World Bank (2008a). *Lessons from World Bank Research on Financial Crises.* World Bank Development Research Group. Policy Research Working paper 4779. World Bank: Washington, DC.

World Bank (2008b). *Global Financial Crisis and Implications for Developing Countries.* Paper for G20 Finance Ministers Meeting. Sao Paulo, Brazil, November 8.

World Bank (1999a). *Gender Dynamics of the East Asian Crisis*, World Bank: Washington, DC.

THE IMPACT OF THE WORLD FOOD CRISIS ON CHILDREN REQUIRING FOOD ASSISTANCE IN ETHIOPIA: A NOTE

Jakob MIKKELSEN
Head, Nutrition and Education Section
WFP Ethiopia

1. BACKGROUND

A wave of food-price inflation is moving across the globe, leaving in its wake drastically increased levels of hunger and poverty. The phenomenon is affecting everyone on the planet, and in some places it is provoking riots and destabilising destabilising governments.

High food prices are, in the words of World Food Programme (WFP) Executive Director Josette Sheeran, a "silent tsunami". They represent the biggest challenge that WFP has faced in its 45-year history. Analysis being carried out by WFP supports World Bank estimates that about 100 million people have been pushed deeper into poverty by soaring food costs.

WFP's Executive Director has also described the current situation as "the perfect storm". This term covers the fact that the current world food crisis is a mix of different, simultaneous shocks and ongoing developments all contributing to the soaring prices. These factors include the fact that global food stocks, according to FAO, are the lowest in the last 30 years as a result of droughts in Australia and Ukraine; restricted trade and tight supply (as in the case of rice, of which countries like India and Brazil have banned export); weather disasters that are more intense and frequent, maybe as a result of global warming; competing demands for food crops, as the market for bio-fuels is growing; income growth and changing diets in emerging economies like China and India that are changing demand patterns on certain food types; and record prices of oil affecting transportation costs.

The situation has been exacerbated by the falling value of the dollar, the currency in which all major commodities are traded. In a bid to protect their own populations, at least 18 countries across the world have imposed export bans or restrictions on certain food types. Of course, this only drives prices up further as food becomes less available.

The people hit hardest by this combination of factors are those living on the razor's edge of poverty. In rich countries, people spend 10–20 per cent of their income on food, so they can afford to pay more. In many poor countries, they already spend 60 per cent, sometimes even 80 per cent, of their budget on food. Therefore, this group of people is much more vulnerable to shocks.

Higher food prices are already causing social unrest around the world. Lives were lost earlier in 2008 in Haiti during several days of unrest, and in recent months there have been protests in at least 25 other countries, including Burkina Faso, Côte d'Ivoire, Cameroon, Gabon, Egypt, Senegal, Indonesia, Bangladesh, India and Philippines.

In developing countries across the world, the price crunch means that families that may have had a bit of money to pay school fees for their children, to go to clinics when they are sick, or take much-needed nourishing food together with anti-retroviral drugs, will suffer as they cut back in these areas. They are starting to cut meals, substituting less nutritious foods in their place.

As they struggle to cope, we risk seeing a major setback regarding the Millennium Development Goals (MDGs) that the world committed itself to reaching by 2015 – the first one being to reduce the proportion of people affected by hunger by 2015. Food is the foundation for six other MDG goals – more hunger and more suffering today points to a potential erosion of the hard-won progress we have made so far.

2. ETHIOPIA'S MALNOURISHED CHILDREN

Ethiopia, the second most populous country in Africa, reported a population of 75 million in 2006, of which some 41 million were children under 18 years of age. Thirteen million children were under the age of five. Of these, the 2005 Demographic and Health Survey by the Central Statistics Agency showed that 47 per cent are stunted (too short for their age), 11 per cent are wasted (too low-weight for their height), and 38 per cent are underweight (too low-weight for their age). Though since 2000 there has been an improvement of 5 per cent in stunting and 9 per cent improvement in the underweight indicator, there is still a long way to go before malnutrition is routed from Ethiopia. If Ethiopia is to meet MDG1, the rate achieved between 2000 and 2005 needs to be doubled.

There is wide consensus about the potential damaging effects that malnutrition can have on a child's physical and mental development. A 2006 report on school children with special needs in the Ethiopian education system suggests, for instance, that a child experiencing malnutrition at an early age might score as much as 15 points less on an IQ test than her/his fellow child who is not experiencing malnutrition. This clearly indicates the potentially severe consequences of early childhood nutritional deprivation on long-term development.

In 2008, close to 4.2 million Ethiopian children continued to receive external food assistance in one form or another through programmes supported by the World Food Programme. This included children of households benefiting from the Productive Safety Net transfers or relief general food rations; malnourished children supported through the Targeted Supplementary Food programme; children who are orphans or vulnerable, including children of HIV positive parents; school children in food insecure areas; and refugee children.

Unfortunately, the lives of these children are being adversely affected by the world food crisis in two major ways. One is that their families have less purchasing power and therefore are in a worse position to provide adequate food, care and health support for the children. Secondly, WFP's ability to assist this increasingly vulnerable group of children is itself being hampered by the rising food and fuel prices, affecting the organisation's ability to distribute the required quantities of food assistance. To give an example, in 2008, it was 50 per cent more expensive to deliver a supplementary food ration to a malnourished child or pregnant or breastfeeding woman than it was in 2007. Simple calculations suggest that organisations like WFP will need to raise, at a minimum, an additional 50 per cent of resources to meet current needs – if not, programmes supporting such malnourished children will have to be drastically reduced.

In the immediate term, the world's rich countries therefore need to rise to the occasion and provide the much-needed additional resources to prevent current shocks from substantially eroding previous gains. In the longer term, cost-effective solutions to dealing with needy children need to be explored further, and supported to serve as effective safety nets. Immediate support has to be targeted especially at the children who are worst affected, like those who are malnourished and at risk of dying.

The world food crisis is not about statistics and figures. It is about fellow human beings, who live under very unfortunate circumstances and who can be assisted if the political will is there.

> **The story of Eneyesh and her son Worke, from the Amhara region of Ethiopia**
>
> Like many village women in the Amhara region of Ethiopia, Eneyesh makes a living by collecting firewood and brewing local beer. However, it is not enough to support her family, which consists of a 3 year-old son and her aged mother.
>
> > "My husband left me because my family couldn't afford to pay the dowry. I don't blame him, but it is very difficult to live without a husband to protect and support the family. I think my son became weak because I am always away from the house trying to get money for food, and I don't have enough time to care for him."
>
> Eneyesh's son, Worke, was identified as malnourished through the "Enhanced Outreach Strategy" (EOS), which provides health services and screening for acute malnutrition for children under-5 and pregnant and lactating women.
>
> > "I was worried about my son because he was getting weaker and did not want to eat anything. I was afraid that he will get thinner and thinner. I saw children die from such conditions," said Eneyesh.
>
> As part of the EOS, Worke received 2 rounds of supplementary food ration to help him recover and prevent him from becoming severely malnourished.
>
> > "I prepared the food in the way the Food Distribution Agent taught me, and made sure that Worke eats it properly. Now he plays and runs around with the other children again. I am very happy that he is healthy again."